The Closest of Strangers

The Closest of Strangers

South African Women's Life Writing

Edited by Judith Lütge Coullie

Wits University Press
1 Jan Smuts Avenue Johannesburg
2001
South Africa

http://witspress.wits.ac.za

ISBN 1-86814-388-0

First published 2004

Selection, compilation and introduction
copyright © 2004 Judith Lütge Coullie

Copyright information for extracts in this volume
begins on page 377, which constitutes a
continuation of this copyright page.

COVER DESIGN BY Bon-Bon
TEXT DESIGN AND LAYOUT BY Orchard Publishing, Cape Town
PRINTED AND BOUND BY Paarl Print, Oosterland St., Paarl

For Ian, Charis and Benjamin.

Contents

Acknowledgements

First and foremost, I wish to applaud all of those women who have recorded, for posterity, their experiences and who have graciously permitted me to reproduce extracts here.

I am indebted for historical information to the *Reader's Digest Illustrated History of South Africa*, Saunders & Southey's *A Dictionary of South African History*, and Cherryl Walker's *Women and Gender in Southern Africa to 1945*. In my own introductions I have relied heavily on these texts, and have thus not indicated sources throughout. Any errors which may have crept in, however, are likely to be mine.

My thanks to Jonitha Rawatlal for wonderfully accurate typing, and to Gillian Bowden for her enthusiasm and for proofreading. Professor Mandy Goedhals made helpful suggestions regarding some of the historical introductions. Noleen Turner's generous sharing of her considerable expertise on *izibongo* is much appreciated. Early on, Naadira Wahid assisted with some of the biographical research. I am grateful, too, to the publishers: Elana Bregin and Frances Perryer for editing, and Maggie Mostert and Veronica Klipp for their confidence in the project and their support.

To Irene Ubuto for unwavering support on the home front, *ngiyabonga kakhula*. Elizabeth Lütge Clarke read and responded to the collection, and has been, at all times, the *very* best friend anyone could ever ask for.

Thanks to the University of Durban-Westville, which awarded a research grant that helped me to bring this anthology to fruition. This material is based upon work supported by the National Research Foundation under grant number 206 3140.

Judith Lütge Coullie

SOUTHERN AFRICA IN THE 1890s

PORTUGUESE EAST AFRICA (MOZAMBIQUE)

Lourenço Marques
Delagoa Bay
Kosi Bay
St Lucia Bay

Indian Ocean

ZULULAND
Durban
Port St Johns
East London
Grahamstown
Port Elizabeth

RHODESIA (ZIMBABWE)
Limpopo R.
SOUTH AFRICAN REPUBLIC (TRANSVAAL)
Pretoria
Johannesburg
SWAZI LAND
1894
1895
1886
NATAL
Tugela R.
Kei R.
Drakensberg

SOUTH-WEST AFRICA (NAMIBIA)
BECHUANALAND (BOTSWANA)
Mafekeng
1896
1894
Harts R.
Vaal R.
1892
ORANGE FREE STATE
Kimberley
Griquatown
Bloemfontein
BASUTOLAND (LESOTHO)
1884
1885
1884
CAPE COLONY
Orange R.
1880
1873
Cape Town

Atlantic Ocean

Railroad
German or Portuguese colony
Republican territory
British colonies
Annexations to British colonies
British High Commission territory
British chartered company territory

Provinces in the mid-1990s

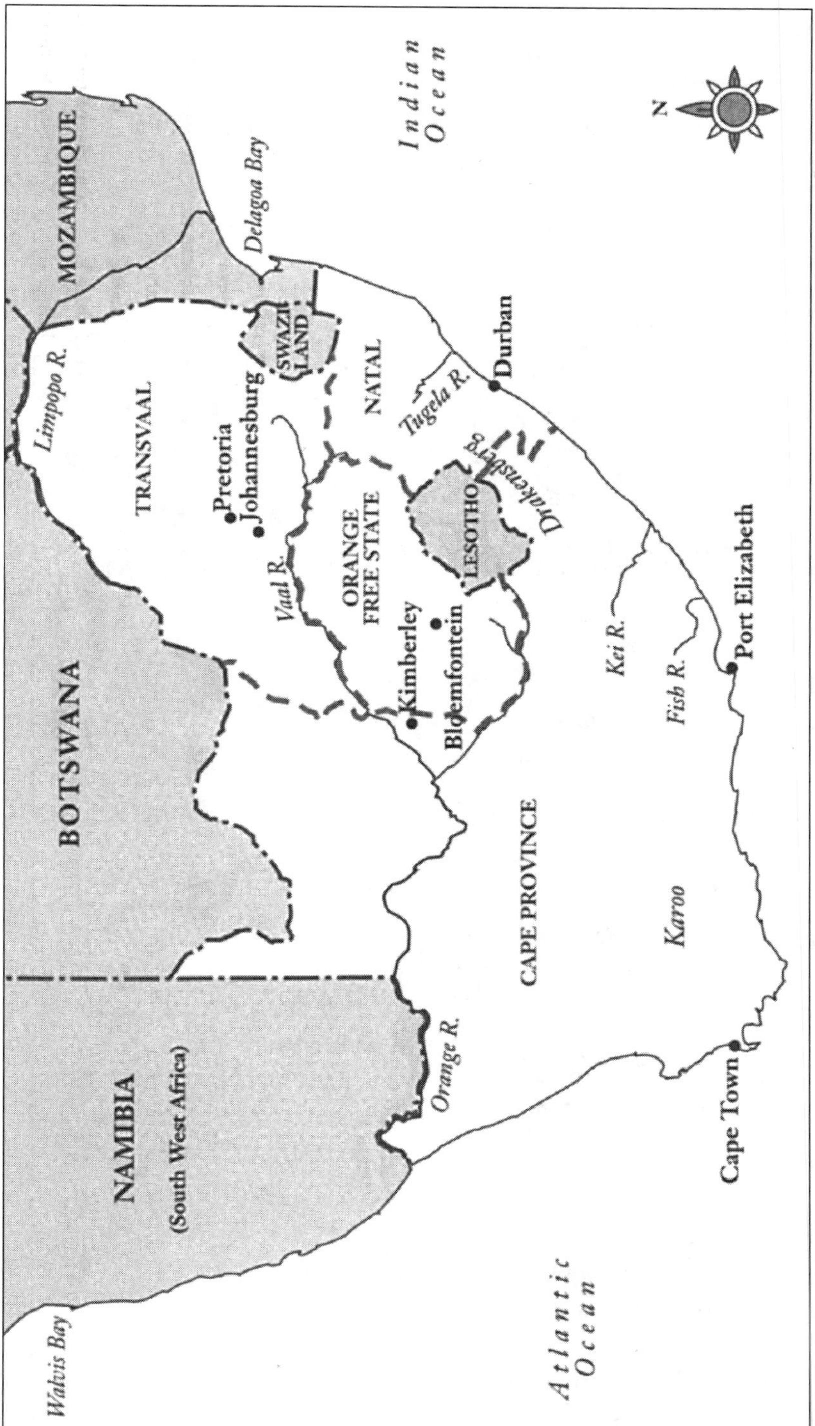

BANTUSTANS

Introduction

The time has come, then, to record the end of a way of life

and, more elusive, the truncated lives of women who were

shaped by a warped society yet who were, all the same,

portents of the future.

LYNDALL GORDON

In the light of the historical rifts between South African women, the title, *The Closest of Strangers*, may appear to some to be overly naïve. After all, what possible closeness could be envisaged between the typical white woman, who enjoyed an exceptionally high standard of living and sent her children to well-equipped, free state schools, and her black counterpart,[1] confined to impoverished rural areas or urban slums and who, *if* she was able, sent *her* children to under-funded, overcrowded schools. Historian Cherryl Walker notes that even before the Nationalist government's adoption of apartheid in 1948, barriers between different groups of women were rigid: 'women's sense of community with other women, the basis of their perception of themselves and their political mobilisation as women, was circumscribed by sturdy boundaries of language, ethnicity and the broader race consciousness around which South African society was organised'.[2] Although the employment of black women as domestic workers in white households became the norm in the twentieth century, this situational intimacy did not develop into empathy or gender-based alliance because of racial, cultural and class differences.[3] And once apartheid became official policy, the fractures of the colour bar deepened into chasms.

This divide – that is, the lack of ordinary social contact between members of different race groups – is reflected in almost all of the life writing collected here. More often than not, the testimonies recount no cross-racial sisterhood,

1

no shared intimacy. On what grounds, then, is the title's claim to closeness between women justified? Ironically, notwithstanding this utter separateness (and even somehow enabled by it), it was common for women to experience long-term mutual dependencies. The black maid was (and frequently still is) an indispensable, if seemingly invisible, feature of the white woman's life. And the white employer's goodwill was often all that stood between the black domestic worker and destitution. For, in the black woman's world, traditional social structures and communities were crumbling, to be replaced by migrancy (with its devastating effect on families and communities), job reservation, and inferior education. In these respects, the relationship was indeed the very closest, even though the strict limits of intimacy – marked by the maid's respectful 'Madam' or 'Missus' and the employer's familiar use of the 'Christian' name of the maid (almost never her mother-tongue name) – were rarely breached.

Few white women, however, readily admit in their life writing either to dependence on black servants or to their racially-based privilege. The late Marike de Klerk, the ex-wife of Nobel Prize-winner F.W. de Klerk, makes a rare confession of what was, in my own experience as a white South African, a common insouciance towards the vast discrepancies between the different race groups' standards of living:

> Like most of my school friends, I simply accepted that black girls went barefoot, wore worn-out clothes and later worked as servants in white homes. [...]
>
> I calmly accepted that black women sat on the floor instead of on chairs or benches in white homes; that black people died illiterate; that coloured people differed from me.
>
> *I in my environment and they in theirs,* I thought, as did most of the children in my class.[4]

Conversely, for an oppressed person like Sindiwe Magona, it seemed that whites were immune to pain or loss:

> It seems strange now, of course, but the idea of, say, white people suffering bereavement never crossed my mind. Even their tragedies were so far removed from my world that I had never stopped to think of white people doing anything they didn't choose to do.

How was I to begin thinking that people like that might be hurt sometimes?[5]

In spite of its implacable divisiveness, however, racism did foster some real cross-racial friendships, particularly during the middle decades of the century when exceptional women of all races, such as Lilian Ngoyi and Helen Joseph, came together in sisterhood to protest against rampant discrimination.

The paradox of ubiquitous racism is that it branded *all* South Africans, in a sense binding them together in their experiences (albeit dissimilar and estranging) of the extremes of segregation. Magona draws attention to the vicious pervasiveness of apartheid which reduced people who were not of one's own kind to faceless ciphers:

> As individuals, we saw we were all caught up in [apartheid's] far-reaching tentacles, be it in the soul-destroying ghettos of the disenfranchised or in the soul-destroying, decadent splendour of ill-gotten wealth.
>
> White women could not escape the privilege which their colour bestowed on them. Black women could not escape the discrimination which theirs made them heir to.
>
> We were all brought face to face with the faceless 'them' we had known, without knowing, all our lives![6]

Thus the paradoxical intimacy and alienation embodied by the title is tragically apt and has resonance for each of the women represented here. But it also, in a sense, embraces every reader, for we are each alone in our selves. For each of us, our sense of who these women were and are, and what they felt, will be determined by the particularities of our own realities. My hope is that these extracts may teach us how to transcend our own narrow concerns and engage with experiences and truths that may differ from our own, even though such imaginative engagements can only ever be partial, fragmentary and crude. In the words of Magona, 'although another may sympathise when I bleed, the tears can only be mine'.[7]

As penetrating and inexorable as racism was during the last century, these autobiographical passages go some way towards fracturing the focus on women as mere representatives of race groups. They encourage readers to engage with each woman on her own terms. To think in terms of racial stereotypes, rather than individuals, is morally and ideologically questionable; the erasure of individuality is precisely what apartheid promoted.

While it is true to say that all South Africans who were not classified 'European' suffered appallingly as a result, and that all South Africans who were classified white enjoyed enormous state-sponsored benefits (circumstances which are manifested over and over again in the life writing), some of these pieces, through their portrayal of black female agency, subvert the cruder racial stereotypes that commonly depict blacks as mere passive victims. This tendency towards the 'victim syndrome' probably arose during the apartheid period out of a fear that any 'positive reporting' would reduce the overall impact of the collective sufferings of blacks.[8] But however well-intentioned (and accurate as a generalisation) this emphasis on victimisation may have been, its unfortunate result has sometimes been to inadvertently reinforce stereotypes and conceal the achievements, victories and heroism of ordinary and extraordinary women. For instance, from the praise poems (*izibongo* and *izihasho*) included here, it seems that black women are less likely to present themselves as victims in oral self-representational texts than they are in elicited researcher-collated testimonies or autobiographies. A possible reason for this may be that, poor and disempowered though these women undoubtedly are, in their own communities where such praises are performed, they portray themselves as agents on the strength of having made active choices in their lives – even when those choices may have been socially discreditable ones, such as being promiscuous or drinking heavily. Researchers, however, may well construe the subjects as victims and thus doubly disempower them.

In its formulation and impact on South African lives, racism has been brutally crude as well as insidiously subtle. It has, moreover, taken many forms, some of them unexpected. For instance, in the early decades of the twentieth century, problems of race, as defined by the whites of the time, frequently related to antagonism between the two dominant settler groups, namely, the English and the Boers/Afrikaners, then to issues of skin colour. The popular understanding of racism as discrimination against 'non-Europeans' is the more apt association, however: from the earliest days of colonisation at the southern tip of Africa, settler interests have ceaselessly eroded the rights of the indigenous peoples. For many whites, Africans were not merely of another race, but another species of human being. Although some interracial mixing and miscegenation did occur, the ruling classes eschewed the idea of a melting pot. Initially espousing the fiction of a 'separate-but-equal' political dispensation, policy makers were not long able to keep up the pretence that they sought equality in the distribution of land, services or even basic human rights.

Given the considerable benefits that accrued to all whites as a result of institutionalised racism, one might reasonably expect to find a significant number of texts by white women at least obliquely indicating support for white supremacy. In fact, very few openly express racist attitudes. Of the 80 or more autobiographical texts in English by white women that I have read (not all of which were selected for inclusion in this collection), the only one that explicitly endorses the apartheid government is Joyce Waring's.[9] (Her husband was, for a time, something of an oddity as the only English-speaking Cabinet Minister in the Afrikaner Nationalist government.) More apparent, but still uncommon are those that indicate a 'partial' or circumstantial approval of racism. For instance, some criticise the cruder aspects of racism (and the Afrikaner government), while arguing in favour of a qualified franchise or the gradual lowering of the colour bar or the massive influx of white immigrants. There is also some post-apartheid revisionism, in which the narrator's past indifference to (or active promotion of) apartheid is regretted. For example, Marike de Klerk records her regret for a lifetime of advocacy for apartheid and Afrikaner Nationalism, but minimises the malevolence of apartheid by focusing on what she depicts as worse cruelties committed by other nations. Apartheid was, she says, 'a mistake' – one that at the time did not seem incompatible with the Christian faith so ardently espoused by its adherents. In this way she seeks exoneration for herself, her ex-husband and other white supremacists.

Also worth commenting on is the large number of autobiographical accounts by white women that fail to demonstrate any real antipathy to racism, or even to document it as a defining feature of their social context. How could these women's lives have been lived – or recollected – without some acknowledgement of the price that the majority paid to secure their well-being? Perhaps the answer, in part, is that the colour bar, and its later incarnation, apartheid, actually worked extraordinarily well to normalise what was grossly abnormal. Whites went to 'whites only' schools and churches; 'Europeans only' signs – displayed prominently all over 'white' South Africa – kept hospitals, post offices, theatres, libraries, restaurants and even parks, beaches and bus stops racially exclusive. Black South Africans – in so far as they impacted upon the white centre at all – served (I use that word advisedly) to keep that centre functioning smoothly. To many whites, the illusion was that whites were actually in the majority, serviced by a minority African labouring class. That all public facilities (and most homes) were cleaned by blacks was the norm – indeed, was 'normal'. For many, the master/mistress–servant relationship was largely incidental to the real business of living with one's white family and white friends, in all-white communities. It is thus perhaps not so surprising that a significant number of white women were able to compose memoirs that seem, in retrospect, so disingenuous; most were seemingly too busy coping with the minutiae of ordinary life to be politically aware.

One should not, of course, discount the fact that for many or even most of these women, insensitivity to the plight of the black majority was facilitated by a deeply ingrained prejudice, a conscious or subconscious belief that black people were inconsequential. But whatever its cause, the general failure of these women to interrogate in their life writing the institutionalised racism which was arguably *the* determining feature of their lives was undoubtedly bolstered by ignorance. Because of the largely irreconcilable class, language and cultural differences between whites and blacks, and the rigid inequities in access to amenities, there was little occasion for social interaction. Most whites took their privileges for granted, thought of themselves as superior, and found few challenges to their complacency. The vigilant Publications Control Board, responsible for censorship, was extremely active, ensuring an almost total suppression of oppositional voices, leaving little chance for consciousness-raising. By the late 1980s, well over 30 000 works had been banned.

Life writing: a century of self-representation

Life writing refers to that range of representational practices in which the subject seeks to depict the lived experiences of her or his own life or another's. This collection focuses on autobiographical accounts. Included in the range are oral and written texts, non-narrative praise poems and narrative memoirs, extracts from full book-length autobiographies, as well as short autobiographical pieces, letters and diary entries.[10]

It is always tempting to regard the autobiographical text as a straightforward representation of somebody's life. This is partly because most autobiographers invite us to take their stories at face value. Sometimes, however, this sense of transparency is compromised; perhaps the woman is a controversial figure, which leads us to question her version. In other instances, style or form may draw attention to themselves and interrupt our ability to imagine the woman and her life behind the words. For instance, the vernacular praise poems can, in translation and in print, appear formulaic and impersonal, challenging western expectations of autobiographical convention. This may also be true of the mediated testimonies of women whose mother tongue is not English. Such texts are important however, since they indicate the rich variety of self-representational practices employed by South African women and encourage us to consider not only *what* has been said, but also *how* it has been said.

Life writing, like all human endeavours, is shaped by the context out of which it emerges – and which, in its turn, it helps to shape. Because life writing undertakes to 'tell the truth' about the experiences of real people, its documentary and polemical value is often more assured than that of fiction. In this regard, I would argue that life writing during apartheid was more important than fiction, which is why it was commonly banned by apartheid censors. Even stories by ordinary South Africans that may seem to be apolitical in nature (such as Maureen Sithole's or Maria Tholo's accounts) are in fact *not* apolitical, because merely to testify to the brutalities of racism before and during apartheid is, in itself, a politically significant act.

Although much of the life writing published throughout the century is not concerned with politics *per se*, there are numerous women who relate their engagement with gender or race politics. Women like Sarah Raal and Emily Hobhouse focus on the devastating effects of British imperialism; Bertha Solomon describes a decades-long fight to improve the laws affecting (white) women. Then there are the even more numerous memoirs of anti-apartheid activists, which demonstrate the justness of the liberation struggle and vindicate its proponents (dubbed 'terrorists' and 'commies' by the state), while exposing the injustices of the 'Christian National' state and its 'God-fearing' agents. Activists such as Ruth First, Winnie Madikizela-Mandela, Helen Joseph, Frances Baard, Helen Suzman and Mamphela Ramphele are a small sample of those whose commitment to the anti-apartheid struggle came at great personal cost.

But social context is also crucial in determining who is likely to want – or be able – to record their experiences, and whose texts will find their way into public expression. From the life writing featured here, a pattern emerges of the gradual increase in South African women's involvement in the world of print. In the early decades of the twentieth century, white males' autobiographies dominated the field. Before the 1960s, no prose narrative autobiographical texts in English by black South African women appear to have been published. The passages by black women that appear in this anthology in the sections covering the first half of the century were either published much later (Phyllis Ntantala recounts her childhood in the 1920s, but her autobiography was only published in 1992) or, like Nontsizi Mgqwetho's text, belong to the indigenous oral tradition.[11] In the early decades of the century, black women seldom published their life stories, largely because of the restrictions resulting from the conjunction of racism and sexism. In general, state-sponsored schooling for Africans was hopelessly inadequate. Until the 1950s, most educational institutions for Africans were mission-run; thereafter, a policy of state-controlled inferior education for blacks, known as Bantu Education, was adopted. For young black women, this disadvantageous situation was compounded by the widespread preference in traditional communities for educating boys.

The first western-style autobiographies published by a black South African woman were Noni Jabavu's *Drawn in Colour* and *The Ochre People* (in the 1960s).[12] Significantly, Jabavu's family was part of a small, land-owning, educated, Christian African élite. Her father was (early in the last century) one of a handful of black academics and she obtained most of her education in Britain. In addition to adopting the self-representational prose narrative mode of the dominant culture, Jabavu seems to address a largely white audience, explaining admiringly – but in detached anthropological mode – the Xhosa traditions from which she has become distanced. Jabavu's texts raise the question: how many black women have been denied access to print because their life writing failed to conform to the conventions of the dominant culture?

The life writing collected here reveals a very gradual – and still incomplete – process of democratisation. Full-length autobiographies by black South African women were slow to appear; they only emerged in significant numbers from the 1980s onwards. The inclusion in the literary record of black women and of the poor and uneducated from all sectors only began in earnest in the last 20 years or so. It was not until the late 1970s and '80s that the testimonies of illiterate or semi-literate black women were published, arising out of the need to allow those who were most disempowered to articulate their own stories. I have included examples from Caroline Kerfoot's collection of autobiographical writing composed by students in adult literacy classes, and from Lesley Lawson's and Helene Perold's *Working Women*. Full-length autobiographies by relatively uneducated black women, usually penned by white women, also began to appear in the late 1970s and '80s. Some of the earliest of these (for example, Carol Hermer's *The Diary of Maria Tholo*) concealed the identity of the subjects behind pseudonyms. The stories of Frances Baard, Katie Makanya and Mpho 'M'atsepo Nthunya (all written by white women) followed.

A similar movement towards democratisation has occurred in the publishing of collections of translated oral praise poems. Until the 1980s, these collections tended to focus on the poems of royal or prominent men (with some royal women included). This is now changing, with attention also being given to the poems of ordinary people. The first praise poem presented in this volume, by Nontsizi Mgqwetho, evinces much that characterises the Xhosa praising tradition, while also manifesting some interesting transformations of custom. For instance, Mgqwetho employs the discourse of the warrior in order to reject male exclusivism (all professional Xhosa praise poets, or *izimbongi*, were male). Examples of less formal praises of rural Zulus were collected by Liz Gunner in the 1970s, and the *izihasho* of Zulu township dwellers were recorded by Noleen Turner's students in the 1980s and '90s.

Collecting South African women's life writing

In selecting texts for inclusion, nationality has been very loosely defined: although most of the women were born in and lived in South Africa, some chose to leave. For instance, Maggie Resha, Hilda Bernstein, Ruth First and Bessie Head went into exile while Nicky Arden, Lyndall Gordon and Prue Smith emigrated. Some were born elsewhere but spent significant portions of their lives in South Africa: Pauline Smith and Emily Hobhouse were British but were profoundly influenced by their experiences in South Africa, while Helen Joseph only came to South Africa when she was in her twenties, but became a fervent activist in the anti-apartheid struggle. Mpho Nthunya was born in Lesotho but educated in South Africa, living in Benoni Location for ten years with her migrant worker father. (Her story reminds us that borders were porous – particularly to indispensable labourers – before and during apartheid.)

The meaning of 'woman' in this country is constantly in flux, inevitably entangled with questions of race, ethnicity, class, religion, relationship to the colonial culture, and so on. Nevertheless, as important and extreme as the differences between women's lives may have been, all South African women throughout the century have been subjected to varying degrees of gender-based discrimination.

For many, colonialism intersected detrimentally with sexism. The codification of customary law by colonial authorities, for example, was generally disadvantageous to African women. For countless black women, racism and its attendant land appropriation, along with forced adaptations to capitalism and notions of western individualism, resulted in extreme economic and emotional insecurity. As black men were emasculated by racism, and as large numbers were increasingly unable or unwilling to engage in stable, responsible relationships with women and children, male exploitation of women and girls escalated in frequency and degree. In white communities, men who learned and perpetuated a sense of their inalienable right to dehumanise black South Africans often felt that they had a similar right over women.

Thus the oppression of women, although unequally imposed, was never confined to any one particular race group, and the brutalities of the gross infringements of human rights that apartheid bred necessarily seeped into – and continue to sour – gender relationships in this country.

An inevitable question that arises in a collection of this nature is, why concentrate on *women's* life writing? There are many reasons for this, chief among them the fact that a collection of women's life writing challenges any notions of an essentialised, universal femininity upon which the subjugation of women relies. This remains a pressing issue in the otherwise enlightened climate of contemporary South Africa. In spite of the new Constitution, which guarantees gender equity in theory, women – regardless of age, race, class or creed – are still suffering the consequences of gender systems that retain as their central tenet the oppression of women. Another compelling reason for a collection like this is that women's lives and contributions to history have long been obscured, both through deliberate design and unwitting neglect. Although this is changing, historical record is still disposed to keep men in the spotlight. This collection is an attempt to correct that distortion.

In order to place the women in history, the passages are grouped chronologically in terms of the time frame in which the narrated events occur, and a brief historical summary introduces each section. Most of the accounts are so manifestly marked by the passage of time – by transformations of the landscape, economy and political, social and familial relationships – that any other design, for instance by theme, would be spurious. It would simply cloud the larger narratives of industrialisation (with its attendant creation of an impoverished black working class), urbanisation and increasing racism in which these accounts are embedded. Any different arrangement would obscure, too, what is often paramount for the autobiographical subjects – the inexorable force of these currents on the women themselves, and their efforts to negotiate a self within the parameters of what was, for many, a bewildering transformation.

The resulting collection of women's life writing provides a fascinating patch-work record of the period 1895 to 2000, and the role that women played in the shaping of their history. Many pieces lay bare experiences or events that highlight the known or expected: the racism, forced removals, police brutality, banning and imprisonment, black poverty and white privilege, during a century of the most profound social changes in southern African history. Others record less familiar circumstances, such as English–Afrikaner antagonism, a glimpse into the lives of Indian South Africans, or the anarchic face of the transition to democracy. But whether familiar or strange in their subject matter, all of the testimonies provide insights into history from the unique perspectives of women who have lived through and engaged with the historical and political process.

In my choice of texts, I was motivated by a desire to give a diverse range of women – the unemployed, illiterate and disempowered, as well as the educated and privileged – the chance to be heard. Although texts by white women con-tinue to predominate in the literary field, I have intentionally included in this collection a greater number of pieces by black women, rather than duplicate the racially imbalanced patterns of textual production.

Extracts were reproduced with as little editorial interference as possible, with few cuts and correction only of obvious typographical errors. Generally, my amendments or notes are indicated by square brackets; those in parentheses are those in the original text (inserted by either the author or the editor). To assist readers to understand unfamiliar terms, we have appended a glossary at the back of the book.

My hope is that readers will be inspired by these autobiographical samples to read the full texts; also, that these accounts will encourage other South African women to recount their experiences. In post-apartheid South Africa, the need for South Africans to re-examine the past, to 'write off' personal history and to re-write themselves is, it seems to me, particularly pressing. This need is tacitly acknowledged in the call to the nation, to the citizens of the 'new South Africa', to testify before the Truth and Reconciliation Commission.[13]

For most whites, political transformation has meant an abrupt shattering of apartheid's cocoon-like illusions. Much recent life writing by white women (and this is more marked in women's writing than in men's) is characterised by shades of guilt, self-doubt and some retreat from the kind of narratorial confidence that, until recently, typified white writing. In the 'new South Africa', the old certainties of the ruling caste have succumbed to the erosions of disclosure. Accepted truths have had to be questioned, and many informants seek in their narratives to construct new truths. The desire for closure and a fresh start, for the horrors of apartheid to be conclusively consigned to history, is reflected in much post-apartheid life writing. Some writers attempt their own personal versions of the Truth and Reconciliation Commission by reviewing their experiences of apartheid with a view to effecting reconciliation – with themselves, their compatriots, and their redefined nation. In *Country of my Skull*, Antjie Krog recognises gratefully that it is through the Truth and Reconciliation Commission that a new South African-ness is emerging:

> because of you
> this country no longer lies between us but within
>
> it breathes becalmed
> after being wounded
> in its wondrous throat
>
> in the cradle of my skull
> it sings…[14]

The long struggle against white domination is won, but the longer struggle is far from over. In post-apartheid South Africa, activism has taken a new direction, as women and men of all races and classes join forces to take up the fight against the HIV/AIDS pandemic. The testimonies of women who are HIV-positive remind us that every day, women and children are being infected with HIV by strangers, lovers, husbands, and even fathers and grandfathers, many of whom contribute to the abhorrent rape statistics in present-day South Africa. Challenges to the gender system have never been more urgent than they are today. In the light of these realities, I can find no more fitting conclusion to this introduction than to quote journalist Charlene Smith, herself a rape victim, who reminds us that: 'In the end women's liberation in Africa is not about the right to workplace equality, it's about the right to life.'[15]

Notes

1. The apartheid government divided South Africans into four basic racial groups (native/ Bantu/black, Asiatic/Indian, coloured and European/white), with the nomenclature changing over the decades. For the most part, I use the terms black, white, Indian and coloured to denote the four broad sectors of the population. At other times (in common with looser, post-apartheid usage) the term 'black' denotes any individuals who would not, under apartheid, have been classified as white.

2. Walker, 1990: 343.

3. Walker, 1990: 11.

4. De Klerk, 1997: 167.

5. Magona, Sindiwe. *Forced to Grow.* Cape Town: David Philip, 1992: 126.

6. Magona, 1992: 129.

7. Magona, 1992: 69.

8. Mamphela Ramphele, 1995: 67.

9. Unfortunately, Waring's *Sticks and Stones* (1969, Johannesburg: Voortrekkerpers) was one of many texts that were not included because of limitations of space or because of failure to secure permission from the copyright holders.

10. Because of the limitations of time and space, biography, autobiographical fiction or drama, lyric poetry, polemical writing or journalism have not been included.

11. However, Nontsizi Mgqwetho's praise poem (*izibongo*) was published in a Xhosa-language newspaper.

12. Regrettably, extracts from either of Jabavu's autobiographical narratives could not be included since we were unable to secure copyright permission from the author.

13. The Truth and Reconciliation Commission's objectives, as defined in the legislation, were to establish 'as complete a picture as possible of the causes, nature and extent of human rights violations'; 'to facilitate the granting of amnesty to those who made full disclosure of the facts relating to acts associated with a political objective'; and 'to restore the human and civil dignity of victims and recommend reparation measures'. These three goals were to be addressed by three committees. The Chairman, Archbishop Tutu, was particularly concerned that the experiences of the ordinary and unknown victims be heard (Krog, 1998: 23).

14. Krog, 1998: 278–79.

15. *Mail & Guardian*, World Aids Day Supplement, 1–7 December 2000: 5.

The Birth of South Africa

1895 to 1910

Before 31 May 1910 there was no unitary state in southern Africa, and South Africa as we now know it did not exist. The area and its peoples were under the political control of either the Boers or the British.

Before Europeans arrived here, the region was peopled by the relatively egalitarian hunter-gatherer San and the herder Khoikhoi groups. The San (also called Bushmen) were the first known human inhabitants of the sub-continent. The Khoikhoi (called 'Hottentots' by the Dutch) probably appeared in the Cape about 2 000 years ago. It was they who would have been encountered by the first Europeans – the Portuguese – to land on the southern shores of Africa in 1488 in their quest to open a sea route to the East. The Iron-Age Bantu-speaking peoples, who were pastoralists and agriculturalists, had migrated south in the first millennium. They established villages and formed more powerful, patriarchal states than the San and the Khoikhoi, and thus put up more resistance when encountered by whites in the 1770s.

The first colonisers were the Dutch who, in 1652, opened a refreshment station in Table Bay for ships of the Dutch East India Company travelling from Europe to the East. Six years later came the first party of slaves, who with their 'kitchen Dutch' are credited as being crucial to the development of creolised Dutch, or Afrikaans. The Dutch retained power until the Napoleonic Wars when the British occupied the Cape to safeguard the sea route to India. The Cape was formally ceded to Britain in 1814. The hostility between the Dutch farmers (or Boers) and the British was to endure for more than a century.

But just as the Europeans were divided, the indigenous Africans were diverse: in addition to those collectively referred to as the Khoisan, there were also the Sotho-Tswana groups in the interior, and the Nguni along the east coast. The main Nguni groups were the Xhosa in the eastern Cape and a number of clans further to the north, most of which consolidated to form the powerful Zulu state under Shaka in the second decade of the nineteenth century. These groups were not always at peace with one another, as vernacular literatures testify.

As it happens, any antagonism there may have been between different groups of Africans was soon overshadowed by regular clashes between the indigenous peoples and the Europeans that began just seven years after the first settlers arrived in the Cape and continued throughout the eighteenth and nineteenth centuries. Strife occurred over an ever-broadening front, as British and Afrikaner expansion north and east gathered momentum. Indeed, the eighteenth and nineteenth centuries are a catalogue of annexations and land-grabbing by the settlers, whose fear of the natives would eventually provide common cause for union of the four European-controlled states after the South African (or Anglo-Boer) War.

Relations between the Dutch colonists and the British before Union in 1910 were fraught with distrust and enmity, and did not seem likely to lead to an alliance. The Dutch Voortrekkers' attempts to escape British hegemony by venturing into the interior were of limited success: the Republic of Natalia established along the eastern seaboard in 1838 was annexed by Britain in 1843; the Boer republics north of the Vaal River – united to form the South African Republic in 1860 – were annexed by Britain in 1877. The Boers fought back in 1880, but once considerable deposits of gold were discovered in 1886, Britain determined to regain control of the region. Fears about Britain's ambitions led to the Boer declaration of war in 1899.

The Anglo-Boer War (known to Afrikaners as the Second War of Independence) was enormously costly. Fought from 1899 to 1902, the war caused large-scale suffering: 31 000 Boers were exiled and 110 000 imprisoned in concentration camps. Fatalities on the Afrikaner side are estimated at 7 000 soldiers and 28 000 civilians (most in concentration camps). An estimated 22 000 British troops and 20 000 Africans died. The war concluded with the Boer surrender of independence, and all four separate regions (the British colonies of the Cape and Natal, and the Boer republics of the Orange Free State and the Transvaal) were federated under British control. In 1903, a common

15

'native policy' was drawn up and in 1908–9 an all-white National Convention met to draw up a constitution for a united state. The South Africa Bill was passed by the British Parliament, and the Union of South Africa was inaugurated on 31 May 1910.

Kathleen McMagh

Kathleen Liesching, pictured here next to her Granny, was a fifth-generation South African of German, Dutch and 1820 British settler descent. Born in 1888, she spent her childhood in the Cape Town home of her grandmother. After the latter's death in 1902, she joined her parents on the family farm in East Griqualand (on the eastern slopes of the Drakensberg, south of Natal). Her parents' financial struggles made it difficult for Kathleen to proceed further with her education, and she became a teacher. Her first post was in Waterval Boven, where she met Irishman Joseph Patrick McMagh, whom she married on 6 November 1911.

This extract from her autobiography, *A Dinner of Herbs, Being the Memoirs of Kathleen McMagh* (1968), recounts a journey from Cape Town to Durban undertaken by the young Kathleen, her sister and their grandmother in 1895.

A trip to Durban

Of all the treats [the one] I loved best was being allowed to sleep in Granny's bed. Had I had my own way I would have enjoyed this privilege nightly; but Granny firmly believed that an old person drew life and vitality from a child during sleep, and she would not allow it.

Our domestic staff consisted of a series of transient 'Rosies', with whom Aunt Bessie did not seem to be able to see eye to eye. These maids reeked of patchouli, a pungent perfume from the East and much favoured by the Cape-Coloured girls in those days. Worse still they loved to sing at their work and they walked out with scarlet-coated 'Tommies'. More than once there were urgent and mysterious comings and goings by night, when a cab would roll up at our huge barred back-gate, whereafter we saw that particular 'Rosie' no more.

Granny used to sigh for the days when Fleurie, of old and faithful slave stock, had been the cook. No poffertjies were as light as those Fleurie had fried, no konfyt of green fig or water-melon had been as transparent, crisply green without and tender and juicy within, as that which Fleurie had boiled. Granny often said that in the days of the slaves servants took pride in their work and did not think of 'flankeering' (gallivanting) with low class white men.

Old Sally was our washerwoman. She lived at Rose Court, a slum dwelling of dubious quality down a lane off Long Street. Sally was very black, tall and of commanding appearance. She remembered and was proud of her slave ancestry, indeed she looked an aristocrat and had spirit. Granny once gave her a pound of pale Cambridge sausages explaining that they were English. Next wash-day she asked the old soul her opinion of them. 'Well, all I can say is,' said Sally in her downright manner, arms akimbo, 'If the English are as insipid as their sausages, then they are a very insipid nation and I don't want to have anything to do with such people.' Sally used the French word for sausages, 'saucisse' which she pronounced 'saucaisse' as we all did, she always referred to my grandfather as 'Die ou Sieur', a relic of the language of the Huguenots.

In our backyard was a washing stone, a slab of mountain granite worn smooth by use and placed tablewise on two supporting legs of stone. This was where Sally operated on washday. One Monday Ruby and I teased her and she upped and gave us each a well-aimed box-on-the-ears with a well-soaped pillowcase. We ran crying to Granny but she would have none of our tales.

'Sally is a decent black woman old enough to be your grandmother. If you want her to respect you, you are to respect her. Go and tell her you are sorry,' so with tear-filled eyes and soapy ears we had to go and eat humble pie.

It was about 1895 that Granny got bronchitis and, as the long cold wet winter was imminent, the doctor advised her to go to sub-tropical Natal for six months. And so it happened that we prepared to voyage to Durban in the steamship *Greek*. We were due to sail at dawn so went on board in the late afternoon; but I refused the evening meal in the hot stuffy saloon and it soon became evident that I was far from well. I tossed in my narrow bunk all night and next morning when the ship's doctor appeared he took one good look at me and did not like what he saw. He notified the captain and said that I was probably sickening for scarlet fever, this would mean quarantining the ship so we were ordered ashore. Poor Granny, ill and no longer young!

Aunt Bessie had to pack up hurriedly and the four of us found ourselves on the quay on a raw damp morning with nowhere to go, for our house had been let furnished for the six months together with the services of the excellent St Helena woman, Sarah, who had succeeded the stream of transient 'Rosies'.

A solitary hansom cab came ambling along and, hailing it, Granny told the cabby to make a tour of the hotels and boarding houses. None of them would take us in. When they heard that there was a sick child in the party they said they had no vacancies. Eventually Aunt Bessie thought of her friend Miss Metlercamp, the proprietress of Madeira House, a comfortable boarding establishment on Tuin Plein near Government House. Here we found sanctuary and I was soon being attended by our doctor. He pooh-poohed the idea of scarlet fever – these young doctors did not understand children, he growled. I had a feverish cold and nothing more serious than that. He was right for in ten days' time we were ready to set forth once again. It was then decided that we should go by train as far as East London and take ship from there, a short voyage of twenty-four hours.

Railway travel was quite an undertaking in those days and our journey was to prove no exception. We had to change trains several times, times when poor Aunt Bessie had to collect all our belongings, roll up the bedding for the four of us and, above all, see that nothing was left behind. On looking back I cannot imagine how this little aunt – she was only four-foot-ten in height and slightly built – performed the Herculean task of coping with an ailing mother and two small children and baggage.

The sort of carriage we travelled in would today be a museum piece. The compartments were in pairs, each pair sharing a lavatory. There was no through corridor and when the conductor came to punch our tickets he had to walk along a nine-inch step that ran outside the coach, along its length. I can still see this peaked-capped official, with his arm around the frame of the open window, examining our tickets; and I never wearied of watching the rise and fall of the telegraph lines as the train sped along. It was a phenomenon no one could explain to me.

These trains provided little comfort. There were no beds. The bunks were fixed and Aunt Bessie would spread newspapers on the none-too-clean floor before making up a bed for Ruby and me on it. There was no electric lighting. A Coloured man came to our carriage at dusk, when we happened to halt at some station, to fit a paraffin lamp into a socket in the ceiling of the compartment. I wept in terror lest it fall on us.

There were no dining-cars. The train stopped at certain stations where the passengers alighted to take meals at the restaurant on the platform in the twenty or thirty minutes allowed. The restaurant was generally a small crowded room having walls of corrugated-iron lined with varnished ceiling board. Granny declared that the soup was always so hot, the meat so tough and the knives so blunt that one was able to eat practically nothing. The price charged was half-a-crown. This nightmare journey must have taken about three nights and days, for there were halts and delays at various junctions where we spent many hours waiting for connections; and what Ruby and I must have looked like by the time we reached East London where we boarded our ship may well be imagined! We reached Durban after a voyage of twenty-four hours but were not able to land because the 'bar' was up, so we were transferred to a tug by means of 'the basket' – a huge wickerwork affair like a giant clothes hamper having a little door in it. Standing like a half-dozen fear-stricken sardines we were hoisted by crane from ship to tug and when we eventually reached the wharf we were landed in the same way.

We found Durban most intriguing. There were no hansom cabs and we did not know whether to be amused when we were invited to enter rickshas drawn by huge bead-festooned Zulus who picked up the shafts and trotted off effortlessly with their huge freights. When our ricksha boy leapt into the air with a wild cry we were tilted perilously and tried to re-assure ourselves by remembering that there *was* a little safety wheel placed especially at the end of an iron stanchion at the back. Granny reasoned that no one else seemed alarmed so we need have no fear, the main thing to remember was that 'Panzi' meant 'down' and 'Pendula' meant 'turn'.

The winters in coastal Natal are dry as a rule, but there were occasional showers when an army of small dark Indians, macaroni-thin, clad only in turbans and loin-cloths, appeared to sweep the streets clean of mud. Their women folk, each called Mary, just as the Indian males were known as Sammy, hawked fruit and vegetables in flat baskets, the design of which they had brought from their native land when they had come as indentured labourers to work for the Natal sugar farmers half a century before.

The betel-nut-chewing women wore gold studs in their nostrils and lips, rings on their toes, earrings and bangles galore. It seemed to us that the Asiatic made his wives the repository for his wealth, such as it was. In those days the Natal Indian and his several wives were humble unlettered folk walking barefooted and wearing flimsy cotton garments. They were alien to us, for at the Cape the only orientals were Malays.

We found life pleasant in Durban. Here we learned the habit of drinking tea at eleven in the morning and we grew accustomed to seeing Zulu males employed as house servants, 'house boys' as they were dubbed. Clad in white cotton tunics and short pants bound with scarlet braid these black men wore huge earrings of wood or horn and masses of tight bangles of copper wire round their legs.

We were comfortably lodged at a boarding house next to the theatre in West Street and, staying there as well, were two families with several boys. One of the mothers seemed to spend most of her time darning black-wool socks which festooned every chair in the drawing room whilst she carried her needle and darning shell, her darning wool and scissors in her hands.

This worried Granny, and after consulting Aunt Bessie, she decided to give her excellent fitted work-basket to this poor soul. My dear old grandmother was very tactful and asked Mrs Darnall whether she would accept the basket, it being large enough to hold her mending. Mrs D. took it with a very bad grace saying, 'It's an old basket, but it'll do,' and never a word of thanks was spoken. I, who had spent many a happy hour unpacking and re-arranging what I believed to be the most beautiful basket in the world sorrowed greatly at its loss.

We might have lodged at this boarding house for the duration of our stay but for an unfortunate incident. One day when I was playing alone in a corner of the empty courtyard a tall Zulu, one of the domestic staff, came to me and, drawing me towards him, lifted my dress. I gazed up at him quite unafraid although he seemed so huge, but some instinct made me suddenly break away and I made my way with all speed to Granny.

I told her what had happened and she, white as a sheet, turned to Aunt Bessie and said, 'Pack the portmanteaux. We must leave at once.'

Sarah Raal

Born in the 1880s in the Orange Free State, Sarah was in her early twenties when she was drawn into the hostilities between Boer and Briton. Her account of her active involvement as a member of a Boer commando is unique. Her four brothers were the first to be called up to fight, later joined by her father, who was subsequently arrested, followed by her mother, younger brother and sister. Finally, Sarah too was detained.

The events recounted here are taken from **The Lady Who Fought: A Young Woman's Account of the Anglo-Boer War** (2000), originally published in Afrikaans as *Met Die Boere in Die Veld* in 1936. They relate to the period after Sarah escaped from the concentration camp in which she was interred and joined her brothers' commando. The money to which she refers was her parents' savings of £500, which she had sewn into her dress. With amazing ingenuity, she managed to conceal this money from her compatriots and captors alike, and was able to give it to her parents when they were reunited at the end of the war.

It was a short skirmish, but one of the bloodiest I ever saw. We sat on the other ridge watching the fight. Two of our burghers had been captured. Then my uncle was wounded. He was shot through the hip, and the Commandant told him to ride away. Behind a rock lay one of the burghers and near him, behind another, lay an African. The burgher was ready to shoot should the African raise his head. My uncle, who knew nothing about this, galloped between them. Just as he did so the burgher fired and my uncle was hit in the heart, falling from his horse. His young son Andries, who was with us, became hysterical, and we had to restrain him from running to his father. Two more burghers were injured, but there were no further fatalities. Of the English seventeen were dead and many wounded, and the burghers had captured their horses and rifles by the time the fighting was over.

Then we had to establish whether or not my uncle was dead. My younger brother Abram and another young man, Roux, said they would go and check. They'd not gone fifty yards when they were peppered with bullets, but they made it safely and saw that he was indeed dead. They took his horse, which was still standing next to him, and his rifle, and galloped back. His horse, saddle and bridle were given to his son.

We moved a short distance before stopping to take care of the wounded. This was usually a difficult task as we could use no light for fear of betraying our whereabouts, and it was very difficult to treat wounds in the dark. We made a sort of screen by tacking blankets together with thorns. A few burghers then stood and held these to allow enough room inside. They stood on the blankets so as not to allow even the faintest glimmer of light to escape and betray us. Sometimes we were short of candles, and then we had only the light of matches in which to work with the wounded. When we finished we had to carry the wounded in blankets because they couldn't endure the bumping of the wagon. We moved off in the direction of Slagkraal, and arrived there at first light the next day.

The wounded had to be treated in a section of the house that was still standing. A few of the burghers, my brother, whose wound had not yet healed, my cousin Andries, who was still grieving and weeping about his father, and I stayed in the house. Commandant Nieuwoudt set up camp a short distance away, but close enough to be able to see what was happening at the house. During the night there was little chance of sleep as the wounded moaned and groaned, wanting first this, then that. Morning had just broken when Commandant Nieuwoudt ordered the wounded to be put in the back of the wagon and sent off. He ordered the rest of us to flee.

The English had surrounded us during the night. Before we knew what had happened, the house was showered with bullets and we had to catch and saddle our horses under deadly fire. Commandant Nieuwoudt told me I could choose for myself whether I wanted to make a run for it or hide until the wounded had gone, after which they would return and provide cover to enable me to escape, for it didn't look as if there were very many English. But I wouldn't hear of it. Imagine if Gosling, the 'women Commandant', got his hands on me! What a terrible thought! So I told the men I wanted to ride with them, and that if I was shot and killed they should ask the English for my body, take the money I still had on me, and give it to my parents.

On the stoep of the house we saddled up and prepared to ride out, all at the same time. First off was the wagon carrying the wounded. They almost died, poor things, because there was no way to steer and the two mules pulling the wagon just ran through the veld – all the bumping and shaking must have driven them half mad with pain.

Bullets rained down on us as we rode out from the stoep. Despite the fact that we lay as low as possible on our horses, I still felt as if I might get a bullet in my back at any moment. I felt my horse give way under me, and when I came to I was lying on the ground. It all happened so quickly that my companion was two hundred yards ahead of me before he realised that I wasn't there. Luckily I wasn't injured, and when I looked round to see what had caused my fall, I saw my horse had got both his front feet stuck in an aardvark hole. I jumped up, grabbed the bridle, and got him out of the hole. By the time my companion looked round to see if I was wounded or dead, I was back on my horse galloping as fast as I could to escape the line of fire.

Once we were all safe again we decided to go and scare the Khakis a little. This caused the English to fall back immediately as there weren't many of them, and from this we deduced that their main body must be close by and that they were probably on our trail. It certainly looked as if the enemy didn't want to give us any peace. So we decided to head in a completely different direction, as we needed time to rest. Our horses' legs were finished, the injured burghers' wounds had had no opportunity to heal with all the moving about, and we ourselves were exhausted.

In front of us lay a long line of ridges and we wanted to move through them, but we weren't at all sure where the English troops were located. For all we knew they might already be in the ridges. There was a long endless plain to be crossed, and if they were in the ridges they would allow us to get up close and only then let loose their cannon fire at us, exposed on the open veld. That would undoubtedly be the end of us.

I called the Commandant and said to him, 'Commandant, lend me your binoculars and I'll ride to the ridge. I can scout there, and see what's going on. If all is safe I'll raise a white handkerchief, and if you don't see anything you'll know the English have captured me.'

'We'll never shelter behind you, especially when you're so scared of being recaptured,' he retorted.

'But, Commandant,' I repeated, 'they won't shoot me if they capture me – all they'll do is send me back to the camp. Our animals are finished. We have to come up with a plan, and I'm determined to go.'

He then said I mustn't blame him if it didn't go well with me, and that he wasn't going to lend me his binoculars as he'd then be without them if they captured me. I asked him to organise another pair for me. My brothers were greatly opposed to my going, but I told them I'd already made up my mind. Then they insisted that I give them the money because the English would only take it from me if I was captured, but I wouldn't hear of it.

I mounted my horse and quickly rode out to the ridge. When I was some distance away the commando started to move. They came slowly, hanging back far enough so they could easily turn tail and flee if something went wrong.

When I reached the bottom of the ridge I stopped and studied it through the binoculars. I was so terrified that every stone and bush looked like an Englishman to me. I was actually shivering on my horse, and called myself a fool for ever risking such a thing. I wanted nothing more than to turn round, but pride and the thought that the burghers would think me a coward made me ride some distance up the ridge. There I halted, and proceeded on legs that could scarcely carry me a step further. Finally I reached the top. I promptly sat down and got out the binoculars. I concentrated, looking in all directions to see if I could see anything, listening to hear if I could hear anything, when suddenly a steenbok jumped out of the bush next to me. I fell off the stone I was sitting on, legs in the air, but nevertheless shouted, 'Hands up!' After a while I started looking for my revolver, and my only comfort was that the burghers would thankfully never know of my embarrassment. I didn't want them to lose their good opinion of me.

I picked up the binoculars and looked carefully round once more, but saw nothing. Then I broke a stick off one of the broom bushes, tied a white handkerchief to it, and waved to the burghers. They saw it quickly and hurried to the ridge. When they arrived it was decided to let the horses rest there until late that afternoon, while the scouts went off to find a safe place for us to rest for a few days.

We were hungry, for food was very scarce. The occasional cow or sheep we came across was so wild that we had to shoot from a distance. We had hardly any clothes left on our bodies, and our ammunition was getting dangerously low as time went by. It was a struggle to endure it all, and still to keep going and maintain courage.

That evening it was decided to split the commando. Two groups would move in different directions in order to confuse the enemy, for they had about twelve to fourteen companies in convoy. Breaking through their line would not be easy as their horses were well fed, and they had plenty of food and ammunition, while we were particularly badly off in these respects. They fought when it suited them, took plenty of rest, had enough doctors and nurses, and there were more than enough 'joiners' and Hottentots to guide them, and to locate and reveal our hiding places.

Our large commandos were now mainly in the Transvaal and in the Cape Colony. After our commando divided, the group I was with moved up the ridge because somewhere ahead was a convenient place where both we and our horses could rest for a while. If only we could get our hands on some food! I had a few pieces of biltong which I had looked after very well, for in our desperate circumstances you really couldn't blame anyone for stealing food, and if anyone so much as saw your mouth moving, they would ask what you were eating and whether they could have some. So we had to eat the few scraps we could find in stealth.

That same day we captured a Khaki-Boer on a fat horse. His legs were bound and he was wearing khakis – a real traitor. We took him some way with us and gave him nothing to eat. First he had to get really hungry. Then a couple of burghers stayed behind with him while the rest of us continued on our way. They wanted to 'shake him out' – send him into the blue yonder minus rifle, horse, clothing or boots. What happened to him after that I don't know, but I do know that the stripes on his back and his empty stomach would make him think twice before betraying the Boers again.

At about midnight we arrived at our intended place of rest. Here the mountains formed a sort of crescent and, after our scouts had been deployed, we rested as it looked safe and there was plenty of food and water for us and the animals. At eight o'clock the next morning the scouts were relieved, and everything still seemed safe. We then set about looking for food. Some went off to shoot game, and by afternoon we were all busy cutting biltong and hanging it in the trees so that it could at least be wind-dry before we had to move on. Wherever you looked you saw groups of Boers sitting around fires with pieces of meat on sticks, cooking them over their fires. The meat was scarcely pale on the outside when it was cut off with a knife and devoured; then more meat was held over the fire in the same way. All the leftover meat was stuffed into our saddle bags, for who knew when we might have to set off and where would we again find meat this easily?

That night we had to move on. The plan was to go to Kalbasdrif, where there were high mountains that could provide shelter and rest for some ten or twelve days. It started raining heavily, and it was so dark you couldn't see the person next to you. We struggled on, and every so often someone would call 'Halt!' That usually meant that the ambulance had fallen into a ditch or was stuck in the mud. Oh, what a terrible night that was. If anyone had told me I would live through such times I wouldn't have thought it possible, but the longing for freedom, a deep empathy with our people suffering in the camps, and the blood of the Afrikaner nation flowing for freedom and justice, inspired us to continue.

I often felt pleased that my parents knew nothing of how hard things were for me, for they'd brought me up in a refined and Christian way, and it would have broken their hearts to see me in shredded clothes, tanned brown, and thin from hunger. If only they were still alive we could make a new beginning together after the end of the war. I was still young and could be of great assistance, and my brothers could once again ease the burden of farming for my father. The thought of them dying in a concentration camp and being buried like dogs, wrapped in a khaki-blanket, used to drive me mad.

Emily Hobhouse

Born in England in 1860, Emily Hobhouse was an active campaigner for the rights of Britain's most exploited workers – miners and children. When the Anglo-Boer War broke out, she became honorary secretary of the women's branch of the South African Conciliation Committee and in 1900 organised a women's protest meeting against the war. As reports of Boer farm burnings filtered through to Britain – the result of Lord Kitchener's scorched earth strategy, which entailed the destruction of farms, crops and livestock – Emily decided to visit South Africa in order to render aid to women and children. Her campaigns to improve the plight of Afrikaner inmates of the concentration camps resulted in her deportation from South Africa under martial law in 1901. She subsequently wrote a book entitled *The Brunt of the War and Where it Fell* (1902), which did much to arouse sympathy for the Boers who had suffered greatly during the hostilities.

She also initiated a campaign to promote home industries amongst impoverished Boer women. In 1923 she published a translation of a Boer woman's diary, *Tant' Alie of Transvaal, Her Diary* (1880–1903); her collected translation of Boer women's reminiscences, *War Without Glamour* (1927), appeared in print after her death in 1926.

The letter reproduced here, to her aunt, is from ***Boer War Letters*** (1999), which Emily wrote in 1903 on her return to South Africa after the war. The Boers had surrendered their independence in May 1902. Britain's promises of reparations for goods and livestock requisitioned by troops, as well as assistance for the reconstruction of the shattered Boer republics, were seldom fulfilled and the ranks of the 'poor white' class were swelled by thousands of destitute Boer families. Predictably, the atrocities suffered by the Boers served to fuel Afrikaner nationalism.

To Lady Hobhouse

Bultfontein Farm
12 June 1903

I am writing this in the bedroom of a Boer, and if being kindly treated makes you comfortable, then I am comfortable. It would be also impossible for any English person to be critical under the circumstances, for these well-to-do folk, the Rheeders, have been ruined by the war and I am in a burnt farm, where one half of the family is living in the waggon house and the other in the patched-up back rooms of the burnt and roofless house.

Mrs. Rheeder has given me her own bed and turned her children out of the room and she cannot do more. The ceiling is made of reeds, the floor covered with sacks and little goat-skin mats, and there are a few articles of furniture such as they have been able to scrape together since the peace. Not a penny of compensation has been received and the question, I notice, always raises an incredulous smile. In fact except two months' rations fetched eighteen miles from Bloemfontein weekly and the offered loan of oxen for ploughing after someone else had used them (which made it too late), no help whatever has been received. Even the Jingoes say in Bloemfontein: 'The word "compensation" has lost its charms.'

We all had our meal together at 6.30. It consisted of coffee, bread, biltong and confiture of some fruit which they eat with the bread and biltong. That was all. (This fare was of course luxury compared with that possible for the majority.) The man behaved and did the honours exactly like a gentleman, which in mind and manners he certainly is. His wife speaks good English and kept herself alive in Bloemfontein Camp 23 months by dressmaking.

My escort, Mr. Enslin, has been provided with a mattress on the floor of the adjoining room. He and I and Jacob, the Kaffir boy, started from Bloemfontein today at 10 a.m. Our four mules brought us along fairly well and we got here shortly before sunset, just time enough for me to make this rapid sketch of the farm. We outspanned for lunch near a dam halfway across an endless veld, and though there was thick ice when we started, I was baked and scorched all day.

One of the women here was 'out on the veld' all the war, and in consequence there is a group of pretty, healthy children, the youngest aged three, having been born in the war out on the hills.

To-morrow by 8 o'clock we are to be up and away.

It is a great jump from the luxury of the Fichardt's house, with fires, electric light and hot-water bottles, to the barrenness of this devastated place where I write by the light of the cart lantern with my feet upon my rolled-up bed.

I omitted to tell you that yesterday afternoon, before I left Bloemfontein, I spent with Mr. and Mrs. Fischer upon their farm, or estate if you like to call it so. It is so much easier to understand people in their own surroundings and Mrs. Fischer is a personage in her own domain, proud of her gardening and her plans for beautifying the place.

The house is built on the top of a kopje and is surrounded by orange trees hung thick with fruit, gold and green; paths and steps run down the sides of the hill to various avenues of gums and firs in the dale below and other little kopjes ornament the ground. Over the dam hung the willow trees still clothed in autumn gold. The farm is seventeen miles in circumference but the central position is so commanding, the air so clear, that you can see it all at once, and oddly enough it does not look large – in fact you look far beyond it some seventy miles towards Boshof, eighty towards Hoopstad, forty towards Brandfort, and so on. Size and distance are so deceptive here. The vegetable garden full of fruit trees – orange, lemon, loquat, almond, apricot and many others – seemed about four acres, but is in reality nearly seventeen acres and so on. Of course all the destruction wrought by the Military who occupied the farm was pointed out to me, and in the house itself only three rooms are now temporarily furnished, all Mrs. Fischer's furniture and silver having disappeared. And thereby hangs a tale which is both amusing and painful but too long to write. Some of his silver Mr. Fischer found in Government House where it was being used, and Mrs. Fischer's carriage came back from the same place. As to the rest of his silver – let us cast a veil. I learnt a great deal during my afternoon with them – of sweet veld and sour veld and all sorts of things that ought to be learnt in this country.

13 June. Strijker's Farm. We got here at 5 p.m. today. I got up early as agreed, for we were to start at 8 a.m., but alas! in the night the mules had stampeded and there was nothing to be seen of them. It took Mr. Enslin and the Kaffir hours to find them, so I occupied the time by sketching another ruined farm across the river. At 11 o'clock we got off and now after two days of driving, I feel myself dried up by sun and air, just like a piece of biltong.

We rested at noon at the Steenekamps' farm, where was the same story of no Government help – claims sent in but not a penny received; the people living in patched-up rooms at the back of the house; no oxen to plough with and another season lost. If they could but get £100 apiece *now*, it would be better than the full claims a year hence. But will they ever get anything? I begin to doubt it and so does Mr. Strijker, Field Cornet, of this farm, and so does everyone.

It is very difficult to write with a row of Boer children watching me.

For lunch we outspanned at the Aswegens' farm, and there found great poverty. They had not even coffee, and it is dreadful to a Boer to have no coffee to offer to a guest. I gave them some I am taking round with me and some rice. Ten days' rations (with an account) when they left the camp, but not another penny of help from Government have they had. No cows. Some hens which cannot lay for want of food. They live on goats' milk, hares and birds which they trap, and springbok which they shoot. You may ask how do they shoot without guns? Well, the answer shows what use may be made of the Constabulary – the only use I have yet heard that body of men to be. When they come to a farm with their guns this Boer says: 'Lend me your gun and five or six cartridges and I will show you how to shoot springbok and give you one.'

Thus he gets his supply and keeps the official in good-humour.

The springbok are coming back again after the war and I saw crowds today racing across the veld. It is nice to see the veld being re-peopled with something living.

14 June. Boshof. I wrote the above at Strijker's farm, but the sun set, leaving me suddenly in the dark and I had to stop. There was more hospitality and kindness than anything else at the Strijkers', but I had a bedroom given me, while the entire family, parents and six children squeezed themselves I don't know where. It was all quite clean.

I am afraid I hurt Strijker's feelings somewhat by bringing in my own *pad kos* instead of eating his, but I was tired and hungry and *could* not. And when he learnt I intended to continue my trek on Sunday instead of staying over with him I fell low myself and brought the English people lower still!

Poor Strijker! such a handsome, sad-looking man, a real God-fearing Boer. The Peace was to him a bitter wrong on the part of his own people, a distrust in God which is like a sin to him. Satisfied, he says, he is not and can never be. 'Give me,' he said, 'my Land, my Capital, my President, and take from me everything else and I will be satisfied. Never unless.'

He thinks it is God's will to try them a little longer before giving them back their country. He is not a wealthy farmer, but a man whose character makes him of some influence and importance. In common with the other Boers far from the towns, he can get no Kaffir labour, for the Military have spoilt them with high wages and they will live near the towns to have a good time. We all sat round the table for family prayers, when he read to us in Dutch and prayed a long extempore prayer and all sang.

This morning early, about 5.30 a.m., I was awakened by more Dutch prayers in the *eet-kamer* (eating-room), and the rise and fall of the hymn singing. Just after the sun had risen we inspanned, and snatching what breakfast I could we departed in a biting wind, wrapped in fur rugs and cloaks.

I forgot to say that yesterday we called at Mrs. Venter's to breathe the mules as we passed. I went in and talked to the woman who was ill in bed. She told me how during the war she was standing on her stoep talking to Mrs. Willman, a neighbour, whose child of two was in her arms. Three English soldiers shot at them and a bullet went through the child's head, killing it on the spot. Another grazed her dress and passed in at the door. When the men came up and saw the dead child they said it was shot by the armed Kaffirs who were, however, much farther off, and young Venter, who also told me about it, said he watched the affair from the kopje near and saw the white men shoot.

We drove for two hours and then stopped to breathe at Piet Nel's of Palmietfontein. The house, which was burnt to the ground, is a large one, and Nel, having a good deal of money, has been able to rebuild it, and has made it very habitable. But he has lost heavily. He is an old man and the day they were captured was a bloody one and stands out in their memory. Hearing a column was near they prepared to flee to the hills close by and hide. The women were in an open cart and Nel was in front with the waggon of goods. The soldiers fired at the women in the cart and shot Christine Nel, a girl of fifteen, through the head. Nevertheless, though the girl was dying, the house was fired, the outhouses destroyed, 28 horses killed and between 4 000 and 5 000 sheep slaughtered in the kraals. The bleached

bones are there still to tell the tale. They took me to the sheep kraal to see them –
masses of white skulls and countless bones strewed thick over the wide kraal and
piled in heaps upon the veld outside. All the bales of wool burnt too. They were all
taken on towards Kimberley, the wounded girl dying on the way and she was
buried at the next farm. In Kimberley Camp they were fifteen months. Another
child died in the camp. Miss Nel spoke of Miss Mellor, our representative there, as
very kind. This family has had no Repatriation help, has received nothing for
claims, and could not get even the loan of a waggon from the board to bring out
material for building from Boshof.

They were very polite and served us with coffee* and so we left the Nels'
farm and their bones behind us. But bones are never quite left behind –
bleached bones lie everywhere, in groups or singly; the poor animals have been
slaughtered beside every road.

We outspanned for lunch and built a fire at Quaggafontein where I visited
the Groenewalds. Both of these (a young well-educated couple) spoke English
well; the wife had been in Bloemfontein Camp with her two children who were
always sick there and have never really recovered from it. They look white and
ill now, utterly different from those hardy children I had recently seen who
were always on the veld. The man returned from prison to find he had nothing
but his wife and two children, but grateful to find them alive. He is now a
tenant farmer at a rental of £36 a year and is living on almost nothing. Claims,
as usual, sent in, but nothing paid.

He said some excitement was caused this week by the fact that 25 men
in Boshof District had been compensated. But they were *all* hands-uppers
supposed to be under the special protection of the British, and now they all
seem to think it would be just as well not to have been thus protected. Coetzee,
who lived close at hand, had claimed £250, and had been handed a cheque for
£15, but as he had been given a month's rations on leaving camp, £6.15s was
demanded back in payment for that, so £8.5 s was his compensation. And he
had surrendered under Lord Roberts' first proclamation! Ah! it makes them full
of bitter mirth.

Another man, Mr. Schrinder of Kaalplaas, whom I saw later in the day, also
under our protection, deported, sent to prison, brought back, sent to a camp, his
wife also in a camp, his house burnt, etc. claimed for £1 450 and received £48!
How they laugh!

---

* Please remember that when coffee is mentioned it seldom means that berry. Many curious things mas-
queraded under that name. The coffee used ran at that time from 6d to 9d per lb.! (E. H.)

Neither is the compensation equally doled out, for another claiming £96, and another claiming £50 both got £14. All these things are noted in their book. The *wilde Boer* in his own heart feels the three million pounds of the Vereeniging terms will never come his way.

Can't anything be done in Parliament to ensure a juster and quicker distribution of the promised help? Cannot at any rate pressure be put to get the payment of the military receipts for which Chamberlain has given his word? Money *now* is so needed. Already a second seed-time has passed and sowing cannot be done. Yet help should come to enable the sowing of mealies and potatoes in the autumn months (the spring here).

They are wonderfully brave and plucky, and the Groenewalds' house was so exquisitely clean and fresh, all they could borrow having been spent on doors, windows, roof, etc.

We trekked on, and by and by, after losing our way, halted a few minutes at Kaalfontein. Here we went into the house and coffee was brought.

Mrs. Van Niekerk, a former widow, lived there and had a military receipt for £70 unpaid. It was for a cart and horses which they took, and Thorneycroft gave the receipt. She was in Brandfort Camp at the time. This is another instance to add to those already sent. Unfortunately, as I learnt in Bloemfontein, they purposely lose these receipts at the Office after the Boer has sent them in and get out of payment in that mean way. So now the lawyers are advising people always to insist upon a *receipt* for their receipt, so as to have proof.

Can't the Liberal members get these paid? This widow in question is not so much in want of money as are many, but she had *no* relative fighting and ought to be repaid. Since peace just lately she has married again and is now Mrs. Rheeder.

Directed by these people we went on, and after an hour or so saw a tree. It stood against the sky and beneath it was a bell-tent and beside it a broken house. So we got out to find water for the mules and three young men issued from the tent. To my surprise two were called Lotz, whose sister I have often corresponded with, and the third, Mr. Jacobs, late under the Free State Education Department. They said the place was called Enkelboom (one tree), and they were overjoyed to see me drop as from the skies upon them. They said it was 14 June, the anniversary of the day their Commando laid down its arms, and they were keeping it very sadly and only solacing themselves by reading my book, when lo! I suddenly appeared! They were very nice, gentlemanly fellows, and belong to an important family here. But not believing in Government loans or Repatriation Boards at all, they determined to club together and go their own way. Borrowing from other sources through a law agent they bought sheep in the Colony, are tending them themselves, and proudly showed me 450 lambs of this season. They are young, unmarried and full of vigour.

But I must finish as this will catch the mail tonight.

Leontine Sagan

Leontine Sagan was born in Budapest in 1890, of Jewish stock. The fortune made by her father on the Kimberley diamond fields had soon dwindled and, after a spell in Europe with his young family, he returned to South Africa. In 1899 the family was reunited in Klerksdorp, which was part of the Boer Republic of the Transvaal. After the eight-year separation, during which mother and children had (financial worries notwithstanding) enjoyed the sophistications of Vienna, the family battled to settle into a unit again. They had, furthermore, to contend with the outbreak of the Anglo-Boer War. As *uitlanders* (foreigners), it was felt that they would be safer in the Cape Colony, but they were forced by circumstance to settle in Johannesburg, which was little more than a shanty town. In August 1902 Leontine and her mother travelled to Europe. The events described below, in an extract from *Lights and Shadows: The Autobiography of Leontine Sagan* (1996), occurred on their return in 1905. Leontine went on to become famous as an actress and producer in Germany and England. She died in 1974.

After two years' absence, we returned to Johannesburg and to a festive family reunion. My father had rented a small house and I was installed in one of its rooms as a bookkeeper to my brother who ran a vinegar factory. But mother insisted that my education should not be neglected, so twice a week I climbed the hill to a former German teacher who gave me lessons in literature and once a week I spent the afternoon in a labyrinth of peach trees, mimosas and cacti with a French lady who taught me her language. She was a weird old lady but her Gallic charm and worldly wisdom fascinated me more than the pedantry of the German *Fräulein*. We read *Manon Lescaut*, Murger's *La Bohême* and other endearing love-stories which inspired me to go to her and leave the German mistress on the hill. As a bookkeeper in my brother's office, I did not score much success. The boredom of the daily routine reduced me to a state of stupor; my additions were always wrong, and my poor brother wished I would go to the devil.

When the first flush of reunion had passed, our domestic life soon relapsed into greyness. After Europe, Johannesburg seemed very shabby and monotonous. The contrast was too painful. Johannesburg served only one god – Gold – and the Stock Exchange was its temple. All sections of the community, from the mining magnates down to the office boy, were possessed by speculation. When there was a boom on the Exchange, all business prospered, the population became giddy, and the golden sovereigns rolled lustily. But alas, when there was a slump, he who had owned carriage and horses yesterday would travel on foot today, his furniture would be auctioned, and he would disappear into parts unknown or be reduced to a lowly livelihood. Bankruptcies were the order of the day but, even while the victims were brought down, they firmly believed that that strumpet, the Stock Exchange, would soon take them back to her bosom. Nor were they far wrong, for any number of people continually climbed up and down the steps between poverty and wealth. Some were interesting personalities – good material for a professor of sociology – but as far as culture and intellectual pleasures went, Johannesburg was a vacuum. Art, music, and drama did not exist. Amateurs had the time of their lives because nobody could compare them with anyone else; they strummed on the piano and scratched on the violin to their hearts' content. It must be said, however, that the *joie de vivre* of this youthful crowd was so great that it animated their enjoyments.

Amateurism lost its rancid flavour in this bubbling hotpot of a mining camp. One could be poor today and rich tomorrow, so there were no social barriers. If a woman was beautiful, it made little difference whether she was a barmaid or a lady. Social life was not restricted to different races and nations; only the English kept more or less to themselves; for the rest, all classes of Europeans and a few Americans and Australians, moved through the drawing rooms of Johannesburg. One might have expected such conditions to lead to stimulating intercourse, but it was not so. Social life presupposes a foundation of tradition, yet most of the men and women who had left their countries and migrated to South Africa had not had time or opportunity to absorb the culture of their fatherlands. Poverty had caused their transplantation. In their new surroundings they had to struggle hard again to stay above water. And though it may have been their ambition to retain the values of Europe, they were handicapped by adverse circumstances.

As the wealth of the city grew so did the feasibility of visiting opera and theatre troupes, which would tour the few towns before returning to England. They were not always the best representatives of their art and in any case belonged more in the realm of entertainment than of art. Likewise, the local – and reasonably good – theatre troupe led by the hard-working Leonard Rayne, did not lay great emphasis on high artistic standards. The South African landscape, moreover, discouraged rather than encouraged Europeans. It is so massive and unyielding in its vastness that most people can bear it only by ignoring it and creating a pitiful picture in their gardens. The circle in which I lived praised the climate but complained about the emptiness of the terrain. In this respect, and in many others, I did not fit in with my environment. The exposed Transvaal landscape had a boundless fascination for me; it was infinite as if at the beginning of time.

I was at an age at which I longed for emotion and so social conventions tormented me. I did not know what to do with the fullness of feeling that I had brought back from Europe. In this state of impatience, I despised the people around me and struggled inwardly against quotidian life. Then one day I met a man who spoke to me of music and art. On my fifteenth birthday, he presented me with two books by Ellen Key, a Swedish writer and champion of women's rights. It was as if the door of my prison had opened. He was a friend of my younger brother, a geologist and a very worldly and fascinating man. He treated me as a grown-up and encouraged my inner revolt. Our friendship intensified when he lent me books by Zola and Maupassant, which I read secretly because mother would never have allowed it. I read through half the night by candlelight and, when that faint flicker seemed too risky, I read by moonlight at the open window. In order to talk more freely, we met in secret and wrote each other long letters which I received poste restante. He enlightened me on books, life in foreign countries, women and love. But he always remained tactful, tender and admiring. As our rendezvous on solitary nights might have betrayed us, we decided to meet in his office in town, and there he kissed me. But, now that I was so close to love, I delighted in picking each feeling to pieces. The more he tried to convince me of the beauty of love, the sharper did my critical mind penetrate it. It was not that I feared seduction; I just treated this affair in the same way as I treated my books over which I talked at random. It was a most curious relationship between a fifteen-year-old girl and a man of thirty-five. He was at heart an idealist and he did not want to harm me, but it fascinated him to influence my intellect, to awaken my mind and my senses, to use me like an instrument on which he played.

In spite of all the books I had read, I knew nothing about the realities of love, least of all of one's own body. I had a good figure and a piquant face; he explained my body to me like a work of art. He worshipped beauty as I did when I touched the marbles in the Vatican gallery. His adoration of my young body did not make me vain but grateful that I too should be an object of beauty. In no way did he physically corrupt me, but spiritually he exercised a tremendous influence over me. We now wrote to each other every day, and I kept a diary in which I dissected our friendship. I kept his letters and my diary – an open exercise book – on a shelf behind my little library.

One day I noticed a remarkable change in the behavior of my family. Their faces were drawn and pale and whispered conversations went on behind closed doors. Immediate fear seized me that my secret had been discovered. I searched for my letters and my diary; they were gone. Days of sinister silence followed. My friend's visits to the house ceased and I was ordered to remain at home. For days the 'terrible secret' lay between me and my family and I was at a loss to know what to do. One evening the storm broke. I was alone with mother. We sat in the dining room; I read while she sewed. Suddenly her words interrupted the brooding silence and she asked me questions which became hysterically persistent in cries of despair. She hit me and, in the flash of a second, she picked up a knife and stood over me like a goddess of vengeance. I screamed and ran to my room, locking the door. The next morning she was calm and quiet. The dreadful event of the previous night was never mentioned between us, neither then nor later, and I always hoped that she might have forgotten it. For when I grew older, I understood what a terrible infliction I had imposed on her proud, passionate heart and how she must have suffered, believing the child she loved so much spoiled and depraved. I loved her more than ever for it. But she was wrong – I was neither spoiled nor depraved. I had simply followed the path of my intellectual curiosity and I was [lucky] to encounter a man who understood my early maturity.

The months that followed were hard and bitter for me. I was kept like a prisoner under supervision. Wherever I went, someone accompanied me. But, in spite of all the precautions, my friend managed to smuggle letters to me and at last I learnt what had happened. My brother had had a violent scene with him, severed all connections and threatened him with the police if he had anything more to do with me. The irony of the whole experience was that, only now, in this clandestine correspondence, did our friendship change to a love-affair and we pledged our troth to each other until I was old enough to marry him. It must have been a reaction after the shock, for we never saw each other again.

I began to hate my family and when, after a time, freedom was restored, I was determined to earn my own living. Having borrowed enough money from my sister for lessons in shorthand and typewriting, after a few months I secured employment in the Austro-Hungarian Consulate. From clumsy beginnings I became an efficient secretary, but I did not like office work and stuck to it only because it gave me a salary and freedom from home. I managed to combine my taste for books and my duty of reading the monthly mining and trade reports by hiding the former under the latter. Reading remained my foremost occupation, good books as well as trash – in fact, everything I could get hold of – and in between I filled my diary with reflections on men and life. But this time, I kept it locked in my desk.

The most curious assortment of people came to the office: stranded travellers seeking help for their return passage to Europe, Austrian aristocrats who were going big game shooting, adventurers great and small, disappointed wives seeking divorce, servant girls and prostitutes. I took an excited interest in them all. Once I even persuaded my mother to engage a young abandoned girl for the house but, when she disappeared after a short while with my dresses, my philanthropy was checked by the ridicule of my friends.

In the course of only a few years, the social strata of Johannesburg had shifted. As some individuals became wealthier, class distinctions developed, and the democracy of the mining camp disappeared. A series of degrees emerged: (a) the mining people; (b) the merchants, doctors, and lawyers; (c) the proletariat of poor Jews and 'poor whites' (Afrikaners). The rich lived in Parktown, the middle class in Doornfontein, and the poor in Fordsburg. The Rand Club, the fortress of the upper ten percent, stood arrogantly in the centre of town. My family lived in Doornfontein where my brother had built himself a house on the outskirts of the suburb, close to the open veld. From its verandah, we could see the *koppies*, those barren, stony hills of the Transvaal, wizards of light and colour, ever bewitching one into different moods – into a mad joy of living in the morning, into voluptuous lethargy in the brooding heat of noon, while, in the magic hour between five and six in the afternoon, they cast a spell of melancholy longing. Our house stood amidst typical Transvaal scenery, and I loved it for this very reason. When I left the office at five, I looked forward to my walk home. It was thrilling to anticipate the moment when veld and hills would appear in the soft light of dusk. I usually started running then and roamed about in the veld until it was suppertime. Every Sunday morning I climbed the koppies and lay there, dreaming away the time until lunch which was signalled to me by mother waving a white flag.

My family became reconciled to my eccentricity about nature. Now that I was independent, I grew more and more away from my people. I went to dances, and when theatrical companies came to town from England, I never missed a night. My cavaliers were good-natured, jolly fellows with no pretence to highbrow ideals; at least, so I thought, for I divided my world into 'inside' and 'outside'. I had no knowledge of other peoples' psychology. Characters in books aroused my passionate feelings, but the cares of my family who worked twelve hours a day left me cold. I could not forgive them for the theft of my letters and diary. How terribly seriously youth takes itself! Nothing in the world could shake my belief that I had every right to my own young life for which I was seeking expression. But I had no means of expressing myself – no profession, no art. I found reason to hate but no reason to love.

After I had been at the Austro-Hungarian Consulate for a year, I received three weeks' leave which I spent in Durban. For the first time I travelled alone. I was seventeen years old. Never had there been a girl more intoxicated by her freedom than I. I had friends in Durban who had taken a room for me in a boarding-house on the Berea. The first days passed in the usual turmoil of dances, picnics, and sea bathing and I only came back to the boarding-house late at night. But one day, I did lunch at home. At the crowded table, there was an empty chair next to mine and when the meal was half done, a man came in and sat beside me. He was loudly welcomed by the others and I learnt that he stayed there only when business brought him to Durban. I rose from the table first and took my cup of coffee on to the verandah. Shortly afterwards this man followed and asked if he might keep me company. I was in such a holiday spirit that I would not have minded even a fat little fellow and, this one being tall and slender, I nodded delightedly. Our conversation flowed as smoothly as if we had known each other for years and when he asked me whether I should be in for dinner, I immediately said yes, although I knew I had an engagement in town. In the evening again we sat on the verandah with our coffee. Then he invited me to come for a walk and I flew upstairs to fetch my coat. He wanted to know whether I would like to see the electricity works at night. So we drove down and he showed me the stamping machines and the roaring furnace.

Would I go down to the beach? Anywhere – to the beach, on to the sea ... I did not care what happened; I trod on air. At that time there were no lights on the pier. Only the beam of the lighthouse cut through the darkness. There was not a soul about. In complete silence we walked on the soft sand. At midnight we returned to our boarding-house, whispered goodnight and, with a bumping heart, I reached my room.

The following day I roved about restlessly, avoiding my friends and waiting for the evening. In silent agreement we disappeared immediately after dinner and again walked, this time through the scented lanes of the Berea. Again deep silence and suddenly I was in his arms. For the first time in my life I was in love, so happily in love that for once I did not listen to my eternally critical mind. Even when he told me he was married and even when I thought over our short acquaintance, I could not react.

Then came the third evening. I put on my best evening dress; we dined in the same hotel where five years before I had dreamt of *Romeo and Juliet* and, after dinner, we went to a second-rate theatre to see *Charley's Aunt*. During the interval we left and climbed the hill back to the Berea past the gardens which were so still that I could not believe there were houses in them. On and on we strolled and I wished that we would never stop, that there might be no way out of all those twisting and turning alleys whose flowers scented the air. Breathlessly

I walked through this enclosure of enchantment. We came to a gate, a garden in whose deep shadows lay a spooky little house. He unlocked the door and went to light a lamp. I did not ask to whom the house belonged or why he had a key. I did not even go in. Anxiously I guarded my fairyland. We sat together in a big armchair on the verandah; confused emotion passed into sleep and, when I woke at dawn, I was lying huddled in his arms like a sleepy little schoolgirl. We returned to the boarding-house. I had four more days before returning to Johannesburg, but we wisely avoided the magic circle of that night. And yet my dream was not ended. A few hours before my departure, he asked me to leave my family, offering to leave his wife and to join my life to his. But I lacked the courage; my critical mind relentlessly guided me back to my Consular office, to my jolly admirers and the familiar routine of my existence.

Life was the same, yet I had changed. I did not look upon my physical sanctity as a piece of good fortune; on the contrary, I felt ashamed. I felt shabby and small. My love-story at fifteen, which passed pretty near the danger-zone, had been merely curiosity. This time I was really in love. I hated my persistent reasoning that reiterated: 'How could you have given yourself to a married man of whom you know nothing, and gone with him to British Columbia or wherever he wanted to elope with you – and ruined your future?' My future – that was the pivot around which all my yearnings circled. For that distant purpose I studied books; I collected experiences. The future should give me all that the present owed me. And yet my heart would remonstrate: 'What sort of person are you, longing to seize life and to hold it, but when the first opportunity comes, you creep back to the safety of convention?'

After a while, letters between us ceased. We never met again. I locked his letters away with the signet ring he gave me and decided to pick up the threads of life where I had left them. Twenty-five years later, on a visit from Europe, I enquired about him. But nobody I asked knew him. I feel that I ought to be deeply grateful to fate for having preserved for me, by unfulfilment, a youthful memory ...

Unions and Divisions

1910 to 1929

Opposition to the pro-white terms of union of British colonies and Boer republics had been expressed in 1909 by a delegation to Britain that included prominent Africans and William Schreiner (the brother of the novelist, Olive Schreiner). The response in Britain was poor, as many Liberals hoped that a strong union would eventually prove beneficial to Africans, in spite of the fact that the Union's constitution established the colour bar and denied the franchise to all blacks other than those on the Cape voters' roll.

The new South African Parliament promptly began to pass racist legislation, partly in an attempt to unify Afrikaner and English whites around a common cause but also because the ruling class feared that massive social and economic upheaval set in motion by the discovery of gold and diamonds would sabotage social control. In order to constrain African workers, the 1911 Natives' Labour Regulation Act made it an offence for Africans to break a labour contract and required all male African workers to carry passes. In 1913 sharecropping was prohibited (in order to compel Africans to sell their labour), and in the same year the Natives' Land Act divided South Africa into 'white' and 'black' areas and prohibited Africans (67,3 per cent of the total population, according to the 1911 census) from owning or renting land outside designated reserves (7,5 per cent of the land).

The devastating effects of these Acts were apparent almost immediately as thousands upon thousands of African families were evicted with nowhere to go and no prospect of earning a decent living. Still, racist legislation continued to emerge, creating separate administrative structures for the rural native reserves (1920) and establishing urban 'locations' for temporary accommodation of Africans who needed to be near cities in order 'to minister to the white man's need' (1923). In 1924 job reservation was legalised, and in 1927 the Native Administration Act afforded the Governor-General wide powers of control over Africans. There were, moreover, incidents of human rights abuses, the most prominent being the massacre at Bulhoek of 183 members of an African religious sect.

Bitter and betrayed, educated Africans (who since the late nineteenth century had eagerly embraced Christianity and the colonial lifestyle) reacted to the Act of Union by forming, in 1912, the South African Native National Congress (SANNC, the forerunner of the African National Congress).

Clearly, assimilation was not on the agenda for whites. Systematic discrimination included restricted female mobility and urban residence rights, while a national system of customary law secured the patriarchal authority of chiefs and homestead heads in order to tie African women to homestead production, thus freeing men to seek work in urban areas. Protests by Africans took the form of representations to government (South African and British), boycotts, strikes and anti-pass campaigns. Most unnerving to whites, however, was the formation of the Industrial and Commercial Workers' Union (ICU), which by 1927 had a membership of 100 000 and an even broader base of popular support. White fears were to prove unfounded, however, for by 1930 the ICU was a spent force.

Some historians have argued that in the years leading up to the formation of the Union, white worker hostility towards Africans was exceeded by that towards Indians. Between 1860 and 1910 over 152 000 Indians arrived in Natal, most as indentured labourers. Anti-Indian legislation began in the Boer republics as early as 1885, followed in Natal by a tax on Indian workers to encourage repatriation and (in 1896) limits imposed on the Indian franchise. In 1897 trading restrictions were enacted and voluntary Indian immigration curbed. Mohandas Gandhi, the Indian-born, British-trained lawyer who had arrived in Durban in 1893, rose to prominence in the Natal Indian Congress, a resistance movement founded in 1894. In the Transvaal, a pass law for Indians led to the adoption of Gandhi's famous policy of *satyagraha* (truth force, or passive resistance). Britain and India's indignation at Gandhi's arrest and brutal police reaction to the spread of strikes and protests in 1913 resulted in small concessions (the discriminatory tax on indentured workers was scrapped and Indian marriages were officially recognised); however, the Union government then prohibited all further immigration of Indians.

The spirit of resistance was flourishing among coloureds (those of mixed blood but also those who were descended from the Khoikhoi and San tribes). The African Political Organisation, formed in 1902 in the Cape under the leadership of the grandson of a slave couple, objected to Britain's failure to extend the franchise to coloureds in the former Boer republics after the Anglo-Boer War. Originally, the APO sought to integrate coloured people into white society, but later (by 1910 membership had grown to 20 000) the organisation co-operated with African protest organisations to fight all racist discrimination.

Boer society was in a crisis at the turn of the century, with thousands of impoverished and unskilled Boers drifting into urban areas, away from the farms destroyed by British 'scorched earth' tactics and then drought. The rallying call for renewed Afrikaner pride came in the first decade of the twentieth century when a young journalist, Gustav Preller, began infusing the creole language (a mix of Dutch, English, Xhosa and Malayan words), disdained by many as a *Hotnotstaal* (Hottentot's language) with more Dutch words, and publishing a popular newspaper in this emergent language. Increasingly accepted as a white man's language, Afrikaans replaced Dutch as an official language in 1925.

Attempts to appease Afrikaners after the war had led to the weighting of the rural vote in the Union's constitution (this ensured future Afrikaner domination of national politics) and the appointment of the Boer general, Louis Botha, as the country's first Prime Minister. Nevertheless, anti-British sentiment festered and caused dissension in Afrikaner ranks, and in 1914, Barry Hertzog led an anti-British, pro-German split from within the governing party (the South African Party) to form the National Party. The same year there was an unsuccessful Boer coup attempt. The founding of the Afrikaner Broederbond in 1918 was another expression of this burgeoning Afrikaner nationalism.

In sharp contrast was the loyalty to the Crown demonstrated by Africans. When WWI broke out, SANNC delegates who were in London (seeking British intervention regarding the 1913 Land Act) immediately offered to raise 5 000 troops to serve in German South West Africa. Undeterred by Smuts's rejection of citizens 'not of European descent' for combat, the SANNC then offered to assist in the recruitment of African non-combatant servicemen: 83 000 Africans volunteered (along with 2 000 coloureds and 146 000 whites).

Between 1907 and 1922 South Africa was racked by conflict between mineowners and mineworkers. Protests by African miners occurred repeatedly from 1916 to 1920, when miners were forced back underground at bayonet point. The rebellion by white miners in 1922, seen by striking Afrikaners as a forerunner to the restoration of the defunct Boer republics, was an attempt to protect white jobs against the growing threat of competition from (less well paid) black workers. Out of this turmoil the Communist Party of South Africa was founded in 1921. Although it initially sought to promote radicalism amongst whites only, on orders from Moscow that it should work for a 'Native Republic' it became the only non-racial party in the country.

Pauline Smith

P auline Smith's mother and doctor father arrived in South Africa from Britain in 1880. She was born in the ostrich-farming capital of Oudtshoorn in the Cape on 2 April 1882, but left South Africa at the age of 12, when she was sent to boarding school in Scotland. As an adult, she settled in England. A lonely, self-deprecating woman, she was encouraged to write by her close friend, the novelist Arnold Bennett. Sickly for most of her life, she never married. She died on 29 January 1959.

This extract from her journal, *Secret Fire: The 1913–14 South African Journal of Pauline Smith* (1997), recounts her experiences on returning to South Africa for an extended working holiday to gather material for her writing. According to Harold Scheub, the editor of *Secret Fire*, the raw material for much of Smith's work, including five of the stories for her best-known work, *The Little Karoo* (1925), the play *The Last Voyage* (1927), and the novel *The Beadle* (1926), was amassed during this trip. Smith's unsentimental sympathy for poor white Afrikaners and her refusal to support the 'racial' divisions between English and Afrikaners, which still festered after Union in 1910, were perceived by many to be politically radical.

Dutch and English

Tuesday, August 19, 1913

Over the river with Aunt Jean to get warm. A very cold dull day. Home by Miss Blant's. Found her sorting out magazines…. She wanted to know if I was a suffragette. I said I was not political at all. 'Oh well, it is wicked, wicked for women to be suffragettes. I don't know how any thinking woman can *be* a suffragette. The Bible is so clearly against it. And the harm they do!!'

P[auline].: 'Oh, well, it's the wild unthinking ones who do the harm.'

Miss B.: 'But they're *all* unthinking and all wicked. No thinking woman *can* be a suffragette. The Bible says it's wrong.'

So I got off the subject on to D.'s lace shawl which I said was now used as an opera cloak, because I think she *wants* it to be used somehow, for she began explaining how she'd cut a hole in it to let her head through and so make it drape a skirt. I said you did not want to spoil it by cutting it, and were *very* proud of it, so we forgot the wickedness of the suffragettes in pleasanter matters …

In the afternoon, U.T. [Uncle Tim Smith, her father's brother, an attorney] and A.M. [Aunt Maud, his wife] went across the river, and I walked up to the Stegmanns. Marie … told me some of her experiences in Attie Murray's office with his old Boer clients. The old man speaking of the bad weather, a great deal of wind at the end of winter, said, 'But what can you expect? God put the Outeniquas between us and the sea to keep the wind out, and now *mense* (people) have made seven holes through the mountain and *natuurlik* the wind comes through and the weather is now changed. It is always so if *mense* go against God.' Another old man comes always to give Marie news of his health. Tells her if he has taken a dose of castor oil, and gives details as to the result. They spoke of the old man who died haggling over the price of his coffin. And of another old man who wept and wailed over his wife as she lay dying, asking her and the others around her where he was to find her equal. Within a fortnight of her death, someone had been recommended to him, and he had inspanned and gone off to make his proposals. When Mrs. S. (i.e., Marie Stegmann) expostulated, he said, 'Well, but I go by the Bible. The Bible says, "It is not good for men to be alone," so *natuurlik* I must take me another wife.'

Mrs. S.: 'But surely if you cared so much for your wife as you say, you could have waited a little longer?'

'*Ag nee wat*, the Lord gave me my wife, and the Lord took away my wife, so she is no longer mine, and I no longer have a wife, and it is not good for a man to live alone so *natuurlik*, like the Bible says, I must get me another.'

They say the feeling between the Dutch and English is much more bitter now than before the war, and blame both English and Dutch for it. I'm afraid English as intolerant of the Dutch as X and Y are in every way must do a great deal of harm, though they will not see it.[1] Their attitude gives the Dutch a certain advantage. They run down the country on every possible occasion. Then naturally, say the Dutch, they ought not to take a country that they hate from people who love it. Let them clear out of this country they hate and leave it to us. But X and Y will never see that they have themselves to blame. One of X's clients asked him the other day why, if he hated the country so much, he lived in it. X said to me afterwards, 'He had me there, certainly. But I said one can't always live where one wants to.' But if they are so isolated and lonely and bitter as they make out, what on earth do they gain by their sacrifice in staying? Is it for the country's good or their own? It gets tedious to hear constantly at meals that 'So and so stopped me, and asked if I wasn't glad to be home again, and I just said, "No, certainly not, shouldn't mind if I never set foot in the place again." The *idea* of asking me if I wasn't glad to get back to a country like this from a country like England.' They speak so often of the advantages of English life, of how they, being English, are so superior to those who have been born and bred out here. How people out here *can't* have the culture that they, being English born and bred, *must* have. Colonials haven't seen things and haven't *heard* things, travelled, etc. But, as Uncle Tim came straight out here from Boston at the age of 19, and as A.M. followed him when still just a young girl, from Boston, I don't know exactly where it was they heard and saw those things which give them a culture so much superior to the culture of the people around them. It is terrible, they say, how quickly English people coming out get hold of colonial ideas. Even the teachers get quite different ideas from English people (that is, from English country conservatives like the Lincolnshire farmers). Only X and Y in all the district have remained English to the marrow bone. Isn't it terrible, they ask, that it should be so? What is more terrible to me is that they should be so sure that only *they* possess any 'culture' or any regard for the English nation. I'm not upholding the colonials. As far as I can see just now, the country is possessed by a generation in its transition stage, and that is always a troubled time. In this district, wealth has come so suddenly and so easily to colonials, Dutch and English alike, that most of them have lost their heads.[2] The English all have motor cars, and the Dutch who don't have cars have all got rubber tyres to their cart-wheels, say the Stegmanns, and ease is all they think of. Their education has only just begun, among the Dutch I mean, and they will have to soak and season in it for several generations yet before they can use it to any good purpose. So far, it has helped them to *verneukery* and *slim*ness. The new generation of Boers despises the old, resents its religion, despises the English and resents their pose of superiority, despises the Jews, and learns all it can from them in sharp practice. But you will find just the same meanness and snobbishness and lack of culture in any country town in England. I think X and Y don't quite understand how it is that the awfulness of the Dutch outlook isn't awful to me at all. It interests me, doesn't irritate me. I keep saying that we must remember they are a foreign nation. We are tolerant where Italians, French or Russians are concerned, why can't we be tolerant with this little people too? I can't despise them anyway. They once said that Father was one the very few men who had made himself so much respected throughout the district that his influence is felt to this day, and people still act in public affairs to some extent guided by that influence. They seem to look upon this as showing an extraordinary lack of appreciation on the part of the Dutch and colonials to the superiority of *all* English ideas. But it doesn't seem to dawn on them that Father must to a certain extent have understood and sympathised with the people first before they could trust him as they did. They have never sympathised with anything Dutch, or honestly tried to understand the Dutch nature. If they had, Uncle Tim might have been looked up to as Father was, though never to the same extent, for he had neither the interest nor the strength of character needed. Y said once that she knew I thought them prejudiced, and I'm afraid they are. But we always are quite friendly in our discussions, and I lie low, like Brer Rabbit, and say very little and think all the more....

The New Curate's Loose Teeth

Wednesday, August 20, 1913

Miss Spence told me last night that she had been to Julia's, and Aunt Jean was not very well, in fact she had asked for brandy at 6 o'clock that evening. So I went up early in the morning to see her. Found her curing her old trouble with a dose of castor oil. Julia very miserable with a bad cold, but Aunt Jean feeling much better. Stayed some time, and just as I was leaving, standing at the gate in the monotocca hedge, Julia pulled me back, whispering, 'Here comes someone that I *must* introduce you to,' and suddenly hailed a miserable looking clerical object hurrying down the street, and introduced me to the new curate, Mr. Jackson, minor canon of Winchester Cathedral.

He is thin and intense, with clear blue eyes, a set of too big false teeth which he clicks all the time, pressing the lower set back frequently with a forefinger, and catching the upper with a click of the lower, the lower projecting about half an inch. His clothes *very* badly in need of sponging and brushing and doing up, but his fierce eyes, somehow making me think uncomfortably of mad eyes, and his teeth spitting out at you all the time are what hold you most. He talks *awful* fast, catching back and clicking his teeth all the time. Waved a *Church Times* in our faces, began reading aloud an article in which a canon confutes an agnostic. Hadn't time to finish, produced a pencil and licked it, marked the article. Thrust it upon Julia and me, talking, spitting, clicking hard all the time. Fished out a scrubby bit of note paper with a long list of names of people on whom he must call (he has only just come). Where should he find them? Mrs. Tim Smith, where should he find her? Looked fiercely at me when I explained that I was Mrs. Tim Smith's niece. What he missed was choral celebration. But the two countries were not to be compared. People hadn't called on him here, so he must call on people. At 'King' (King William's Town), only one man had called on him at all. A Mr. Bond, so Jackson had said it was a Bond of union between them. (What was Miss Morris laughing at?) Mr. Yeo down on his list too, but Mr. Yeo at present yodelling in Cape Town. Again, what, might he ask, was Miss Morris laughing at? (Miss S[mith] felt too exhausted even to smile.) Just had a letter from Frank Sutton. Must go off and answer it. Of course, we found it impossible to live without church services.

Oh goodness, by the time he flew off, I was afraid that he was really a little insane, but conclude now that he is only wildly enthusiastic, convinced that only Church of England members, and regular communicants, can get salvation and contemptuous in a wildly fluttering way of all other denominations, Jews and nonconformists alike. Julia took me exhausted back to the house, and showed me a book of church ethics, all marked and scored and noted, which he had sent her to read. Said Julia, 'You know, P., I can't understand it. I read it over and over and I can't make sense, and then he comes and asks me questions. I think I'll get him to lend you the books instead.'

P.: 'Well, if you do I shan't read them. I'm not going to have anything to do with him. His teeth worry me too much.'

Julia: 'There now, and I *did* think we'd got somebody here that would be a nice companion for you this visit!' and really quite sorrowful about it.

Came home, and Letty said a Mr. Thomas was in the drawing room with the missis. Half an hour later, the missis came through, saying Mr. *Jackson* had paid her a long visit and just gone! She got on better with him than I did, as he knows Boston and other Lincolnshire churches, but his teeth worried her considerably too. [...]

Uncle Tim's Yarn

Thursday, August 21, 1913

... After supper, A.M. and I walked up to post, then on to Stegmanns. M. took us through to smell the pantry, which I used to love to do when I was a child ... Told us stories of old Mr. Truter whose lies are very wonderful. His pumpkin vines grew so fast that the pumpkins all had one side worn off being pulled along. His soil is so fertile that his seeds sprout before he has finished sowing, his aim so good that he has shot five wild duck with the same shot, and that was a ramrod (he had no bullets handy) which strung all the birds and was so hot that it brought them down roasted.

No one to call after we returned, and Uncle Tim told me yarns instead. One very curious one, about the first murder case to be tried in Oudtshoorn. A Kaffir (Xhosa) in the district owned a lot of cattle, and a Hottentot (Khoikhoi) lived with him. One day, the Hottentot came into the village with the cattle, saying the Kaffir had sent him to sell it. Sold it, and went off with the money. Was seen in the district again, and spread the report that the Kaffir, having received the money, had gone back to Kaffirland, as he had often spoken of doing. No suspicions aroused. Then, some time after, some men shooting up in the Cango hills came across a leopard's vomit in which was a human thumb. They brought the thumb back to the village and put it in spirits, and it was taken to the court house. Police went out to Cango to investigate and get the leopard if possible. After some time, a skeleton was found, and with it a knobkerrie. It had evidently been buried, and then dug up by the leopard. In the skull and spine were found two rough-cast bullets. They found that the Hottentot some time before he sold the cattle had cast bullets similar to these. Also, that after the Kaffir's disappearance, he came into possession of money which could not be accounted for. The Hottentot was arrested and tried, and condemned to death on circumstantial evidence. There was no gallows in the gaol here, and the gallows had to be brought up from Cape Town, but no transport rider could be found to get it up from Mossel Bay. They all refused to ride it. After some weeks delay, someone more courageous than the rest brought it up, and the man was hanged. The gallows was then to be sent back to town, but not a transport rider throughout the district would now touch it, and it was left lying about the prison yard for years, as Uncle Tim well remembers …

Notes

1. The editor, Harold Scheub, explains that X and Y refer to Uncle Tim and Aunt Maud (1997: xxii).
2. In 1913, Oudtshoorn was experiencing an ostrich boom (Scheub 1997: xxvi).

Phyllis Ntantala

Phyllis Ntantala's parents were Christian converts and part of the black 'landed gentry'. Phyllis was born in 1920 in the Transkei. This rural area, peopled largely by Xhosa-speaking Africans, was annexed to the Cape Colony in the latter years of the nineteenth century, but administered as a separate unit, which permitted African ownership of land.

Educated at Lovedale College, the leading mission high school for Africans of the time, and the University of Fort Hare, Phyllis married the pioneering scholar A.C. Jordan. They had three children. In the early 1960s, as conditions for black South Africans worsened under the apartheid government, the Jordans went into unhappy exile in the United States.

The following passage from her autobiography, *A Life's Mosaic: The Autobiography of Phyllis Ntantala* (1992), describes the family home of her childhood in the 1920s. The high regard in which her father, 'Tata', was held by black and white alike and his position of prominence and economic security were to be increasingly undermined as first the 'Colour Bar' (segregation on the basis of race) and later apartheid destroyed traditional social networks of black South Africans.

The home of a man of means in the rural areas is a huge establishment, where all sorts of people gather. Ours was such a home. Here came relatives, close and distant, on short or long visits, sometimes bringing their children with them. Some of them came to ask for blankets and clothes to see them through the next winter. One such was Sis' Dinah, a distant niece of Mama. After she had been bought this and that by Mama, she always went to the washing-basket and picked a few more things for herself and her children, especially my dresses for her daughter Ntombentsha, who was my age. Mama would discover this after she was gone. Sis' Dinah was able to get away with it because the washing-basket was in the store-room for the convenience of aunt Ma-Mlambo, who could get to it whenever she came to do the washing, so she did not have to wait for Mama.

Some arrived because of some dispute with a husband or a son and came to ask Tata to intercede on their behalf; others came because they had not seen us in a long time. None of these people could be sent away empty handed. Many of them proved of great help while they were here. They helped in harvesting beans, sun-drying the pumpkins, getting the corn into the silos, grain-pits and tanks. They helped in the ploughing fields, hoeing and around the home, putting new plaster onto the rondavels. Then on the day Tata went to sell his bales of wool, those who came for a blanket or coat were taken along and came back, not only with the blanket or coat, but with other articles of clothing. There would be joy all around. They were grateful and pleased. Tata would be pleased too that he had been able to fulfil his obligations. When relatives arrived because of trouble at home, and the husband or son eventually came along, the family heads were called, and the dispute was settled; and after getting her share of presents for having tarried with us so long, each of these too left at last.

Then there were the travellers, who stopped here asking for water to drink and to rest under the trees. These travellers could not be given only the water for which they had asked, but would be given tea and food before they resumed their journey. It was unthinkable to send them away without feeding them. Some of the travellers were saleswomen or salesmen, hawking their wares from village to village. They were usually women from Mndundu and Rhamrha in Gatyana, Mfengu women selling tobacco, mats, baskets and pottery. Word would have gone around that travelling saleswomen had been spotted somewhere in the neighbourhood. We, the children, would be asked to look out for them, and tell them that our parents wanted to buy something from them. For days we would be on the lookout, and when we spotted them, would run off to call them, asking them to stop at our place. Tata seemed to prefer their tobacco to that bought at the store.

Then these women would arrive, driving their donkeys laden with bags of tobacco, while they themselves carried their mats, baskets and pots on their heads. On the veranda or under the trees their wares would be displayed, and Tata would buy what he wanted, while Mama would be looking at the mats and baskets (seldom the pots, for we did not need them as we did not brew any of the home-made brews from corn). She too would pick what she wanted. While all this was going on, a warm conversation between our parents and these women would ensue. We, the children, would be busy making tea for everybody and getting food ready to feed the starving saleswomen. They, too, could not be sent away hungry.

Engrossed in their conversation, they would forget that time was passing and not waiting for them. Late in the afternoon would be heard exclamations of 'Yho! Is it this late already? It will be dark by the time we cross Thethiswayo (a ford in the Nqabarha River). We do not want to cross that part of the river in the dark. It is not safe.'

'And even after you have crossed, you still have far to get home,' one of our parents would observe.

'Yes, you are right. We were not aware it was getting late already.'

'You might as well stop over for the night and resume your journey tomorrow,' one of the parents would suggest.

This would be agreed upon and the saleswomen would be our guests for that night. Nobody thought it strange. This was as it should be.

Then there were the daily drop-ins who came for a chat and would remain here for the midday meal and sometimes for the evening meal. In addition there were those who came to help with the daily chores – cleaning the yard, plastering, hoeing, harvesting, mending the cattle-fold or the fence, and all the chores around a home. Though this was 'free' help, they all expected to be given something when the chore was done. Another category was those who came to work in the fields to earn cash or kind. These, too, expected to be fed when they had finished and before they went home. This meant a big pot every day for people known to be here and even those who still had to decide whether to stop or not.

Then there was the central core family – the family itself, the helper in the kitchen, the yard-man and the herd-boys (four, aged ten to fifteen). Tata usually had four herd-boys – two for the small stock and one for the cattle and an older one floating between the cattle and the yard-work. This core group lived as a family unit, with all grown-ups wielding authority over the children. None of us dared to say to Sis' Ma-Zangwa, our kitchen help, or to Bhut' Nobhula, our general factotum, 'You are not my parent; you cannot order me about,' or tell them that they were being paid for what they did. Such talk would have meant punishment and they would not have hesitated to take the matter to our parents, for though they were servants, they were not our servants.

The men earned a beast a year (usually a female beast) or ten sheep, which they could send home or keep with our stock until they left. Some of the workers, especially the herd-boys, became as brothers to us. In the kitchen at night we taught them the three Rs. Nose, who had come to us at the age of ten and left at fifteen, learnt to read and write in our kitchen. He had become so much part of our family that his mother was concerned he would never want to go back to his home again. Fearing this, the mother came to plead with Tata to release him. 'He is my only child. He is so happy here. I fear he will forget us. You know, whenever he comes home, we cannot eat without saying grace first. These are things he has learnt here and he likes them.' At fifteen Nose left us with four head of cattle and twenty sheep. Tata always said to him: 'Just tell me, how many young men who have been to Johannesburg have as much stock as you?'

Nose was not the only one who learnt to read and write in our kitchen. There were many others who did. Sometimes living with us would be children who had come to our school for Standards 5 and 6, because the schools in their areas only went up to Standard 4. They never paid any boarding fees. Now and again, a parent would send some contribution in kind – beans, pumpkins, vegetables or a harmel – towards the upkeep of the child. In a setting like this, children learn to live with and adjust to all sorts of people. Seldom does one find clashes of such a nature as to make life intolerable.

Each child had a chore to do, and woe to those who neglected their chores. If you had a puppy, it was your duty to feed, wash and clean up after it. If your chore was to feed the chickens, it was your duty to see that they were fed in the morning and given fresh water, the eggs were collected at the appropriate times, and the geese were let out to go to the river for their swim. Those in the chicken yard had the responsibility of opening the gate in the afternoon for the geese to come in. There were pigs to be fed and given water. Sometimes a ewe would die in childbirth and Tata would assign the responsibility of raising that lamb to one of us, with the promise that if it survived, it would be that child's own. The child would then nurse that motherless lamb, feeding it warm milk, cleaning its feeding bottle and finding some ewe that had lost its lamb to suckle it. We earned a few sheep this way.

It was we, the children, who saw to it that the stamped mealies for the next day's pot were ready the night before. In the morning there was no time for that before school. And if this was not done, Sis' Ma-Zangwa would say in the morning, just as we were getting ready for school: 'Hey! I do not know what they will eat when they come back from school. I am going to help in the fields today.' And she would do just that. Sis' Ma-Zangwa, our kitchen help, had more say than Mama about what each of us had to do. She would announce: 'I am going to the stream to do the washing today and Ethel is coming with me. Nonkululeko, you remain behind to make tea for Bhuti when he comes home. You did not make it yesterday, because you were late coming back from school and Ethel had to.' Or she would pick one of the kids to go to the store with her. She nearly always picked Ntangashe, for she was quiet and would not come back with reports of all the people met on the way or at the store, as my sister Somhlophe did. On those days when she was going to cook for the workers in the fields, she would assign the family pot to the children, and there was no questioning that command. This was good training, making children grow up responsible people. None of us ever considered it harsh. It was life, and these things had to be done.

I still remember of a morning during the ploughing and hoeing season Tata, standing early at the kitchen door, saying: 'There are some women in the fields today. Please see to it they are fed before they leave for home.'

'Yes, Bhuti!' Sis' Ma-Zangwa would respond.

'Did you hear what Bhuti said?' – this to the children. 'I am going to cook for those workers in the fields. You will have to take charge of the family meal.' So saying, Sis' Ma-Zangwa would drop everything and busy herself with preparations for the meal for the workers in the fields. In fact, she never even cooked for them, for once she had set the pot, she would go to the fields to chat with them, leaving us, the children, to mind her pot.

At noon the workers would come back from the fields, sit under the trees, and ask for water to drink and wash their hands. Sis' Ma-Zangwa would join them under the trees, keeping them company. And when her 'pots' were ready, she would feed them. Their work was not measured by hours. Some days they would sit there, chatting until it was time for them to go home. Then they would have their sugar weighed out and given to them, or their bars of blue soap, or kerosene, for which they had come to work. Very few of them came to work for money.

When there was a big job in the fields or around the home – re-roofing the rondavels with new grass or re-plastering them – then a work party would be organised. My parents would delegate one of our neighbours, someone with the reputation of being a good organiser. Days before the party, this individual would come with her helpers to prepare the food for that day – to stamp mealies, brew *marhewu*, bake bread. Depending on the size of the party, one or two sheep would be slaughtered. It was on such occasions that we tasted *marhewu*. After this beverage had been brewed and fermented well, the woman who brewed it would bring Mama a beakerful, saying to her: 'Please do have some, before it all goes. It is so tasty. It is the best I have ever brewed in all my life.' Because this brew was not part of our daily fare, I never acquired a taste for it. And yet those who know it say it is very nourishing, good for people working in the fields.

My people! How they seemed to take life in their stride.

Starting School

A younger child in a family, I think, is always at an advantage over older siblings. Such a child moves into the world of children sooner, getting to know all the things that the siblings are doing; and if precocious, as I was, absorbs most of the things the older children are learning.

At four years old I was ready for school. Even though I could not write, I knew my alphabet from A to Z and I could count to twenty. [...]

I was ready for school and my parents knew it. So all the rules about age were waived and I went to school. And as Mama said to all those who remarked upon it, 'If and when she gets tired, she will stop and stay home.' I never stopped. Even the three-and-a-half miles to and from school did not deter me. I had walked that distance on Sundays, going to church with my parents. Doing it for five days in the week was not going to be so forbidding. Anyway, what teacher, manager or even inspector of schools could say 'no' if my parents wanted me in school?

Everybody at home was enthusiastic about my going. Somhlophe volunteered to carry me piggy-back part of the way. As she had so many friends, some days I never walked, for her friends took turns carrying me. They liked it and so did I. It was only on my way back home that I would walk those three-and-a-half miles, for Somhlophe, in the upper classes, could not leave with us.

The schoolchildren accepted and welcomed me the very first day I got there. For were they not, most of them, my sister Somhlophe's friends? On that first day, one of her friends, Nozipho Ntshona, came to say 'Hi, Phyllie' during recess, and shared with me some of her wild turnips she had dug up. These wild turnips were very popular among schoolchildren. The teachers, who on many Sundays came to eat dinner at home, were no strangers to me. I knew them and they knew me. School was no strange place to me. I moved into that setting as if I had always belonged there, and I liked it.

And yet for all that, Mama was somewhat apprehensive. I remember her saying, as she was tying up my *kappie* (bonnet) and straightening my dress, 'When the teacher asks you a question, speak up and answer the question. Don't cry, Philli-girl.' She said this because my sister Ntangashe, shy and quiet, took a long time to adjust to the school atmosphere of lively, loud, strange children. However, by the time I went to school Ntangashe had got over her fears and had quite a number of friends, too, among the schoolchildren. Little did Mama know that there was no need to tell me to speak up when spoken to. I answered questions even before they were directed at me.

We were late coming to school that morning, and as the custom was, late-comers had to wait by the door until the teacher-in-charge came to find out why the students were not on time. Miss Dlova was conducting a religious instruction lesson across the hall not very far from the door. 'Who can tell me what the Eighth Commandment is?' asked the teacher. And before any of the class answered, a tiny voice from those by the door called out: 'Thou shalt not steal.' I had taken Mama's advice seriously and was answering the question asked. Anyway, I knew the Ten Commandments from my Sunday school. Later in life, whenever Miss Dlova congratulated me on my achievements, she would say: 'I knew you would do well. You passed with honours even before your name was in the Admission Register.'

I must have taken Mama's advice too much to heart. That whole day in class, whenever the teacher asked a question, my hand shot up, ready with an answer.

I do not recall if I knew every answer and I doubt if I did in fact. At the end of the day our teacher, Miss Ntshona, took me aside and asked why my hand went up every time she asked a question. 'Mama told me to speak up and not cry,' I shot back. She laughed, helped me with my *kappie* and sent me home with the others.

One day I had on a beautiful new dress. I must have been proud of myself. That whole morning I never sat for longer than fifteen minutes in the classroom. Whenever any girl wanted to go out, I volunteered to go along with her. We were allowed out in pairs, so we would troop up to the teacher with our 'Please, Miss, may I go out?' (Why we had to make this request in English, I have never been able to understand. I suppose it was part of our education.) As we were coming back from one of these forays outside, the teacher called me: 'Phyllie, you have not sat ten minutes in the classroom. Why?'

Extrovert that I am, I pointed to my new dress. 'Don't you see?'

She had to laugh. Now what teacher does not like a child like that?

Before the end of my first year in school, when I was four and eight months, Mama died. She had been ill early in the autumn, but recovered. Then she went down with pneumonia late in October and died within a week. She had been nursing aunt Daisy, Tata's sister, who had been brought very ill from her home to Grandma's house. Shuttling between the two homes – ours and Grandma's – Mama caught the pneumonia virus that was to kill her.

The family doctor, Mrs Thompson, was called in twice to see Mama. Her last visit was on the afternoon of the Saturday she died. The doctor told both Tata and the patient that the pneumonia had not peaked yet, but with the drugs she was leaving, it should peak by the next day. She left, promising to come back on Monday.

My cot was in the room where my parents slept. On either side of the room were their beds, with a table in the middle, a dresser on the side of Tata's bed, and my cot between Mama's bed and the dresser. I woke up that Sunday morning, and looked across at Mama's bed. She was lying on the mattress on the floor, and her bed was folded and put behind the door. Tata was sitting on the edge of his bed, dressed, and on one of the chairs in the room Oom Papana, Mama's cousin, was also sitting. Somhlophe came in with a tray of morning coffee, set it on the table, stood at the foot of Tata's bed, and looked across at the mattress on the floor. Then Tata broke the news to her: 'Nonkululeko, Mama has left us, my child. She died early this morning.'

Nontsizi Mgqwetho

Izibongo (Praise poetry)

The divergent customs of praising – usually a male-biased tradition – can be traced back hundreds of years in the histories of the Sotho, Tswana, Swazi, Ndebele, Xhosa and Zulu; mutating in response to social change, the tradition remains important (if less prevalent, particularly amongst urban Africans). The vernacular terms, *izibongo* (Zulu and Xhosa), *lithoko* (Sotho) and *maboko* (Tswana), are preferable to the English term, 'praise poetry', for these 'oral IDs' (as Noleen Turner calls them) do not always praise their subjects. Rather, they *hail* the subject of the poem (which may be clans, individuals, animals or even inanimate objects such as bones), identifying characteristics that make the subject special. They are performed in social circumstances that warrant the 'naming, identifying and therefore giving significance and substance to the named person or object' (Gunner & Gwala 1994: 2). *Izibongo* are performed in formal, ritualised social circumstances, when the praises are likely to be complex, intricate and long, as well as informal gatherings, when the poems are often short and simple or even (as in the case of contemporary Zulu *izihasho*) satirical and crude.

The reciting of *izibongo* is always a communal activity, with auditors participating in the performance. They 'are more similar to song and music than to a piece of western poetry which is supposed to be read and appreciated in individual study. They are also similar to dance, because of their marked rhythm of delivery' (Canonici 1996: 8). Moreover, generally the poems are most accurately described as auto/biographical – with the slash remaining a permanent feature of the nomenclature – since the western distinction between autobiography and biography is usually irrelevant. Not only is it common for a person's praises to be added to or even composed by other members of the community, but they may also be performed by someone other than the subject of the poem in order to honour the person identified in the poem.

Jeff Opland, in his study of Xhosa praises, *Xhosa Poets and Poetry* (1998), mentions that the original version of Nontsizi Mgqwetho's *izibongo* first appeared in the Xhosa newspaper *Umteteli wa Bantu* ('The People's Spokesman') of 12 January 1924. He explains that in the absence of other information about her, all that we know of the poet, Nontsizi, must be gleaned from the more than 90 Xhosa poems that she published in *Umteteli* between 1920 and 1929.

Opland, Mgqwetho's translator, argues that Mgqwetho's poems are riven with contradiction and reveal the tensions typically experienced by those caught in profound social transition. A committed Christian, she rejects the culture that brought Christianity and destroyed traditional African values. Constantly lamenting the sorry plight of urban women and outspokenly championing women's rights, Mgqwetho's feminist stance is, however, undermined as she assumes a masculine voice in speaking as an *imbongi* (praise poet). Her poetry, while traditional in form, simultaneously breaks with tradition by the mere fact of appearing in print and by adopting certain western literary conventions.

Mgqwetho's poetry is especially significant, as Opland points out, because 'no woman has ever published a volume of poetry in Xhosa' (1998: 196).

Peace, Nontsizi, renowned for your chanting,
Your poetry's the nation's treasure.
No elephant finds its own trunk clumsy.
Peace, mother hen, Africa's sheltering wing!

Hen shepherding chicks
Safe from the talons of birds of prey,
The nation knows you, lofty she-python,
The poets' clique shuns you.

Upset Phalo's land, Mgqwetho,[1]
Loom over nations and sap their strength.
Wild beast too vicious to take from behind,
Your associates tremble in tackling you.

Peace, dusky woman, storehouse of stories,
Your stench reeks like the river snake.
Mercy! Elephant browsing the tops,
You've made a name for Mgqwetho …

Peace, Nontsizi, African rivermoss,
Your poetry goes to the core
And the peaks of the nation swivel
As you sway from side to side …

Peace, poetess, Vaaibom's flamingo,
Who tucks up her feet for take-off
Untucking them to land:
Animals come out to bask in the sun.

Peace, newsy duck of Africa,
Ungainly woman with ill-shaped frame.
Oh, Nontsizi, African rivermoss,
With bow-legs like yours you'll never marry!

Peace, poetess, Africa's sheltering wing,
Make way, they're hot on my heels.
Peace, starling perched in a fig tree,
Your poetry puts paid to pleasantries …

Peace, Nontsizi, match-stick legs scratched
From prophesying in clumps of thorn;
Oh, peace, poetic sybil,
Watch out, the wild bird's flapping its wings …

Oh peace, Nontsizi, African rivermoss,
Woman, the winsome song of your voice
Sets Africa's walls thrumming,
Utterly shaming all the lads.

We'll hear of the day of your death, Nontsizi.
The commando's horse has lost its way.
Oh, peace! And to you, Ntsikana,[2]
Who prophesied in thorn brakes.

Notes

1. Phalo is an ancestor of the Xhosa chiefs; the land of Phalo is Xhosa territory and, by extension, the whole country (Opland 1998: 333).
2. Ntsikana (who died in May 1821) is the revered Xhosa prophet of Christianity (Opland 1998: 333).

Prue Smith

Prue's father, Leslie Pryce, was born and educated in England. At the age of 17, he joined the Electrical Engineer's Volunteer Corps to fight in the Anglo-Boer War in South Africa. After serving in what was the precursor to the RAF in the First World War, he returned to South Africa, bringing with him his new wife.

Prue, pictured here as a baby, was born in Johannesburg in 1923. After studying at the University of the Witwatersrand, she won a scholarship to Oxford. She was delighted to escape from South Africa and, along with raising a family of 'four healthy children' with her husband Michael, pursued a successful career in broadcasting. She died in Oxford in 1999, before her memoirs, made possible by the 'untold blessings and releases in the freedom of Mandela', had appeared in print. The following extracts, from *The Morning Light: A South African Childhood Revalued* (2000), focus on her relationship with her nanny, Lottie.

Lottie

She had, when I was young, no children of her own. I can tell now, and am sure I could then, that she gave me the care and love, though perhaps not the iron discipline, that she would have given a daughter of her own. The care was total except, I believe, for breast-feeding, which my mother for some reason, in later days, often assured me that she had performed herself. In almost every other way Lottie was my carer and keeper, bather, dresser, feeder and watcher and singer-to-sleep.

I have very early memories of the feeding, in particular. She had to sit with me at table – until we were about ten or eleven John and I ate with our parents only for Sunday lunch; otherwise always in the day nursery. John used to bolt his food and then be allowed to 'get down', but I was a reluctant eater, it seems, and so was given my food on a special plate kept hot by having a sort of pewter chamber underneath for refilling with hot water, as the meal dragged on. Lottie was patient and resourceful. I would complain that the food tasted like soap, or dirt, or *kak* or any horrible thing I could think of. '*Aikona!*' Lottie would exclaim. 'Oh no! It can't be! Let me smell it!' – and in this satisfactory way, once Lottie had seen that in spite of many encouragements there was no future between that meal and me, the lump on the plate would piece by piece disappear into some bag or cloth on Lottie's lap, with many ecstatically funny faces pulled by both of us at the strange flavours which I was inventing. Unless memory will one day take me back to the cradle itself, this may be my earliest intimation of Lottie's skill and wisdom in managing her tricky position of surrogate mother, on the far side of an enormous cultural divide, without either criticising or (noticeably) deceiving her employer.

As I grew up, and my mother had no younger children, Lottie became more my companion and confidante, while in the household her duties changed to the charge of the everlasting laundry (which in very early days a turbanned *dhobi* used to do, carrying huge bundles of it over his shoulder, on his back – never a bike, never a cart – kicking out, poor man, at the dogs), and to the training and supervising of the *ntombi*.

We did not have a high turnover of staff in our family, though some of our neighbours were always hiring and firing. My father was a kind and just employer, very paternalistic. Like many English in those days, he wanted only Zulu servants – there are signs of a British-Zulu *entente* even today. It is rather surprising, seeing that the Zulu are the only nation in southern Africa to have inflicted defeat on a British army. Nevertheless, the defeat (or victory) of Isandhlwana forgotten (if it was known about), Zulu is what our servants had to be and, for the most part, they came from one village too – Taylor's Halt, to the west of the Valley of a Thousand Hills, in Natal, KwaZulu-Natal. When the season came for one of the men to go home for ploughing and sowing or harvest, a relative would be sent in his place. But this applied only to the men.

Lottie was not part of that system and moreover she was a Xhosa, from the Eastern Cape. She had a husband, called Meshak, who was a delivery-cart driver for Solly Kramer's bottlestore in town and lived in Alexandra Township. That is all I know about him, and I did not once see him, in fourteen years. He was not allowed to come to our house. That is how it was.

On Sunday mornings and every other Thursday Lottie would put aside the blue overall and starched white apron with its top that covered her great bosom and travelled over her wide shoulders to descend down her back in broad bands to a crisp bow at her waist; put aside, too, the starched white cap which concealed her many tight little pigtails. On Sundays she would put on a dark, smart, sober, high-necked and long-sleeved dress, whatever the heat of the day, and on her head either a *doek*, a scarf tied at the back, or a dark cap of crochet-work coming over her brow and almost concealing her ears. It was Church, of course. I do not know whether Meshak joined her at the church – if he did, I suppose that he would have had to conceal his connection with the bottlestore – or whether they had any home life beyond every other Thursday.

On those Thursdays, she dressed quite differently. In the first place, she wore quite a different sort of cap. All the caps, which were rather like acorn cups, she made herself. I watched her, so many times, with a stout crochet needle and thick thread, black for Sundays, white cotton for everyday, but for Thursdays coloured silk – pink, yellow, green, bright. She made them by beginning at the middle with a round disc which ends up, when the cap has been completed, on the crown of the head; this disc is then progressed round and around, and outwards, getting larger as the hook is poked in and out of the circle just completed, Lottie's quick brown hands, with the pink palms, twitching the thread around. But it doesn't end up as a flat circle, as a doily, although there were many of these on the surfaces around her bedroom, and indeed around mine, which she made for me, and in a lighter thread with beads round the edge hanging (against the flies) over our jugs of milk or home-made lemonade. She taught me, in time, to make stunning doilies; but caps are a different matter. They have to conform to the shape of a head, so once the crown is big enough, they have to start to go roundly downwards and this is an aspect of the art which I could never learn. If I, no matter how closely supervised, took two or three stitches together into the hook, to begin to reduce and redirect the circumference, things got very lumpy, out of hand and off the hook.

On Thursdays Lottie wore no makeup or jewellery except modest earrings. Her going-out dresses were always plain and matronly, but on Thursdays they were much brighter than on Sundays; and Thursday caps were no less than joyful, with little arabesques or points around the ears. Her Thursday demeanour when we said goodbye was also bright and joyful; loving, but smiling and eager to go. I was always asleep by the time she came home, and she never told me anything about life in Alexandra Township, and was never willing to answer any questions about it.

I didn't often visit the laundry. If Lottie was in it, poking the boiling copper with the old cricket bat, or drubbing with the Gorgonzola, she would be too busy to talk. It was in the ironing room that nearly all our reading took place – that is, my reading to her – but the greatest pleasure of all was if she asked me into her bedroom, in her free time.

Lottie's bedroom had a black iron bedstead with a white coverlet she had crocheted herself, and her pillow lay in a white pillow-cover with the word 'Home' worked on it and shown up by a pink backing. A tin trunk covered by a large, white embroidered cloth served as bedside table. Upon it was an alarm clock, a candle in a blue-and-white enamel candle-holder (we had electricity but not in the servants' rooms) and a beer bottle full of sea water which I brought her, by special request, every year from Durban or Cape Town. All these objects sat upon doilies of their own, and a china cake-stand which was also on the 'table' supported, on a very big and fine doily, a battered Bible. There was a chest of drawers and washstand with enamel jug and bowl. A wooden fruitbox, covered with a pretty cloth, supported a hand-operated Singer sewing machine which she sometimes took away to Alexandra on a Thursday, balancing it, of course, on her head. [...]

Comities and amities

[…] My first experience of a real somewhere else, outside, came about when Lottie was 'lent' to my brother's preparatory school in Johannesburg. She took charge of the black women staff there during some crisis, while a new – white – matron or housekeeper was looked for. The headmaster and his wife, Mr and Mrs Hadland, were close friends of my parents, and Mrs Hadland was one of the few adults whom I felt to be a friend to me. She was a masterful sort of person, though kind and quite jokey in her manner, and she always, when visiting my parents, came to find me and have a talk, knowing that at the first sign of visitors I used to rush off to the safety of the ironing room or to hide 'under the bridge', in the big culverts that took the stormwater under the roads into our big ditches. Sometimes Mrs Hadland brought me things for my museum. I remember a deformed double tomato which gave immense pleasure, before it rotted, because it resembled a bright red human bottom; and a sort of glass phial in which there were layers of differently coloured sand, or ash, from Vesuvius. When Mrs Hadland realised the heartbreak which the lending-out of Lottie was causing to me, she had a long conference with my parents, and then with Lottie, and it was decided that I could go and stay with Lottie at the school!

A little bungalow, the school sanatorium, at the far end of the grounds, beyond the playing fields, well out of sight of the pupils but near the servants' quarters, was thought to be a suitable temporary home for Lottie and me. It was understood that it was to be a rather secret arrangement, and that if any little boy came down with an infectious disease, or needed any nursing care, I would have to return home. Lottie slept in the bed next to mine. This was in itself a great treat, for both of us: at home, if my parents went out at night, Lottie used to come and sleep in my room, but not in the spare bed; she brought her own bedclothes and had to sleep on the floor. She did not complain but I can remember myself crying and fussing about it. And at the Sannie we had our meals together in the kitchen, and Lottie cooked only the things I would eat without persuasion, and our reading was done either lying down on our beds or grandly in a tiny sitting room. The whole thing was a wonder. For the first and only time, Lottie and I were together as mother and daughter. […]

'Mind you don't suck the railings!' Whenever Lottie and I set off for the Zoo, this bizarre piece of advice was issued by my mother, in the attentively automatic way that she would also put a handkerchief into my pocket or adjust the ribbon in my hair. In those days the Johannesburg Zoo was one of the very few public places, in fact I can think of no other, where blacks and whites were allowed to be together on an equal footing. There were separate 'conveniences', but for the main actions – even the elephant rides, even the swings – there was mingling. Commercial considerations, I suppose. So what was in my mother's mind about the railings? It was the uneasy thought that I would be climbing onto, or looking through or otherwise getting intimate with, railings which were being used by black children, or adults, in the same way. 'Mind you don't suck the railings!' is something I still say, an arcane family joke, to my own grown-up children as I see them off to foreign parts.

The Zoo was always an enormous treat, for Lottie as well as for me. It had been quite difficult to arrange, at first; or we thought it was going to be, since the Zoo was the other side of town, my mother did not drive in those days, and public transport was segregated. The solution was found by my father. Sometimes it was permitted for the conductors of 'white' buses and trams to allow blacks to occupy the two rear seats upstairs. Knowing they had discretionary powers, therefore, my father gave Lottie some cards to show to conductors, with his name and address and a polite request 'to whom it may concern' (as on the men's Passes) to allow 'nurse-girl Lottie' to accompany his daughter on the public transport. He had such firm, regular and authoritative handwriting that I had complete confidence in these cards. Rightly so. There was never any trouble. I was always allowed to sit in the tram next to Lottie at the back, upstairs, though I am sure my parents supposed that by the force of my father's card we would be allowed into the 'whites only/alleen vir blankes' seats in the front.

The trams in those days were very high and narrow, shaped in general like a box of dates, rounded at the ends. Since they ran on rails they were not able to turn around, only to reverse; so for the return journeys the backs of the seats, which were made of wooden slats fixed to iron frames and hinges, could be flapped over, at each terminus to enable the passengers for the return journey to face the direction of travel. At the termini the conductors did this at great speed, passing down the aisle and stroking the seat backs so that they would all go in sequence *'skwee-CLAP! skwee-CLAP!'* After the first rather nervous trip to the Zoo, we gained confidence and would ourselves flap over (gently and secretly, no *skwee-CLAP*) the seat in front of Lottie's, so that we had our own little compartment to ourselves; we could face each other, or put our feet up, or use it as a parcel rack. It was an enormous privacy and somehow a sock in the eye for – whoever it was. It was an important part of the thrill of going to the Zoo. [...]

Dissolution

My father died, suddenly and unexpectedly, in his early fifties. I had just turned fourteen. It was during the Christmas holidays and on the day that his death was discovered (for he died alone), meaning well, I suppose, my mother sent me to stay with a school friend some distance outside Johannesburg. My friend and her family, also meaning well, I suppose, did not mention my father during the fortnight or so that I was there. I can remember asking my friend, after a few days, if she knew about my father. She said 'Oh yes' in a hurried and frightened way and plunged the conversation into dogs, or horses, or clothes. By the time I returned home the funeral was over, no more friends were calling at the house, my mother was distraught with business affairs, negotiating to sell the house to the school, acknowledging wreaths and flowers and letters.

Whatever course world and time, chance, likelihood or supposition had marked out for my life was blown to fragments by his death; not fragments even, not so solid: blown into vaporous gases so that the universe was blasted free from whatever before had tethered it to sense and solidity. I feel, after all this time, the terrible pain and pity of it. Whenever there have been other deaths, especially that of my husband, at every blow near to me, and many that are far – disaster and sorrow, cruelty, genocides, wars, famines – the pain and the pity move in predatory circles around my heart. The death of my father was the fundament of all other sorrows; it was the bedrock on which have been laid, over the years, the sediments of all other griefs. Grief, like loneliness, courses down the riverbed of memory, laying down its detritus, in flow after flow stirring up and augmenting its gravels. [...]

A little while before my father's death I had been told that Lottie had to go home on a visit to her village in the Eastern Cape. I realised at the time that this was unusual; normally it was only the men who went home at certain times of the year, to help with harvest and planting. So I was surprised as well as dismayed when Lottie went; but she seemed to want to go, and my mother said she would soon be back.

But my father's death and the dissolution intervened, soon after. No more servants, no more dogs; only nothing, nothing. We stayed on a while in the house, and the new term at school began. At break-time one day, at the school, one of the cleaning maids came up to me and said there was a visitor for me – 'at the gate, *nkosazana*. She said you would know.'

I rushed to the storm drain so as not to be seen going out of the school gate, crept down it under the road, under the bridge, and came to the gate where I had so often admired Lottie welcoming and instructing the strangers. She was sitting on the pavement, dark dress, dark cap, bowing over a baby which she was breastfeeding. I recall only confusion and distress and a conflict in my mind about which to deal with first – my father's death, or her return and her baby. It was sorted out, with many hugs and tears. She had heard about my father; she wanted me to tell her, to the smallest detail, what I knew, which was not very much. I told her all I could, both of us sobbing. I felt as though I had not been able to shed, or share, any of my shock and grief until that day. She had not gone home to her village, but to Alexandra Township, to Meshak. She had come to see me because of the death, though she also wanted to show me her little new daughter. As we sat on the pavement's edge, she found a way of hugging me with one arm and supporting the child with the other, so that I could watch the little brown face, solemnly sucking, close to mine. For some of the time Lottie was keening as well as crying, swaying from her hips, to and fro. I know now that this is a natural movement of grief.

I learned the truth about her 'going home' – sent away, of course, for pregnancy. 'But that didn't mean she had to sit here, on the pavement, out in the road? Her room was still there, the bed, the chair; there would be food in the kitchen ... she could show the baby to my mother ...' She would not; she would not come, she would not show, she would not eat, she would not let me go and fetch. She had been sacked. In the end she won this battle, as most others. I forsook school and walked with her to the queue for the Alexandra bus. She unwrapped the baby from her back and let me hold her in my arms as we queued, until the very door. I watched her driven off in a shaky and overcrowded old vehicle, driven off, out of my life, her new child in her arms.

In a strange way I have come to think, after all these years, that my opportunity to spend that little time with Lottie grieving for my father, sharing it with her, set me free to live at least adequately without him, without the reliance upon him which had shaped my life; and I seem to see in these memories of impressions and emotions a correspondence between that meeting and the way in which the setting free of Mandela and all that has followed have enabled me at last to write about my childhood that I had thought was lost. I cannot explain it; but I know that there are many Whitefellows who, whether living abroad or not, have felt themselves set free and in deep ways re-created by the freedom of Mandela – in spite of the rages and resentments which that freedom of itself has in some, both black and white, set free.

I sat on the crowded pavement of the Alexandra bus stop a long time after her bus left. I remember the black legs and dusty feet or worn shoes gathering round me, discussing me, and wondering, I suppose, what to do about me that would not land them in some kind of trouble. I knew from the shifting crowd of legs that there must be quite a large gathering of people. A group of women led by one who spoke English tried to question and to help me. Each time that I tried to explain to them, my sobs made my words unintelligible. In any case, what help or what solution could there possibly be? One of them said the others should go away and she would wait with me; which she did, just quietly sitting down beside me and waving others away, exactly as one would need. When I had calmed myself and when I thought school would be safely over for the day so that I would have no re-entry problem, I thanked this woman so fervently that she was embarrassed; and I went home to tea.

My mother was sitting on the *stoep*, with the flowery china and silver teapot and lace tablecloth. She was worried, distracted, as usual. I told her, with difficulty, about Lottie and the baby; but she could not deal with my problems as well as her own. She must have known, too, that I wanted to hurt her with the news, not only because of the sending away but because I had been deceived about it and now had the truth. She did not let herself seem troubled or hurt at all, if she was; only politely interested. I tried again with what I thought must be a deadlier thrust – 'And she has called her little girl … Prudence.' My mother briefly laughed, as though this were some kind of joke, or rather flattering piece of impertinence.

Enfranchisement and Disenfranchisement

1930 to early 1940s

In the first decades of the twentieth century, women – black and white – generally remained marginal to key political developments. Domesticity was a cornerstone in both settler and indigenous gender systems. Urbanisation among black women occurred only slowly in the early twentieth century because the migrant labour system, which drew men to the mines, depended on women to remain in the rural areas to maintain agricultural productivity and traditional homesteads. In addition to the often disastrous effects of migrancy on black families and communities, the fact that growing numbers of women were obliged to act as heads of households (contrary to the custom in strongly patriarchal traditional cultures) led to further tension within rural African society. Nevertheless, women were inevitably sucked into the maelstrom of proletarianisation and urbanisation, and this too put pressure on indigenous gender systems. In the towns, black women were often drawn into domestic service, street hawking, illegal beer brewing and prostitution – in many instances because they could no longer rely on a male provider. Cherryl Walker (1990: 20) points to a widening cleavage between 'respectable' and 'unrespectable' African women, with an implicit class differentiation.

After the First World War the numbers of white women employed outside the home as nurses, teachers and clerks grew. More white women (particularly Afrikaners) entered the labour market during the 1920s and '30s, mostly in the garment and food industries, thus undermining to some extent the settler ideal of female domesticity. Educational opportunities for women continued to expand during this period. (The South African College in Cape Town had been the first tertiary institution to open its doors to women, in 1886.)

By and large, the women's suffrage movement was made up of white, English-speaking, urban, middle-class women, whose conception of 'woman' was, Walker argues, shaped by an overriding identification with their own race, ethnic group (Afrikaner women seldom participated) and class (1990: 313–45). Furthermore, the fight for women's suffrage implied neither antagonism to the principle of supreme male authority, nor a commitment to a transcendent gender-based loyalty. Pragmatism necessitated adjustment of the initial goal of securing the vote for women on the same terms as for men. This meant that early hopes for the extension of the qualified franchise – tied to class-bound qualifications of property and education – to black women in the Cape gave way to a demand for an unqualified franchise *for white women only*. This shift in policy caused one of the woman's suffrage movement's chief protagonists, Olive Schreiner, to distance herself from the group. It also played into the National Party's hands and became a useful weapon in its attempts to weaken the significance of black voters in the Cape. Black voters amounted to less than 20 per cent of the Cape electorate in 1929; once white women had been enfranchised in 1930, the pro-portionate strength of black voters diminished considerably to just under 11 per cent of the voters in the Cape, and less than five per cent nationally.

Black women in the Cape were thus specifically excluded from the qualified franchise. Although they were not at this time prominent in national politics, they were also not politically quiescent: there had been campaigns by black women since the turn of the century. However, African women generally did not assume leadership positions and black women's suffrage was not on the agenda of women activists, as politics was considered to be a male preserve. Indeed, women were not even recognised as full members of the African National Congress (ANC) until 1943. The preoccupation of resistance move-ments was with racial power.

In the 1930s, the covert, neo-fascist, male organisation known as the Afri-kaner Broederbond (brotherhood of Afrikaners), managed to secure a firm foothold in almost all of the country's cultural, economic and political activi-ties. Together with organisations such as the Nasionale Pers (National Press) newspapers and Afrikaner financial institutions, Afrikaner leaders took advan-tage of the economic crisis to mobilise poor compatriots around the cause of a unified *volk* (nation). The Depression was at its worst in South Africa in the early 1930s, and in 1933 a severe drought gripped the country, further hasten-ing proletarianisation. The Carnegie Commission calculated in 1931 that out of a white population of 1,8 million, 300 000 were living as paupers. As a result, the government embarked on a 'civilised labour' policy that guaranteed work for whites at the expense of blacks.

The idealised concept of the *volksmoeder* (people's mother) served to blur the profound class divisions amongst Afrikaners, while the ideology of white superiority was consolidated, along with women's role in its preservation (Walker, 1990: 22). Immense popular enthusiasm for the nationalist cause was whipped up in 1938 during the centenary commemoration of the Great Trek, and Gustav Preller and other writers created a largely mythical history in which a united Afrikaner people, chosen by God, had been oppressed by the English.

After South Africa had abandoned the gold standard in 1932, the economy recovered and expanded, but the rise in the standard of living was enjoyed only by white South Africans. Although more and more Africans, coloureds and Asians were drawn into the economy, the real wages of farm labourers and black mineworkers remained static, or actually declined, between 1911 and 1970.

Political divisions amongst whites, temporarily healed in 1934 when the National Party and the South African Party joined together to form the United Party, soon re-emerged. In 1939, Afrikaner nationalists who were against South African participation in the Second World War were outvoted. Jan Smuts became Prime Minister and led South Africa into the war, but amongst Afrikaners anti-British, pro-Nazi sentiment thrived. In 1940, J.B.M. Hertzog and Malan formed the right-wing Herenigde Nasionale Party (Reunited National Party).

Hertzog's attempts to remove blacks from the Cape voters' roll had provoked a revival of African political activity, leading to the formation of the All-African Convention in 1935. Their programme of moderate protest failed to prevent the abolition of the Cape African franchise in 1936. This came as a cruel blow to Africans throughout South Africa who had valued the Cape vote, not because of the political clout it afforded but because its existence was grounds for hope that it would one day be extended to the whole of South Africa. Supposedly as compensation, the government established the Natives' Representative Council and blacks were given a separate voters' roll in order to elect four senators to represent them. The Natives' Trust and Land Act made provision for the extension of the Natives' reserves from 7,5 per cent to 13 per cent of the total land in the country. (However, the same Act also barred rural Africans from acquiring land outside their stipulated areas.) Resistance at the time was ineffectual: the ANC was dominated by leaders who preferred moral argument to open confrontation, and political splits within radical protest movements had led to the weakening of the Communist Party and the virtual collapse of the ICU. Africans, moreover, had been devastated by the Depression, which had hit them far more cruelly than it had whites.

Dr Goonam

Kesaveloo Naidoo was born in 1906 in Durban to R.K. (an immigrant from South India) and Archie Naidoo (from Mauritius). Her parents were well connected, moving in the same social circles as Gandhi and other prominent South Africans of Indian descent, such as Monty Naicker and Strinivasa Sastri. Her favourite uncle was the philanthropist M.L. Sultan, who founded the college of the same name in Durban. After attending Tamil and English schools, Kesaveloo's fierce independence eventually won through and she persuaded her reluctant father to allow her to embark on a virtually unprecedented (for a South African Indian woman) medical career. Since no medical school in South Africa would admit her, she set sail for Scotland in 1928, returning to South Africa in 1936 after qualifying as a doctor at Edinburgh University. When she set up her practice in Durban, she dropped the name Naidoo because of its caste connotations and adopted the name Goonam. She was one of the doctors who led the 1946 Indian Passive Resistance Campaign against the Anti-Indian Land Act, and was imprisoned 17 times. She died in 1999, aged 92.

This passage from her autobiography (written in collaboration with Fatima Meer) entitled *Coolie Doctor: An Autobiography by Dr Goonam* (1991) tells of some of her experiences as a young doctor in Durban in the 1930s.

During my home visits [house calls], I discovered the depth of Indian poverty. The staple diet was mealie rice, dholl, herbs, potatoes and pickles. Protein was sadly lacking, meat, fish and chicken being beyond their reach. I enjoyed the visits, but felt helpless against the poverty and superstition. I couldn't teach them to think logically. Tact and diplomacy did not go very far with them. The all pervading 'evil spirit' kept them constant company and clouded their vision. All illness was due to divine chastisement and they often obstinately turned their backs on medical treatment.

Tradition, superstition, ignorance and ritual dominated Indian life and I am afraid I had practically no patience with these things.

I was shocked when a child suffering from bronchitis after a bout of measles was not allowed 'English' medicine because the Goddess Mariamma had sent a visitation to the home and medicines were taboo. Instead a thanks-giving prayer (puja) was conducted to appease the wrath of the goddess for sparing the child's life.

One day I witnessed a horrendous scene that remains inscribed in my memory even after forty years. I was on my rounds when passing a temple, I heard the most awful swish of a sjambok (whip) and saw a young boy being chased by a man who was shouting and screaming.

The boy's voice reached a crescendo and tailed off to almost an inaudible cry. I stopped, got out of the car and looking hard at the youngster, recognised him as the case of bilateral tuberculosis I had diagnosed a week earlier. Only now he was even more emaciated, and his eyes were sunken, and his face wreathed in a sweat as he fell into a faint on the bare ground. There was bleeding about his face, legs and chest. His mother was lifting him to make him drink 'holy water'. When she saw me she said simply, 'He has the spirit, but just now he will be better.' The boy died two days later.

But it was not all tragedy, there were idiosyncrasies that accompanied orthodoxy.

One early morning, I was called out of bed to attend a maternity case. I knew the family and had attended to one or two members occasionally. The tin shack was on top of a hill and I had to do some mountaineering.

The patient, a pregnant girl, was lying on the floor and had been in labour for a whole day. There had been a midwife in attendance, but she had left when I was called.

After some strenuous manipulation, I delivered a child with a huge head, hydrocephalic, as medical people call it, with gross facial deformity and distortion. The grandmother strode into the room, took one look at the infant, spat on the floor, turned towards me with a scowl and screaming angrily said, 'Take it away … it is a devil!' She made me feel as if I had brought it with me in my black bag. As I went outside to wash my hands, she gave me a fiendish look, and hurrying back to the room covered the crying infant with a heavy blanket.

The young mother drew me closer and in a whisper pleaded with me to take it away, and pointing to the river down the valley, said I should throw it there. 'It will bring us bad luck.' Her eyes welled with tears. I realised that the old lady would make her life intolerable and I did some quick thinking. Where could I take the baby? I bundled him and took him down the steep hill to my car, and placing him on the back seat, sped to St. Aiden's Mission Hospital which tolerated my oddities and idiosyncrasies with a true spirit of human feeling. On the way, the baby cried lustily and when I stopped at the traffic lights, I got suspicious looks from the passengers in the cars alongside mine. It seemed an eternity before the lights turned green.

The matron was most cooperative, she accepted the baby and placed him in the nursery. But despite her care, the unfortunate infant died within a week. The corpse was preserved in formalin because of [its] highly unusual characteristics and finally claimed by the medical school.

I went to see the patient the day after I had delivered her and found the family immersed in a great ceremony. Incense was burning, a priest with a snow white cap and dhothi was chanting from the holy book throwing bits of twigs and ghee into the container of hot embers (hawan). The mother had a talisman tied to her wrist and the floor was smeared with cow dung to ward off the evil spirit. The [hatchet-faced] old girl, busying herself with the priest, gestured to me to be gone as soon as possible. I was definitely not wanted there. Surprisingly, even the young mother didn't inquire as to what I had done with her offspring. Was it a deliberate act of indifference or was she so fear-ridden by her mother-in-law?

The father of the child however came to see me at the surgery to hear what had been done to his son. He made me promise not to discuss the matter with any of his relatives. My services were never sought again by that family as long as the old matriarch lived, but I did meet the young woman a few years later. She had had two normal births and looked pleased with life. Subsequently, she came to me with her fourth pregnancy after the old lady had died. It was a successful delivery of a much wanted boy baby at the hospital.

There was also a lot to laugh about.

The orthodox women at the clinics would not utter their husband's names and I teased them to tell me the names, but they never caught on that I was playing games with them.

'My child's father has a bad cough, I want some medicine for him.'

'What's his name?'

The woman's reply would be a whispered mention of the first letter of the name 'M'.

'Is it Moonsamy?'

'No.'

'Is is Muthusamy?'

'No.'

I would purposely go on.

'Malayandi?'

'No.'

'Murugan?'

A smile would play on her lips when I hit the right one. While it was near blasphemy for the Indian woman to utter her husband's name, the husband mentioned his wife's with impunity, although many husbands preferred to refer to their wives as the mother of their eldest child, 'The mother of Ranga or the mother of Seetha'.

The old Telegu woman with rings on her ears and rings on her nose would be sitting complacently smoking, the lit end of her cigar inside her mouth and would spring to attention when her turn came. That breed of traditional smokers has fast disappeared. I found it interesting to watch their skill in not burning their lips. The old woman would rattle away in Telegu, noisily demonstrating her intractable condition of indigestion. It was mental gymnastics for me to keep switching from one language to another – Tamil, Telegu, Hindi, Zulu. I invariably made a hash of it. But the patients were too well mannered to laugh at me. They were kind and tolerant.

We found great fun translating phrases literally into English. At the clinics, I had to acquaint the sister with the meaning of such expressions as 'green egg', 'cold touch', 'vein pulling', 'sawing in the chest', etc. The question of 'hot medicine', 'cool medicine', 'blood heating medicine', 'blood drying medicine', were communicated in great detail by patients who wanted to ensure that such conditions were kept in mind when dispensing medicines.

They would complain that their blood was either too hot or too cold and requested something to counteract the specific condition. If they had a cold or congestion of the lungs or any inflammatory lesion, their blood had become cold, and needed something to warm it up. If they had a boil or come out in a rash, their blood was hot and needed to be cooled.

Whilst we could explain the therapeutic nature of the medicines prescribed, we could not satisfy their queries about the thermostatic effects in their bodies. It was difficult to prescribe diets as they would want to know what effect each known vegetable and fruit had on the system. 'Can I eat cabbage or will it cool my blood?' The sister had a lot of walking to do, to and from my room, to where the patient was to tell him/her about the rationale of the body and its effects on these vegetables. 'Can I eat chicken or will it warm my blood?' Apples, grapes, pawpaws, mangoes, all were carefully gone into for their effects on the body.

Our compounder had stock mixtures, ready in all available Winchesters, for the weekend regulars. They were good at taking their medicines, and there was no need to mask the bitter taste of drugs, as black people said the [more] bitter the medicine the better the result. The avoidance of salt was no hardship to them.

Herbs, cress, leaves such as young pumpkin leaves, leaves of certain plants regarded by whites as weeds, made a tasty dish. We would encourage them to include them in their diet as they had a laxative effect. The ground chutney made from curry leaves, coriander leaves, mint, etc, left all their vitamins intact, and I would stress the need to include these in their daily diet. Yogart [sic] formed the basis of many people's food.

The younger people's complaints gave us tea time levity. They had their own way of explaining it. 'I didn't have my bath for three months.' Sister would then wonder if there was a water shortage where she came from. It meant that she did not have her periods for three months. Then there was a girl who did not translate from her language but said she was 'fragrant' (pregnant) for two months. One bright Johnny who was a motor mechanic by trade came to us to have his wife dismantled as she did not have her period for two months. He had three children and didn't want any more. Whilst I was keen on Family Planning, I couldn't possibly 'dismantle' her.

Mr Kumar came on a busy Monday morning, very anxious to see me, but since my nurse let patients in, in strict order, Mr Kumar had to bide his turn. Eventually when the nurse looked for him he appeared to have vanished. All of a sudden we heard a loud knocking on the back door. When it was opened, in came an agitated Mr Kumar. 'It is very bad, the water works Dr!' he said, shaking his head. 'Yes,' I agreed with him. The toilet attached to my surgery had been giving us a lot of trouble, due to our country patients who would inadvertently turn off the stop cock. We tried to keep a vigilant eye on it especially when country patients used it, but on busy days it was not possible to keep it constantly in mind and the trouble would be repeated. So when Mr Kumar complained of the water works, I told him I'd get the matter seen to right away, and forthwith instructed the nurse to rectify it. The nurse returned to tell Mr Kumar that he could use the toilet now, it was in order, but he looked at us in consternation.

'Come on, there are other patients doctor must see,' the nurse admonished. His consternation increased and there was a look of utter confusion on his face.

'Nurse has seen to it – it is in order now,' I reassured him.

'Dr, please, you must come to my house ... the wife's water works ... she is bedridden!' stammered the man.

'Oh ... is that what it is ... she can't pass water?'

Suddenly a semi-smile of relief broke on his face. At last I had got the message. So it was a case of retention of urine and not a stop cock. It was an urgent matter.

'But why didn't you tell?' ... I stopped short, he was trying to tell me all the time. How stupid I had been, I should have comprehended.

'Right, let me finish these cases quickly and I'll go with you.'

Mr Kumar's home was 20 kilometers away and we were soon speeding along the sugar belt on the North Coast Road. There was an oppressive hot wind, the sun had dried up the earth and the green blades of the sugar cane looked parched and limp, hanging their tongues out for water. There was a rumble of thunder now and then. It looked like rain and I was hoping it would keep off till I had finished the call, as the road was impassable on wet days, the rain made it skiddy and slippery and the wind congested it with dead branches and leaves. Mr Kumar, a little anxious about my state of preparedness, asked, 'Have you got your tools, Doctor?'

'Oh yes ... yes ... yes. I have everything,' I assured him. But how right he was associating my job with a plumber's as indeed it was.

We reached his house, a rambling brick farm stead. The terraced frontage was a mass of bourganvilla [*sic*]. As we climbed the steps to the verandah, I had the sense of anxious eyes following my every step. 'Could this slip of a woman handle this case?' they seemed to be asking. A man, better still, a white doctor would have inspired more confidence in them; but then this sickness dealt with a part of the body that required a lady doctor.

As I approached the sick room, I heard a lusty piercing scream, intimating a healthy, vigorous woman, rather than a bedridden dying patient. I had to wade through a large number of people, some standing, some sitting on the floor, some almost on top of the sick woman, before I could reach the patient. Every window was barred and bolted, there was not a breath of fresh air in the room. I felt an immediate sense of suffocation and proceeded to open a window and tactfully cleared the room of its large audience, leaving just one young girl of about 16 to assist me. The patient had stopped screaming by now and remained completely silent as I questioned the young girl on the history of her condition. I gathered that the urine trouble and the 'bedridden' condition was of less than 18 hours' duration. The girl was still explaining when Mr Kumar appeared, to tell me that the patient had also 'lost her tongue'. His appearance provoked his wife into a fresh bout of lusty screams. The family had diagnosed the illness. They were simply seeking a cure for it. She had been bewitched by a ghost set upon her by her daughter-in-law's family in retaliation to a slinging word match they had had. The patient had gone into her garden following the fight at the inauspicious time of 7 pm when evil spirits are particularly active. She had seen the ghost behind a tree, 'a bad tree' haunted by ghosts of dead people.

I examined the patient, gave her a shot of morphia which relaxed her, catheterised her and applied abdominal pressure to the full bladder. There was a dramatic gush of urine. The young girl, seeing the free flow of water uttered a cry of joy 'Bhagwan!' (Oh God!). The others, hearing her, rushed into the room, knocking each other in the stampede to reach the bed and see the pool created by Mrs Kumar. I was now acclaimed a miracle worker. They pulled my hands and stroked them, took them to their eyes and kissed them. It was moving, flattering, but at the same time suffocating and embarrassing. The patient, in the meantime, was enjoying a deep and sonorous sleep after her exhausting time with the ghost.

The following morning, Mr Kumar appeared in the surgery laden with a huge bunch of marigolds, a collection of choice vegetables, including a pocket of home grown rice – offerings fit for a goddess!

A week later, the 'bedridden lady' arrived looking none the worse for her ordeal. She gave me intimate details of the 'plot' to kill her and declared that the injection saved her life, and lowering her voice to almost a whisper and edging close to me, informed me that the evil tree in question had been set on fire and was now completely destroyed. For good measure, the priest had come and conducted prayers for three days to eliminate all trace of bad spirits, and again lowering her voice another decibel, confided, 'Ghosts don't like the chanting of mantras.'

Everytime thereafter, whenever I smelt marigolds in the surgery or saw prize vegetables I knew the lady from North Coast Road was somewhere in the waiting room.

Hers was a textbook description of hysteria with retention of urine the predominant feature. Soon I discovered that Indians had the 'Spirit complex', Africans the 'Tagaati (witchcraft) complex', Europeans the 'Neurosis complex' and coloureds a mixture of all three under the spell of black magic.

Katie Makanya

Katie Manye, pictured here with Margaret McCord, was born on 28 July 1873 at Fort Beaufort in the Cape, then a British colony. As a young woman, in 1891, she travelled with her sister Charlotte to England where, as members of the Jubilee Singers, they were presented at Court to Queen Victoria. At a time when medical services for black South Africans were almost non-existent, Katie was Dr James McCord's indispensable assistant in the establishment and running of McCord's Zulu Hospital in Durban. She was his interpreter, dispenser and nurse for 35 years.

Katie married Ndeya Makanya and bore ten children, four of whom died in infancy. Katie herself died in Natal in 1955, shortly after having told her story to Dr McCord's youngest daughter, Margaret. *The Calling of Katie Makanya* (1995), from which this extract is taken, is a mixture of biography and oral testimony arising out of the taped conversations held between Margaret McCord and Katie in 1954.

The narrative reproduced here begins in the 1930s, after another paranoid outburst by Katie's seventh child, Livingstone. His mental illness was especially difficult for Katie to accept since all through childhood he had excelled at school and Katie had had high hopes that he would become a doctor.

That night after they had eaten, Samuel, Ndeya, Josephine and Katie were sitting at table in the kitchen when Livingstone got up to put another stick on the fire. Suddenly and without any warning, he whirled around and clubbed Samuel on the forehead with all his strength. Samuel lost his temper, jumped up with the blood pouring down his face and went for his brother. But Livingstone leapt out of the way and threw himself at Katie's feet.

'Don't let him kill me, Ma,' he pleaded.

'I'm not going to kill you,' Samuel shouted. 'I'm only going to give you a big thrashing. I'll teach you not to hit me.'

'Stop it, Samuel,' Katie yelled. She looked down at Livingstone and very gently asked why he had tried to fight.

'I don't know,' he whimpered.

'Poor child,' she murmured, stroking his face as though he were still little. 'I think you must be very tired. Come. Let's go to bed.'

He went with her obediently, and she lay beside him all through the night, never sleeping but always quick to lay her arm across his chest and whisper soft and loving words whenever he stirred. Ndeya and Samuel took turns guarding the doorway. Early the next morning men from the asylum came to take him away.

Livingstone did not want to go with them. When they came into the house he started to yell and fight. But they were strong, and with Samuel's help they strapped a canvas sheet around his body so that he couldn't move and tied him down on a stretcher. As they carried him outside, Katie leaned forward and tried to pat his cheek. But he jerked his head away. When the men tilted the stretcher to push it into their ambulance, he looked at her for the last time. She felt as though she herself were dying when she saw the fear, anger and childish confusion mixed up in his eyes.

Katie went to visit him just once in Pietermaritzburg. He was kept all alone in a room like a prison cell so that he could not hurt other patients. When he heard Katie speaking to him through a little window in the door, his cheek began to twitch and he shouted out angrily to the men in charge that she was not his mother. The nurses at the asylum told her not to return until he improved. But Livingstone got worse instead of better, and finally he was transferred to an asylum in Bloemfontein for the incurably insane, hundreds of miles away.

Every few months Katie wrote to the European superintendent of the asylum to ask if there was anything she could send her son – a bag of toffees, perhaps, or a new shirt. But the answer was always the same. She realised then that there was no longer anything she could do for Livingstone.

After her trouble with Livingstone, Katie felt very old and discouraged. Indeed, she was old. It was almost forty years since she had started working for the Doctor, and he too was growing old. Yet strangely, to her he seemed no different from when he'd returned from America after the Great War.

Therefore, on the day in 1939 when she read that England was going to fight another war, she asked the Doctor when he and Dr Pearson would put on their uniforms and leave for duty as they had done at the start of the last war.

He laughed. 'I've grown too fat for that uniform. Anyway, I'm too old for the army now.'

'I'm glad. Because then you stayed in America too long.'

'But Katie,' he hesitated, no longer smiling, 'pretty soon I'll have to retire. I'll be seventy next April, and all the missionaries have to retire when they're seventy. I've been planning to talk to you about this. Dr Taylor will put someone else in charge of the dispensary, and I don't know if you want to go on working –'

'I only work for you, Doctor, not for anyone else.'

'Then you'll retire also?'

'Yes, Doctor.'

It was strange to think of retiring, of not coming to the dispensary. On the hot sunny days when her rheumatism did not trouble her too much, Katie did not think she could live without all the excitement of 86 Beatrice Street, without the hum of different languages spoken all at once, the shouts of the rickshaw men and the honking of the motor cars, without the mingled smells of flowers, petrol, garlic, fish and body sweat blown around by the sea breezes, without the vivid colours of the Indian women in their saris and the bright patterns of African beadwork. Yet, at other times when the rain crowded the patients onto the benches in the waiting-room and the pain in her knees grew tiresome, she dreamed of a small country dispensary where she would work with the Doctor in the mornings and plant her garden in the afternoons.

On Christmas Eve he brought presents for all the workers at the dispensary. For Katie he had a bag of toffees, a tin of Baumann's Biscuits, and two large photographs, one of himself and one of Mrs McCord. 'So you won't forget us,' he said. This talk of forgetting puzzled her. As she travelled out to Adams and during the Christmas service in the mission church, and afterwards when she showed her friends his photograph hanging on her wall, she kept wondering what he had meant. Had she complained too much about the rheumatism in her knees? Did he think she would leave him and come back here to Adams when their work in the dispensary was finished?

On the first day after the Christmas holiday she waited uneasily for the sound of his motor car, and as soon as he arrived she followed him into his consulting room.

'Please, Doctor, where are we going to have our new dispensary after we retire?

'What are you talking about?' he asked her as he put on his long white coat.

'Don't you remember? You've always said that when you retired, we'd find a place in the country where the people would need us, to have a small dispensary?'

'Oh.' He sat down behind his desk, not smiling. 'That was a long time ago. When we are young we don't know what it's like to grow old. Now you and I know. Neither one of us has as much energy any more. It's time for us to sit back and enjoy our children and our grandchildren.'

'But our people still need you. You're not too old to doctor them.'

He smiled sadly. 'The Bible says a man's too old when he reaches three-score years and ten.'

'But not you. You're still strong. You're still the best doctor.'

'That's the way I want to be remembered.'

'But what will I do?'

'You'll go back to Adams to live with Ndeya. When it's warm you will work in your garden, and when it's cold you'll sit by the fire and tell stories to your grandchildren. And you will be happy there. Do you hear me, Katie?'

'I hear you, Doctor.'

'Then you had better start calling in the patients.'

That last day was the same as all the other days of their many years together. She passed around the bread and tea, waited for the Doctor's car to come at nine o'clock and, as soon as he had changed into his long white coat and picked up his stethoscope, she called in the first of the patients. The day was no different from all the others. Late in the afternoon the Doctor called out for her to bring his tea into the consulting room. 'With two cups,' he said.

When she brought in the tea tray and laid it on his desk, he motioned her into the chair across from him and opened up his tin of biscuits. 'There aren't many left, so we might as well finish them off,' he said.

'Thank you, Doctor.' Not knowing what else to say, she rolled the sweetened crumbs around on her tongue.

'Well, Katie, we've come to the end of a long road.'

'Yes, Doctor.'

'You've made my work easy.' He hesitated for a moment and cleared his throat. 'We've been through much together, you and I.' He paused again, finding it difficult to speak, and again cleared his throat. 'You've sacrificed much for the sake of our work. I want you to know I've always been grateful.' He paused again, but in that moment there was no need for words between them. Katie could read his thoughts and knew that he loved her as he loved all the people and loved Africa and that he did not want to go away.

'I, too, am grateful,' she said.

'Now it's time for each of us to have a long, long holiday.'

'Yes.'

'If you ever need anything after I'm gone, anything at all, go to Dr Taylor.'

'Yes, Doctor.'

Katie knew now that everything was finished. How could she live when he was gone? In front of her his face blurred until the wrinkles disappeared and he seemed like a young man again and his laughter was shaking the earth.

She felt the rush of movement, his hands grasping her shoulders. 'Steady there. Good! Now put your head down on your knees.'

The floor steadied under her feet.

'Drink this.'

He was holding her cup of tea to her mouth. Even with plenty of sugar it tasted very strong but she had to swallow quickly because he was tipping the cup against her lips. At last she pushed it away.

'I'm all right now, Doctor.'

He stepped back and half-leaned, half-sat on his desk. 'For a moment you startled me. I thought you were going to faint.' He chuckled softly. 'Like that first day you came to work, remember?'

'I remember. I was very frightened that day.'

'But still you came back. That took courage.'

Her tears came then. 'But now I've no more courage,' she sobbed. 'I'm very frightened. Because I never thought you'd leave us. I thought we'd bury you here.'

He tried to make her laugh. 'I'm not ready to be buried yet.'

'You know what I mean.'

'Yes, I do know. But Katie, a man needs to go back to his homeplace.'

She nodded silently, remembering Mbambo, who left her to go back to Umgeni when he was dying.

'Oh, Doctor, will you ever come back?' He did not speak, only looked down at her, unable to find any words. But because he was a true man and had never lied to her, he shook his head.

The silence between them was long. Then he stepped forward and reached out that right hand, the one with the two fingers missing, and very lightly touched Katie's face. His words were low and between them alone. 'Who can see into the future? But one thing I think you know already. My heart will be here always.'

'Here? In Africa? You mean like David Livingstone?'

'You remember that too?'

'You gave my sister Charlotte a book once about David Livingstone. She left it with me and I have it still.'

Miss Ball's voice jarred at them through the door. 'It's the hospital, Doctor. They want you on the phone.'

'All right, I'm coming.' He dropped his hand from Katie's face. 'This isn't goodbye. I'll see you again, many times, before I actually leave.'

'Yes, Doctor.'

But it was goodbye. She saw him again only at the parties and receptions in his honour during the month before his ship sailed.

Ntombi Dhlamini

This song was composed by Ntombi Dhlamini and recorded by Hugh Tracey – the legendary ethnomusicologist – in Durban in the1930s or '40s. Tracey comments that Dhlamini had been a domestic worker in a Durban home for many years. For recreation, she organised a choir, for which she composed many songs. Jeff Opland reproduced an English translation of the song in *Words that Circle Words: A Choice of South African Oral Poetry* (1992). This song – thought to be autobiographical – is narrated by a disillusioned woman who rejects her lover. As Opland observes, the song's evocative image of two people whose worldly possessions can be contained in a pillowcase or in the hollow of an armpit reflects their impoverished status as part of a growing African proletariat.

I thought you loved me,
Yet I'm wasting my time on you.
I thought we'd be parted only by death,
But today you've disappointed me.
You'll never amount to anything.
You're a disgrace, worthless, unreliable.
Bring my things. I'll put them in my pillow.
You take yours and stuff them under your armpit.
You deceived me.

Foundations of
Apartheid

1940 to 1949

Social change in South Africa was rapid and radical. By the end of 1939, after South Africa had joined the war against Germany, 137 000 men were under arms and volunteers were still pouring in. (Ultimately, some 390 000 men and women volunteers served in the armed forces.) But not all white South Africans supported the Allied forces. By 1940, the pro-Nazi, Afrikaner Ossewa Brandwag (Oxwagon Sentinel) claimed a membership of double the number of those who had signed up. In 1942 its military wing, the Stormjaers (Stormtroopers), embarked on an anti-war sabotage campaign. This included blowing up pylons, power lines, post offices, shops and banks, as well as beating up soldiers and Jews (who, in 1936, comprised about four per cent of the white population). Ossewa Brandwag members included Afrikaners who subsequently rose to prominence in the apartheid government, such as B.J. Vorster, who was to become Minister of Justice, Prime Minister and State President.

In general, though, South African voters backed the war effort. During the war, countless families opened their homes to Allied troops from the many ships that passed through South African ports, and knitting was enthusiastically taken up by thousands of white women. A Durban woman, Perla Gibson, became famous for singing to the troops through a megaphone from the quayside in Durban. Always dressed in white, the 'Lady in white' sang up to 250 songs per day. On one occasion, her rendition of 'Waltzing Matilda' brought so many visiting Australian troops to the wharf side of their ship that it listed and the masts crashed into a grain elevator. The war boosted the South African economy and, as a result, pass laws were relaxed, permitting large numbers of Africans to pour into the towns in search of work.

Such changes affected gender relations. According to Cherryl Walker (1990: 25), by the Second World War a particular ideology of gender had become dominant across all racial and ethnic groups in southern Africa: this was rooted in the western and Christian model, in terms of which the concept of 'woman' was organised around domesticity (more frequently in the nuclear rather than the extended family), subordination to male authority, childbearing and childcare. Nevertheless, in African communities, older, indigenous gender systems continued to operate, particularly outside the Christianised or urbanised groups.

In general, black South Africans supported the war effort. For them, the ideological dangers of Nazism were only too apparent. Since they were not allowed to carry arms, 123 000 black South Africans served in non-combatant roles such as driving, digging trenches, cooking and stretcher-bearing. The focus on racism and human rights occasioned by the war did not, as many had hoped, affect the structures of South African society. When the war ended, the government applied racially discriminatory cash and clothing allowances for discharged servicemen: whites received £5 in cash and a £25 clothing allowance, coloureds received £3 and £15 respectively, while Africans received only £2 and a khaki suit worth £2. Neither did the benefits of burgeoning industrialisation and the strengthening economy filter down to black workers. In 1941 the African Mineworkers Union was formed, which by 1944 claimed a membership of 25 000. The government's response was to ban union activity in all mine compounds and, in 1946, a strike by more than 60 000 African mineworkers for a minimum wage of 10 shillings per day was brutally and swiftly repressed by the state: 12 people were killed and more than 1 000 injured. Although the strike failed to achieve its objectives (it took another three years before mine-owners granted African workers a threepence per shift increase), the strike ushered in a new era for African politics.

In the 1940s, resistance by black ghetto-dwellers became more strident: there were the Alexandra bus boycotts (between 1940 and 1945) and the Sofasonke squatters' movement. The latter was in response to the virtual cessation of new housing provision by local government in Johannesburg for blacks during the early 1940s. This had resulted in horrendous overcrowding and situations such as that in Pimville, the ghetto outside Johannesburg, which had only 63 taps for more than 15 000 people. Gangs flourished, as did alcoholism and crime. The state's solution to mushrooming squatter settlements was to force most

Witwatersrand squatters into massive 'matchbox' housing estates by the end of the decade.

Black militancy was encouraged by the Communist Party, whose fortunes had improved markedly once Russia had entered the war against Germany. In the early 1940s, the ANC's transformation into a mass movement began, largely due to the influence of the new president, Dr Alfred Xuma, who centralised control of the organisation in the presidency and the five-person executive and sought to broaden the base of paid-up members to blue-collar workers. He also permitted the establishment in 1943 of the more militant Congress Youth League which, in the next five years, broadened its support base within the ANC.

The victory of the National Party in the 1948 elections and its adoption of apartheid policies (the term, meaning separateness, was coined to denote complete segregation and the promotion of tribal affiliation) enabled the Youth League to persuade the ANC to adopt a Programme of Action in 1949 which called for new methods of struggle, including boycotts, strikes and civil disobedience.

Pauline Podbrey

Pauline Podbrey's family immigrated to South Africa from Lithuania in 1933 because of growing unemployment in Europe. Her intense commitment to communism led to her involvement in the development of the black trade union movement and in the anti-apartheid struggle, along with legendary activists like Dr Goonam, Ruth First and Hilda Watts. It was through her political activism that Pauline met and fell in love with H.A. Naidoo, a leading communist figure of Indian extraction, whom she married in

Cape Town in 1943. After the National Party came to power, Pauline and H.A. fled South Africa. H.A. stowed away on a ship, while Pauline travelled on a borrowed passport. They worked in Budapest for three years, where their experiences led to a very painful disillusionment with communism. Pauline and H.A. had three daughters. She now lives in Cape Town with her second husband.

This extract from her autobiography, *White Girl in Search of the Party* (1993), deals with her experiences of racism as a young white woman dating an Indian man in Durban in the early 1940s.

Sunday 27 September 1942 was a milestone in my life. That was the day on which the Communist Party of South Africa Durban District Committee held a mass rally and pageant at Currie's Fountain to call for a second front in Europe and invited me to be one of the speakers. It meant sharing the platform not only with H.A. Naidoo and Wilson Cele, but also with national leaders like Advocate Harry Snitcher from Cape Town and, from the Central Committee of Johannesburg, Michael Harmel and Dr Yussuf Dadoo. I was awed by their presence and shaking at the prospect of standing up in front of all the thousands of people we expected to attend that day. It was one thing to address a small indoor meeting or to speak from a soap-box on a street corner. Those were challenges I had come to relish but this was different. This was a proper mass rally and I was an official Party representative. Should I prepare notes? Should I write the speech out in full? I'd never done this before, I'd always stood up and talked, saying what was on my mind. But this was different. I tried to put my thoughts on paper and to fill them out with rounded, resonant phrases but it soon became all too clear to me that that was not my style. I could only speak as I had always done – spontaneously, with conviction; I had to appeal to my audience directly, without any bits of paper coming between us.

There's a photograph of me talking to Ismail Meer before the meeting. I'm in a white knee-length pleated skirt with a red blazer, drawing nervously on a cigarette while he smiles at me reassuringly. A week earlier Dorothy Naylor had asked me why I'd started to smoke. 'It's easy to look intelligent,' I'd answered, 'without saying anything.' Puffing away at a fag denoted anything you wished it to do. It could indicate deep thought, superior judgment, commitment or withdrawal. But now I did have to say something and my throat went dry as I watched the huge grounds filling up with a sea of faces. In the front row sat Father, a pocket handkerchief covering his thinning hair to protect him from the hot afternoon sun, conspicuous among the black and brown faces surrounding him. Father had brought my young brother, Maurice, to hear his big sister speak – it was Maurice's first mass public meeting and he was looking round with unabashed [curiosity]. H.A. passed by, deep in conversation with our important visitors who gave me not a second glance. He broke away from them, walked over to me and patted me on the shoulder: 'Don't look so worried,' he said. 'You'll do all right.' I cannot remember now what I said and how I said it. All I recall was my relief when it was over. When I sat down to the usual applause I looked down at Father and he was smiling encouragingly. The thought crossed my mind: I think he's quite proud of me. It was one of the rare occasions when Father showed approval.

I grew up believing that I was a disappointment to Father. Whatever my achievements, Father would invariably ask, 'Couldn't you have done better?' If I came second in a test, Father would want to know why I wasn't first. I cannot remember a single occasion when he offered praise. Some months later when I announced that I was going to leave home and it led to the inevitable argument I blurted out, 'You've always been ashamed of me; you've never approved of anything I've done; you've never even liked me!' Father looked at me in amazement. 'You don't know what you're saying! Me, ashamed of you? Why I'm proud of you, proud of everything you've done. I'm forever boasting about you, ask any of my friends. And you think I don't like you? Nobody could love a daughter more than I've loved you. How could you not know it?' 'Because you never once said so,' I muttered. All those wasted years when I might have basked in my father's approval, unhappy teenage years which would have been so much easier to bear if I knew that I had my father's uncritical love. Father looked at me as if he were seeing me for the first time. 'Naturally, I thought you knew,' he said. 'Wasn't it obvious?' He paused for a while. 'I can't help it if words don't come easily to me.'

I asked my parents if I could invite H.A. to dinner at our home. Father knew him by repute and Mother said 'Of course, if he's a friend of yours.' They welcomed him and Mother cooked a special Friday night meal with chicken soup and *kneidlach*. Eight-year old Maurice gazed in awe as Father and H.A. talked politics. Father was enjoying himself; here was a man with whom it was a pleasure to exchange ideas, one he could respect; informed, intelligent, dispassionate. 'Now there's a real Communist for you,' Father said approvingly after H.A. had gone, 'Probably the only one left in this country, I shouldn't wonder.'

H.A. and I were falling in love and with the passing of each day the bond between us strengthened. We tried to see each other whenever our hectic programme of activities provided an opportunity. Sometimes, after a meeting, we would slip up to his room and spend a blissful hour together. By now his landlady, Mrs Chetty, accepted me with better grace; she'd welcome me with a wave and a smile as we slipped though her kitchen to get to H.A.'s small back room. Afterwards H.A. would hail an Indian taxi and see me home to Umgeni Road. We were grateful for the blackout; we could sit close together holding hands as we drove through Durban's darkened streets. By now our love affair was common knowledge among our comrades. I no longer tried to dim the light in my eyes when he entered a room and he, for his part, whilst maintaining the strictest impartiality during meetings, made no secret of his preference for me above all other women. In the wider world outside our circle we continued to pretend that our association was purely political. Politics alone was enough to rouse the ire and hostility of most people without introducing the explosive subject of sex across the racial barrier.

Finding a place where we could be alone together was not easy. We couldn't always get to his room and sometimes we'd slip into empty offices after working hours. Once we thought we'd found a place – the office of the Jewellery Workers' Union. H.A. had borrowed the key of the office and when the staff went home we crept in, turned the key in the door and switched off the light. We were locked in each other's arms when we heard voices outside; someone was trying to turn the handle of the door and complaining that it hadn't been left open, as it should have been. 'Oh, damn,' H.A. muttered, 'They're having a committee meeting here tonight.' Frantically we began to straighten our clothes. 'They mustn't find us like this,' I whispered. 'It's too humiliating; let's jump through the window.' I opened the window and leaned out. We were two floors up and there was no ledge. Outside, the early arrivals had been joined by others. Now there were ten or twelve of them and then their secretary arrived and he had a key. When he opened the door H.A. was standing on the table, pretending to fix the light bulb; I rushed past the surprised committee members, trying to hide my face in embarrassment; they gaped and giggled.

Travelling together by public transport was also difficult. He was restricted to the last three seats on the upper deck of the tram and I was not allowed to sit next to him. When I decided to defy this discriminatory by-law and settled down next to H.A. at the back of the tram, the conductor challenged me. 'These seats are for non-Europeans only,' he said, looking at me suspiciously. 'You must move.' He sometimes had to order blacks and Indians out of the white seats, not usually the other way round.

'How do you know I'm not an Indian?' I demanded. This brought him up sharply. How indeed could he prove my race merely by my appearance if I chose to declare otherwise? He stammered in confusion then marched away. In a country like South Africa the races had mixed ever since the arrival of the white man and appearance was in fact the only yardstick used by racists. All the same, I could see the conductor's dilemma: if she can pass as White, why travel as black?

'I can't stand this secrecy,' H.A. said one night. 'This hole-in-the-corner way of meeting is humiliating. I want everyone to know that I love you.' 'I too. I'd love to shout it from the rooftops,' I told him. 'But what can we do?' 'Let's get married.' I stared at him in amazement. This was something I had not considered. 'But I don't believe in marriage,' I blurted out. 'In a normal world we wouldn't need it,' he agreed, 'but here and now I think it would help. I can't keep on pretending that you're just my comrade.' I thought about what he'd said and had to agree that he needed the extra security which marriage would give him in this crazy society. There was a kind of finality about marriage which even bigots had to accept whereas a love affair between a white girl and an Indian could only be explained by them if the white girl were no good, if she were 'white trash'. Not only whites. Non-whites, too, looked askance at a white woman who walked with a black man.

The previous Sunday afternoon, as H.A. and I were strolling down a quiet side street in the Indian quarter, fingers touching, a group of garish, over-painted coloured women loitering on the corner saw us approaching and, shouting something incomprehensible, made a rush towards me. Their threatening postures and violent abuse amazed and frightened me. 'What's the matter with them?' I turned to H.A. 'What are they saying?' Before he could answer they were upon us, aiming blows at my head, my shoulders, my back. Like a band of enraged furies they pelted me with their fists and swung their handbags at my head. The curses which poured out of their mouths and the hate which blazed in their eyes left me gasping. I couldn't understand why they were doing this; to the best of my knowledge I had done them no harm; I didn't even know them. H.A. did his best to protect me but we were greatly outnumbered; the blows kept coming with ever greater ferocity as our attackers became more frantic and their insults grew more foul. I tried to defend myself but they were tearing at my clothes and yelling obscenities, pushing their faces within inches of my face; I could smell their sour breaths and look into their broken, misshapen teeth. Then a car appeared at the end of the road, a man poked his head through the window and shouted at H.A. and me to get in. 'Jump in quickly,' the driver shouted. We did and he drove off at great speed, followed by a shower of stones and curses.

'That was lucky,' H.A. said as he turned to the driver to thank him. He didn't know him but the driver recognised H.A. 'Glad to help,' the man said, 'it looked like real trouble.'

'What's the matter with them?' I demanded of H.A. 'Why did they behave like that? Why do they hate me? I've never seen them before in my life.' 'They think you're encroaching on their patch; they reckon it's unfair competition.' H.A. tried to calm me. 'Oh my God,' I said as I burst into tears, 'they thought I was one of them, one of those dreadful harpies, a prostitute!'

The encounter left me feeling soiled and humiliated. I had never met a prostitute before but the mention of the word made me shudder. I'd read about them in books but I couldn't imagine how any woman could defile herself to the extent of selling her body to any man who could pay. The very notion appalled and repelled me. In theory I could argue that it was the fault of the system: women were forced into prostitution by poverty, lack of opportunity, unemployment. Change the system and you'll abolish prostitution. That was my belief intellectually but it still left me with a chasm of the imagination, a failure to comprehend, a shying away from the flesh-and-blood woman who actually practised this trade. And here I found myself called a prostitute! Was not the difference between me and a prostitute clearly visible to the naked eye? The humiliation hurt more than the physical blows.

'There's a flat we could have in Wills Court,' H.A. announced one day and my spirits sank. 'I can't live like Vera,' I told him. 'I can't sink into a ghetto existence.' All the same we went to look at the tiny two-room flat on the third floor and I realised that we had no choice. If we were to live together it would have to be in the overcrowded quarter to which the Indians were restricted. Rich Indians had a wider choice but we were not among them. The block of flats beyond the Indian market to which H.A. led me was shabby and unpainted; the entrance smelled of urine and a pall of dejection hung over it. I hated the thought of making it my home. And on top of all that was the thought that weighed me down: how was I going to break the news to my parents? How would they take it? I didn't expect an enthusiastic reception for my news but I tried to draw comfort from their respect for H.A. After all, I reasoned, they know and like him, they're not like other whites – they're not racists. They may not like my news but they'll accept it. I tried to introduce it to them gradually, talking about H.A. and telling Mother stories about him and his family.

'Do you know how H.A.'s grandmother came to this country?' I asked Mother rhetorically. She looked at me warily. 'She was kidnapped,' I announced dramatically. 'She was a girl of 17 and already a mother of two when she and some of her friends went bathing in a river one day, near their home in South India. A recruiting agent for the Natal sugar estates tricked them on to a ship lying nearby, pretending to show them round. When they were on board the ship pulled up anchor and set sail. The girls never saw their families again.' 'It is a terrible story,' Mother agreed. 'But why, out of the millions of girls in India, did they have to choose H.A.'s grandmother?' So, I thought, she does suspect and she doesn't like it but she's bound to accept it. I couldn't have been more wrong.

When I was arrested on the picket line at the Rubber Workers' Strike outside Dunlop's factory and charged with kicking a policeman on his shin, both Mum and Dad surprised me with their loyalty and support when I told them that I would have to appear in court. I would have preferred to keep this from them but I guessed there would be press publicity and I decided it would be better to prepare them for it.

'They were trying to break the picket line to bring in the scabs,' I told them. 'We linked arms and they drove into us, lashing about with their truncheons. I was lucky not to get coshed on the head. Two of the pickets were badly hurt. I honestly don't remember kicking the policeman but I might have done, in the melée. I was so angry at the police always siding with the blacklegs. They're supposed to be impartial but they're just bosses' stooges.'

I anticipated much blame and wringing of hands but all Mother said was: 'You must wear your good navy suit in court and don't let them frighten you.' And Father added, 'Of course the police side with the bosses, didn't you know that?' Then he asked, 'Were you the only white girl on the picket line?' I had to admit that I was the only girl there. 'H'm,' Father said; 'I'm coming to court. I'll be there.'

The magistrate was odious. He fined me £15 – a not inconsiderable sum in those days – but it was his comment that was so offensive. 'Girls like you,' he glared down at me, 'are a disgrace to the white race. Getting mixed up with natives!' He snorted his disgust, 'You lower our prestige in front of them.' Father flushed with fury. He clenched his fists and made to follow the magistrate as he swept out of the court room. 'How dare you speak like that about my daughter?' he shouted after the departing figure. 'It's you who are a disgrace.' My lawyer, Rowly, restrained Dad from chasing after the magistrate and led him out of the court room, still fuming.

My parents' staunch support in the face of slanted press publicity and snide remarks from friends and neighbours gave me courage to confide my plans of marriage. I expected opposition and argument, but I was quite unprepared for the deluge that descended on my head. Mother cried out, as if in pain, and she burst into tears, a thing she rarely did. Father went ashen grey and had difficulty catching his breath. 'Heavens,' I thought, 'he's going to have a heart attack and it will be my fault.' He recovered sufficiently to shake his fist in my face. 'Never, never,' he panted. 'Over my dead body.' I couldn't believe my ears. This was my father – my Communist, liberated, anti-racist father. I was prepared to deal with opposition but not with this kind of desperation.

'But you like H.A.; you know him!' I pleaded. 'That's not the point,' Father shouted and became incoherent with distress. I could see this was no time to argue. The atmosphere was too charged and was liable to erupt. I left the house and found a room in a sad little boarding house near my office. I hoped the storm would blow over and they would come round sufficiently to talk it over calmly. In the meantime I'd keep out of their way. I was reminded of Sholem Aleichem's Tevye der Milchiker who, when he discovered that his beloved daughter was going to marry a goy, 'sat *shiva*', mourning her as though she were dead. Tevye was a God-fearing *shetetl* dweller, ill versed in the scriptures but devoutly steeped in tradition. One could feel superior to him but there was no doubting his searing pain. He loved his daughter and longed to embrace her but would not, could not, allow himself to betray his God. Now Tevye was my father – wrong and irrational but desperately hurt.

The weeks that followed were miserably unhappy for all of us. Father was like a man demented; he shouted and pleaded, threatened and reasoned. He called on Comrade Rowly Arenstein, the District Party Secretary and begged him to prevent this marriage. 'It is not for me to tell them what to do, Mr Podbrey,' Rowly told him primly. I was angry with Rowly when he recounted this interview to us, smugly self-satisfied at having followed 'the correct line'.

'You might have shown a little compassion,' I told him. 'Couldn't you see how he suffers.' 'But your father then threatened to go to the press and accuse the Party of encouraging mixed marriages,' Rowly said. 'Do you think he'll do it?' he asked anxiously. This was something the Durban press would have scooped up with relish. What a stick to beat us with! And what damage a story like that would have done the Party. 'Of course he won't,' I snapped at Rowly indignantly. I knew my father and not for a moment did I believe that he would stoop to such a tactic. But the mere fact that he could demean himself to make such a threat proved how desperate he was.

'How does your mother feel about our marriage?' I asked H.A.

'She's not at all happy about it,' he said, 'but she wants to meet you. And so does my grandmother. You know,' he told me, 'I've always called my grandmother, Mother, and my mother, Sister.'

H.A.'s mother, Valliyama, was ten years old when she married and fourteen when he was born. His father used to visit them at weekends; the weekdays were spent with his first wife who was unable to bear him any children. H.A. remembered his father, but dimly. Kunjebihari Naidoo was a prosperous businessman and a higher caste Hindu who was considered to have honoured the young Villiyama by marrying her. He delighted in the three children that she bore him and was generous with his support. H.A. recalled how he longed for Fridays when his father brought him sweets and gave his mother money. Grandmother Pooranam built the family home in Tatham Crescent and felt satisfied that she had done well in arranging the marriage. Then the father disappeared and some days later his body was fished out of the harbour. The family were convinced that he was murdered by relatives of the first wife who feared that he was about to forsake her in favour of the second wife. Nobody went to the police with their suspicions; they were far too fearful of what the killers might do to them. The family were left destitute and once again Grandmother Pooranam took charge. She arranged a second marriage for Valliyama with a man old enough to be her father. But he turned out to be a feckless drunkard and he died after siring six more children on Valliyama, two of whom died in infancy.

One day her teen-age son surprised Valliyama, sister/mother, in bed with a man. H.A. recalled how furious he was, lashing out at both of them with his fists, abusing and upbraiding his mother. He related this incident with a sense of indignant justification, convinced that he could not have acted otherwise. One may excuse a child's jealousy, I told him but it seemed to me as if he still thought he was entitled to set himself up in judgment. Didn't he think his mother was entitled to have a lover? Wasn't his attitude a bit priggish? It was clear that it had never occurred to him before. My remarks caught him by surprise but he didn't reject them out of hand. He remained thoughtful. Most men, I guessed, would react indignantly when their diehard attitudes were challenged, especially where these related to sexual mores. H.A. was different: he was no bigot; his mind was not closed to new concepts.

The grandmother was old and frail when I met her, but her indomitable spirit still glowed in her rheumy eyes. Two fingers of her right hand were missing; she had lost them when, as a young woman, she'd tackled a man who was trying to kill his wife with a machete. She, alone on the sugar estate, went to the wife's rescue; she lost two fingers but she saved the young woman's life. Had she ever tried to find her first family in India? I asked H.A. 'She never did. She felt guilty and ashamed,' he told me. 'She was convinced her first husband would long ago have disowned her, as though she had sinned by being abducted, made herself unclean.' In Natal Pooranam became one of the indentured labourers on the sugar estates and for seven long years she was tied to the sugar barons as though she were their slave. When her indenture ended, she left the sugar estate, married again and started another family.

To help support the younger brothers and sisters H.A. left school early and found a job in a clothing factory. It was there he met George Ponnen and the two became inseparable. Together they signed up for evening classes; both were eager to further their interrupted schooling. They were fascinated by the art of public speaking and on Sundays the two boys would go for long walks in the country where, away from mocking onlookers, they declaimed to the trees, trying to emulate the long words and convoluted phrases of the traditional Indian leaders in Durban. At work the two friends did well. They both gained promotion and their wages rose. At night school they passed their exams and they looked forward to gaining qualifications which would lift them up into the higher clerical grades. Their personal ambitions to make something of themselves by hard honest labour and diligent study did not prevent them from active participation in youth group activities. Here, too, their personal qualities marked them out and both Ponnen and H.A. were elected by their fellows to play leading parts. H.A., the chairman, and Ponnen, the secretary/treasurer, took their duties seriously.

Their lives might have continued on this sober, pre-determined path had not an unexpected event occurred at the factory. In November 1934 an Indian worker was caught stealing some material and was sacked. As an object lesson to the rest of the staff, the employer then drilled five three-quarter-inch peep-holes in the black workers' lavatories and appointed a guard to keep constant surveillance. The women workers were incensed at such humiliation and walked out on strike, appointing H.A. and Ponnen to act as their spokesmen. For the first time white and black women workers stood solidly together; they forced the boss to plug up the holes and gained a few other concessions but their own trade union refused to back them. The Union Secretary, J.C. Bolton, went so far as to inveigle two white women workers to testify against H.A. and Ponnen when they were charged with leading an illegal strike. They were each fined £2, which their fellow workers paid for them, but both were fired from their jobs. Attempts to find work in other factories failed; they had been placed on a blacklist. H.A. and Ponnen might easily have drifted into street-corner impotence as so many other young Indians did, aimlessly resentful of the injustice meted out to them but unable to find a way out. But not long afterwards, as H.A. and Ponnen were strolling down Berea Road, they came across Eddie Roux selling *Umsebenzi* on the corner of Grey Street and from then on their futures were set on a predetermined course.

This was my first visit to H.A.'s family home, a place he'd left some years before and where he was now received with affectionate respect – not only as the eldest son but also as the leader. The old lady, the matriarch, sat in a corner of the small, sparsely furnished room, smiling benignly with toothless gums while her children and grandchildren vied for the honour of serving her. The mother, Valliyama, was now the effective head of the family, and her six children, all except H.A., were still at home, some with their own children. All the grown-ups contributed to the joint income which Valliyama administered. By astute management she had succeeded in saving enough to buy a large house set in extensive grounds. Here she raised fruit and vegetables and bred chickens to help support her large brood. Thanks to her capable management, the family was now enjoying a higher standard of living than they'd ever had before. H.A. was the maverick, the son who'd left home, the one who contributed nothing to the family income. But Valliyama felt no irritation or sense of grievance; she was proud of her first-born and beamed with pleasure when he arrived. She knew about the work he was doing and the reputation he enjoyed in the Indian community – her neighbours were always telling her what a fine son she had.

As in our household, the two generations spoke different languages. H.A. had very little Tamil and neither his mother nor grandmother knew any English,

107

so communication was difficult and stilted, even more than in our family. We spent the afternoon of my visit smiling and nodding and drinking tea. The family regaled us with an endless supply of syrupy, over-sweet pastries, made from semolina, honey and nuts, which they kept on pressing me to eat. It was difficult to explain without risking offence that, delicious as they were, a few were more than sufficient. After we'd smiled our good-byes and shaken hands, I asked H.A., 'Well, what do you think? Did they like me?' 'Oh yes, they did,' he answered. 'But before I left they told me: "Think carefully about marriage. It's better to marry one of your own kind."'

One morning Benson came running to the boarding house where I was staying with an urgent message.

'Your father is standing outside the office and he's telling everyone to go away. He's shooing them off, saying that there's going to be no work today. He seems very upset. Perhaps you'd better stay away while he's there.' I did so and waited in my room while Benson brought me bulletins from time to time. 'There's a long queue outside the office and they're wondering what is happening.' And later, 'Your father is lying stretched out on the floor outside the office door, not speaking to anyone.' Eventually, at about 11 o'clock, Father rose and went away. What, I wondered, did he hope to gain from such an undignified gesture? Such extraordinary behaviour, so out of character!

Years later I found out just how miserable my whole family's life became when the news about my intended marriage leaked out, as it was bound to do. 'Your sister's going to marry a coolie,' the kids in the street shouted after Maurice, waylaying him every time he left the flat. One by one his old pals deserted him, leaving him lonely and isolated. He was miserable and vulnerable but he never conceded defeat. 'My sister's a lot better than your stupid sister,' he would shout back and then he would take them on, in one lot of fisticuffs after another, arriving home bloody-nosed and bruised, but proud and unbeaten. He didn't tell Mother why he had to fight so much but my nine-year old brother remained stalwart in my defence. When Mother applied for her usual ticket to attend the synagogue on Yom Kippur, she was allocated a seat at the back of the pews. After the service, when friends and relations greeted each other, Mother was cold-shouldered. She was left in no doubt that the mother of a girl like me was not fit to rub shoulders with respectable, God-fearing folk.

'We have to speak to your parents, to make them understand,' H.A. said. We persevered and eventually, after many messages were left unanswered,

Father agreed to meet us. Mother refused and left the flat before we arrived. Father had aged since we'd last met, barely six weeks earlier. His face was more wrinkled and the outside corners of his eyes drooped downwards, as did his mouth. His suffering was plain to see but there was no bitterness in what he said, only resignation.

'Do you think,' he told us, 'that I don't know how you feel.' He turned to me. 'I can understand why you fell in love with him.' Dad pointed to H.A. 'He's one of the finest, straightest men I know. And he's handsome.' He sighed. 'Oh, yes, I can see the day coming when white girls will vie for the favours of young Indians; they're much better looking than the whites.' He sighed again. 'But not now, not yet.' I tried to say something but he motioned me to be quiet. 'What sort of life do you think you'd lead in this town, shunned by the whites and even by a lot of the Indians? Would you be prepared to lose yourself in the Indian community like your friend Vera has done? And not only that, think what future your children would have in this ignorant, stupid, prejudiced society.' Then he added, almost as an afterthought, 'Not to mention the humiliation and pain of your mother, brother and me.'

'Daddy,' I pleaded. 'What can we do? We really and truly love each other.' 'I'll tell you what you can do,' Father said and it was clear he'd given the matter a lot of thought. 'You must leave the country. Go right away from here. Go to England, America, anywhere. For your sake and ours you must promise me that you'll not get married in Durban. Promise!'

'But Mr Podbrey,' H.A. said, 'our work is here. We're committed to the Party, the trade unions, the national movement.' Father spoke doggedly. 'That's for you to work out. All I ask is your promise that you'll leave the country if you decide to marry.' 'We've got to think about it,' H.A. answered. 'You've got to give us time. We'll let you know.' And so we were left with a choice which seemed to me insoluble, yet we had to decide.

In the days and nights that followed we argued for and against each course of action so often and so plausibly that I felt my head would split. I could not bear to think of leaving the African Commercial and Distributive Workers' Union just as it was beginning to gain stability and *de facto* recognition from employers. Membership was growing daily and it would not be long before we would get the bosses round a negotiating table and begin to show real gains for our members. As for H.A., to remove him from the Durban scene would be like pulling out the linchpin from the movement. What would the Sugar Workers' Union, the Nationalist Bloc of the Indian Congress, the Durban

Communist Party, do without him? And what about the other trade unions, the Liberal Study Group, the Non-European United Front? But if we stayed, could we work together, see each other every day, yet have to live apart? We knew it would not be fair to our comrades to seek their help in making up our minds. No one could help us. This was something we had to work out for ourselves. [...]

When the answer did come it appeared to be heaven-sent or as good as. It came from the very top of the Party, from the Central Committee itself and the messenger was Jack Simons, a lecturer in Native Law and Administration at the University of Cape Town and a leading member of the Central Committee. In the years that followed I came to love and admire Jack for his sharp, clear mind, his ability to convey the complexities of Marxism/Leninism without resort to slogans or clichés, and for his kindliness, courage and sardonic sense of humour. Jack came to Durban to tell us that as the Central Committee was now established in Cape Town it had been decided to make it more representative by co-opting leading members from the different provinces. H.A. had been chosen by them and he'd be required to move to Cape Town.

We had all welcomed the move of the Central Committee from Johannesburg to Cape Town. Up in the Transvaal the Party centre was riven by petty squabbles and unseemly in-fighting. We had greater respect for the integrity and political judgement of comrades like Moses Kotane, the General Secretary, Ray Alexander, Jack's wife and a leading trade unionist, and, of course, Jack himself. The Durban comrades were proud to have H.A. represent them on the Central Committee but, 'What about his work here?' some of them objected.

'No one is indispensable,' Jack said. 'There are enough capable young men among you to take over his duties and we do believe that his role in the Central Committee, helping to shape national policy, is even more important.'

As for me and my job, Jack said, 'It is best that an African union should have African leadership. You did a good job to help get it started and to initiate Comrade Benson. He seems the obvious person to take over now.'

To H.A. and me privately Jack said: 'You'll find Cape Town a far more liberal, congenial place to live in, compared to Durban. The atmosphere is more tolerant and you'll be able to marry and settle down. Give it a try, anyway, and if later on you find that you must leave the country and go overseas, we won't stand in your way.'

110

When I told Father of our decision, he accepted it with resignation. 'I'd have preferred you to go overseas,' he sighed, 'but I hope you'll be happy in Cape Town.' Mother still refused to see me.

Travelling separately, we reached Cape Town at the beginning of 1943. Jack was right. The air was freer, the atmosphere more relaxed. The city was beautiful and the comrades were warm and welcoming.

Norma Kitson

Norma Cranko – first on the left – was born in Durban in 1933 into a wealthy Jewish family. She left school at the age of 14 to work as a secretary for a gold-mining company, an experience which reinforced her sense of the injustices that pervaded South African society. She became a member of the Congress of Democrats (the anti-apartheid organisation for whites) in 1953, and in 1955 went to London where she met fellow communist, South African David Kitson. Discovering she was pregnant with

David's child, she was determined to have an abortion, but her resolve faltered just as she was about to be wheeled into theatre. She and David were subsequently married on 14 July 1956. They returned to South Africa in 1959 to continue their anti-apartheid work, for which David was arrested in 1964. He was sentenced to 20 years' imprisonment. Norma was also arrested and tortured. In 1966, she and her two children went into exile in Britain. There she founded the City of London Anti-Apartheid Group. In 1984, a full 20 years later, she was reunited with her husband David. She died in 2002.

This extract from her autobiography, **Where Sixpence Lives** (1987), describes her privileged but unhappy childhood in Durban's élite Berea suburb in the early 1940s.

My dad was an early-to-bed, early-to-rise man all his life. He was a warden during the war and he knitted socks on four needles. I didn't bring friends home from school because I was scared they'd see him knitting. He was a quiet, almost mysterious man, who came from a very poor family. His father had died in the Boer War in a cattle truck on his way to join his wife and six children in Krugersdorp outside Johannesburg. Dad was the youngest in his family. His brothers lived in Johannesburg but Dad had to live by the sea because of his yachting.

Joan explained to me years later that my father was a homosexual, frightened of women because of his mother. Belle Cranko was a five-foot martinet, adored by her five sons and feared by everyone else. But I don't think my father was frightened of women. He adored my mother. He would sometimes gaze at her with astonished adoration as if he did not know how such a beautiful butterfly could have landed so close to him. They never had much to talk about and she complained that he kept her like an ornament in a glass case. But he would not have a word said against her and made the servants and us tiptoe around the house when she was having 'her rest'. He took us on drives and in his yacht to the Bluff to 'give her a break' and her needs were sacrosanct in our house. Although she often drove him to hair-tearing frustration, he seemed to admire her illogicalities and impulsiveness with a worshipful awe. He thought it was charming that she did not read. Sometimes he would raise his hand and ever so gently stroke her hair, careful not to disarrange it, and a soft look would come into his eyes.

My mother used to tell us our father was 'of Spanish extraction'. Then, when they wrote a biography of my cousin John, they said the Crankos were Hollanders – something *European*. But you can still see Cranko Road in Cape Town and you can still see them all lying buried in the Coloured cemetery there. And where did I get my frizzy hair from?

Unlike the other men in my family, who owned factories and hotels, my dad always worked in a job. He had been a brilliant student who matriculated at thirteen and at eighteen he was a fully qualified chemist. He had gone to England to pass his exams as there was no pharmacy college in South Africa then. He studied the plants at Kew Gardens and learned how to roll pills. During the First World War, he told me, after he had returned to South Africa, he set up a corrugated tin roof in an alley off Smith Street. It wasn't such a main street then. Now it's almost as important as West Street that runs through the town to the sea. He ordered a small quantity of drugs from England and then sold them to the local retail chemists. He made lifelong friends with the Durban chemists, as far out as Pinetown – that was where mostly Indians lived. His orders got bigger and bigger and eventually he ordered a large shipment of supplies from England. When this shipment was under way, the Second World War broke out and the drug companies could not send further supplies to South Africa. The rich wholesale chemists, South African Druggists in Johannesburg, wanted to get their hands on both his order and his clients, so they offered him a job and directorship. They built a Durban office in Smith Street and my father remained there until he retired.

My mother was from a Polish family who prided themselves on being aristocrats. My mother and her sisters never worked. My grandfather, Mark Stiller, had emigrated from Lodz as a young man. On his way to South Africa, he met my grandmother, Bertha Zeffert, a Polish Jewess, in London. When he was settled, he sent for her to join him. The Polish Jews considered themselves superior to German Jews – although Russian Jews were the best. The Stillers had the reputation of being dead rich, well known for their millions – houses, factories and hotels. My mother lived for parties, cards and coffee mornings. She would spend hours in the bath, painting her finger- and toenails, putting on face masks, shaving her legs, creaming her skin. She loved to gossip and spent hours on the phone to her sisters and friends exchanging chitchat, and was always irritated when my father showed no interest. She slept during the day and went out every night and my parents passed each other, uneasily, until the ritual Sunday lunch of roast chicken with the children.

I know that my mother felt she suffered terribly from the war. We couldn't get white flour and we had to have government sugar. That spoiled all the recipes. But the worst thing was brown bread because you couldn't get white flour. My mother hated it. And she couldn't buy Wrigley's spearmint chewing gum, which she loved and chewed often to sweeten her breath. Even her CTC cigarettes were sometimes out of stock in the shops. And Dad was always nagging her to save petrol. Eventually she befriended an American family who visited Durban and so she got supplies of the things she missed most. She and my father would argue about this when they thought we weren't listening. He thought we should just get on with it and that it was unprincipled to make an issue of the things we had to do without. After all, he said, 'There's a *war* on!' But it was a matter of pride with my mother that she should always manage to get the unobtainable.

But my mother did do her bit for the war effort. Every Tuesday afternoon she had volunteer war-work women in the garden knitting for the 'boys'. They made thick white waterproof sweaters for English sailors. I remember my mother saying, 'They can sit in the garden – I will not have them in the house. And if it rains they can sit on the stoep.'

'Why?' my father asked.

'My God, you should just see some of them!' she said. 'Honestly, you don't know where some of those women have been.'

My father held his head with both his hands and scratched his scalp.

'What have I said? What did I say?' my mother asked shrilly. 'It's true. You haven't met them, have you?' My father had no answer. He would shrug in amazement, pick up a book and go and sit on the stoep and read or disappear in his old green Dodge.

My mother also helped hostess at the Durban Jewish Club, which ran a canteen for British servicemen, and at one time our huge house in Essenwood Road became a convalescent home, when a shipful of wounded Scots landed in Durban. They slept in a long row on the front stoep and VAD nurses would come and look after them – wheel them around the garden and read to them. My mother did first aid for a long time and I was ashamed of her because, although I had passed from first grade to second grade at school, she never passed into second aid.

I thought our home was quite normal, as children do. Once I stole some white sugar to give to Phineas because it was a treat.

'*Ai kona!*' (Oh, no!) he said. 'I don't want no white sugar. There's people dying in the war, Miss Norma.'

'That's got nothing to do with sugar,' I said, feeling hurt. 'I got it for you specially.'

Phineas looked at me sadly. 'It *is* about the sugar and about all the good things – this war's about all those things, Miss Norma,' he said.

Phineas was my friend and he was always saying funny things like that.

Edith was an old black woman with no teeth who ran our house: ordered the food and looked after the linen and cooked for the servants. She was passed on to us by my mother's oldest sister, Auntie Ettie. She had married Uncle Cyril who owned KO Bang, the wholesale fisheries, so they were rich. Auntie Ettie graduated to getting a Coloured woman, who cost more. You couldn't talk to Edith properly because she was scared of losing her job. She would say 'Hau! Miss Norma,' in horror, admiration, shock or interest. When she laughed she put her apron over her mouth so we couldn't see that she had no teeth. Sometimes, in the kitchen, I would hear her speaking loudly to the other servants in Zulu and it sounded as if she was complaining. She was frightened of my mother, who was always threatening the servants with the sack. Nurse McGrath complained constantly that Edith ordered too much food for the servants. 'They go through the mealie meal like a dose of salts,' she'd tell my mother, who would flick her hand dismissively and say, 'Oh, do sort it out, McGrath.' Edith's husband had died many years before, as had her five children. Once she showed me her shrunken breasts when she was explaining how her milk dried up and one of her babies died. She hit her breast with her hand as if blaming it for letting her down. She used to go to church whenever it was her 'off' [day] because she was very religious.

A 'girl' came in to do the washing and ironing every day. She wasn't a live-in servant and there was a new 'girl' every few weeks, usually a woman with a baby tied to her back. Sometimes they came straight from the *kraal* – village – wearing bangles around their ankles and beads around their necks. Some didn't have proper English names yet. I remember one wash girl called Ntembi who came with her baby. I crouched behind the banana trees watching as she bent over the zinc wash tub and scrubbed on the rubbing board with Sunlight soap. Her skin gleamed and her baby slept in the sun on her back and she sang to it, and every now and then she would untie the baby and swing it round and look deeply at it, croon and cuddle it. I don't think she had learned yet to be frightened of white people because when Nurse McGrath gave her her money one day, Ntembi started yelling and screaming and holding her baby up and Phineas rushed up to translate.

'Madam, she says the madam said she would get more for a day's work. Madam, she says her child is hungry and she cannot feed the baby with this money.'

Nurse McGrath looked at Phineas icily. 'Tell her if she is not satisfied, she can go. I have no power to increase the wages.'

When Phineas had transmitted this news to Ntembi she spat on the ground near McGrath and shouted loudly at her and walked away.

But the following week she was back. Her skin looked dusty and the baby was sleeping with its eyes half-open. She had taken the bangles off her feet and the beads from around her throat and Sarah gave her an apron so that she looked like a proper servant. When Nurse McGrath handed over her money, she dipped her knee and raised her hands together to her head.

But after a few weeks there was another wash girl scrubbing at the rubbing board.

Sarah did the cleaning and was my mother's maid. She took my mother's breakfast up to her in bed every morning at 11.30 and would stand by while my mother ate bits off the tray. A mouthful of an avocado from the garden, a teaspoonful of egg, a bite of toast, a peeled apple quarter, a spoonful of grapefruit, a biscuit with Joseph's home-made cumquat preserve.

Sarah was in charge of our mother's clothes. She was an angry young woman who banged about a lot when she wasn't with my mother. She aped my mother behind her back, catching her mannerisms and foibles in a move or a look. She was resentful and fearful of losing her job. Every day my mother would try on this dress and that scarf, these shoes and those stockings, with that hat. She discarded dresses, shoes and scarves here and there while Sarah picked them up and brought new ones from the cupboards, and the heap of cast-offs mounted on the green velvet chaise longue. Posing in front of the mirror, my mother would ask her, 'How does this look?'

'Very nice, madam.'

'Nice? These are the wrong shade of stockings with this dress. Get me the navy dress with the white spotted belt.'

'Yes, madam.'

'No, dammit! Not *that* navy dress. Don't tell me my lovely navy dress has been pinched. Oh, yes, *that's* the one. Well, but maybe I should wear red today, what d'you think?'

'Yes, madam.'

Then my mother would say 'Oh, you stupid girl,' but I knew that Sarah was very clever because she knew how to keep her job.

This would go on for about an hour every morning and then Sarah would go down to the kitchen for her lunch and regale the servants with the morning's events, tinged with humour and fraught with bitterness.

Sarah was always at war with the ironing girl. She had to be sure that there was not a single crease in anything that went in my mother's drawers and cupboards, so she would inspect each garment and then harangue the 'girl' to improve her ironing. It was a petty fruitless existence for intelligent Sarah and she was totally dependent on it to keep her children. Meek and unresponsive as she was with my mother, she was sometimes rough and angry with Ronnie and me. I think we were a constant reminder to her of her own children and that she was unable to be with them while they were growing up.

Phineas did the floors and the garden and was our waiter. He was cheerful, friendly and helpful to everyone. He would sit outside his tin room in the full heat of the sun and make sandals out of old car tyres so that he wouldn't have to go barefoot. He had learned to do it when he was a ricksha boy on the Durban beach. Zulus used to be famous warriors led by their king, Tshaka, and wore beautiful headdresses, beads and skins, and carried shields. Their skins shone and they were very tall and strong. Now they did not have enough to eat and many looked puny, with discoloured skins. Now the Durban Corporation licensed them to act like horses, carrying tourists in their carts. But they liked them to wear their warrior clothes – for the photographs. Phineas had to give it up because his chest got sore. My dad said ricksha boys only lived till they were thirty-five. They died from the strain of it. Phineas sometimes disappeared for a couple of hours and we would see him sitting on a kerb in the neighbourhood, playing his guitar and singing.

Sixpence, Sarah's eldest child, came for a few weeks a year and helped everybody. He was a shy, solemn boy, seven years older than I, whose delight was to polish my mother's blue Wolseley car. When he was with us he did jobs for everyone, cleaning shoes, emptying the dirty water from the tin washing basin, carrying buckets of water from the garden tap to the servants' rooms, helping my brother Ronnie catch frogs to sell to the snake park, running to the shops for everyone – although he was not paid, he spent his holiday with his mother working very hard for our family. He used to make me lucky-bean bracelets and necklaces.

The servants lived in tin rooms behind the tennis courts. A grove of banana trees screened their quarters from view. Ronnie used to carve buddhas out of the banana trees and then we'd pray to them and the servants would laugh at us. We'd kneel down and say 'Allah! Allah be praised!' and touch the ground with our heads. Ronnie said a man told him it was good for our souls.

When I wanted to be near people I would sit on the tomato boxes by the banana trees near the servants' rooms, where it was cool and there was always someone to talk to. They missed their families and often talked about not having enough money. I used to say, thinking about Mom's Dimple Haig bottle with her tickey (threepenny bit) collection, 'Ask my mom, she'll give you some.' They'd smile and pat me on the head and Edith would sweep me onto her lap and say, 'Haai, Miss Norma!' as if I had used bad language. Sarah missed her other three children – Sixpence was the only one who ever came to our house. I often told her to let them come and live with us and she'd say, 'Haai! You spoiled kids!' and slap my leg.

Bertha Solomon

Bertha Solomon was born in Minsk, Russia, to Jewish parents. Her father, Idel Schwartz, left for South Africa in the 1890s in order to avoid conscription into the Tsar's army. Bertha, her mother and sister joined him in South Africa when she was four years old. They settled in Cape Town. Her autobiography, *Time Remembered: The Story of a Fight* (1968), records her experiences of South Africa's turbulent history in the first half of the twentieth century: from the Anglo-Boer War (1899–1902) to 1958, when she retired from politics. Solomon became an advocate of the Supreme Court and an activist in the struggle for women's rights. For four years she campaigned to achieve women's suffrage (granted to white women only in 1930). She served for five years on the Provincial Council and twenty years in Parliament and was a founder of the University Women's Association, which continues to award bursaries to women. She died in 1969.

Her narrative recounts her protracted battle against the legal disabilities of married women. This culminated in the Matrimonial Affairs Act of 1953 (popularly known as 'Bertha's Bill'). Jan Smuts, then Prime Minister, is said to have remarked of her tenacity: 'What this House needs is more Bertha control.' The passage below records her continued fight (in 1949) for the Bill to be drafted – a fight made more difficult due to the National Party's unexpected victory in 1948 (by a narrow margin of five seats), thus placing the United Party (of which Solomon was a member) in the opposition.

When the new session of Parliament opened in 1949 I was ready again with my questions. Was the Married Women's Disabilities Report printed and, if not, why not? As I look back, I see that my insistence on the publication of the Women's Legal Disabilities Commission Report must have been very irritating to Mr. Swart, but my insistence achieved its purpose. Irritating or not to the Minister of Justice, in April of that year the Report finally did appear, to my great relief. It was well received, and its moderate recommendations approved on the whole, though there was some grumbling among the diehards on both sides of the House. Now the next question in my mind was how to persuade the Minister to take action on the report. He himself, I well knew, was not in favour of any change in the law, yet as he was the Minister of Justice, for a Government Bill based on the report, the initiative had to come from him. And I wanted a Government Bill! True I could introduce one, but I felt it had to be a Government Bill. If I were to introduce it as a Private Member's Bill, those who were not particularly interested would simply follow the Minister's lead and vote against it. And that would be that. So once more I tabled a question. 'Would the Minister introduce a Bill embodying the recommendations of the Women's Disabilities Commission?' The Minister's reply was non-committal. 'His department was considering drafting a Bill.' And with that I had to rest content for the time being.

The work that session was heavy. The Nationalist Government had won its sudden and unexpected victory largely on its slogan of 'Apartheid' (Separation), a word evolved, it is said, by Mr. Paul Sauer, the new Minister of Lands. But to the United Party's persistent questions of 'What is apartheid? What do you mean by apartheid?' it became evident from the Government's evasive answers that, at that stage, apartheid was still only a slogan; useful as a slogan but vague in content. The Government had clearly not yet thought out the implications of it, or what it would mean to the country to implement apartheid. Apartheid had been then merely a good stick with which to beat the United Party in the election. Its actual interpretation was to come only later with the appointment in early 1950 of Dr. Eiselen as the new Secretary for Native Affairs, as it was then termed, i.e. as the permanent head of the department dealing with Africans.

It was Dr. Eiselen who first put body and meaning on the bare bones of the slogan and made of it a policy. Dr. Eiselen, tall, austere and with icy blue eyes, had never been a civil servant, so considerable uproar in Parliament followed on his appointment from outside the civil service to so senior a position in that body in the teeth of civil service disapproval. But the Government made it clear in its official statement in the debate that Dr. Eiselen had been appointed because his 'special knowledge' and his views on Native policy, i.e. on apartheid, coincided with those of the Government. It was not often that I spoke on Native Affairs. There were so many others always anxious and ready to do so that the Party's list of speakers was almost too long; and beside I had my hands full with my own specialities. But on the occasion of the Eiselen uproar, by chance I got the opportunity to get into the debate, and seized it. It happened that some time before I had read and noted a lecture on the new policy of apartheid delivered by that same Dr. Eiselen before the People's Forum in Johannesburg, and I challenged the Government with extensive quotations from it. Were these views of Dr. Eiselen's really the Government's views on apartheid, I asked? And if so, were the Government's followers aware of them? For even in 1948 at the date of his lecture, Dr. Eiselen was obviously already visualising Bantustans as a necessary concomitant to apartheid, and talking of the 'great sacrifices' that would be necessary to bring apartheid and the Bantustans into being. Were Dr. Malan and his followers prepared to make such sacrifices, I asked, and were they as Afrikaners prepared to change the centuries old way of life of South Africa with its reliance on African labour, that Dr. Eiselen envisaged? To these questions I got no answer; not even a dusty one from the Government. But General Smuts liked that speech and congratulated me on it in caucus. Meanwhile, although the speech from the throne at the opening session of the new Parliament had foreshadowed various Eiselen-inspired steps to implement apartheid, the Government was in something of a dilemma. True, it had a majority in the House of Assembly but in the Senate, which was still the Senate of the former United Party government, it was in a minority. The United Party still had control there and, since Bills had to be passed by both Houses, the Government would be seriously embarrassed if the Senate turned down its legislation. Another source of embarrassment for the Government was that, just before the session opened, there had been serious trouble in Durban. The Africans had run riot in the Indian quarter (the Africans are always inclined to resent the Indian) and many shops had been looted and some fired. The Government had had to call up the Active Citizen Force to suppress the riot, as well as to fly police reinforcements down from the Rand. It had also had to set up camps for the homeless Indians. The number of casualties was ultimately said to be one hundred and eleven dead and a thousand injured in the riots, and the Government proclaimed special measures to stop the rioting. Nevertheless there were further clashes between the police and the rioters when they tried to attack the camps in which the Indians had taken refuge. Naturally, Durban and Natal generally were still seething with unrest and, further, the 'no white bread' trouble, the rising cost of living, etc., all of which the Nationalists had capitalised on in the election, were still with the new Government and likely to continue for some time. It was reported that women fainted in the long queues outside the offices of letting control. Accommodation was desperately scarce and some foods were in short supply. Nevertheless, it was not essential bread and butter legislation with which the Government was concerned. The Government was obsessed with ideological legislation, with concern for Afrikaner hegemony. Because of its fear that the Afrikaner would be 'ploughed under' – that was the favourite phrase then – and swamped, almost its first action had been to put an end to General Smuts' farsighted post-war immigration scheme of 1946, under which immigrants had been pouring into the country at the rate of thirty thousand a year. (At the time of writing this, the Government, belatedly realising the need for increasing the white population, has re-started the United Party immigration scheme, without acknowledgements – and is now proudly boasting of the thirty to forty thousand immigrants a year it is bringing in.) Then having put an end to further immigration, the Government moved on to deal with the immigrants already in the country. It introduced a new Citizenship Bill whereby it would take five years for any British subject (and for a non-British subject, six years) to become a South African national. Further, both would now have to make definite application for citizenship. This was quite a new departure as regards British subjects. Until the new Act, an immigrant from Britain or any Commonwealth country automatically acquired

South African nationality after two years' residence in the country. There was no need for him or her to apply. Inevitably the United Party opposition fought the Bill vigorously. Telegrams of protest streamed in from all parts of the country. There was a marathon debate until the Government imposed the guillotine. Finally there was an all-night sitting before the Bill was passed, but all to no avail. The Bill went through. Incidentally, those occasional all-night sittings during my twenty years in Parliament, though they were exhausting, had an odd fascination for me. To go out on the terrace of the House in the small hours and look down on the sleeping city gave me a sense of remoteness and aloneness; as if the brightly-lit House and its activities constituted an island in space, cut off by the surrounding darkness from the world outside.

Mpho
'M'atsepo Nthunya

A Mosotho, born in 1930 in Lesotho (then the British Protectorate of Basutoland), Mpho experienced extreme poverty with her family, barely subsisting in their remote homestead in the mountains. When she was eight, her father – who was a migrant worker in Benoni, South Africa – sent for his family. They lived with him in the location for ten years, and Mpho was able to attend the local mission school until she was married. Like so many black South Africans she speaks several languages, (in her case, eight). In 1948 she married Alexis Nthunya and had six children, only three of whom survived. Forced to turn to domestic service after the death of her husband in 1968, she supported 11 people on her meagre salary as a cleaner at the University of Lesotho.

Her story, *Singing Away the Hunger: Stories of a Life in Lesotho* (1996), was dictated to and edited by K. Limakatso Kendall, a visiting woman American academic, with whom Mpho developed a close friendship.

Before the Beginning

Making this book is a strange thing to me: in Sesotho we say *mohlolo* – a miracle, or a wonder. Most of the people in my life – my family, my friends, my neighbours – most of them cannot read. Almost none of them can read English. You go into any house in my neighbourhood, and you will not find a book, unless it is one of the children's school-books, wrapped in brown paper the way the nuns tell them to do it. Books are not part of our lives.

Even me: I can read English because I learned it in a school in Benoni Location, in the Union of South Africa, when I was a girl. I like books very much; when I see a book I always want to know what's in it, especially if it has pictures. But I have no time to read anything. If I am at home, the children are coming in and going out and needing things all the time. At the end of the day I am so tired all I can do is sleep. If I am at work, my arms are in soapy water or I'm ironing or cleaning the floors. When can I read? I see that some of the young Basotho like to read books; I see a young person sometimes with a book that's not even for school. I am glad for that. But the people of Mafikeng, where I live, will never read my book. It will not mean anything to them.

I am telling my stories in English for many months now, and it is a time for me to see my whole life. I see that things are always changing. I was born in 1930, so I remember many things which were happening in the old days in Lesotho and which happen no more. I lived in Benoni Location for more than ten years, and I saw the Boer policeman taking the black people and beating them like dogs. They even took me once, and kept me in one of their jails for a while.

I was married with a good Mosotho man, and we left Benoni and lived in the Maluti Mountains where we had many children, raised sheep, grew maize, and listened to the quiet. At the beginning we were hungry and our children were hungry; but after many years of working hard we were no longer poor. We had many animals and fields. Then my husband died, and I had to come back to my mother's home, in the Roma Valley, to find work. I lost or sold the animals and left the fields and my houses in the mountains. Now I live in Mafikeng, the village at the gates of the National University of Lesotho. I have worked at the university cleaning houses since 1968. It is at the University that I meet Limakatso, I call her *motsoalle oa ka*, my very good friend. I tell her my stories and she writes them down in a computer to make them a book. *Mohlolo!*

Talking to Limakatso, I remember many things which I forgot for a long time. This is a good thing for me. I'm looking back, and it's like looking at an album of photos from my whole life. If other people can look at it too, that's fine. But it's my album, and it pleases me to look at it. I'm telling stories for children and grown people in other places, because I want people who know how to read and have time to read, to know something about the Basotho – how we used to live and how we live now, how poor we are, and how we are living together in this place called Lesotho. I'm also telling stories for Basotho like my grandchildren, who read books but don't know the old ways of their own people. If they can read these stories, maybe it will teach them where they come from. And maybe it can help them to learn English, so they can find work.

I tell these stories in English to my *motsoalle* so she can write them in the computer. I can tell these stories better in Sesotho. When I tell stories in Sesotho, the words roll like a music I am singing with my heart. When I speak *Sekhooa*, the white people's language, I start and stop. I stare at my *motsoalle*, at the ceiling, looking, looking. I say, 'What can I say? What is the word for this?'

I am like a car trying to start on a cold morning, coughing and stopping. Limakatso says people who read *Sekhooa* never get to hear the stories from women like me, and I think it must be true. When would we write them? I have only a Standard Five education, went to Standard Six for a little while but didn't finish it. I don't know the people who publish books, don't know where to send a book if I could write it. Limakatso says people are hungry for these stories. They want to know. So I say, '*Ho lokile*. Fine. It's OK with me. We can write them.' Maybe I make a little bit of money to buy maize meal for the children.

I try to imagine what I can do with a book written by me. I think of my mother. I imagine that I can give this book of English words to her, and because of the wisdom of Heaven she can read it. I say to her, 'Take this book and see your story: when you were married, and what happened to your daughter, who always loves you. Here are the stories of your daughter's children, and their children. None of this would be, without you. And now others can know your story.' So I say this book is my album for my mother, Valeria 'M'amahlaku Sekobi Lillane, who passed away. Others can look at it if they like. [...]

Two Marriages, One Husband

One Sunday when I was eighteen, I was sitting in church with ribbons in my hair like a crown. I was thinking about Lesotho, trying to remember. I thought about the hunger and the beauty of the place. My mother took me from there in 1938, because of a dream that came three times. Now it was 1948, and I was sitting in church, but I did not hear the prayers at all. I was tired of living in Benoni Location, and I was beginning to be homesick.

A Mosotho miner who was also living in Benoni saw me in church that day. He asked a girl who was a friend of mine, 'Is this a Mosotho girl?'

My friend sees that this miner is interested in me, and she says, 'Yes. She is living in Benoni Location with her parents, in Number 32 of Fourth Street. You can find her there.' That was the beginning, and I came to love Alexis Nthunya before his family kidnapped me and forced us to marry.

Right there outside the church in Benoni, the first time he ever saw me, Alexis said to my friend, 'I love this Mpho. I want to marry her.'

'I don't know,' my friend said to him. 'Her father is very fierce, very *bohale*. He won't have any nonsense with his child.'

My friend came to me later and told me what happened. I told her I wanted to see that gentleman. I wanted to see who loved me and wanted to marry me, when he never even spoke to me. So she told me she would ask him to come to church the next Sunday to meet me.

So we go. After church the girl calls me and says, 'Here is Alexis Nthunya, the gentleman I was talking about. He says he loves you and he wants to marry you.'

I say, '*Hei*! I don't want to be married.'

She says, 'Why? You want to stay in Benoni so you can make children without fathers?'

I say, 'No. My mother will pray for me not to have children.' I don't say that I am tired of Benoni. I just watch Alexis and see how he looks at me.

He says, 'I want to take this Mosotho girl back to Lesotho, because I see she is a good child. I want to take her home.'

I began to fall in love with this man. He was very handsome; all the girls who saw him wanted him. He was medium-brown complexion, with a big nose; large, soft lips; and huge, round eyes. He was tall and muscular, and he loved to dress well. He always wanted to wear peg-legged pants, and when he was riding a horse, with his blanket over his shoulders, he looked like a chief. Whenever he went anywhere dressed up, on his horse, people would bow to him and call him *Morena*, Chief.

We met many times, always at church on Sunday because I could not see him any other time. My father was very strict; if he saw me standing with a boy he would hit me like a dog. So I just met Alexis in church, but he was always very nice, and he always looked at me in that way, and I began to fall in love with him. He was a quiet man, and gentle. Not like many others. I saw he was a good man.

When Alexis went to the mines he wrote me letters in Sesotho, and I wrote back to him. One day my father found a letter and said, 'Where does this letter come from?'

I said, 'I don't know.'

My father took the letter and said he would tear it up, and I went to find my friend who introduced me to Alexis. I told her my father has this letter and I knew he was going to beat me. This young woman went to my father and said, '*Ntate*, this child is big enough. She must have boyfriends. How can she marry without knowing any boys at all? There is one Mosotho boy from the mines; he wants to marry her, so he wrote the letter, speaking about love. So don't tear the letters, and don't beat her. She is big enough to have a boyfriend.'

Ntate says, 'OK, because you have told me this, I will leave the letters. From where does this gentleman come?' And we talk.

He asks me, 'Where does this man see you?'

I say, 'In the church only.'

He says, 'He must be a good man. He goes to church. You are talking with him about love?'

I say, 'Yes'.

He says, 'Where is his home? Who is his family?'

I say, 'His home is Marakabei, District of Maseru, in the Maluti Mountains. His name is Nthunya.'

My father thinks about this. He looks away for a long time, and then he says, 'Yes, he must be a good gentleman. You must not take any *tsotsis* for boyfriends.'

I say, 'Yes, father.' This is in 1948.

Some time later my father got a letter from the parents of Alexis. They asked for me. They said, 'Our son wants to marry your daughter, Mpho.'

So my father asks me again, 'Do you know Alexis Moalosi Nthunya? Do you?'

I say, 'Yes, *Ntate*. He is the Mosotho I told you about, the one I met in church, who writes me letters from the mines, speaking about love.'

'Yes,' my father says. 'Here is a letter from his parents. They want you to marry their son, and they will pay nice *lobola*, bride-price, for you.'

So it was decided. My mother and I came to Lesotho to receive the *lobola*, and I went to school at St. Mary's to learn hand-sewing, so I could be a good wife. My *lobola* was nine cows, twelve goats, and one horse, and we had to find people to look after those animals in Roma, Lesotho, which was our real home. I enjoyed learning to sew and getting ready for my marriage. I made myself two dresses of the small-print cloth Basotho women like to wear – we call it *seshoeshoe* because it is a cloth of Basotho women, even though it is made in England. Then we took my new dresses, packed them, and went to Gauteng to make more clothes for me and a white dress for the church wedding.

Early in the morning on the day after my mother and I came back from Lesotho, I was sitting at the table trying to write a letter to Alexis, because I wanted him to know I was back in Benoni. I heard a child say, '*Ausi* Mpho, two ladies are calling you outside.'

I leave my pen and writing pad on the table and go find the two ladies at the gate. They say, '*Ausi*, come with us halfway to the shops, there. Your gentleman wants to talk to you.'

I say, 'Who?'

'Alexis Nthunya wants to talk to you. He heard that you were back here.'

We go. We get to the first store. We don't find him. A lady in the store says, 'No, he says he will be there, in Tenth Street.' We are in Fifth Street.

We go. When we arrive there, nobody. Another lady says, 'Oh, maybe he was here but he sees that you are late. He must go to work in the afternoon. Maybe he's at that house close by.'

She points to the house, and one of the two ladies with me says, 'Let's go quickly, because I'm afraid of Mpho's father, if he finds us.'

When we go to that house, we knock. A lady says, 'Come in.'

There are two men: my gentleman, Alexis, and an old man. I greet them. They answer me, and the lady of the house gives me a chair and says, 'Sit down and talk quickly, because I'm afraid of Mpho's father.'

Alexis says, politely, '*E-a, 'M'e*' (Yes, Ma'am).

We talk. He asks me about Lesotho, and how many cows did his father bring for *lobola* to my house. I tell him nine cows, twelve goats, and one horse. He asks me now, why did we come to Benoni again, after the *lobola* is paid. I say, 'I'm coming to buy some clothes for marriage.'

He says, 'Oh, I understand. Because even myself, I want to have nice clothes for marriage. So you are going to buy a white dress?'

I say, 'Yes, a white dress. I want a white dress for my marriage.' And we speak of many things.

But suddenly the time is gone, because since I arrived I see three hours have passed. I am surprised when that lady comes again and says, 'Mpho, you are not going anywhere from now.'

'*Hao, 'M'e!*' I ask her why. I say, 'I must go home. My parents will worry.'

She says, 'No. You have been paid *lobola*, but your parents brought you to Benoni again, where *tsotsis* will come and take you. So we don't want our cows and goats and horse to go up and down for nothing. You are no more going out of this house.'

I say I'm going out.

She says, 'So we shall see. You can't.' And she looks at Alexis and says, 'You didn't tell this girl that there is no more going out?'

He says, 'I'm afraid to tell her,' and I know it is because he loves me and doesn't want me to be afraid.

And she answers Alexis, 'I'm not playing with you. It's true, she can't go out. My father brought cows and goats and a horse to her family in Lesotho. After that, her parents brought her here again. They have the cows. They should leave her in Lesotho to wait for you. No. You must tell her she is your wife, and she is not going out. If you are afraid to tell her, I will tell her.'

Alexis and I feel shy, then. So the lady goes in another room and takes a new blanket and puts it on my shoulders. I throw it off.

She says, 'It's a pity, because you are going to put it on. You are not going out, totally.' So she goes out and my gentleman is now very scared and frightened. He does not want me to be unhappy or afraid, but his sister is quarrelling with him.

I say, 'Why do you do this to me?'

He says, 'It's not me. It is my sister, 'M'athuso, who does this. I'm ashamed, because your father is looking for you now. We waste time by sitting here, but now I don't know what I can do, because now you have been given the blanket. We are married.'

I say, 'I'm going out.'

But the lady has locked the door and the windows. She says, 'This girl is a *tsotsi*. She will fly. I am taking the key. I am locking the windows.'

She goes away and finds the headman in that part of the location. We call him the Chief, or *induna*. She comes back with this Chief and he asks me, 'What is your name?'

I tell him.

'What is your father's name?'

I say, 'Johannes Lillane, from Fourth Street, Number 32.'

He writes it down and he says, 'You know this gentleman?'

I say, 'Yes.'

'Did you ever talk about marriage?'

I say, 'Yes.'

'He has given *lobola* to your father's house in Lesotho?'

I say, 'Yes.'

Then he says, 'Look here, this gentleman is your husband from now, my dear, because he has given *lobola* to your family, and his family has given you the new blanket. So the relatives of this gentleman say they don't want you to be taken away by the *tsotsis* here. The *tsotsis* like to take pretty women your age and put them to work. But remember those cows, goats, and horse. You must not worry from now. Sit down, my dear, and know that this is your husband. I am going now to your house and tell your father not to worry because your husband has taken you home.'

It was now late. Because I was seeing children passing from school as I was looking out the window. So I stayed there, doing nothing but talking to my gentleman. He was shy because he didn't like what his sister was doing, quarrelling with him in front of me. At five o'clock he was supposed to go to work, so then I was left with the ladies. I was worried because of my mother and father. I was not feeling all right, and I did not sleep well.

Early in the morning, about six, the Chief came back and said he has been to my parents. 'The mother of the girl says she is glad to learn the girl is here, because she was worried. She was afraid the *tsotsis* had taken her, and she could not see how she could give back the cows and the goats and the horse. But she says you must bring her back to go to church for the marriage.' Then the Chief went away.

Right then the brother of the ladies went and got one sheep. He brought it back to the house where I was staying and made it stand by the door. They said, 'Come and see your food. We have a sheep.'

I looked, and I went back and sat down. The ladies were sewing a new dress for me to wear, a grey one of *seshoeshoe*. After they sewed it, they dressed me in it. The men were killing the sheep, and they took two ribs and put them on the fire and then gave to me to eat. So from that day, they told me, 'You are married. Alexis is your husband.'

I ate the ribs, and my husband's family ate the sheep, and we had *papa*. I was feeling better, because I knew my parents were not worried any more, but I wanted to go back for a church marriage. I began to talk to them, to work in the house with the new grey dress on, and it was no more feeling bad.

Because Alexis was working night shift we could not be together at night during that week, so it was not until Saturday that we shared the blanket. His sister told me what would happen when we shared the blanket, because I did not know these things.

We had a room with a bed, and when we shared the blanket it made much blood. When I woke up in the morning, his sister came for the sheets to be sure there was blood, so she would know it was my first time to share the blankets. She took the sheets away.

I said, 'Why do you take these sheets? I am embarrassed. I was going to wash them.'

But she says, 'No. I'll wash them.' And she looks pleased.

Sunday Alexis and I were together again, and on Monday he went to work the night shift. I did not like sharing the blanket because it was my first time to do it, and it hurt. In the morning when you wake up, you feel shy when you see the other people. You know they are looking at you and knowing what happened.

I stayed there eight months without going out, until Christmas holidays. I never went to my parents' home from that day. My mother was just seeing me in the church; my father too. They asked if I was feeling all right. I said I was all right, no complaints. And from there, in December, Alexis took me to Marakabei, where my baby came and died in April.

Apartheid Escalates

1950 to 1959

In 1948, the same year that Alan Paton's *Cry, the Beloved Country* was published, the Reunited Nationalists (renamed the National Party in 1951) won the election on the promise of reinforced power for all whites, but especially for white Afrikaners who then took control of the civil service. There was a perceptible increase in political separation from English-speakers, and Afrikaans became closely associated with apartheid, despite the fact that most coloureds were also mother-tongue Afrikaans speakers.

From the outset, the National Party set about introducing more extensive racist legislation, which would regulate every aspect of private and social life: in 1949 and 1950 respectively, the Prohibition of Mixed Marriages and Immorality Acts outlawed inter-racial sexual and marriage unions; the Population Registration Act (1950) allowed for the classification of people according to 'race' (based on physical appearance as well as 'repute'); and the Group Areas (1950) and Reservation of Separate Amenities (1953) Acts reserved residential suburbs and public areas for specific race groups. This legislation involved massive social upheavals at enormous cost to those affected. Later provincial ordinances implemented 'petty apartheid', reserving beaches, park benches, playground equipment, bus stops and even lifts for differentiated use by specific race groups (with whites being blatantly favoured).

The ironically named Abolition of Passes Act (1952) required Africans – including, for the first time, all women – to carry 'reference books' at all times; and the Bantu Education Act (1953) introduced a system of vastly inferior education for Africans. The Illegal Squatting Act of 1951 and the Native Laws Amendment Act of 1952 extended government control over the movement of Africans in all urban areas; while the establishment in 1951 of a network of labour bureaus effectively restricted the mobility of rural Africans. The official justification for the National Party policy was that Africans would be stripped of all rights in 'white' South Africa, while being given political rights in the reserves. Legislation passed in 1951 established a tiered system of 'tribal' authorities that would, in time, provide the foundation for African self-government. In 1951 and 1954, respectively, an independent commission and the government's own Tomlinson Commission found that the African reserves were already grossly overpopulated: their recommendations were disregarded.

The new government scrapped parliamentary representation for Indian and coloured voters and passed the Suppression of Communism Act in 1950. It also responded to the ANC's policy shift towards greater mass action at this time. The 1952 Defiance Campaign, in which protestors broke curfews, entered 'Europeans only' areas and refused to carry passes had attracted the attention of the United Nations and helped swell ANC membership from 20 000 to 100 000. The state reacted by arresting nearly 6 000 people in October 1952 and Parliament passed the Criminal Law Amendment Act of 1953, which made it an offence to protest against any law, or to incite others to campaign or protest. The Communist Party, with all its members 'listed' and its meetings banned, went underground. The ANC then took the lead in the Congress Alliance (the combined anti-apartheid front which included Indian, coloured and white activist organisations) and in the drawing up of the Freedom Charter (adopted in 1955), which provided a blueprint for a non-racial, social democratic future for South Africa. Africanists within the organisation rejected multiracial co-operation and broke away to form the Pan African Congress (PAC) in 1959, under Robert Sobukwe.

Resistance by women of all races in the 1950s was significant, although this was not the first time that women had publicly protested. As early as 1913, African women had protested against the planned implementation of pass laws in the Orange Free State. But in 1954, the ranks of protesting women swelled: the Women's Committee for the Defence of the Constitution organised a mass march of women to protest against the government's efforts to have coloureds removed from the voters' roll. This event was followed in 1955 by the birth of the Black Sash, named after the black sash which protestors wore to symbolise mourning for the government's treatment of the constitution. In later decades, the Black Sash was to become an unyielding thorn in the apartheid regime's side and a stalwart defender of the rights of apartheid's victims. In 1955 the Federation of South African Women and Congress of Trade Unions were formed and in 1956 about 20 000 women demonstrated their anger when they marched on the Union Buildings in Pretoria. There were also massive boycotts, such as the one in Alexandra in 1957. Such widespread opposition, however, only served to provoke an intensification of government hostility and in 1956, 156 activists were charged with treason. The Treason Trial lasted until 1961, when those still facing charges were found not guilty. By the end of the 1950s it was clear that a new strategy for anti-apartheid resistance was required.

In 1958, H.F. Verwoerd became Prime Minister. The next year apartheid was extended to higher education (admittance to particular colleges was determined by ethnicity) and the 'bantustans' became self-governing under the control of co-operative chiefs. The Bantustan policy had been formulated by Verwoerd and his Secretary for Native Affairs, partly in response to mounting international pressure on South Africa to give some political rights to Africans. A government spokesman later explained the policy of separate development thus: discrimination was not based on race or colour, but on nationhood, granting to each nation 'self-determination within the borders of their homelands'. In reality, however, it was designed to maintain and strengthen white supremacy in the greater part of the country. Not all whites supported apartheid: in 1959 the Progressive Party was founded by eleven liberal MPs (one of whom was Helen Suzman), who rejected the opposition United Party's ineffectual challenge to apartheid.

Marjorie Michael

Marjorie met her husband-to-be, George Michael, when visiting a friend in hospital. He was a big game hunter who swept her off her feet. They were married when she was 21. 'Very much a town person' before she met him, Marjorie found herself living an exciting and different life from that of her single days. The couple travelled extensively in Africa, filming wildlife and leading hunting expeditions. They produced a television series on African wildlife, which was well received in Britain and America. George also made a feature film, 'Blood on the Veld', and published an autobiography, *African Fury* (1954).

It was the 'hundreds and hundreds' of letters that Marjorie received, asking her what it was like to have a hunter for a husband, that prompted her to 'write a letter for the world to read'. The result was her autobiographical account of life with George, titled *I Married a Hunter* (1956). In the extract reprinted here, Marjorie realises that childbirth for a 'native' woman is very different from childbirth for a white woman like herself.

Before George and I were married he would sometimes tell me tales of native beliefs, or of happenings out in the bush that seemed to me, a town girl, so unreal that I just could not bring myself to believe them. I was sure that he was making them up to impress me or astound me, and several times I told him so. He never argued the point. 'All right,' he would say quietly. 'You can think what you like, but just wait until you've done a few long safaris with me, Marge, and *then* we'll see who's right!'

And I must say that when I came to travel the bush with George I had to admit that many of the things I had refused to believe were, in fact, quite true, and just as he had described them. But of them all, I think that the native attitude to childbearing is probably the hardest for any Western woman to understand, and on our way home from the Kruger Park I had this brought home to me very forcibly.

I must explain that for some time after the birth of my second daughter, June, I was seriously ill, and the doctor ordered me to remain in bed for nearly a month, and then to take it easy for several more weeks after that. He said that I had been trying to do too much work about the house too soon after the new arrival, and that I would just *have* to rest until I was really strong enough to do all the things I wanted to do.

Sitting on the edge of my bed one evening, a few days after my return from the nursing home, George jokingly remarked: 'You know, Marge, you modern women are far too soft. You can't even have a child without a whole lot of fuss and bother!'

'What do you mean?' I replied, a bit put out by this piece of male superiority.

'Every woman has to go through a great deal of pain and physical exertion which leaves her weak and useless for several days. You know that quite well.'

George's reply really surprised me.

'That's where you're wrong,' he said. 'Consider practically any of the native women in the bush country. When their time for confinement arrives they just go behind a bush, have the baby, do all that's necessary themselves, pick up the newly-born child and then carry on with what they were doing. There's no fuss at all. It's part of their accepted way of life, birth, marriage and death. Most of them don't make half the fuss and palaver at any of these occasions that we do. They are more realistic about things. They take them in their stride.'

'Rubbish,' I retorted. 'Who on earth has ever heard of such a thing?' He saw that he had irritated me, and tactfully changed the subject. Afterwards, on my own, I thought over what he had told me and wondered whether there might be some truth in it. I have often found in the past that when I have scoffed at something George has told me, I have been forced to admit that, unlikely as I had thought it, he was right and I was wrong. I had half a suspicion that this might also be the case here.

For although I would have liked to dismiss the tale as being altogether too fanciful, I had to remember that my own native girl had had two confinements in her room, in the servants' quarters behind our house. Although she had neither doctor nor nurse to help her, she did have a sister or a friend with her at the birth, and on each occasion she was back in the house doing her work after only two or three days in bed.

But I could never bring myself to believe that a woman could have a baby entirely on her own, and then carry on with her normal woman's work, just as though nothing unusual had happened. I had to wait until we were on our way home from the Kruger Game Reserve to learn that what George told me was quite correct.

We had been travelling over rough country, for we took a round-about road back home, and the constant bumping had broken one of the pipes in our radiator. We used up all the spare water we had with us, but still the leak grew worse, until it seemed that water was running out almost as fast as we could pour it into the radiator. George decided that we had better stop at the first native village we could find, and he would try to improvise something that would last us until we could reach the next garage, about fifty miles away. So we drove on slowly in our steaming station wagon until at last we reached a small Swazi village, where we were at once surrounded by dozens of naked children and mangy dogs.

The place was very poor and primitive; little more than a cluster of mud huts built near a small, shallow river. A few pigs rooted half-heartedly in the dirt, as if they had not much hope of finding anything to eat, but felt they had to go through the motions of looking. The people who came out to stare at us, or who watched us through the open doorways of their homes, had the lack-lustre eyes and the resigned faces of the very poor.

A tall native, rather better looking and better fed than the rest, and obviously the head of the village (everyone stood back respectfully when he arrived), came up to us and offered his assistance while George busied himself trying to mend the leak. He found it in one of the small pipes at the core of the radiator and began to squeeze pellets of soap all round it to try to seal it. After a while he straightened up and wiped the perspiration off his face.

'Now let's try and see if we've cured the leak,' he said. He turned to the Chief, who all this time had been standing in silence behind him.

'Could you ask one of your fellows to bring some water from the river?' he asked. The Chief nodded, and called to a woman to fetch some water. She stepped forward to collect a can which George held out for her, and then she stood there for some time talking to the Chief. I knew snatches of their language; enough to understand that he was telling her to go down to the river for the water, which I later discovered was about half a mile away, while she did not appear to be keen on making the journey. I noticed that she was very pregnant and said to George that I did not think it right for a woman in her condition to be sent half a mile for water.

He shrugged his shoulders.

'Don't let it worry you, Marge,' he said. 'The Chief knows what he's about. I know it seems hard to you, but we can't very well interfere and start countermanding his instructions. We'll only end up by making ourselves unpopular, and it won't do the woman any good, either, for he'll still make her get the water.'

He turned back to the engine again, and I began to rummage about in the back of the wagon, looking for some coffee. Now that we had stopped, we might as well brew up, for then we need not make another stop farther on, and we had a long way to go that day. When the coffee was ready, we sat in the shade of a tree, chatting, and suddenly, looking at my watch, I realized that there was no sign of the woman with the water, although she had been away for nearly forty-five minutes.

'Please send someone else down for that water,' George told the Chief. 'The woman must have got lost or something, and we'd like to be away as soon as possible. We have a long journey ahead of us.'

The Chief sent a youngster into the nearest hut, and he brought out a little water in a calabash, which we poured into the radiator. Then the boy went into the next hut, and while he was away I saw the native woman returning with the can of water from the river balanced on her head.

But – *was she the same girl?*

I stared at her in amazement. Yes, she *was* the same girl – with an important difference. Whereas less than an hour ago she had been a pregnant woman, swollen and slow in her movements, now she was slim and graceful. And, in her arms, wrapped in a shawl, was a newly-born baby!

I just stood there gaping, hardly able to believe my eyes. George saw the expression on my face and burst out laughing.

'*Now* will you believe what I told you when you were laid up – that native women treat childbirth as a very small thing to be taken entirely in their stride?'

'George,' I replied, 'after this, I'll believe anything.'

I learned a little later that the birth had been brought on after she had filled the can with water and was actually lifting it up to put on her head. When she felt the symptoms, she had prepared herself near the water's edge, delivered the baby, performed the necessary ablutions afterwards, then wrapped up the child in her shawl, placed the can of water on her head, and walked the half-mile back to the car.

When the head man realized my interest in what was to him and the other villagers, a very ordinary performance, he told me some of the remedies that the Swazi women use for various ailments.

When these women are expecting their first child they frequently complain of painful and swollen nipples. Their cure for this is simple. The wise matrons of the tribe heat a quantity of cow dung in a pot, and then place it, like a poultice, as hot as can be borne, on the breasts of the mother-to-be. This process is repeated several times until all the inflammation is drawn out. Then they apply the juice from a type of bitter aloe, which toughens the nipples.

This bitter juice is also used by a mother who wants to wean her child. The juice is so unpleasant that the baby, after having a few tastes of it, cannot be induced to suck at the breast any more! To us, I agree, the treatment sounds crude and unhygienic, and, of course, so it is. But it does have one redeeming value; it works.

Sindiwe Magona

S indiwe Magona was born in a little village in the Transkei (then a 'Bantu homeland' reserved for Xhosas), and her family moved to a squatter camp on the outskirts of Cape Town when she was four years old. *To My Children's Children* (the first volume of her autobiography, published in 1990 and translated into Zulu in 1995 as *Kubantwana Babantwana Bam*) is her narrative of her life up to the age of 23, by which time her husband had deserted her, leaving his pregnant wife to eke out an existence for her two small children from odd jobs, such as hawking sheep heads and marijuana. In addition to the harsh discrimination to which she was subjected in apartheid South Africa, she had to live under a cloud of disapprobation, earning the reproachful label of *idikazi* reserved for 'husbandless' women in Xhosa society. The second volume of her autobiography, *Forced to Grow* (1992), describes her 'rebirth' and growth, a period of remarkable achievement culminating in several degrees, including an Honorary Doctorate from Hartwick College in New York and a job in the United Nations' Public Information Department. Magona has also published *Living, Loving and Lying Awake at Night* (1992), *Push-push and Other Stories* (1996) and *Mother to Mother* (1998).

This extract is from **To My Children's Children**, which she wrote as a 'letter from a Xhosa grandmother' to give her grandchildren some sense of their history. In it she recounts her experiences of Bantu Education, the Xhosa puberty ritual and her confirmation as a Christian in the mid-1950s.

The year I left Primary School was the year that education became racially segregated. Hitherto, white pupils, African pupils, coloured pupils, and Indian pupils could, theoretically, attend the same school. Indeed, there were cases of African pupils attending coloured or white schools. After 1955, the law forbade that practice. Henceforth there would be different Departments of Education for the different race groups. Understandably, the examinations set would not be the same since the examining bodies would be different.

Protesting against the Bantu Education Act of 1954, many African teachers were fired. Others were arrested. Some left the country, going to the newly independent African states, or to Britain. There were a few, I heard, who even went to Russia and elsewhere, countries I didn't even know existed.

Then, before I knew it, I was no longer a child. This seemed not to take everyone else the least bit by surprise. For me, however, when it finally came, it did so with alarming suddenness: one day I was envying the bigger girls their breasts; the next, I had sprouted these objects of my fervent desire.

'Sindiwe, tomorrow after school I want you to come to me at work.'

My heart leapt. The next day was a Friday. We attached a great deal of importance to Friday in my family. That was the day on which father got paid. The first thing that came to my mind was 'a dress'!

'No, you are not getting a dress. Your mother just made you one,' replied Tata, to my disappointment.

Still optimistic nonetheless, I pestered him with guesses. But all he would say was, 'If I told you what we'll be doing, you would have nothing to do with the information. So, wait and see. And besides,' he added as an afterthought, 'this way you can't go broadcasting it to your chums.'

Not even Mama would satisfy the curiosity that duelled with excitement for first position. I knew well though, what I could count on: the five or so men who worked with Tata as petrol attendants were bound to give me some money. So would Tata, who never otherwise parted with a penny by giving it to his children.

That night as I ate my supper, stamped mealies, our staple food, I could already smell the fish and chips I would buy for myself with some of that money.

The hour or so I spent waiting for father to knock off from his job went without a hitch. I greeted his colleagues, who told me I had grown a lot since the last time I had come there. How I wanted to believe that! Grow, to me, meant added inches. That is something I didn't do well, and evidence thereof is my height today.

I had, as I had expected, been sent to the café to get cigarettes, matches, and cool drink.

'Take the change and buy yourself some sweets.'

'Here,' said another, 'get yourself more.'

Father worked the petrol pumps six to six. Thus a little after that hour, still without any illumination as to where we were going and why we were going there, I set off with him, mystified but uncomplaining.

A fifteen-minute walk took us from Observatory to Mowbray, where we took a bus. A short ride and a longish walk thereafter down a sandy footpath, guarded on either side by such a thick hedge of maitland it could well have been a brick or concrete wall, and we were, of all places, on a livestock farm.

What was more astonishing, however, was that we were not there to visit a relative working there – the only conclusion I could reach after seeing our destination.

'This weekend,' said my father, 'we are going to celebrate your becoming a woman. Therefore, you are here to choose the little piece of meat we will offer our relatives, our friends, and our neighbours whom we have invited for these rites.'

The farmer, like most farmers in this country, is white. Also, the probability is very high that he is an Afrikaner.

He called out to one of his African or coloured men, '*Wat soek hy?*' ('What does he want?')

The man conveyed father's reply and instructed us, from his boss, to wait. The farmer was busy with someone else, a white man; customer, friend or neighbour – I couldn't tell. He strode over to us as soon as he was free, with another of the servants in tow.

'Ask how much he can pay!' said the farmer in Afrikaans.

Father replied in English, directly to the farmer.

'Ask him whether he needs the delivery van,' persisted the farmer, in Afrikaans, via his man.

After more of this 'trialogue' we were eventually conducted to the stalls or stables. Here, as father had requested, we were shown the young heifers. Father asked me to pick out the one I liked best.

I did.

'Thirty-five pounds,' announced the farmer. Father replied he didn't think the heifer was worth that much as it was a bit on the thin side.

'Ask this boy how much he has in his pocket. I haven't got the whole night to waste,' roared the farmer, once more via his interpreter.

'No, nkosi (boss), I can pay twenty-five pounds.'

'Take this one.'

'That one is not right. It is too old.'

After more haggling, we finally got the first heifer. Father paid twenty-seven pounds and ten shillings for it. We were leaving, half-way down the footpath, when the delivery van shot past us blowing a mini sandstorm in our way.

A hundred or so metres past, it lurched to a halt and one of the 'boys' hollered:

'Niyayifun'ireyi?' ('Do you want a ride?')

Running forward, father indicated we did and urged me to hurry. I did.

Within three-quarters of an hour, the van came to a stop in front of my home. Father was the first to jump out and then helped me down, for there was no platform from the back of the truck. The two farmhands followed. They and father immediately started dragging the heifer out. The beast was secured by rope onto one of the poles supporting the wash line.

Father then went to the van's front compartment and thanked the farmer profusely for his kindness.

Seeds of ingratitude must have lurked somewhere inside me, even then. Father's profuse thanks irritated me.

Why was he thanking the boer for humiliating him? Father, my father, sharing the back of the van with a beast. I seethed, not at the farmer. Father should have refused the ride, I felt. I, for one, had no problems with the fare we would have paid had we made our own way. The time it would have taken us to get home, to say nothing of the inconvenience, were of little consequence to me. Fear of being kicked to a bloody pulp by the cow greatly added to my indignation. How dare this boer make us sit at the back? How dare he hog the front compartment, clearly roomy enough for three? Of course, I wasn't the least bit bothered by the two workmen's position. They could ride with a whole herd of cows as far as I was concerned. That was their job, after all.

By Sunday afternoon, the whole extended family seemed to have come. Men were seated outside in a circle in front of the house. Women filled the house. The younger were cooking. Some in the kitchen on the primus stoves – our two, and four others borrowed from neighbours. That food would be served to

145

those deemed 'elevated' – by age, wealth or education, the usual criteria for such distinction.

Outside, a little beyond where the circle was emitting a collective cloud from the numerous pipes, a makeshift fireplace proudly displayed four-gallon tins, once containers of paraffin, wherein now bubbled meat, vegetables and stamped mealies: a feast in the making.

Although everyone present knew the reason for the feast, at some point, before *umqombothi* (the home-brewed corn and *amabele* beer) went to the head, an announcement would be made:

'Will her mother or one of her aunts on her father's side, bring her out?'

Since father and I had returned from our little shopping, I had been in seclusion. Only mother or one of my father's own sisters were allowed near me. Now, mid-afternoon, I was summoned.

'Here she is!' Mother left me standing alone right there in the middle of the circle, now joined by the more mature women.

Uncle Masondo, the master of ceremonies, began a brief historical presentation. He had not quite finished when the bard of the clan deemed it fit to speed things up:

'*Mzukulwana kaNophuthukezi,*	'Grandchild of Nophuthekezi,
Ntombi kaSingongo, kaMbhuti	Daughter of Sigongo, of Mbhuti
KaMali, kaVongothwane!	Of Mali, of Vongothwane!
Mdengentonga!'	Tall by deeds!'
'*Dlangamandla! Zulu! Tolo!*	
Mchenge, Mabhanekazi	'(The praises of the Tolo Clan)
Vumba lempongo liyanuka!	
Mafungwashe kwezakwa-	(She by whom out of those of
Vongothwane!	Vongothwanes they swear!)
Thokazi leZizikazi	Heifer of a Zizi (Clan) woman
LamaZiz' amnyama neenkomo	(The Zizis, black as their
zawo!	cows!)
Camagu! Mpilo Nde! Amabutho	(Blessings! Long life! May
Akowenu akulondoloze!'	Your Ancestors guard you!)'

Ubulunga (the necklace woven from the tail hairs of the cow slaughtered for this rite) adorned my neck. Less ornate (and thus, to my mind, of less importance), were the belts I wore: one on my waist, two on each wrist, and a head band.

All these came from different parts of the same 'insignificant morsel'. They would protect the woman for whom they had been made throughout her life but especially during her child-bearing years.

I wore these bands for at least three months. Whenever I left the house, however, I wore only the waist-band hidden well underneath, nestling against my skin.

If I had any doubt or sense of embarrassment about any of this, I wisely kept that to myself. Besides, the objective, to affirm, protect and enhance my womanhood, guaranteeing my fertility and safety during child-birth, was not something I was inclined to waive my rights to.

'My child, a good daughter pleases the parents. Your parents are very proud of you. Mind never to disgrace the Magona name. Mind never to disgrace the Tolo clan. Remember, a good wife is like a good daughter to her husband. She is also like a loving mother to him. We are all proud of you. Continue with school and learn so that when we are old we will have someone who can help us; someone to lean on.'

'*Dlangamandla, uzigcine ukhulile ngoku!*' ('Dlangamandla, look after yourself, you are grown now!') Those were the words from the women of my clan, said to me towards the end of the ceremony. I did not ask how I would protect myself. I did not ask where the danger lay. I was too busy feeling grown-up.

After the weekend celebrations I would go to school as usual. I had come to accept the existence of two far from compatible worlds, the one my world of traditions, rites, and ancestor worship and the other, the world of 'civilization' that included school. No word about what had happened to me would I whisper even to my most trusted friend once I was at school. By this time I was in high school.

The high school I had entered had been chosen unanimously. At that time, the Langa High School was the only high school for African students in the Western Cape. Students from as far away as Paarl, Stellenbosch, and Worcester commuted daily to this school. I was lucky to be living a mere nineteen-kilometre distance from it.

That year, 1956, Langa High School must have had some of its youngest students entering high school. We would, during breaks, gaily play jump-rope and ball games, and run around screaming, laughing and being thoroughly disgusting and undignified, according to some of the older students, who accused us of turning the school into a crèche. We were anywhere between twelve and fourteen.

I must have struck a rather pitiful-comic figure. Small, I was beuniformed in long gym-dress (father believed a woman, and to him that was any girl above the age of ten, should dress to cover not only the knee, but a good five to ten centimetres below it).

'Shame, poor thing, why does your mother make you wear such a long gym-dress?' I was asked by two young married women, complete strangers, one day. That event led to the only conspiracy I remember between mother and me. Mother put in another set of buttons on the shoulder flaps of the gym. This permitted me to have two lengths – the first set of buttons were for father, giving me about seven centimetres below the knee, and to be used on my way home, between Salt River and home where the likelihood of bumping into him existed. The second set gave me knee-length and teen-aged respectability.

That same year I was attending confirmation classes. Every Saturday afternoon found me in a group inside the one-room shack we called church. There, the senior preacher, Mr Ntenetye, quizzed us on the Catechism. Here, I fell hopelessly in love with the seductive melody of the Liturgy. When the day came, we went to St George's Cathedral in Cape Town for confirmation by The Right Reverend Joost de Blank, the Archbishop of Cape Town. The whole ceremony had an air of unreality for me. If someone had told me I was already in Heaven, I would not have disputed that. Black, white, coloured, and everybody else was there. All under one roof. And what a roof it was. Wherever did the saying 'as poor as a church mouse' originate?

148

Maggie Resha

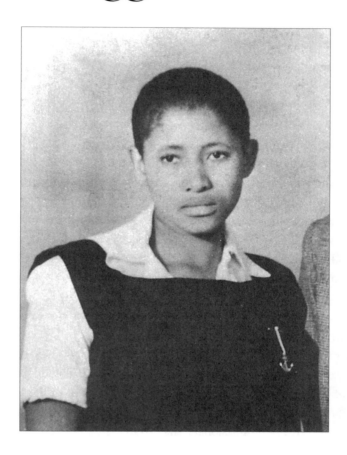

M atabello Mmamolise Tsiu, of the Bafokeng clan, was born in Matatiele in the Cape Province in about 1926. She met Robert Resha at Pretoria Hospital, where she was working as a nurse, and in 1948 they were married. Both Robert and Maggie were key figures in the ANC during the mass struggles against apartheid in the 1950s. In May 1960, Maggie was jailed for about 25 days. In 1963 she led the ANC Women's League delegation to the World Congress of Women in Moscow. She lived in exile in Algiers until 1973 (the year in which Robert died), then relocated briefly to London, returning to South Africa in 1976.

This excerpt from her autobiography, *Mangoana O Tsoara Thipa Ka Bohaleng: My Life in the Struggle* (1991), recounts her involvement as one of the organisers of the massive 1956 women's demonstration against the planned extension of the Pass Laws to women. The event was a huge success in organisational terms, but it only succeeded in delaying the inevitable. These laws were finally extended to include African women in 1963, radically undermining their rights to live and work in the urban areas. With the advent of democratic government in South Africa in 1994, the day of this historic march, 9 August 1956, is commemorated annually as 'South African Women's Day', a public holiday.

Maggie Resha died in 2003.

It goes without saying that the Pass Laws were one of the main pillars of apartheid. Indeed, when the Nationalist Party took power in 1948, one of the many harsh laws the regime added to the Statute Book was to tighten the Pass Laws on men and extend them to include the women. For their part, the women knew exactly what they were faced with; they knew they were faced with Afrikaner diehards and villains of racial segregation, who would stop at nothing. To these, the Africans have been seen as nothing else except tools of labour. To extend the Pass Laws was to pull down the wall which protected the women from the humiliation of carrying these documents. To do so would be to dispel the belief that womanhood and motherhood deserved respect and honour in society, irrespective of race or colour.

Under the direction of the ANC, the Federation of South African Women, which was formed in 1954, and the African National Congress Women's League, called upon women throughout the country to resist this callous move. Women, in towns as well as in the rural areas, staged demonstrations against local chiefs, Native Commissioners, magistrates. In 1955, 2,000 women from the Transvaal went to the Union Building with a petition to the then prime minister Strijdom, who snubbed them, and to which the women responded by organising a demonstration to the same place by women from all over the country.

However, right at home, in Western Native Township (WNT), there was a bit of a hitch. Ida Mtwana, who had been President of the Federation as well as of the Women's League before Lilian Ngoyi, had sort of drifted away from women's activities, and she had half of the WNT following her lead. After we had discussed this snag at the Federation Executive, Lilian proposed that, as I had worked with Ida longer than anyone else had done, and that since we both resided in the same region, I should go to tackle her to join the march. I was a bit reluctant to see Ida because there had been reports that she was not satisfied about not being consulted on some issues concerning the organisation. Anyway, the thought of the anticipated success of the march subdued the fear of my going to talk to her. And, thanks to Lilian's tactic, Ida agreed that we should sink our differences and that she would join the march.

On my way to Ida's house, I passed Kate Mxakato's and successfully persuaded her to accompany me. Kate lived in WNT – but she was not in Ida's new group. She was a militant woman and later became provincial secretary of the Women's League. We both convinced ourselves that seeing two people would make Ida see how we still believe her contribution valuable in the struggle.

I was very relieved when Ida agreed to join the march, and I there and then told her that I would be delivering leaflets and petitions to cover Western Native Township. With the help of the male comrades of the Congress Alliance, thousands and thousands of leaflets were cyclostyled and distributed. These leaflets explained what the march was about, and called upon all women to organise their neighbours as well as women on buses and in trains. The country was flooded with leaflets. It was accompanied by petitions, which were to be signed by women only, whether they were going to join the march or not. In these petitions there was an emphatic 'No!' to the proposal to extend passes to women, as well as a scathing attack on all racist laws. When all the copies were collected on 9 August 1956, there were over 100,000 signatures.

I do not know whether to claim that this was the busiest time for the women, because we seemed to be busy all of the time. It was just a year after we had been engaged in organising for the Congress of the People, and just before that there had been the campaign against the removal of Sophiatown, which kept us on our toes day in and day out, about which I wrote in an earlier chapter. But what made the organisation of the march difficult was that we had to go around carrying leaflets, and no one could be sure as to whether or not she would not be caught by the police. So we had to be on our guard all the time.

I remember that, two days before we went to Pretoria, I thought that there might be some women we might have missed because Sophiatown was so overcrowded. So, coming home from work in the afternoon, I decided to go to organise in the street in the north of the township. I was carrying some leaflets and petitions in a little suitcase. At the corner of one street I met two women who were carrying their babies on their backs. As I was talking to them, explaining about the march, a black SB [Security Branch policeman] passed near us, in a rush. I did not know whether to drop the leaflets I was holding because I was trying to tell the women that, since they had babies, they could just sign the petitions. But the SB man said to me: 'Oh, Mrs Resha, I thought you were carrying equipment in your case for delivering babies, but it seems that you use it for leaflets as well!' I took no notice of him, and he left us alone.

As the women were signing the petitions, the one said to the other: 'You know, we can go to Pretoria with our babies; our mothers used to go to the fields and come back, carrying a large *seroto* (large grass carrier) of mealies on their heads, with their babies on their backs'. 'Yes,' replied the other, and then continued, 'In any case, when we are arrested for pass offences, we will either have to go to jail and take our babies with us, or be separated from them.' There and then they asked me to put their names on the list of those who would be going to Pretoria the next day.

In the morning, I met them at the bus rank, and we took the same bus to Pretoria. Those two women were now the ones preaching about the evils of the Pass Laws to the others. I was happy, but I was also amazed by their determination, and I saw what conviction could do to a person. In Pretoria, they were even more happy to see that there were many, many thousands of other women who had come with their babies, and that even women who were highly expectant had made the journey. Those are the women of South Africa; the women who are prepared to fight because they want health, happiness and security for their children.

This demonstration, which was well-organised beforehand, was planned for 9 August 1956, and Strijdom was notified, in advance, that he should be available to receive the women. The regime panicked, as usual, and tried, unsuccessfully to disrupt the march by putting various obstacles in the way. Transport was cancelled in many areas. Women from Natal, the Cape Province and the Orange Free State paid large sums of money to book carriages to take them to Pretoria. Many women from the Transvaal went to Pretoria overnight to avoid the disruption of the transport.

I remember that I was, with several other women from our area, part of a bus group who went to Pretoria. Our bus was stopped at a police roadblock, and two white policemen, both young men, climbed aboard. As they came in, we started to sing a hymn. This made them look at us in great puzzlement – perhaps they thought we were going to a funeral. After a few minutes they allowed the bus driver to continue his journey. While we felt jubilant, we were not absolutely sure that we had passed our last roadblock.

A few days before the day of the demonstration the regime had announced a ban on all gatherings of more than three people. It became a real problem then to walk together in a group, since even walking was technically a breach of the law. So we each took different ways and streets, never stopping, through Pretoria, as if we were just pedestrians in a large city. Everyone knew where the Union Buildings were; no one could get lost. By ten o'clock, 20,000 women had assembled in the grounds of the venue, around the statue of Louis Botha (1862–1919) on horseback, impressive in his wide-brimmed hat, looking across the city. To many women from the Transvaal, who had visited these grounds, the statue was familiar. But to many others, who had come from other provinces, one could see the curiosity in their faces as they read the name on the statue of the man who had become the first Prime Minister of the white union of Boer and Briton in 1910.

From the bottom of the gardens to the buildings itself must be about half a mile; we had to climb hundreds of steps and terraces, each of which was filled with gardens of the loveliest flowers. Because of the vastness of the crowds who were assembling, many people had to trample over the flowers in order to get to the Amphitheatre. Some, including myself, had sore feet from going up these hundreds of steps with our shoes on. But it was like a real invasion when the women surged forward and ever upward towards the building. I don't think that at that stage anyone even thought of the ban upon a gathering of more than three; this was a multitude of angry and defiant women of all races from every walk of life – some were carrying babies on their backs. But each one of us held a petition denouncing the Pass Laws and all other racist laws. What was noticeable was the absence of uniformed police, while there were scores of Special Branch and many journalists.

Because of the volume of petitions to be presented (there were 100,000 in all), we needed a delegation of ten or eleven people to carry them all. But the representativeness of the delegation also had to be considered; for example, a representative from each racial group, and a representative from each province. Lilian Ngoyi and Helen Joseph, respectively President and Secretary of the Federation, were to lead the delegation to the Prime Minister's office. I was not part of the delegation. Many of the nurses who were present had been asked to keep a watchful eye on the crowd. Anything could have happened because of the strain of going up the steps and because of the scorching sun.

But, thanks God, there were no mishaps. Before we could settle down in the Amphitheatre, we were met with stink bombs. Everyone had to put her hand on her nose. What a welcome! Nevertheless, the delegation was determined to press on. By the time it went up, I could see clearly the anger on Lilian's face.

The magic sweat she once talked about which she had during the Cape Town ship incident in 1954, was rolling down her temples. It was at this moment that the Union Buildings came to a standstill. When I cast my eyes up to this pompous building with its two domes (signifying the union of the Boers and the British), the verandahs of the building were covered with hundreds of pink faces, giving the impression of hanging like linen on a drying fence. The workers inside had abandoned their desks to come to witness a spectacle that had never been seen since the formation of the Union – black women in occupation of the Amphitheatre: a no-go area for an African even as gardener or sweeper. The Amphitheatre, I had been told, is the holiest of places for the Boers – only their President or Prime Minister stands there when giving important announcements about war and peace.

The secretary to the Prime Minister told the delegation that his boss was unavailable. The women, in their anger, dumped the petition outside his office. Yes, the 'Lion of the North', as Strijdom was called, had lost his courage to face this army of angry women.

Lilian asked the crowd to observe a thirty-minute silence in protest. During this period not a cough, not a child's cry, was to be heard. It was like a calm lake whose waters were undisturbed by even a breeze. A thirty-minute silence is unprecedented in my experience. I could hardly believe my ears when I heard Lilian call for it. Yet, because of our anger, the time seemed to pass almost in a flash. Following that silence the women burst into a taunting revolutionary song, which had been composed by the Natal women at a previous conference: '*Heyi Strijdom! watint abafazi, watint'-imbokotho uzokufa*' (Strijdom beware! Now that you have touched the women, you have struck a rock, and you will die). It was only one of several songs that were composed against him. For instance, in Sophiatown they sang, '*Koloi ena haena mabili, sutha sutha uena Strydom. Haosa, suthe, etla uhata*' (This wagon has no wheels. Clear off, clear off, Strydom. If you don't, it will crush you!).

Before the day was wound up with '*Nkosi Sikelel' iAfrika*', Lilian's voice echoed from the walls of the Union Buildings as she cried out: 'A ... frika!' The atmosphere seemed electrified by the power of her voice, and the crowd responded: '*Mayibuye!*' (May it Return!). By this time, many of the women, myself included, were weeping quietly. Yes, the women had done it! Women from the ghettoes of the locations, from the farms, from the villages, young and old, had dared to invade the very citadel of oppression in order to express their indignation and detestation for apartheid laws.

To see how heartless and thoughtless the leaders of the white regime could be, the following day they issued statements complaining bitterly about the damage done to the flowers at the Union Buildings terraces and grounds, the cost of which they put at hundreds of pounds. They also complained of the litter that had been left behind. It was most thoughtless of a repressive regime to cry for flowers; it did not cross their minds what a sacrifice it had been for the women, who had left their sick, their old, their homes, their young, to travel, under difficult conditions, risking arrest, to get to Pretoria.

Although the leadership of the ANC were concerned about the risks involved, when the idea of the march first came up, it now declared the 9 August as 'South Africa Women's Day' in order to honour the gallantry of the women. That day has since that time been added to the calendar of the ANC struggle against apartheid, as one of the landmarks of our history.

Winnie Madikizela-Mandela

Nomzamo Winifred Madikizela was born in the Transkei in 1934. She became involved in the ANC after moving to Johannesburg and, in 1958, she and Nelson Mandela were married. They had two daughters, but, as she records in the extract below, they were never given the chance to lead a normal married life. In 1962 Nelson was arrested and Winnie was banned. In 1964 he was sentenced to life imprisonment and, for a quarter of a century, their sole contact took place under the watchful gaze of prison warders. In 1969 Winnie was detained under the Suppression of Communism Act and spent a long period in solitary confinement. She was jailed again in 1974 and 1976, and in 1977 was banished to the small Free State town of Brandfort, where she remained for eight years.

On her return to Soweto, she organised the Mandela United Football Club, which reputedly engaged in a series of acts of terror in the late 1980s. In 1988, one of the members, Stompie Seipei, died after a severe beating, and Winnie was subsequently convicted of kidnapping and being an accessory to the assault of four young men. In 1992, two years after his release from prison, Nelson announced their separation and in 1994 they were divorced.

Although controversy continues to dog her, Winnie has, throughout it all, retained much of her popular support base. She resigned her post as Member of Parliament in 2003, after her conviction on 57 counts of fraud. Her refusal to apply for amnesty from the Truth and Reconciliation Commission in 1998 'because we were fighting a just war' was in keeping with her contentious political style. The TRC found her guilty of gross violations of human rights.

Part of My Soul (1986), from which this extract is taken, was banned in South Africa for many years. Compiled by Anne Benjamin and Mary Benson from tape-recorded interviews, it is a moving account of the life of the woman who earned for herself the title of 'Mother of the Nation'.

Life with Him was Always a Life without Him

Meeting Nelson Mandela
'We never had him physically to share that love he exudes so much of. I knew when I married him that I married the struggle. The liberation of my people.'

I saw Nelson Mandela for the first time in the Johannesburg Regional Court. He was representing a colleague of mine who had been assaulted by police. I just saw this towering, imposing man, actually quite awesome. (*Giggles.*) As he walked into court, the crowd whispered his name. He doesn't even know about this incident.

The second time was in the company of Oliver Tambo and Adelaide Tsukudu (later his wife). Oliver comes from Bizana, the same village I come from, so I knew him slightly, and Adelaide and I were living at a hostel, the Helping Hand Club, and were close friends. I had just got off the bus from Baragwanath

Hospital and they drove by and offered me a lift. Adelaide said she was starving so we stopped at a delicatessen. Oliver found he had no money but they noticed Nelson in the shop and Oliver said, 'Tell him to pay.' Which he did, and when he came out with Adelaide, Oliver introduced me as 'Winnie from Bizana'.

Soon after, I got a telephone call from Nelson. He invited me to lunch and said he would send a friend to fetch me. I was of course petrified – he was much older than me and he was a patron of my school of social work. We had never seen him, he was just a name on the letterheads; he was too important for us students to even know him. So when I got this call, I couldn't work for the rest of the day. And when I prepared to go and meet him, I took out every schoolgirl's dress I possessed. Nothing seemed suitable – in those days we had almost knee-length frilled dresses that made one look even younger and more ridiculous. And when I ultimately found something more dignified – it wasn't even mine. I felt so uncomfortable.

It was a Sunday. He always worked right through – Saturdays, Sundays, Mondays, the days were the same. I was driven to his office where he was buried in files, there were stacks and stacks of files all over, and it was just about lunch-time.

We went to an Indian restaurant. I tasted Indian food for the first time – a little country bumpkin from Pondoland. I had associated most of the time with my professional colleagues and I hadn't really known much about Johannesburg social life. It was such a struggle to eat. I couldn't swallow. I was almost in tears because of this hot, hot curry. And he noticed and embarrassingly gave me a glass of water and said, 'If you find it too hot, it helps to take a sip of water.' And he was enjoying that hot unbearable food!

As we were eating, he couldn't swallow one spoonful without people coming to consult him – it was an impossible set-up. It went right through that very first appointment. And I felt so left out, I just didn't fit in.

Leaving the restaurant, going to his car, we took something like half an hour. Nelson couldn't walk from here to there without having consultations. He is that type of person, almost impossible to live with as far as the public is concerned.

He belongs to them. I didn't know that that was to be the pace of my life. I was just stunned and fascinated.

When we got back to the office it was the same story – there were people everywhere. So we drove out of town and walked in the veld, and he told me he had in fact phoned to ask if I could help raise funds for the Treason Trial.

He never even asked me what my political affiliations were or whether I had any views at all. And I never dreamt of asking: how do I fit in, in this whole complex structure?

When we were walking back to the car, the path was rocky and my sandal strap broke. I was walking with difficulty, barefoot, so he held my hand as my father would hold a little girl's hand, and just before we got in the car, he said, 'It was a lovely day,' and just turned and kissed me.

The following day I got a phone call to say I would be picked up when I knocked off from work. He was there in the car dressed in his gym attire. He was a fanatic from the fitness point of view, so he was in his training clothes. That's where I was taken, to the gym, to watch him sweat out!

That was the pattern of my life right through the week. I was picked up – one moment I was watching him, then he would dash off to a string of meetings. He would just have time to drop me off at the hostel.

Even at that stage, life with him was a life without him. He did not even pretend that I would have some special claim to his time.

So if you are looking for some kind of romance, you won't find it. What he always did was to see to it that one comrade was there to pick me up. Even if I didn't see him for a week, I would be industriously collected and taken back to the hostel every day, and then of course the car must dash back to fetch him and take him to his meetings. I never had any frivolous romance with him – there never was time for that.

He took me to meet a lot of his friends. Almost every night there were consultations in the suburbs; there were meetings in the townships. Nobody asked questions, people were just comrades. I was also extremely involved in my own way, in my social work, in a lot of cultural activities and a large number of women's organizations.

One day, Nelson just pulled up on the side of the road and said, 'You know, there is a woman, a dressmaker, you must go and see her, she is going to make your wedding-gown. How many bridesmaids would you like to have?' That's how I was told I was getting married to him! It was not put arrogantly; it was just something that was taken for granted. I asked, 'What time?' I was madly in love with him at that stage, and so was he with me in his own way. It was such a mutual feeling and understanding that we didn't have to talk about it.

He arranged for me to be driven to Pondoland to tell my family. I got there and for a whole day I couldn't bring myself to speak of it to my father. And then I couldn't do it directly, I told him through my stepmother. He was very shocked.

Nelson was held in such high esteem and was such an important person in the country that my father couldn't imagine how I had found my way to him when I had been sent to do social work. My father was extremely proud.

But the family were also very concerned about the fact that Nelson had three children[1] and that I might not be able to cope. I never knew when he actually got divorced: I couldn't bring myself to ask such a thing right through our so-called courtship. And they were concerned about Nelson's future – after all, he was on trial for treason. Well, they were able to read history better than I was. But one became so much part and parcel of Nelson if you knew him that you automatically expected anything that happened to him to happen to yourself, and it didn't really matter. He gave you such confidence, such faith and courage. If you became involved in our cause as he was, it was just not possible to think in terms of yourself at all.

For him it was a total commitment which goes back to the days of his youth. Growing up in that tribal set-up in the countryside seemed to give him his background; he is a traditionalist. I don't mean in the stifled, narrow sort of way. Rather in the sense that what he is in the struggle, he is because of the love of his country, the love of his roots. He used to philosophize about the elders – white-haired, heavily bearded old men smoking their pipes beside the huge fireplaces outside the *kraal* – about their wisdom which he admired so much. It was those elders who instilled that pride in him, and love of his people. It's an incredibly strong bond – he himself as a person comes second to this love for his people, and the love of nature.

In June 1958 he was granted four days' permission to leave Johannesburg for us to get married – besides being an accused in the Treason Trial, he was also banned – and I insisted on getting married at home in Pondoland, because nothing could have pleased my father better and I wanted Nelson to see my background. It was an initiation for the kind of life we were heading for anyway because we had to dash back without even completing the usual marriage ceremony in the traditional manner. After the marriage in my home, we were supposed to then get married in his home as well. As far as the elders in the family are concerned, we haven't finished getting married to this day.

It was both a traditional marriage and to some extent a Western ceremony. Of course Nelson paid *lobola* for me; I never found out how much it was. It is not talked of in terms of money but in terms of cattle. (For years, Brigadier Coetzee, who is now head of the Security Branch, kept Nelson's letter from my father, in which he acknowledged the *lobola*. And during my interrogation in

1969, I remember this horrible Swanepoel saying: 'Poor Nelson, he must have been terribly stranded to pay so much for a woman like you!')

The day Nelson comes out of prison, we must go and complete the second part of our ceremony. I still have the wedding cake, the part of that cake we were supposed to have taken to his place. I brought it here to Brandfort. It crumbled a bit when they dumped our things. It is now in my house in Orlando, waiting for him.

Note

1. Nelson's two sons and his daughter lived with their mother in Johannesburg.

Winds of Repression

1960 to 1969

In 1960, the same year that Harold Macmillan delivered his famous 'winds of change' speech to the South African Parliament, warning that the winds of African nationalism were blowing throughout Africa, H.F. Verwoerd announced that South Africa would withdraw from the Commonwealth and that the Pan Africanist Congress and African National Congress were banned. This was in the aftermath of strikes and protests around the country, the most notable being at Sharpeville on 21 March 1960 when 69 unarmed, PAC anti-pass protesters were shot dead and 180 injured by police. This was widely perceived as a turning point in liberation politics. A State of Emergency was immediately declared and many leaders fled into exile. In 1961 (the same year in which the sensational Treason Trial ended with acquittal, and in which ANC President-General Albert Luthuli's restriction order was lifted just long enough for him to receive the Nobel Peace Prize), the now illegal liberation movements decided to set up military wings. Nelson Mandela was appointed as chief of staff of the ANC's multiracial *Umkhonto weSizwe* (Spear of the Nation) or MK. He left South Africa illegally for military training in Algeria in 1962; on his return, he was arrested and sentenced to five years' imprisonment. MK began its sabotage campaign and between December 1961 and mid-1963, 200 attacks on government buildings and electrical and railway installations were carried out.

Government response was to intensify repression: the Sabotage Act of 1962 enabled the Minister of Justice to place political activists under house arrest, and the Ninety-Day Detention Act (1963) allowed for detention of up to 90 days for the purposes of questioning (without a warrant for arrest or access to a lawyer; in 1965 the period was extended to 180 days); moreover, persons convicted of political offences who had served their sentences could be further detained. (The Terrorism Act of 1967 further strengthened state powers by providing for indefinite detention without trial.) In 1963, the police swooped on Lilliesleaf Farm in Rivonia and arrested virtually the entire High Command of the ANC's *Umkhonto weSizwe*. The Rivonia Trial concluded in June 1964,

162

with all eight accused being sentenced to life imprisonment. Mandela, who had been brought from his prison cell to face the charge of high treason, was also sentenced to life imprisonment. He and the rest of the black accused were taken to Robben Island.

With the crushing of opposition movements, the promotion of Afrikaner nationalism and grand apartheid seemed to be on track. On 31 May 1961, with a mandate from 52 per cent of the white population, the government broke with British imperialism when South Africa declared itself a republic and left the Commonwealth. Independent of British influence, the redefinition of blacks as non-South Africans began. In 1963, the Transkei was the first bantustan (for those of Xhosa extraction) to be granted limited self-government. (Full 'independence' was only granted in 1976.) 'Black spots', that is, black residential enclaves within areas that were declared 'whites only', were being wiped off the map and millions of Africans were to be relocated to the tribal 'homelands'. Indians and coloureds were also affected and, in 1966, Cape Town's District Six was declared a white area. Two years later, coloured representation in Parliament was abolished and a new law prohibited non-racial political parties. This further devastated the white opposition; the Liberal Party dissolved and the Progressive Party was forced to become a white party. (The following year, the ANC in exile opened its membership to whites.) In 1969, the Black Consciousness-inspired South African Students' Organisation (SASO) was founded under Steve Biko.

As early as 1950, political censorship had reduced the flow of information when the Suppression of Communism Act banned the Communist Party newspaper and prevented banned and listed persons from being published or quoted. In 1963 a government-nominated Publications Control Board was created which could – and did – ban publications for any of a number of reasons. In the 1960s, many dissident writers had their work proscribed. Some Afrikaners rejected the government's authoritarianism: a group of non-conformist Afrikaans writers (including Ingrid Jonker, André Brink and Breyten Breytenbach) became known as 'die Sestigers' (those of the sixties); the Afrikaans cleric, Beyers Naudé, founded the anti-apartheid Christian Institute in 1963; and in 1965, Bram Fischer, the Communist Afrikaner barrister who had defended the accused in the Treason Trial and the Rivonia Trial, went underground. He was arrested in 1966 and sentenced to life imprisonment.

By the end of the 1960s, the Afrikaner nationalist government's dream of a white South Africa seemed close to realisation. The assassination of Verwoerd by Demitrios Tsafendas in 1966 was not construed as anything more than the insane act of a crazed man, and B.J. Vorster, undeterred by the event, took over as Prime Minister. Internal dissent in the new Republic was largely stifled as leaders were either in prison or in exile. During this period, South Africa was experiencing unprecedented economic growth (as indicated by the defence budget, which swelled by 1 200 per cent from 1960 to 1973), in part due to harsh labour laws and massive foreign investment.

International condemnation, however, was becoming more strident. In 1962 the United Nations urged members to isolate South Africa and, in 1966, it revoked the country's mandate over South West Africa. The Organisation for African Unity, founded in 1963, was equally condemnatory.

Lyndall Gordon

Lyndall Gordon (née Getz) – front row, extreme left – was born and raised in Cape Town in the tight-knit Jewish community. In 1963, she and Siamon Gordon were married. She is the prize-winning author of works such as *Virgina Woolf: A Writer's Life* (1984) and *Charlotte Bronte: A Passionate Life* (1994).

Shared Lives (1992) recounts the rituals of a past era, the 1950s and '60s, when, as Lyndall puts it, 'we were the last virgins, growing up in an increasingly fantastic colonial tribe'. The passage below (from *Shared Lives*) describes how, as not-quite-adult university students, Lyndall and her best friends Flora and Rose wrestled with the temptations of passion and the imperatives of an early marriage.

Passions were difficult for that last generation of virgins, who were not exactly chaste. Our mothers and grandmothers had a clearer code of conduct. 'You are behaving like an engaged girl,' Granny once reproved me for holding hands in public. My mother's stories extended to a sedate kiss in the garden in the course of a ball: 'Roy Fennells took Monica outdoors and asked her to kiss him, and she said no; then he took me, and I said no; then, finally, he took Lilianne, and she kissed him; she was thrilled, until we told her that she had been his third try' – such were chums' stories of clean fun. In middle age, they spoke of men as rather absurd, pitiful creatures whose more unpredictable moves should be treated, if possible, as a joke. Their strongest feelings were maternal. Monica, who had been Head Girl of old Good Hope, best at hockey, and winner of all the prizes, devoted herself to having children. Normally reticent, in her forties she confided to my mother that a well-spring of bliss had begun to rise in her in the middle of the night.

'When he sleeps,' she said rapturously, 'I'm filled with love. When he wakes, I hold him in my arms, looking into his dear eyes.'

My mother, taken aback, thought that Monica had become uncommonly excited about her rather placid, pipe-smoking husband, Bill. 'Why, Mon,' she said, fingering her pearls uncertainly, and looking briefly at the ceiling, 'how *very* nice for you.'

There was a brief silence.

'He can't drink enough,' Monica went on, her glow deepening.

'Oh … you meant the baby!' cried my mother, suddenly enlightened. 'You've fallen in love with little Selwyn.' They chuckled at the absurdity of my mother's mistake.

Lilianne's husband was a little 'difficult', to use their word. Bertie Henry was a Scottish farmer who grew apples along the cool top of Piketberg mountain, on the route to Klawer. A thickset man, he had a masculine air of wilfulness that Lilianne rather enjoyed in the way that women used to enjoy the challenge of a dominant male while they indulged his lesser foibles. When Lilianne joined this rough creature on the mountain-top, the isolation was at first a little daunting, and she was fearful of gigantic African insects which emerged from the thatched roof of their farmhouse. In later years, when Lilianne came to town, she would relate her story of the spider and the penis.

In the early days of their marriage it had been Bertie's habit to strip after work and lie naked on the bed, reading the *Farmer's Weekly*. One day, to Lilianne's consternation, she saw a spectacularly large and hairy spider descend on its thread from the thatch until it hung, suspended, just above the equally novel phenomenon of Bertie's penis. The look on Lilianne's face changed from consternation to horror as, suddenly, with an exclamation, Bertie leapt to his feet, gave a howl of pain, and leapt in agony around the room. Lilianne showed us how quickly she rushed to the kettle for water, how efficiently she filled a basin into which she dropped antiseptic, and how assiduously she chased the still-bounding Bertie, trying in vain to get the basin lodged firmly under the penis in order to bathe the injured organ. Bertie, still howling and hopping, seemed to

166

reject these efforts with furious impatience until, as the pain died down, he was able to explain that, as he'd leapt from the bed, he had stubbed his toe.

For all this, nothing was said about women's bodies, their own needs: unarticulated, these bodies didn't appear to exist except to nurture the next generation. Flora's awakening desires, her public declarations and wilder demonstrations, seemed excessive, if not outrageous, in the context of the passive female manners of the time. My grandmother warned us not only against the dangers of licence, but of the tactical inadvisability of showing emotions. She was not analytic; she simply passed on the rules of women in what was still a man's world. Initiative of any overt sort was unwomanly, demanding, indecent. Flora defied these messages, not physically so much – since it was still obligatory to be a virgin – and not in any calculating or ideological way, but simply by admitting honestly, in outward gesture and plain words, to an impulse that did not arise solely in answer to male invitation.

'I've got a draft up my shaft,' she announced one day as we sat together, between lectures, overlooking the Cape Flats from the windy steps of Jameson Hall.

So began our secret fashion. Too lazy to wash our panties, we went without, not ever on dates but on varsity days, enjoying the wild rush of the south-easter – a daring fashion, given the strong gusts of the Cape. It was a variation on the more admissible pleasure of swimming naked against the silky buffeting of the great waves, far out to sea, on the grey, blowy days when the beaches were deserted.

Of course this was no real answer to the trials of virginity. The main trial was self-control. The decent male attitude could not be faulted. It was: do whatever you think right. This might go with a certain amount of scoffing at the 'platter' ritual: society's barbaric offer of a woman's virginity as a prize for the best bidder. There was no regard for purity as such; it was tolerated as a state which might be harmful to overthrow.

There was one attraction in virginity, and this was the element of mystery. At that time 'nice' girls had only a dim idea of what a grown man looked like without his clothes. There were paintings and sculptures, of course, but we had an idea that the real thing might differ, though no mention was made of erections when the facts of life were relayed, rather as a joke, from one relatively ignorant girl to another in the school playground. Joking was one way of coping with mysteries that might, we feared, come to unromantic ends, as in *The Bell Jar*, when Esther, model college-girl of the '50s, saw that the genitals of her date, Buddy Willard, looked like turkey-gizzards.

Where Esther sought out the gory details for the grim satisfaction of knowing, we held to our innocence, deploring the passage of time that propelled us towards adulthood. Curiously, anorexia was unknown in our milieu, despite its vogue for diets, and this may have had to do with the fact that, before the permissive society of the '60s, the rules that guarded licence provided some protection from pressure to mature too fast, and from the finality of sexual experience as men have shaped it. Schoolgirl confessions of revulsion held no fear of frigidity; rather relief that complete adult temptation had not yet come one's way. And as passions awakened, they were granted a certain freedom of play by the very rules that forbade their final form.

'We were the last of the great kissers,' recalled Leonora Carey, who met Flora later in Johannesburg. 'We did it for hours because we could do nothing else.'

Complicating this interplay of passion and restraint was the brevity of the time-limit before marriage-pressure came into play. My grandmother said that it was silly for girls of eighteen to get too serious over boyfriends.

'I agree,' I said. 'I won't start thinking of marriage until twenty-three.'

'Now that's going too far,' she said.

She was certain that plain speaking was for a woman's 'own good'. She told her niece, Sarah, who was twenty-eight and unsure of her feeling for a reliable businessman: 'You are not going to get any younger – or prettier. Marry him. Or else leave him and find someone else.' The urgency of the situation was not lost on Sarah, who married the man at once. And there were numerous Sarahs who, not calculating by nature but made so, married in haste for fear of being 'left behind'. Two weeks after my return to Cape Town, Rose brought up this subject:

Saturday, 30 January 1959

It is taking longer to draw towards Rose than Flora, but the other day we went to bioscope together and at interval, while they collected money for the Coalbrook Mine disaster, Rose (who has just turned 19) started telling me how already she is suffering from marriage pressure. I hate the way Jewish girls are supposed to get married before they are 21 otherwise everyone gets sorry for them. Flora is already feeling sorry for girls one year older than ourselves.

This age coincided with leaving university. That was the customary time to announce an engagement – preferably to a professional man, definitely to a Jew. This left only three years after school to find the right husband. No wonder my schoolfriends cut lectures so as to concentrate on the social chances of the Union.

Where my mother saw life in terms of moral tests (even illness was, to her, a test), and where Flora saw life in terms of social success, Siamon looked forward to mental challenge. In order to remedy the deficiencies of my mind and a feminine lack of purpose, he set me definite and, I thought, impossible goals for 1960.

'Anybody with any intelligence', he said firmly, 'should do well in paltry first-year courses.' So, after the long idleness of Good Hope, and the wasted opportunities of Israel, I settled to work in Jagger Library, ignoring the jeers of old classmates and the tug of the Union, in the attempt to prove that I did have brains after all. It did not take long to discover that, even if lectures were not always good, it was possible, in fact more rewarding, to work on my own. I liked to go to the library on Saturday mornings, when it was almost deserted, to collect facts about Byzantium in a niche smelling of old print and dust, and then emerge from darkness into the brilliant light when the library closed at 12.45, and look across the Cape Flats, across neat, toy-like white suburbs and the unknown clutter of non-white townships, unreal and quivering in the haze of heat, east towards the faint purple splodge of the Hottentots Holland Mountains. One Saturday, I locked this scene in mind and body, knowing that all must change, was changing already, that this period of study was but a respite, a last linger in a place I perversely loved, before being compelled to leave for good.

During these undergraduate years, the most absorbing course was South African history in the second year, 1961. Dr Davenport's unbiased lectures were a revelation after the doctored version of history taught at school. That year, I dropped child psychology after two months because its formulations, at least as they were taught at UCT, seemed pseudo-scientific. Instead, I took up social anthropology which, like South African history, had the verifiable immediacy of the local scene. As Professor Monica Wilson and a black graduate, Archie Mafeje, explained the intricate network of obligation and sharing in African society – say, the role of 'mother's brother' or the manifold burdens on women – the black majority came into focus.

Through my mother's Klawer stories came the impact of a South Africa of which we knew nothing: the old-fashioned Afrikaners of the *platteland* and their inextricable fusion with the harsh landscape of the interior. This was a land for which they would live and die. But that was only a small part of

169

the picture: of black society – the vast Bantu-speaking chiefdoms of Xhosa, Zulu, Sotho, Tswana, and others, who were lumped together as the marginal 'Natives' – of them we knew even less. Such oblivion was the triumph of apartheid, specifically of the Group Areas Act, which decreed that non-whites 'develop' separately from whites, on the distant peripheries of cities or in small, underdeveloped and often infertile wastes called 'homelands'. [...]

By the mid-'60s almost all overt opposition to apartheid had been eliminated. Those who were not detained and tortured felt guilty for having survived. And with increasingly rigid segregation, liberal aims for a mixed society seemed more futile than ever. Anthropology promoted this impression, for what it taught me – unintentionally, of course – was the hopelessness of factual knowledge: no one, I thought, but a black could fully understand a black society, and my hefty textbook on the Tswana, for all its plethora of social detail, was extraordinarily dull and empty of human truth. As the actuality of Israel had made me doubtful of Zionist ideology, so now I doubted not only the easy platitudes of white liberalism, but the very nature of political thinking with its reductive categories that left out the vital nuance of individual circumstance. We were irrelevant to a black country, I thought, and must leave. This was a common conclusion, and a constant topic of conversation, though many deferred their leaving until renewed unrest threatened their safety. [...]

At the time that Flora became 'Florian', Rosie became 'Rose'. And as she took on the glamorous, made-up face of 'Rose' – she never appeared without her nail-polish, her silver eye-shadow, and pencilled perfection of round lips – she seemed to vanish, that sparkling, hilarious Rosie I had known at school. Even her jokes had a contrived air, as though she were playing to herself, practising for some future which she did not expect us to share.

What I had not understood was the import of that long letter of 1959, when Rose declared that to gain a boyfriend at an early age was the most defining of social triumphs; that such a girl, glorying in her safety, would look down on less-fortunate friends. It had seemed to me that she was projecting a notion of outdated crudity, and I dismissed it as passing nonsense. Such an attitude belonged to Jane Austen's silliest mother, Mrs Bennet, to be rejected by her sensible daughter, Elizabeth, and upheld by the frothy Lydia. *Pride and Prejudice* has been called Jane Austen's 'Jewish novel', in view of Mrs Bennet's unrelenting pressure on her marriageable daughters. Such pressure is deliciously funny, but

Mrs Bennet may be rightly concerned with her daughters' fate in a society in which marriage is a woman's only respected career. To intelligent Charlotte Lucas, who is not in her first youth, marriage appears to be 'the pleasantest preservative from want' and for the sake of this preservative, she accepts a fool. Such women are sensitive to family wishes: they prefer not to burden the father or brother who may, it is true, jar them with every movement, but to whom they are bound by inextricable ties. To such bonds and concerns, Rose, at eighteen, had already succumbed, and with all the superadded sensitive anxiety of an intelligence too discriminating for her environment. This fine intelligence was compelled to subscribe to a view of marriage as a market, with men as buyers: the most desirable goods would go first; the least desirable would be left. Thus the care with make-up, the closed-off smiles, and studied jokes. All through those pressured years at varsity, she was saying to herself, 'smile', and alternatively, 'Don't *strain* … RELAX.'

Those girls who could not announce an engagement at the close of their third year at varsity went to Johannesburg. To 'go to Johannesburg' was a euphemism for hunting a husband – for some a last resort, for others like Rose a hope of more exciting 'talent' than might be found in the well-worn circle at home. Greta, the twenty-nine-year-old daughter of Mrs Gevint's friend Feige, had gone as the last resort, and she returned home in triumph – not unmixed with trepidation.

'Ma,' she said over the phone from Jo'burg, 'he's not handsome.'

'Just bring him home. *I'll* decide who's handsome.'

The whole family, with Mrs Gevint and Flora, waited at the airport.

Down the steps came Greta and, behind her, Max, a fat, bald man with a mouth full of enormous teeth. Slowly, Feige eyed the paunch as Max approached. He was, after all, well off, and she could see the anxious crease on Greta's forehead.

'A *scheine*,' she cried, opening her arms to welcome Max, 'a *feine*! (a good-looker, a fine man).'

'A *scheine*!' echoed the whole family in relief. So Greta was settled ever after.

In Johannesburg, Rose met a leading gynaecologist. There she married and lived in a spacious house with a large garden. I visited her in the late '60s, en route to Cape Town from a dark apartment in one of the sleazier uptown streets of New York. It was strange to see Rose in this setting – a composed wife of a successful man, a mother, my Rosie of unconventional judgement at the bottom of the school grounds. This Rose drew me over to the cot and, softly, a hum came from under her breath as she bent over the tiny, sleeping head.

So Rose, as I'd known her, vanished. With the farewell wave of that disturbing letter,[1] she disappeared into her time and place, assuming that I had gone before her – changed, changed utterly by the paired mode of being that women's magazines of the '50s hailed as 'togetherness'. In the mid-to-late '60s, I used to wander along Broadway or Madison Avenue, looking for my generation, which seemed to have vanished, as Rose had vanished, into marriage and motherhood. By 1965 I, too, was a mother, and my family disapproved of continued study. Columbia itself disapproved. When I asked for a loan, Dr Ridgeway, behind the administrator's desk, said brusquely: 'We don't give loans to mothers.' I, too, was vanishing – a homesick alien, silent in Trilling's class, intimidated by the forbidding style of his Jehovah pronouncements, in tow as 'wife' and 'mother'.

Flora, turning into 'Romy' in the mid-'60s, retained to an extra-ordinary degree her intransigent and buoyant self. She revived me from postpartum depression in the winter of '67 when she came to New York. Her stories of teaching maths to the E stream at Greenside High made me laugh again. She got on famously with fourteen-year-old intellectual duds. Though she had no hope for their maths, she found they worked better to the strum of a guitar: a boy played it softly in the corner, while Romy kept watch for the Head. She became a little apprehensive when the Inspector arrived at the school, and turned the pages of the hopeless books.

'Your ticks are too large,' said the Inspector severely, his eyes bent on the Bardot neckline.

Romy said: 'For one moment, I thought he was inspecting my breasts.'

Yet, voluble as she remained, she was loyal to the men she loved, and more discreet than of old about doubts, waverings, and imperilled virginity. She, too, vanished intermittently into two successive loves during the decade that she debated the question of marriage.

Note

1. In 1959, Rose had written to Lyndall saying that she felt theirs was a schoolgirl friendship, one that could not survive out of that environment (Gordon 1992: 104–5).

Frances Baard

Frances Goitsemang was born to Herbert Maswabi and Sarah Voss, both of Tswana origin. Although her exact date of birth is not known, Frances believes it to be in October 1908. She was a trade unionist and political activist and was imprisoned from 1963 to 1969 in terms of the Suppression of Communism Act. A fearless fighter, Baard was a prominent figure in the ANC Women's League and later in the United Democratic Front, an umbrella body formed in 1983 to unite organisational opposition to apartheid. She died in 1997.

This extract from her autobiography, *My Spirit is Not Banned* (1986), describes her experiences of banning and imprisonment.

The start of a bad time

In the beginning of 1963 the police came to my house again and they gave me my banning orders, you know, that I mustn't go out of Port Elizabeth, and that I must go to the police station every week to show that I am still there, and that I am not allowed into any coloured area or any township other than New Brighton, that I am not allowed to talk to any other banned or listed what-what person or attend any meetings or gatherings, even social gatherings. I even had to make a special application to be allowed to attend church! Those banning orders came from Vorster! That was when he was minister of justice, before he became prime minister.

Those banning orders were a great nuisance but it didn't worry me too much because I had been expecting this sort of thing. But what must one do? I just carry on with my work as much as I can. Of course I couldn't go to the trade union offices any more but I still carried on working and talking to people and organizing as much as I can.

Then, on the 18th October when I was still banned, the police came to my house again! This time they came to arrest me. They also arrested some other people at the same time, friends of mine.

That time there were four children in my house who I was looking after. There were my own two sons and I was looking after one of Mildred's children and one of Eleanor's as well. The one was about five years and the other was only about three years, still small children. Those children were staying with me alone because my husband had already died by then. We were all sleeping that night, and the house was very quiet. Then suddenly, in the middle of the night: KNOCK! KNOCK! KNOCK!, the police came knocking on the door like they always do, very loud. They wanted to search the house and so forth. They came inside making a noise and putting the lights on and everything. The children woke up wondering what was happening now. They were standing there in their pyjamas in the middle of the night, watching, looking. 'What is happening with these people? What is Mama doing?'

When the police had finished in the house they took me to where a police car was standing by the gate, in the road. The children came with me in the dark as far as the gate. Then the police put me in the car. I looked at the children standing at the gate and my heart was just as if it would fall down. It was too pathetic to leave children at that time of the night alone in the house. And so I left in the police car, and that was the last those children saw of me until after so many years. It was 10 years or so, a very long time, until I saw them again.

During that time the cases were never spoken in Port Elizabeth. They used to take us out to some other place around there. I can't remember which place it was that time, but they took us to court and told us that we were arrested for such and such a thing, working for a banned organization and so forth. They found the other people who were with me guilty and sent them to jail, but they discharged me. I was the only person discharged then. But immediately I got out the doors of the court they arrested me again and took me back to jail in Port Elizabeth. Most of those other people got two years or two and a half years. But they took me back to Port Elizabeth and put me into solitary confinement. That was in North End police station I remember. It is called Baakens Bridge because of the bridge right near it.

Solitary confinement

That was terrible. I spent a year in solitary confinement. I stayed there for weeks and weeks. I wouldn't wish for anybody to spend a whole year in solitary confinement. Really, it is a terrible thing. You sit and think. Walk to the window. The window was right up; I had to stand on something – the toilet was next to the window – so I could stand on the toilet to see a little hole there at the window. And you still don't see anything because the cell was downstairs, underground. You stay there in that cell, sit for a while, and then walk for a while. It was quite a big cell. Then I sit again. Sometimes I would sing some songs. You talk to yourself but you don't know what to say! You hear people talking outside but you can't even see them. They take you out for exercise for about five minutes maybe, every day. In the morning they take me out into this little space; I just had to go up and down and then come in again. Sometimes in the afternoon they take you out again and you walk up and down, and then they come and lock you in again. Even when I was doing the exercise I don't see anybody. They didn't even question me, interrogate me or anything; they just left me there for a whole year. I didn't see anyone else except the ones who bring me my food.

They cook food for you there in jail. But when they bring it to you they open the door and they kick it in, and maybe some of it spills but they don't mind. Then you must pick it up and eat it.

When they first put me in that cell there was no water or anything. There was a toilet in the corner of the cell, but no tap or anything, and no water. I had to drink the water from the toilet. I used to wash at that toilet too. But after a few days they brought water for me to wash and drink, and that was better.

I begged and asked them to give me a bible to read, or something, anything. But they refused. A whole year without anything to read and no one to talk to. And a light on in the cell all the time. All day and at night too, the light on. You can't sleep. I was so thin when I came out of there! I remember one person who met me when I came out of there, it was one of those SBs who took me there, one of the black policemen, and he was there when I came out. Whoo! He got a shock of his life. He said, 'Mai! Jhoo! Is that you? Why do you look like this? You never looked like this!'

I said, 'Well, what do you expect? I've been in jail for such a long time.' That man couldn't believe it.

I think they were trying to kill me somehow, but my spirit was too strong. I have always been a church-goer, but they wouldn't even allow me to go to church that time I was in solitary. But my spirit kept me alive because I knew that freedom would come one day, and my faith in God too, kept me strong. The only thing that kept me alive was the hope that one day, what I'm here for, I will get it.

I spent that whole year, a little bit of exercise sometimes, and then just sit and sit, and no-one to talk to, and nothing to read, and I try to look out of the window and watch the cars go past. Day after day with nothing to do. And so a whole year went by. And then after that year they took me to court now for my case.

Jail

When I got to court they said, 'Eh, you will be very surprised to see who is going to give evidence against you.' So I said, 'Well, I don't care who it might be. I left my sons at home, it may be one of my sons ...'

Well now, this person who was giving evidence against me, it was somebody that I worked with. As I have said, at this time we were working with the M-Plan and we had cells in the ANC. This man who was giving evidence against me was the chairman of our group, and so he knew everything that we had done and what we had said. When they told me that this person was giving evidence against me and I saw this man there at the court, I thought, 'Oh, is that you?' and I thought, 'Well, I am not going to say anything, because he knows everything, and they know everything. This man has told them everything. I am not going to make a fool of myself and say what-what, they can just do what they like.' And so they asked him, 'Yes, so-and-so, you worked with Frances Baard?'

'Yes.'

'And what did you do?'

He told them what we did, everything as we did it. Then it came to my side and I had to answer this man.

'Well, I don't know what to say. You can just do what you like, because even if I say I didn't do that, or I did that … I am going to be convicted, ja. So I give you the right, magistrate, to do just as you like.'

So the magistrate said, 'Well, since you've stayed a whole year in solitary I am only going to give you five years to be in jail.'

So I was convicted for five years, and I went to jail for five years. I started at Kroonstad, and I stayed there for about two years. That's where I met those people who had been in the first case and had been sent to jail before me.

Jail is not a nice place. The worst place, jail. When you are there after you have been convicted they give you some khaki things to wear, a khaki shirt and khaki skirt, and they give you a mat and blankets for sleeping on.

There's a bell which rings in the mornings, very early, and they come and open the doors, and there is noise, and you get up and go and wash. They have bathrooms where you can wash. Then you make your beds. After the washing it is breakfast time. We eat outside. Porridge and bread and coffee. A mug of coffee and one slice of bread, perhaps two slices after you have had your porridge.

Then after breakfast you start working. You clean your cells, and if it is washing day you take all the things which they have given you, the clothes of the prisoners, and you have to do the washing. And if there is something to be ironed, then some others will do the ironing. Sometimes when we were at Kroonstad we used to sew with machines, sew things which were torn, and mend things.

Then it was lunch. It was mealies. Mealies only. When you are going to have lunch they lock the cells. You have to have lunch inside the cells. And then you can rest a bit until they come and tell you that time is up now and you must go back and work.

In the evening it was sweet potatoes. (At Barberton they used to have big sweet potatoes!) They would cook the sweet potatoes and maybe some spinach for us. And then after supper, maybe at four o' clock in the afternoon, we are locked up again. And we stay there in the cell until it is time to sleep for the night.

We were all political prisoners together in those cells and we used to have schools there together. We used to teach the others who didn't know how to read and write, and we used to have choirs and singing. We didn't have any books there except some bibles, and they didn't give us anything to write with. But as a prisoner you must have something to write with. You don't care how you got it, and how you are going to get it, but you must have something. So we used to have some writing materials there too. And after we had given lessons we used to examine these people, like a proper school.

After the schools and the teaching in the evening when we go to sleep, we used to unroll these mats that they gave us to sleep on and we used to sleep 1,2,3,4,5,6 ... on this side of the cell and 1,2,3,4,5,6 ... on the other side, like that.

Anyway, I spent some time in Kroonstad jail and then they took us all to Nylstroom where they have a big jail. We had no visitors in Nylstroom jail because it was too far for our families to come and visit us, and a lot of people didn't know which jail we were in. We used to write to our families to tell them how we were and ask them how they were keeping, but many of the letters didn't reach them. So it was very lonely there in the jail. It was as if everyone had forgotten all about us. After a time I smuggled a letter out to tell the people where we were and that we were very lonely and unhappy in that jail, and what could they do about it. Nothing happened for a long time and I forgot about the letter. Then about six months later it finally ended up with a priest and he showed it to Helen Joseph asking her if she knew anything about it. She said, 'Yes, that is Frances Baard who has written that letter.'

So she knew which jail we were in, and she told other people, and she told them that things were not good with us. So those people arranged for a group of women to come and visit us.

I will never forget that day. It was a very special day. The guards came and told us that there were visitors to see us. We didn't know who these women were but they told the prison people that they were our relatives and so they were allowed to see us. We didn't know who they were but we knew that they were from the ANC so each woman said, 'Ja, ja, it is my relative.'

Each woman brought something with her and there was one woman to visit each woman in jail so that each one of us had a visitor. We were so happy to see these people man! I just danced when they came! We had something to talk about for the whole day, for the whole month after that. But the second time they tried to see us they were not allowed. I don't know whether they had moved us to another jail already, or whether they stopped those women, but they never came to see us a second time even though I believe they tried.

While we were in Nylstroom some of those other women finished their sentences and they went out of the jail. Then they took the rest of us to Barberton. There is a very big jail there, and big people! I've never seen such big people as the guards there, big and healthy, and they said, 'Ne, I must tell you that this is Barberton. *Ons het klaar gehoor van julle hier.*' (We have already heard about you here.) So that was the last place, and we stayed there.

Mrs Matomela who was my best friend in Port Elizabeth, she was there too from the first lot of people who were tried. One day they came and they gave her a telegram to tell her that her husband had passed away while she was in jail. She asked them if she couldn't go home, to bury her husband. They said, 'No, you can't. There are some people there that will bury him.'

This poor woman was so upset you know. It was pathetic. You see her sitting in that corner and you go to her, and she'll get up and leave you and go to that other corner. It was too cruel for anyone to tell you that you can't bury your own, own husband, and you are not even a criminal; you are just there because you oppose the government. And so that was that. She went out after her time had expired and she went home. And when she was home she got sick and she passed away after only a few months.

I too didn't know what was happening with my family that time I was in jail. I used to write to them but they never got my letters, and they couldn't visit me because I was so far away in Barberton. I didn't know whether they were well or sick, or where they were. It is very hard to be a mother without knowing how your children are or anything. My younger son got married while I was in jail but I didn't know until after I was out.

At least it was better in jail than it had been in solitary confinement. In jail there were other people to talk to, and things were better. They used to allow us to go to church on Sundays then too. There was a preacher or a minister who used to come and deliver some sermons to us on Sunday mornings. After the sermon we would sing some hymns, and then we would go back to our cells.

At that place they used to call us to the office and say the sergeant or what-what, big-what-*baas* wants to see us. So we get there and there are some questions we have to answer, and then we can go back to our cells. So one day when we got there the women were called into the office one by one. I waited there, and when one of them came back I asked her, 'What is it now?'

'They asked us are we still members of the African National Congress?'

'Oh. What did you say?'

'No. We said no, we are no more members.'

I said, 'Wait until they come and ask me!'

When they came and it was my turn, I went in and this man asked me, 'Are you still a member of the African National Congress?'

'Yes.'

'But the organization is banned.'

'But my spirit is not banned. I still say that I want freedom in my lifetime. I don't care if the African National Congress is banned or what-what, my spirit is not banned.'

'Loop! Gaan hier uit!' (Go! Get out of here!) And I was chased out of there!

Helen Joseph

Helen Beatrice May Fennell was born in Midhurst, Sussex, in England in 1905. A graduate of London University, she taught in India before coming to South Africa in 1931. Her marriage to Billie Joseph did not last. She was National Secretary of the Federation of South African Women in the 1950s and, from 1955 to 1962, served on the national executive of the Congress of South African Democrats, the white wing of the Congress Alliance (allied to the ANC and the South African Indian Congress). In 1956 she was among the leaders of the mass protest of 20 000 women who marched to the Union Buildings in Pretoria to oppose the Pass Laws. Following the adoption of the Freedom Charter in 1956, Joseph and 155 others (including Nelson Mandela) were accused of treason. The resulting Treason Trial dragged on from 1956 to 1961, with all of the accused finally being acquitted. Having failed to halt Helen's activities through legal channels, the apartheid government resorted to banning her. She was given three separate banning orders, totalling 16 years. In 1962, she became the first South African to be placed under house arrest – an experience described in the extract reproduced here. She died in 1992.

Helen wrote three autobiographical accounts of her role in the struggle (all of which were banned in apartheid South Africa): *If This be Treason* (1963), *Tomorrow's Sun: A Smuggled Journal from South Africa* (1966), and **Side by Side: The Autobiography of Helen Joseph** (1986). It is from the third work that this extract is taken.

Learning to Live a Half Life

The 1950s had been a decade of protest, from the Defiance Campaign at the beginning to the Treason Trial victory and the resistance of women to passes at its end. There had been tough battles with the Nationalist government, there had been oppression, but the underlying feeling had been a sense of achievement, even of triumph, despite the setbacks along the road.

Now we came into a new decade – the decade of the worst legal oppression yet known. As the years dragged by, each new security law brought further inroads into personal liberty, into accepted norms of justice.

The 1960s became the years of political trials, of detention without trial, of torture and death under interrogation. The maximum security gaols filled up with hundreds of political prisoners, men who had committed no crime against society but had pitted themselves and their cause against the armageddon of the Nationalist state.

The first half of 1962 brought the General Laws Amendment Act, which had spawned house arrest and other intensified restrictions of personal liberty. December 1962 brought a sinister rider to this Act in Government Notice No. 2130. Its provisions had a devastating effect on the lives of many banned and listed people – the four hundred and thirty seven persons whose names had been published as having been members or supporters of the banned Communist Party. It affected even people who were neither banned nor listed but had once been members or even supporters of an illegal organisation, and this covered members of the now illegal Congress of Democrats.

The effect of the notice was far-reaching, drastic, as it forbade banned and listed people from belonging to any of thirty-six different legal organisations, some of which no longer existed, some of which I had never heard. What they all had in common was their opposition to the Nationalist regime. The Federation of South African Women was included and also the Indian and Coloured Congresses. The ANC, the PAC and the COD were, of course, already banned.

The notice then went much further. It contained a prohibition on being a member, officer or office-bearer of any organisation which propagates, attacks, defends, criticises or discusses any form of state or any principle or policy of the government of a state. It was so broad in its implications that it was breathtaking – once you understood it – for it was worded in such a cumbersome way that I had to read it a couple of times before I understood it myself. It was also published very unobtrusively in the government *Gazette* so that it took a little while before even the people affected were aware that they could no longer work for an organisation which was political. Parliament was in recess and this notice was not even debated.

I was now totally excluded from the Federation of South African Women and had to resign as its National Secretary. This came as a very bitter blow because until I was banned in 1962, the Federation had formed possibly the most important part of my life. From now on I should be permanently cut off from it. Listing does not come to an end when a banning order expires. It is permanent and it still affects my life twenty years later. The earlier five-year ban in the 1950s, and even the more recent restrictions, had brought only difficulties that could be overcome and I was still the National Secretary. But that was over, for this notice undoubtedly covered the Federation – and me.

I also had to resign officially as the Honorary Secretary of the Human Rights Welfare Committee for the banished people. Its political nature was inherent in its very name but I had no intention of abandoning it. We had always held our discussions in private and my name never appeared thereafter in any minutes. After our journey to the banished people and their families, I could not tolerate the idea of giving up the close personal connections that had grown out of it. I continued my correspondence with the individual banished men and women, but only in my personal capacity.

I received a letter from the liquidator appointed for the Congress of Democrats after its banning in 1962. I was invited to show reasons why my name should not be included amongst those of the already listed people, on the grounds that I had been an office-bearer, a member and an active supporter of the Congress of Democrats. I had certainly been all of these and I was proud to have been so. I had also given sworn testimony in the treason trial about my position in the Congress of Democrats. In any event, nothing would have persuaded me to deny my association with my organisation. I ignored the liquidator's letter and my name was duly placed on the list. Now I fell under Notice 2130 on three counts. I was banned, I was listed and I had belonged to an illegal organisation.

Already in 1962, I had written to the Minister of Justice asking for the reasons for my banning and house-arrest orders. I received a reply as ludicrous as the one asked for at the time of my first bans in 1957. It added a few choice extras, for example, that I had associated with listed communists, but as the names of the listed people were published only after my house arrest, I could not see how I was supposed to know who they were. I certainly had not known that Joe Morolong, who had been with me for the whole journey to the banished people, was a listed person, until I saw that one of the reasons given for my house arrest and bans was that I had arrived in Cape Town in the company of this listed person. And I still could not see laughing, friendly Joe as a dangerous person!

At the end of March 1963, the Supreme Court of Justice upheld the minister's appeal against Jack Hodgson's legal victory which had brought us that precious three months of partial freedom, my taste of social life again had been brief but very good, but this time the minister had won and we went back to our half-life under house arrest. I found that I soon slipped back into the former routine. The first shock was over and it was not as difficult as the first time, especially as all the other restrictions had remained in force.

As I moved slowly through the first year of house arrest, it developed its own rhythm. The freedom to move out of my house as early as half past six in the morning didn't mean very much to me. This couple of hours before my office work began seemed a bit of a waste, until I started to call on my friends sometimes to have breakfast with them. I called on others on my way home in the evenings for a quick drink and some chatter – behind drawn curtains if there was more than one other person present, and always watching the time so that I could be sure of getting home before half past six.

For a time, one of my greatest joys was having the Cachalia family, Amina, Yusuf and their two little children, just around the corner from my office, not even five minutes away. I could and did go there often for a quick lunch with them, the kind of meal which only banned people know, always on the alert for a knock on the front door and the hasty retreat into another room with your plate, knife, fork and glass. It was not a violation of my bans to be found in the Cachalia home, but it would be if I were discovered with more than one person.

I had always known that Amina suffered from a heart condition, even from childhood, but the news that she was to undergo major heart surgery came as a great shock to me. I became deeply anxious and depressed over it, fearing that I might lose this precious friend. I suppose it was inevitable that during periods of enforced isolation, such as I had every night, anxiety affects one more severely. I reached the lowest level of depression that I had yet experienced. I could not sleep properly, I wept, I suppose mostly in self-pity, in fear that Amina might die and for my own feeling of being so desperately alone.

Amina recovered from her operation, but her family moved away from the little house around the corner from my office. It was no longer possible for us to share my lunch hour. We telephoned each other often until one night she said, 'Hold on, Helen, there's someone at the door ...' There was indeed – two security policemen who served five-year banning orders on her, while I was still holding the telephone. It meant that for the next five years, we should not be able to speak to each other, yet even this restriction could not destroy our friendship.

After that I could only look at her on Saturdays when she and her husband, Yusuf, also banned and house-arrested like me, would walk with their children to the police station to report. I would get there at the same time, just so that we could smile at each other as I passed in my car or walked in silence beside Yusuf to write our names in the house-arrest register.

Despite all my restrictions, I did not escape attention from the security police. They suddenly instituted a vicious campaign of following me by car wherever I went. It was unreal, sometimes comic, mostly sinister. When I left my home in the morning to go to work, one or even two cars would be parked in Fanny Avenue, a block away, and would pull out behind me and follow me all the way to town. This performance would be repeated when I went to report at the police station too, whether I went there by car, or bus, or walked. When I returned home, they were there again.

For six weeks I went nowhere except to work, for I had no intention of leading these tailing cars to the homes of my friends. I think I drove the entire time with one eye on the rear-view mirror. I had two collisions with other cars during that time. Then this persecution stopped as suddenly as it had begun. Perhaps I supplied a useful exercise in training police recruits to follow suspect cars. Perhaps the police foolishly imagined that I was planning to escape from my irksome house arrest by leaving South Africa. I certainly did not have any such plans, then or at any other time. I had the right, as British born, to leave South Africa, but the bans prevented me from leaving Johannesburg to reach any airport or sea port. So perhaps they really thought I was going to make a dash for it.

It was a gruelling experience for me, but once I got a laugh out of it when my unwelcome escort got in front of me in a traffic snarl and I deliberately followed him, bumper to bumper, until he tired of this reversal of roles and drove away very fast. It reminded me of a time when Robert Resha and I were returning from a meeting one night and realised that we were being followed. We came to a traffic circle and I drove round and round it until it was impossible to say who was following whom. When it finally dawned on the police that I was not even trying to get away from them, but laughing at them, they drove off in disgust.

During the three months when house arrest fell away, I forgot one Saturday afternoon that I should have reported to the police before half past two. I was arrested a few days later and spent a few solitary hours in the police cells before being charged and released on bail. I was held in the same large cell where we had been detained three years before and I was delighted to see that our lipstick and eyebrow pencil scrawls, our defiant graffiti of Congress slogans, were still on the walls.

This dire offence, to forget to report to the police station and write my name in a book, carried an unbelievable minimum sentence of twelve months in gaol. I don't think anyone has ever really understood just why this offence should be considered so dangerous. Over the years almost every banned person has come to grief over this senseless obligation. To forget is not a planned defiance, as no one in his right mind would deliberately fail to report and court twelve months in prison for it.

Inevitably, I was convicted. It was held by the court to be blameworthy negligence. I should have taken adequate precautions to see that I did not forget this vital obligation. I did not of course know beforehand that I was going to forget but perhaps I should have plastered my office with notices, 'Report to the police at lunch time!' It had not occurred to me to do that.

I was sentenced to the compulsory twelve months' gaol but the magistrate suspended it all except four days and I served my sentence in Johannesburg gaol.

It ended up as only two days, thanks to the happy coincidence of a weekend and a public holiday. I handed myself over with a plastic bag containing my toilet things, which was all I was allowed to have of my own possessions, donned the prison garb and was released again the following morning. That part was over, but I still had eleven months and twenty-six days of gaol hanging over my head. This could be imposed, in addition to any new sentence, should I again forget to report.

There came a day, of course, when I did forget a second time. I was totally unaware of it and protested the next day that I had actually been to report, whether or not the house-arrest register had my signature. I persuaded the policeman on duty that I had been there. He believed me and reluctantly permitted me to sign the register for two days. On my way back to the office I tried to reconstruct the previous day, which I had taken off to attend to a number of private matters and do some shopping. Horrified, I realised that in fact I could not have reported to the police station at all.

I generally regard the police as enemies, even the uniformed police, for they are guilty of shameful acts of brutality towards black people. Yet over the years there had inevitably developed some friendly relations with the staff at the police station where I went to report. They had almost always been helpful and courteous. I felt ashamed that I had, even if unintentionally, deceived that young policeman. I was concerned lest his breach of duty might be held against him.

I drove back to the police station and demanded to see the station commander. I told him what I had done, that I was prepared to take the consequences. To my amazement he assured me that he knew about it already and that the police were not going to take any action against me for not reporting. I fancy the security police had not been informed of my omission. I went back to my office with a lighter heart. I knew that if I had been convicted again of failing to report, I might have to face the imposition of the twelve-month suspended sentence as well as any new sentence.

During 1964 I was arrested again, not this time for violating my banning orders, but on two other more serious charges, one for possessing banned literature and the other for furthering the aims of a banned organisation, the ANC. The banned literature charge developed a comic dimension. I had, in fact, thrown it into my office wastepaper basket, still unopened, but addressed to me. It had been 'discovered' by a zealous security policeman who obviously knew where to look for it – on a recessed ledge in the men's cloakroom, where someone must have hidden it. When I protested in court that I had never set foot in the men's loo, the prosecutor accused me of standing in the doorway and pitching the magazine onto the ledge, some eight feet away. Not surprisingly, the magistrate acquitted me on that charge.

The charge relating to the banned ANC had to do with a sum of money repaid to the Federation of South African Women by the ANC in respect of a loan made from the Federation Bail Fund when the ANC was still legal. My defence counsel soon disposed of this allegation of furthering the aims of an organisation by accepting repayment of a loan and I was acquitted.

At this time, the danger of deportation was drawing rather close to me because, although I was a South African citizen, it was not by birth or descent. Conviction under almost every clause of the Suppression of Communism Act could lead to deportation, prefaced by a period in gaol. Fortunately, my only conviction so far was under Section 10 of the Act for failing to report to the police. Although this carried that ominous provision for compulsory imprisonment, it was almost the only clause which did not carry deportation. So I had to be thankful for small mercies and hope that I should be able to avoid any other offence under the Act.

After the end of the treason trial in 1961, I had written the story of the trial as we had known it from the dock. I called it, *If This Be Treason*. It could neither be published nor sold in South Africa because I was a banned person, which made it an offence to quote or disseminate anything that I had said or written.

The book was published in 1963 and a few copies eventually made their way to me. When I held one copy in my hand for the first time, only then did I feel that I was an author. I had a surprise telephone call from London one night, from the party held to celebrate publication day. My brother spoke to me and I think he too could hardly believe that this was all in honour of his sister's book. It all seemed very unreal to me that this should be going on so far away without me there. I felt isolated and elated, both at the same time.

Ever since our journey to the banished people, I had wanted to write the stories of these men and women we had found. We had listened to their stories, only one or two of which had ever been published. South Africa knew almost nothing about these forgotten people, about the stark horror of their lonely lives, the utter hopelessness of indefinite banishment.

My bans did not, at that time, prohibit me from actually writing, only from being published here, but I didn't want to risk the possibility of additional bans to prevent my writing at all. In 1965 I was able to take a few months' leave from my job and this helped me greatly towards writing another book – this time about the banished people. I called it *Tomorrow's Sun*. I had taken the title from Olive Schreiner's book, *Trooper Peter Halkett*.

> Tomorrow's sun shall rise and it shall flood these dark koppies with light, and the rocks shall glint in it. Not more certain is that rising than the coming of the day ... here on the spot where now we stand shall be raised a temple. Man shall not gather in it to worship that which divides; but they shall stand in it shoulder to shoulder, white man with black and the stranger with the inhabitant of the land; and the place shall be holy for men shall say, 'Are we not brethren and the sons of one Father?'

Throughout this period I worked at least one day a week at my office because I did not want to highlight my being on prolonged leave for fear of unwelcome police attention. I spent many days writing in the lovely peaceful garden of the Community of the Resurrection, or in their quiet library. There I could work with a feeling of security, without listening for the opening and closing of car doors as I did at home. But I took care that I was not followed as I drove there and back.

I finished writing *Tomorrow's Sun*. I posted the chapters to London a few pages at a time, as friends completed the typing for me. I waited for the publishers' verdict. It came on a very wet Saturday when I was at home for my house-arrest weekend with no visitors allowed. The post brought the opinion from the publishers' official reader. I was devastated. The opinion was unfavourable, mainly because I had tried to put too much into the book; too many stories, too many people. He said, among other things, that I had produced an amorphous clump of people with unpronounceable names.

I found this accusation ridiculous, even an example of English chauvinism. What right had he, or anyone else, to reject names in another language simply because he couldn't pronounce them? At the end, however, he conceded that he had felt that I was standing at his elbow, saying 'Listen, listen!' and he had had to listen. The publishers urged me to consider rewriting the book, bearing the criticism in mind.

It was the day of Churchill's funeral, broadcast in all its sombre majesty. I thought miserably that I could also hear the death knell tolling for my book. It was a terrible afternoon and the rain kept pouring down. My gloom persisted right through that empty weekend. Write it again? Leave out so many of the stories about the banished people? That was what the book was all about – I had not wanted to write it for any other reason.

My first reaction was to abandon the book altogether. Then I consulted a couple of friends, themselves writers, finally taking their advice that I must try again. I owed it to the banished people, for there was no one else to tell their tragic stories as I could. Their stories would not be told unless I rewrote my book. I cut and slashed and I tried again. This time with success and the book was published. The stories of the banished people were told to the world, even if not to South Africa.

The advance publicity for *Tomorrow's Sun* appeared in London in February 1966. The government acted against me immediately. Within two weeks of the publicity I was served with additional banning orders which prohibited me from preparing any material for publication or even assisting in doing so. The connection with my book was clear enough. I was to write nothing more. This prohibition had not been included in my original bans because this particular refinement had not been thought up then. I could only laugh. The minister was too late, for the book had already been published in England.

When I read the orders more carefully, however, I realised that my laughter was a little too premature. There were other prohibitions, new to me, though often included in the bans of others banned after me. I was now prohibited from entering any building which housed the offices of a trade union or any organisation which produced a publication. I realised with a sort of sick horror that my office at the Medical Aid Society was in the building which housed the Garment Workers' Union and I could not enter it again.

With my usual confidence I was sure that I could find a way out of even this difficulty. It did not take me long to work out an interim plan while I waited for a reply from the minister to my urgent application to be allowed to enter the building where my office was. Meanwhile, I continued my work at home, keeping contact by telephone and fetching and returning work daily; just standing outside the building on the pavement. It wasn't a very dignified procedure but it was better than nothing.

The minister replied with a flat refusal. I realised that he had not only prevented me from writing again, but that my job was now in jeopardy.

Within twenty-four hours I was notified by the management committee that my appointment had been terminated. My suggestion that I might work in an office in an adjacent building was rejected. My employers had had enough of Helen Joseph, despite my contribution to the Medical Aid Society.

I was stunned and humiliated, almost unbelieving. The Society was not ungenerous. It paid me a handsome honorarium, which I wanted to throw back, but commonsense prevailed over dignity. I had to live and I had more than earned that money over the years. It took me some time to see the whole affair in perspective and to accept that the patience of the Society had been sorely tried by this turbulent Secretary. It was not surprising that I had to go when the opportunity presented itself in that I could no longer even enter the building. I sometimes wonder how I managed to survive there so long, fifteen years, for there had been the treason trial, five months in detention and the house arrest and bans.

It was a new experience for me to be sacked. I had to accept that I was almost unemployable, despite my degree and diploma and my long administrative and social welfare experience. I was sixty-one, heavily handicapped by my political reputation and by these new banning orders with their prohibitions, not only on entering buildings but also on teaching or publishing of any sort.

Like so many other banned people, I abandoned any thought of employment at the executive or professional level, which I had enjoyed for so long. No welfare organisation would dare to employ me as a social worker for fear of losing government subsidies.

I went through a few disillusioning weeks of applying for advertised vacancies. Prospective employers would show initial enthusiasm over my experience and qualifications but freeze in silence on hearing who I was. It was necessary for me to say that I was banned because, as both a banned and listed person, I was compelled to inform the police of any change of employment. I knew from the experience of others that a new job was always followed by a visit from the security police to the new employers. It had happened to others. It would happen to me.

Until now my life had been cushioned by the security of my job, despite the problems of being banned and house-arrested. Others had not been so fortunate. Being banned had spelt financial ruin to some and to almost everyone intolerable anxiety over the future, with prospects of lengthy unemployment to be ended only with uncongenial and lower-paid jobs. This had already driven some banned people out of the country and well-meaning friends suggested that I too should go, return to England to be free, reminding me that I was at no age to start job-hunting with so many handicaps. Yet the thought of leaving South Africa was never in my mind. I was convinced I could survive somehow, even if I had to live very modestly, sell my car, perhaps even my home. But not yet. I could battle on.

191

Gillian Slovo

Gillian Slovo's autobiography, *Every Secret Thing: My Family, My Country* (1997), recounts a childhood enmeshed in the secrets that determined her activist parents' lives. Escaping from an ever-tightening net drawn by the Security Police, her father, Joe Slovo, and then later her mother and the children, left South Africa in 1964. In the last years of her life, her mother, Ruth First, worked as a journalist and academic in Mozambique. She was murdered by the South African security forces in 1982. As negotiations between liberation movements and the apartheid state got under way in the early 1990s, her father returned to South Africa triumphant. He was appointed Minister of Housing in the new South Africa. He died of cancer in January 1995. The story of his life up until the 1960s is told in *Slovo: The Unfinished Autobiography* (1995). Gillian's elder sister, Shawn, made the award-winning autobiographical film *A World Apart*.

Gillian lives in England with her partner and daughter. She is an accomplished writer and her publications include the detective thrillers *Morbid Symptoms* (1984), *Death by Analysis* (1986), *Death Comes Staccato* (1987), *Catnap* (1995), *Close Call* (1996) and *Red Dust* (2000). Her latest publication is *The Ice Road* (2004). The passage below from her autobiography recounts the difficulties of being the child of underground activists.

In 1963 we kept on smiling although our life was in the process of splintering into pieces. It started innocuously enough with Joe leaving town. He told us he was going on a short trip and that he'd soon be back and then he drove, illegally, across the border.

At the time he wasn't lying. He expected to be back. He had gone to organise the training of MK recruits throughout Africa, and to plead for guns and arms from sympathetic states. When that was accomplished, he was due to return: to operate underground.

Many years later, I asked him how he could ever have believed that the plan could possibly pan out. Mandela had gone underground and had been caught. Later, Bram Fischer tried it too, and he was also caught. 'How long,' is what I asked Joe, 'did you think you'd last?'

He answered with a slight, ironic smile and a question, 'It does seem crazy now, doesn't it?'

Crazy, because even the newspapers were following his every move. In June they reported that Joe and fellow communist J.B. Marks had gone to Southern Rhodesia where they'd both been arrested. Two days later the same newspapers spotted the two men at liberty in the neighbouring Bechuanaland capital of Francistown, staying in a local hotel. On 8 June the *Cape Times* informed its readership that Joe had, the night before, telephoned his wife.

The furrows on Ruth's face grew deeper. One day she packed us in the car and drove us through the Johannesburg suburbs. We sat in the back seat, licking our fingers for the last taste of the hamburgers in baskets we'd bought from the Charcoal Oven and singing songs. The Beatles were a faint whisper from the mysterious 'overseas'; we stuck to local products, singing that early sixties jokey, whiney, favourite '*Ag* (pronounced gutturally as in the German Ach) *pleez* daddy'. We sang out gustily:

> Ag pleez daddy, won't you take us to the drive-in,
> All six seven of us eight, nine, ten.
> We wanna see a flick about Tarzan and the Apemen,
> And when the show's over, you can bring us back again.

Ag pleez daddy, we sang, pretending that our father was like the others, out at work earning money to buy us our hearts' desires, not somewhere in Africa, bargaining for guns. We loved the song's words, the demands of insatiable childhood for zoos and aquariums and South African boxers who would 'donner'

Yankees to the floor. But best of all, we loved the chorus. We belted it out:

> Popcorn, chewing gum, peanuts and bubble gum
> Ice-cream, candy floss and Eskimo pie
> Ag daddy, how we miss, nigger balls and liquorice
> Pepsi-cola, ginger beer and Canada Dry.

If our mother, usually so fast to pick up on racial insults, noticed our shouting out the word nigger, the knuckles on her steering-wheel did not visibly tighten. Or perhaps I just didn't notice. They were already almost translucent with tension as she steered the car through the northern suburbs of Johannesburg to the Liliesleaf farm in Rivonia. At a farm gate she peeped the horn and a black man appeared. He peered into the car, smiled in recognition and opened up.

A gabled mansion stood at the end of the driveway, its front half opening up on to a rolling lawn. But when my mother stopped the car and we all got out she led us away from the house past the garage and to a set of low concrete buildings, the servants' quarters.

I climbed two low steps up to a concrete platform from which the bare rooms ran off. It was dark inside and each room seemed to be crowded with serious African men. The low mumble of their various meetings was drowned out by the endless background clatter of a duplicating machine. My mother's special friend, and our family favourite, Walter Sisulu came out and hugged us and then he took Ruth off to one side and started talking urgently in her ear. And all the time, we hung about, unable to understand a word of the conversations going on around us, only sensing that our fates were tangled up in that makeshift place. [...]

I remember almost every minute, frame by frame, of that 9 August when they picked my mother up. I was eleven years old and on a constant weekly round of visits to orthodontists and opticians. I remember a ninth-floor office with lime green blackout blinds. I sat on a high-backed chair in the dark, cold iron frames wedged against my nose, struggling to answer the insistent questioning as to which of two sets of circles – red or green – was the clearest. Each time I blinked the focus would change. I could feel the eye doctor's exasperation rising at my indecision, which only made me hesitate more. But finally the ordeal was pronounced over. I walked out of there as I always did, clutching the spectacles that I refused to wear, sure that it wasn't the optician's halitosis but my failure to give him what he wanted that had made things end so badly.

My grandfather was waiting in the entrance hall. Mild-mannered, unassertive, gentle Julius. As a child, I adored him, this one member of our adult world who seemed content to stay calmly in the background. As an adult, I marvel at how little of himself he left behind. There's a passport, a plaque commemorating his eighty communist years and a handful of black and white snapshots. In many of the photos, Julius seems frozen by the camera. He stares out, unblinking, at an unlikeable world – like a man from a strange, unknowable culture trapped in the photographer's unfriendly gaze.

On that day, however, in the optician's foyer, Julius was his usual, calm, silent self. We went out to his car to join my waiting sisters.

He drove us through Johannesburg's business centre and into the suburbs, an ordinary route on an ordinary day. Even today, if I concentrate carefully I can hear a faint echo of my sisters' voices as they ganged up on me, rhyming 'Gilly' with 'silly', 'Jill' with 'ill' and 'pill' in one endlessly unchanging lilting poem. I was almost lulled into sleep by its monotony when Julius suddenly stamped his foot down hard on the brake. By the time I looked up he was already out the car. He was such a careful man yet he left us skewed at an angle to the pavement, the engine ticking over, while he strode across the road to a corner café. I can guess now what must have caught his attention – a newspaper billboard with my mother's name on it. At the time, however, I didn't spot the headline. I just knew that there was something wrong.

Julius emerged soon after that. Clutching a newspaper, he walked towards us and got back into the car. I remember clearly the sound of Shawn and Robyn teasing each other. Julius folded the paper and threw it near my foot. I wanted to pick it up, to read what it was that had turned his face so white. Julius started the car. I left the paper where it lay and looked at him. He didn't seem to notice. Starting straight ahead, he pulled out and drove, faster than he ever had, to our house in Mendelssohn Road.

When we got home we found the iron garden gate open and, in the driveway, a stranger's car. The front door was also open and there was a stranger waiting there. Silently, we walked towards him. I don't remember Julius with us. Perhaps he wasn't there: perhaps he'd dropped us off and fled.

Inside the house every drawer and cupboard, every nook and cranny, was being turned over by policemen. I saw my grandmother and our nanny, Elsie, hovering in the background, their hands hanging uselessly by their sides. My two sisters and I walked down the corridor, conscious of alien faces watching with expressions we couldn't fathom. I held my chin high and felt an illicit childish thrill at the attention.

Ruth was in her bedroom, packing. A man, leaning nonchalantly against a wall, was watching her every move. She greeted us, her face immobile: almost everything she did showed her iron control. I remember her tapered fingers painstakingly holding each piece of clothing and laying it carefully on top of the one that went before. Half-way through, she fetched a book from the dressing table – Stendhal's *The Charterhouse of Parme* – and put it in the suitcase. As I watched it going in, I heard the policeman snort. My mother heard him too. She turned to look at him, her eyes blazing. He couldn't hold her gaze. He pretended to relax, folded one arm into the other and leaned heavily back against the wall.

The suitcase closed with a final click. My mother picked it up and started walking. Men went with her to the door. I followed them. They put her in the car, in the front seat, one on either side of her. Three jovial burly men squeezed themselves into the back seat. My mother looked at me, almost as if she didn't know who I was. I stood, waiting for her to say something. Finally her eyes seemed to focus on me and, leaning closer, she tossed a few loving reassuring words my way, topping them up with one last injunction. 'Look after Robyn,' she said.

The man beside her pulled the car door shut. The driver on her other side turned on the engine and started down the drive. I didn't wait while they reversed carefully out into the sharp bend at the bottom of our drive and then drove off. Instead, I went inside the house in search of Robyn.

I found her in the kitchen, standing close to Elsie who used to wake us, dress us and paint mercurochrome across our cuts and bruises. Shawn was in the garden and my grandmother kept walking in and out, opening her mouth to say things that had no meaning. I stood by Robyn in the kitchen, helping her make apple fritters. [...]

While Ruth was isolated, our lives were open to anybody who cared to pry. Not that most people did. My teachers' smiles just grew more mysterious while my school friends greeted the news of Ruth's arrest with a mixture of silence and incomprehension. How could they have understood? I lived in a house where the desks were fitted with secret compartments; I went with Tilly to deliver food to Ruth and watched a policeman poking tangerines, checking for smuggled notes, smelling asparagus, almost holing Ruth's stocking by the roughness of his handling: such a contrast to my classmates' serene, ordinary world. 'Is your mother a kleptomaniac?' was how one of them tried to get to grips with what had happened. A kleptomaniac, she explained, because compulsive shoplifting was the only reason she could conjure up for the gaoling of that precious South African jewel – a white woman.

One of my teachers was also the mother of my best friend, Susan. She helped my grandmother by occasionally taking me home to spend the night. I knew why she was doing it and so did she. We never discussed it. I never even found out what she'd told Susan. Everything continued as if nothing had happened.

In their care, I paid a tourist's visit to their safe white duplex, to ordinary life where the trouble Susan and I got into was about being polite enough to adults, or cleaning up after a glove-puppet performance. Not that I was a target for reproof. On the contrary, I was a model guest, impeccably behaved. With a kind of desperate gusto, I threw myself into normality. My fixation reached a climax during our school's end-of-term play where I'd been given the minor role of gypsy dancer. My mother wasn't there to watch me: no matter. All my will-power went into articulating each successive step. I stamped the ground, tossed my head, grinned wildly, my body calling on the audience to notice me.

A refrain kept echoing in my head:

Notice me,

notice me,

don't notice me.

I didn't know which I wanted.

While my mother was in prison another school friend, Carol Sutton, had a birthday. Our classes were small and the parents well off and the custom was to be invited *en masse* to each other's parties. Not this time however. With rising apprehension, I watched moon-faced Carol doling out her invitations. When I didn't get one, I tried to pretend to myself that it was the result of some kind of mad bureaucratic error which would soon be remedied. Even after she had carefully folded the paper bag in which she'd brought them, and dropped it in the waste basket, I remained optimistic. Tomorrow, I promised myself, she'd give me one tomorrow.

No invitation came, not then, not later. At first, I feigned nonchalance, pretending it hadn't really happened. But then, in the days that led up to her party, I broke. I played it extra specially nice, flirting my way into her affections. I knew I'd been struck off not because she didn't like me but because her mother didn't like my mother. I should also have known that there was nothing I could do to change that, but I guess I was my parent's child doing battle against the odds. Somehow I thought that if I could only demonstrate how wonderful I was, Carol would force her mother to reverse her ban.

The weekend of Carol's party came and went. On the Monday afterwards she offered me a selection of sweets, beautifully packed in a cellophane wrapping and tied up with a pale blue bow. I almost refused them. I knew that this was what self-respect demanded. But then another memory, more than two years old, stopped the 'no' escaping from my mouth.

It had happened in 1961, in May, a year after Sharpeville when the South African government left the Commonwealth and proclaimed the country a republic. While most white people applauded this declaration by the apartheid state that it no longer cared what the world thought, my parents helped organise the general strike which was the ANC's response. I had a foot, as usual, in both these worlds.

As the Republic Day celebrations reached their climax, I knew each white school child was to be presented with a pocket-sized model of the new flag and a gold commemoration coin. I thought about it often. I didn't want the flag which was a symbol of everything my family despised. But as for the coin, boy, how I coveted it, so much so that I convinced myself that it wouldn't do any harm to take it. Besides, a little voice informed me, if I did take it, no one need ever know.

Aged nine, I stood in my school's line, waiting for my turn, nervous, not that I'd take the coin but that my refusal of the flag would bring [censure] on my head. At last, I arrived at the front of the queue. The flag was proffered, I shook my head, no. While I'd been preparing myself for this act of rejection, my teacher had already anticipated it. She smiled and held out her hand to the girl waiting behind me. To ask now for the coin would have been humiliating. I had no choice. I walked off, coinless.

How I coveted that shining, fresh-minted, Judas coin. How I regretted not asking for one. And so, two years later, I wasn't going to make the same mistake. Instead of knocking the Alice band off Carol Sutton's mouse-brown hair, I took her offering.

There was no way I could win. The package sat like poison on my desk. When I got home, I threw it away untouched.

Not that anybody at home noticed. Our world had gone quite haywire. One day, not long after they'd taken Ruth away, I saw a police car heading up our drive. I ran inside, shouting out a warning. Like a cartoon character, my grandfather panicked, moving frenetically this way and that. I couldn't understand what was the matter with him. I followed his jerky progress down the corridor and to the bathroom where he jumped, fully clothed, into the bath, pulling the shower curtain round him as if its opaque plastic could ever have protected him. I remember standing outside the bathroom door, anxious to protect him, and anxious also that he was so unable to protect himself that he'd chosen a hiding place which even a three-year-old could easily have uncovered.

I needn't have worried. The curtain was never put to the test because this time at least, the police had not come for Julius. They were there because my grandmother, doubly tyrannical in Ruth's home, had sacked one of Ruth's domestic workers.

I think of Tilly now, of her sharply raised voice and her censorious tongue. I cannot understand what drove her on. She had started her working life in a shoe shop, and yet when we were children we hated going shopping with her because of the offensive way she addressed the staff. Looking back, I wonder what it was that fuelled her stern contempt of them, and where on earth had she learned to throw her voice like that. I never got to ask her. All I know is that Tilly could, with one blink of her heavily lidded eyes, intimidate the most articulate of Ruth's friends. No wonder that she was altogether too much for an impoverished, and now unemployed, black woman that Tilly had summarily dismissed. The woman had gone to the police and asked for protection while she collected her belongings. I guess they were only too happy to oblige.

After the squad car drove away, my grandfather vanished from our lives. When I gave him the all clear, he emerged, shamefaced from the shower, got into his car and drove away. I never saw him after that, not in South Africa that is.

Since Tilly's lips sealed over his departure with characteristic tightness, I made up my own fiction to explain Julius' absence. Tilly was living with us, I decided, therefore Julius must have gone to look after their house. As an explanation it didn't hold water – they lived too close for that – but I stuck by it because this was, at least, some way to fill the void of not knowing.

As much as I wanted to, I knew there was no point in pushing Tilly on the subject. She had far too many other preoccupations. Her day was book-ended by a drive to Ruth's prison, where she delivered food and clothes. She went, morning and night, in brightness and during thunderstorms, between the unrelenting school runs and the uncomfortable meal-times where she concentrated on getting us to sit up straight. Her spare time she used to harass senior policemen, demanding that they release her daughter or, at least, provide her with books to read.

How trying she must have found us three, with our stormy quarrels and our menagerie. We had cats and dogs and white mice, and something was always going wrong with one of them. During Ruth's stay in prison the mice went first, developing some fateful rodent virus that slowed their breathing and eventually stopped it altogether. We laid the dying out on flannel-swathed hot-water bottles and used an eye dropper to feed them brandy, but even as we were doing it, I could see the barely concealed amusement in Elsie's face. Not only did she think we were mad to care about those unlovable white things, she knew a lost cause when she saw one. And she was right. Within days the whole mouse colony was dead.

They went the same way as the silkworms we'd pulled from deep within our neighbour's mulberrybush and carefully placed in holed cardboard boxes. Each day, we'd look inside the boxes to see the worms' manic handiwork and imagine the silk we would soon possess. But nature was too slow for us. Gradually we lost interest until finally Tilly would demand permission to throw the moth corpses and their ratty spinnings out.

Our animal disasters did not end there. Our dog Pandy, the black Labrador, had been with the household long enough to rate a mention from Ruth in 1956, the last time she'd been imprisoned in Marshall Square. Now he started breathing laboriously as if in sympathy with the moths and mice.

Tilly couldn't cope with three of us: Shawn went off to boarding school. Meanwhile, despite my mother's parting words, I wasn't doing such a great job of looking after Robyn. She was continually in trouble. I remember sitting in my classroom, in the sweltering heat, and hearing the sound of breaking glass. My heart sank. I knew it was something to do with Robyn. It had to be. And of course it was. She'd put her hand, accidentally, through a window. The teacher's response was to scold and use elastoplast to staunch the blood. Four hours later, after Tilly had picked both of us up at the usual time, a doctor used three stitches to bind the wound.

It wasn't the only mishap Robyn had. She was on crutches, immobilised by a pain that was probably emotional, that day in Zoo Lake when we were having afternoon tea. While Robyn limped off to feed the ducks, I sat in the restaurant by the lake, comfortable between my grandmother and her stylish friend, Annetta, my thoughts drifting in the heat haze that had enveloped me.

Ruth First

Having already suffered severe restrictions under a series of banning orders, Ruth First, a member of the South African Communist Party and the ANC, was detained in 1963 under the new 'Ninety-Day Detention' law. There was no warrant of arrest, no charge and no trial. The cell that she was put in had no ablution facilities, and she was subjected to solitary confinement and repeated interrogation. In spite of enormous resilience, at one point she attempted to commit suicide. Once released, she fled South Africa and spent the rest of her life in exile.

This passage comes from *117 Days: An Account of Confinement and Interrogation under the South African Ninety-Day Detention Law* (1965), Ruth's account of her detention in 1963 which, due to her immediate re-arrest at the end of the 90 days, lasted 117 days. At the point at which the extract begins, Ruth's husband, Joe Slovo, had already escaped across the border and her young children, Shawn, Gillian and Robyn, were in the care of her parents. The Rivonia that is mentioned is the site of the farm that was used for founding meetings of *Umkhonto weSizwe* (MK), the ANC's armed wing, of which her husband Joe was a founder member. The concluding sentence of *117 Days* expresses Ruth's conviction that 'they would come again'; this proved to be prophetic for, in 1982, she was killed by a letter bomb sent to her in Maputo by South African government agents. Her murder was part of an orchestrated series of murders that targeted activists in numerous states friendly to the ANC and other liberation movements. Ruth's murderers were subsequently granted amnesty by the Truth and Reconciliation Commission.

I was called out of my cell one morning and I was sure it was for interrogation by the Security Branch. It was a visit by the children, brought by my mother, and arranged at the sympathetic instigation of a non-political neighbour who had tugged at Colonel Klindt's heart-strings by telephone. It did them good to see that I looked the same and talked not of being locked up but of school and the cat, library books, and holidays. Shawn, a vulnerable thirteen-year-old, seemed closest to tears; serious wide-eyed considerate Gillian exerted her usual tight control; and jolly Robyn was diverted throughout the short visit by a conspiracy of her own. They had handed me a fistful of bubblegum on arrival and when the time came to say good-bye, Robyn whispered in between her hugs: 'It's Ch-pp-'s Bubblegum. There are things written on the inside of the paper, something for you to read!'

I chewed the gum and read the wrappings:

'Did you know the skin of an elephant is an inch thick?' 'Did you know the giraffe has seven bones in his neck?' 'Did you know the stars are hundreds of miles apart from each other?' 'Did you know zip fasteners were first used in the nineteenth century?'

'They'll leave you to sweat a while,' a knowledgeable policeman volunteered. They did. For nine days. One morning I heard the approach of the keys to my cell. The wardress appeared. 'They want you,' she said.

Two men were waiting in the small interview room. The taller was Warrant Officer Nel. Lanky, in a drab grey suit, with sandy stringy hair, blue eyes as cold as a fish in an icy bowl, a toneless voice that I never heard utter a spontaneous sound. Sergeant Smit was ginger, an irritable and jerky man. Liverish, it turned out. There was a high deal table and two chairs. The stuffing floated out of the seat of the one so I was offered the second. Nel perched on the edge of the torn seat, and Smit leaned against the wall. This first encounter was hedged in by formal politenesses.

Did I know why I was being detained? Nel asked.

No, I said.

Patiently he read me the lesson of the day. Clause 17 of the General Law Amendment Act of 1963 states:

> Any commissioned officer … may … without warrant arrest … any person whom he suspects upon reasonable grounds of having committed or intending or having intended to commit any offence under the Suppression of Communism Act, 1950 (Act No. 44 of 1950), or under the last-mentioned Act as applied by the Unlawful Organizations Act, 1960 (Act No. 34 of 1960), or the offence of sabotage, or who in his opinion is in possession of any information relating to the commission of any such offence or the intention to commit any such offence, and *detain such person* or cause him to be detained *in custody for interrogation* in connection with the commission of or intention to commit such offence, *at any place he may think fit, until such person has in the opinion of the Commissioner of the South African Police replied satisfactorily to*

*all questions at the said interrogation, but no such person shall be so
detained for more than ninety days on any particular occasion when
he is so arrested.*

Was I prepared to answer questions?

I could not possibly know, I said, until I knew what the questions were. But I
was being detained to answer questions, Nel repeatedly insisted. Preliminary to
prosecution? I asked. Were they preparing a prosecution? How could I answer
questions if evidence was being gathered against me? I needed to know what
the questions were before I could say if I would answer them.

Like a pet white mouse in a toy ferris wheel, round and round I went. I was
bored, I found to my surprise. I had been through this encounter so often, in
my imagination, lying in my cell, that I was surprised not to hear them say: 'But
you've tried this on us so often before!'

Unexpectedly, Nel took a decision. 'You were a member of the central
committee of the Black Hand Secret Society,' he darted at me.

I answered that question – with an incredulous giggle. I was banned from
some thirty organizations, over twenty-four of which I had never belonged to
anyway. I had heard of a few dozen organizations other than those listed in the
usual banning orders. But the whole country knew that the Black Hand Secret
Society was an invention of the Security Branch. A reaction question, surely, I
made a mental note. I just had time to register the technique when they moved
in with a body blow.

'What were you doing at Rivonia?' I filled in my stunned pause with nervous
repetitive chatter that I could give no undertaking to answer questions till I
knew the full extent of the investigation.

'Why did Joe leave the country?'

'Why did you hold mixed parties?' – 'To mix,' I said.

'What were you doing in South West Africa?'

The questions and the few flippant non-committal fencing replies had
become awkward. I felt the producers were noticing that I was missing my cues
and not hearing the prompt.

The sergeant had been leaning against the wall. Impatiently he pulled
himself erect and said crossly to Nel, 'She thinks she's clever. She's just trying
to probe.'

He was right, of course. I knew enough for one interview. The Security
Branch knew I had been at Rivonia.

Five days later the two came again. And six days after that. They asked no new questions. Was I prepared to answer questions? Was I prepared to make a statement? A statement on what? Answers to their questions, they said. What questions? I asked. Everything, they said. They wanted to know everything. Secrets. Nel improved on that. 'Top secrets,' he said.

Behind the parrying and the fencing we were baring our teeth at one another.

Yes, I said precipitately, I'll make a statement.

Nel pulled sheets of foolscap from his briefcase and held his pen ready.

I said I could write it myself.

I understand from Warrant Officer Nel, I wrote, that I am being detained in terms of section 17 of Act No. 32 of 1963. (I borrowed his copy of the Government Gazette and wrote out the main drift of the clause.) I could not say if I would answer questions until I knew whether I was being charged with any offence and until I knew the nature of the questions. My verbal formula of evasion filled almost the whole of the foolscap sheet. The two detectives carried this sheet of paper away. They looked relieved, I thought, that this time they had a sheet of paper to take back to headquarters.

On the whole I was visited once a week. Never on the same day of the week twice running, rarely at the same time of the day. The attempts at interrogation seemed desultory. Some sessions were a toneless repetition. 'Are you prepared to make a statement?' – 'How can I?' and I was taken back to my cell. Several times the appearance of the two detectives, or Nel alone, was so brief that I believed it was merely to make the file entry 'Saw Mrs Slovo' as proof that he had checked in for duty.

One week there were two different interrogators.

Swanepoel was squat, bullfrog-like. His face glowed a fiery red that seemed to point to the bottle, but he swore that he had never drunk so it must have been his temper burning through, for Swanepoel's stock-in-trade was his bullying. Higher in rank yet deferring to Swanepoel's belligerence was Van Zyl, a lumbering, large man who tried persuasion in a sing-song oily voice. Van Zyl carried 'Granpa' headache powders in his top pocket; he sometimes offered them to his victims. On Sundays he was a lay preacher, on weekdays he was Swanepoel's interrogation partner. The two of them peddled a mixture of noisy vulgar abuse and suspect avuncular wheedling.

I had sat around for long enough without telling them anything, they said. I had been detained to answer questions. The replies had to be to the satisfaction of the Minister.

How did they know I knew anything? I asked. They knew, they said. I must know. I was 'part of the set-up'.

My husband, my father, they said. They knew all about *them*.

Why did Joe, my husband, leave the country, Swanepoel demanded? He raised his voice. 'He's a coward,' he bellowed. 'He's a coward on the run.'

'Do you really think you can tell me anything about Joe ...?'

Swanepoel leaned forward. 'And we know he's sent you money from Dar-es-Salaam.' 'Has he, now?' I said. 'Good, it's about time. And why shouldn't he support us?'

'Not money for you,' Swanepoel snarled. 'Money for the movement ... We know.'

'You know? Well, if you say so ...'

Where did the money come from? the two wanted to know. They kept coming back to this question. Swanepoel blustered and shouted; Van Zyl looked amused when I raised my voice in response. They demanded to know, they insisted I was there to answer questions and answer them I would. 'Surely you know everything already?' I said. 'You keep saying so and look at the bulges in your briefcases, your files must be crammed full.' Their briefcases lay on the table before us. 'Oh, in those we carry our sandwiches and bottles of brandy,' they said. For a moment we were a happy joking family.

Swanepoel tried another tack, then another. He turned to Van Zyl. 'She's too comfortable here. She's having a holiday. We must have her moved to Pretoria. She won't like that.'

Once again he asked why Joe had left the country. 'Joe is no fool,' I said. 'Has it ever struck you that he might have provided for this day? How can you know that I know anything at all? Couldn't he have said to me the day he left, "My dear, when I have gone the chances are that the Security Branch will hold you for ninety days to question you about me ... so I'm going, but I shan't tell you the reason why ... It will be useless for the Security Branch to question you, won't it?"'

Swanepoel's stock-in-trade was to bully and taunt but like most bullies he could not himself stand being teased. His colour rose higher.

'You're an obstinate woman, Mrs Slovo. But remember this. Everyone cracks sooner or later. It's our job to find the cracking point. We'll find yours too.'

Even now I cannot write how it happened but shortly after this I was given two pieces of information that froze my limbs. First leak: a delegate present at a meeting I had attended at Rivonia with Mandela, Sisulu, and others had blurted information to the police. The Security Branch would have a list of those present at these highly confidential discussions, they would have the agenda items and possibly even an account of what each of us had said. Here was one revealing source of information; were there others? Second leak: the Security Branch was investigating my father and my mother. My father I knew about. Swanepoel had made little attempt to hide his interest in him. Would they act against my mother too? If they had detained James Kantor for being Harold's business associate and brother-in-law, what was to stop them detaining my mother as a lead to my father? The prospect of her detention unnerved me. How would she live in the grime and filth of a cell? The children had lost Joe in June, me at the beginning of August. Judging by the questioning of the Security Branch my father might well be in hiding. I had left the children with heartache but I had the comfort of my mother as substitute. If she was taken, they would be abandoned.

I had to find a way to warn her. I spent a day thinking about how to smuggle out a note, another day composing the message. I got out the sliver of lead hidden in the lining of my suitcase. I wrote the message, but then tore it up. For what if it was intercepted? Instead of forewarning my mother I would be drawing Security Branch fire to her. How [to] write so that an innocent construction could be put on the words? This might be the only message I succeeded in getting through; there was no time to exchange views and debate action, the message had to be blatantly clear. I composed another message, and yet another. Repeating the text of the warning I had received would expose my source of information. Admonishing my mother to caution would be dismissed with impatience. The only way to persuade her to act to safeguard her own freedom, I decided, was to insist, for my sake and theirs, that she take the children away. With infinite trouble I wrote thirty urgent words to send a signal by a laborious procedure that had been devised for a time of extreme need. (I had previously alerted my mother that I would use this way to reach her.) I waited several days to send the signal out, so that it would be picked up as pre-arranged, and then settled down to wait for an acknowledgement. Nothing happened the first day, or the second, the third or fourth. By the fifth I was forced to conclude that the signal had not got through. The transmission system had not worked. If I had needed any fresh reminder here it was: I was insulated against contact and my chances of breaking the isolation, even in desperate need, were nil.

During my first weeks in the cell I had been impudently buoyant. I was determined to find the stamina to survive this war of attrition. But now I began to feel encumbered by diversionary actions. My parents, and through them the children, were being pulled into the line of fire. What was the Security Branch planning? Who else was on the list to be detained? Who else had turned informer? I lay and worried, before full awakening in the morning, all day, even in my sleep. I was no longer sleeping well.

They have the evidence of the man at the meeting. Whose else? How had they tumbled on Rivonia? The shock of the Thursday afternoon raid a month ago surged back. Kathy [Ahmed Kathrada] had had his hair dyed red, making him look like the cousin of the Portuguese market gardener. Walter Sisulu with straightened hair and Chaplinesque moustache had dispensed with his suits and sported a pullover of vivid design like a sailor's tattoo; he had had toothache that week, and had needed a dentist. (Did they bring him a dentist in his Ninety-Day detention cell?) Govan [Mbeki] in blue denim overalls had been dressed like a labourer but had always had a pencil in his hand, writing, drafting, planning. A baker's van had inched along the winding driveway. '*Ons slaan toe!*' (Let's get cracking!) the officer in charge, Lieutenant Van Wyk, had said, and the van had disgorged policemen. Walter had leapt for the window but a police dog had brought him down. Handcuffs had been produced for Raymond, Walter, Govan and Kathy, Rusty and Dennis. They had taken Arthur and Hazel too. Policemen had played ball with Nicholas and Paul, the two young Goldreich children, and had asked five-year-old Paul for the names of his father's friends. Labourers and domestics on the farm had been rounded up and put into police vans. Each now sat in a solitary cell.

Sequence and incident became jumbled; I found difficulty in disentangling my fears from the facts. I longed for what seemed in retrospect the untroubled emptiness of the early days in detention. I wrestled with decisions that had to be based on the flimsiest shreds of information, my ability to reason bedevilled, I knew, by the lopsidedness that solitary confinement would impose on my reasoning. Did they have enough to convict me? Who else was in detention by now? Who was talking? What was I on record as having said at the Rivonia meeting that had been denounced? I could not remember: meetings at Rivonia tended to merge into one another, and into meetings held elsewhere: there had been many.

I embarked upon a campaign to accommodate myself to the prospect not of ninety days in a cell, but years. The sooner I got used to the idea, I decided, the more easily I would bear it. Once convicted I would be able to read, study, perhaps even write; at worst I could store experiences and impressions for the day I could write. I would struggle to erase self-pity. Hardest of all, I would struggle not to think about the children. They would be elsewhere, where they could grow up without the continuous reminder of me in a prison, and they would have Joe. I had always needed him so; he would give the children his confidence, his optimism, his humour. It could have been so much worse: Joe might have been sitting in a cell upstairs, and by sheer lucky timing he had got away from the Rivonia raid and the aftermath. I had to stop thinking about the children. I needed all my concentration to handle my own situation … but of course I couldn't stop thinking about them.

Hilda Bernstein

Born in England, Hilda Watts was an ardent communist who worked closely with Nelson Mandela and the leadership of the ANC for over 40 years. The following passage is taken from her account of her last two years in South Africa, **The World That was Ours: The Story of the Rivonia Trial** (1989). Hilda has written a number of other works, including a prize-winning novel, *Death is Part of the Process* (1983), and *A Life of One's Own* (2002), a biography of her father and sister, which was shortlisted for the Alan Paton Non-fiction Award, 2003. The autobiography of her late husband, Rusty (Lionel) Bernstein, *Memory Against Forgetting: Memoirs from a Life in South African Politics, 1938–1964,* was published in 1999.

In 1960, Hilda and Rusty were imprisoned during the State of Emergency that followed the Sharpeville shootings. Rusty was one of the Treason Trial accused. He was acquitted with the others in 1961 but, in May 1962, he was served with an order confining him to Johannesburg and prohibiting him from entering black areas and factories. Already 'listed' as members of banned organisations (and thus subjected to surveillance and restrictions on movement and association) both Rusty and Hilda had also been banned for many years from virtually all public activity. Following Mandela's arrest in August 1962, Rusty was placed under house arrest. In July 1963 he was arrested at Lilliesleaf farm in Rivonia, along with other key members of the ANC. The Bernsteins' daughter, Toni, was 'listed' in 1964 as a former member of the radical white organisation, the Congress of Democrats, and for many months Rusty was not permitted to speak to her. The constant harassment of the family continued, and aware that they would not be permitted to live any kind of normal life in South Africa, Rusty and Hilda decided to flee. This is her account of their escape over the border into Botswana in 1964.

Tonight Eva has another note. Rusty says I must not go without first seeing the children and explaining to them. Eva is strongly opposed to this unnecessarily dangerous enterprise.

She says, 'Can't you go without seeing them?'

'No, I can't, I must see them.'

She says, 'But if you have to choose – to see them now, and through doing that imperil your hopes of ever seeing them again; or to go without seeing them, knowing you will then have a better chance to be re-united in the future? If you think about it that way, can't you go without seeing them?'

After a while, when I can control my voice, I say, yes, I can go without seeing them.

But Rusty insists. So on Wednesday afternoon I leave my refuge and Eva. I kiss her goodbye, a woman I did not know a few days ago but who I now know so well; shut in together we have talked and talked, she has told me of her childhood, and shown who she is. May we meet again one day.

The place of assignment is a public park, and there I go disguised and in borrowed clothes. Keith laughs at my make-up. Frances runs, runs to meet me from over a hill. Patrick is away at boarding school; we will have to write to him as soon as we can.

I tell them we have decided to go away. We cannot go on living like this. 'We are going to try and get to a safe place, and then we will send for you. Toni will look after you.' Frances understands, and just for a moment her eyes redden, then she controls herself. Keith asks, 'How long before you send for us?'

'We don't know. Not too long. As soon as we can.'

'A week?'

'Maybe two or even three. But as quickly as we can.'

A blue van stands on the road at the top of the hill, just outside the park. I noticed it in another place when I was coming. I am uneasy, it is time to go.

Toni looks at me with dark eyes. 'Are you frightened?'

'Terrified!' But I smile to pretend to her that I am not serious. She is not deceived.

I walk away, turning to wave, to take a last look. Toni has her arms around Keith. If we are caught it will be years and years before we see them again. They will be grown, and strange. [...]

From the moment I get in, I am afraid.

That cliché about the icy hand of fear – fear is not an icy hand, it is a burning acid that flows through every vein.

I have never in my life known such agonizing fear, a fear that does not decrease but eats into me hour after hour. Why such fear? There is now too much to lose. Rusty has broken his house-arrest order by leaving home after 6.30 p.m., and the banning order that confines him to Johannesburg; two more charges to add to those they have framed already. His bail will certainly be cancelled. I have not been charged. For me first ninety days, then charges, then a trial. We have staked too much.

All these years we have known fear, all that long time of trouble and tension, of meeting people you could not meet and doing things you were prohibited from doing; the years of raids, of listening for cars at night, anticipating arrests; the time of the emergency with one awful week of mounting tension and crisis; the years of concealed discussions, of watching who may be following, of calculated risks. Fear, yes, but not this kind of fear. Fear when you are in control of yourself and of a situation, when you act deliberately and for a positive purpose. A constructive fear, not this crawling, miserable fear that turns my insides to liquid – the fear of someone who is running away. To be caught doing something worthwhile is one thing, and you have pride and self-respect, and defend your actions, like the Rivonia men. But to be caught for nothing, for running away – I am completely and totally the victim of this abject, nightmare fear.

We have left the lights of Johannesburg and are out on the dark road. It is not so bad when there is no other traffic, but each time we see the headlights of a car far away coming towards us, or even worse, overtaking us from behind, each time the acid fear; I cringe, I close my eyes.

Yet we are not stopped. The car lights appear behind, come nearer and brighter, glare into our car, swerve out and pass, and the rear lights flow red and small in the distance. We go on and on, passing small towns. [...]

And now we hit the road again. Our headlights steady, cease shooting up and down cutting the night at odd angles. The lights behind us have all disappeared. We are the only ones awake in this dark corner. We are nearly at the place where we will leave the road and start walking.

McClipper is driving slowly, looking carefully along the side of the road. He has driven a stake into the soil just off the road to mark the place. In this thick darkness it is difficult to see, but he knows more or less how far down the road it is; and finds it.

As I get out of the car, the tide of corroding fear subsides although I cannot wait to get away from the road and into the concealing bush.

'Now we must walk,' says McClipper. He leaves the boy, his nephew, to sleep in the car. 'The time is right,' he says. Midnight. About seven miles to the border, at least two hours of walking. We will reach the border between two and four. And when we have crossed, how far to Lobatsi? McClipper is vague. 'Oh, three, four miles, a little more. You have a long hard walk ahead.'

He adds: 'I will go half-way to the border with you, then you will go on without me. I can't walk as far as the border and all the way back to the car. Arthritis. My legs.' He pulls his trousers to show us bandages on his legs.

In spite of the arthritis, he sets off with a long stride and light step. I walk behind him with two water bottles slung across my shoulders, and behind me walks Rusty with two canvas airline bags containing a few clothes. In the car I had changed into slacks and walking shoes, and had abandoned high-heeled shoes and some food Rusty had packed.

It is a night of absolute darkness, completely without sound: no moon, and few stars. We walk in this blackness and silence over level ground, through rough grass and among the small twisted trees of the northern Transvaal. McClipper walks easily but I must hurry to keep up with him – his stride is much longer than mine. I do not mind, I am released at last from that cringing terror. I feel in command of myself again and a return to my private belief, temporarily lost, that I can face up to any situation. I am in control.

From time to time we appear to be on some kind of track that deteriorates from hard earth to thick dry sand. It holds the feet, you must work at walking. Sometimes McClipper stops dead, holds up a hand for us to stop, and listens, listens. We listen too, straining to hear what holds him. There is no sound in this lifeless country. It is strange, there are no sounds of insects. The veld at night is always alive, there are always the clicks and rustles of birds or tiny creatures. Not here. No life, even in the trees, even in the grass. I have never known such a completely silent, dead and black countryside.

Then a dog begins barking; we must be near an African village, but we can see nothing. He barks and barks, and as we walk silently by lunges at us with ferocious teeth. Fear of the dog, but a greater fear that his bark will wake someone. We have been warned: don't talk, sound carries far at night in the countryside; don't strike a light, it can be seen for miles, police patrols watch out for lights; don't go near villages, some of the Africans are not to be trusted, they are in the pay of the police; the border patrols use dogs and binoculars; be over the border while it is still dark.

After an hour of steady walking, McClipper says we have reached the point where he will turn back. Whispering, he shows us the general direction we must take to reach the border fence, about another hour's walking away. As we stand with him, far and faint a cock crows in the darkness, then another. McClipper says suddenly, 'You hear that cockcrow over there?' 'Yes.' 'And that one over there?' 'Yes.' If you follow a line that runs between those two cockcrows, you will be going the right way.'

How do you walk between the remembered sound of cockcrows? We have tried to take some sort of sighting of the general direction on a few stars that are now visible, all that can be seen in the intensely black night. There is no more track; nothing is visible in this difficult country in such complete darkness. Sometimes it is heavy sand that drags at our feet, pulling us down at each step; then fields of ploughed earth, waves of churned-up, broken ground over which we climb and stumble, rise and sink. The bushes with their long stiletto thorns are a constant hazard; they are dark patches that cannot be identified until you have walked into them, then they stab at hands and legs, pierce clothes, entangle everything. You must tear yourself out of these thorn traps, they are like hooks that try to hold you. The ground falls away into holes, ankle-twisting pits into which we fall.

The time for reaching the border has passed. The fence is a mirage, a ghost that leaps into sight always a little ahead, then dissolves into nothing as we approach. How many times I have seen that fence, and each time a few more steps and it becomes a bush, an entanglement of thorns, a twisted tree. We change course, thinking that perhaps we are walking parallel to the border. When the ground clears of scrub, against the stars there is a distant hill made visible by the faint glow of reflected light in the sky beyond it. Surely that is Lobatsi – there is no other town anywhere near. So we walk towards the glow in the sky, hour after hour we see it beyond a hill. The hill dissolves, becomes another one, remote and unreachable; the glow remains beyond us, and there is no border.

Suddenly Rusty says: 'A glow like that in the sky, visible from such a distance – Lobatsi is too small. It must be Mafeking.' Have we really been walking for hours in the wrong direction, *back* towards Mafeking? We change direction again, turn away from the trap of the light reflected in the sky.

What time is it? It is too dark to see a watch. We are exhausted and stop to drink water and rest. I thought I could walk any distance, but my limbs are not prepared to take me. One leg has become painful and very stiff; it does not respond properly. The ground is very cold and after we have rested I have the greatest difficulty in walking again. Still the darkness and silence, intense and complete.

We light a small torch only once, to hold it to a compass, and from this we try to assess the direction we must take. Although we try to conceal the light, we are afraid to light it again; even a small glow is visible from afar.

We are without direction, floundering hopelessly in this hostile, stony country where night is a silent curtain. Perhaps we have walked in a circle. The stars have moved down the sky, we have abandoned them for they did not lead us to the border. When it gets light, Rusty says … what point in carrying on? Shall we wait until dawn? Barren, cold ground with no insect-life, where only the sour wind and sharp dry grass survives. I can't rest, I must keep on walking, for if we stop for long I will not be able to stand up again.

I have fallen more than once. The ground falls away into holes again. Rusty stumbles into one like a pit, up to his waist. We'll break a leg or ankle, he says, this is useless. For the third time we try to stop and rest, for the third time I know that rest is fatal. It is hopeless to continue, but impossible to stop. Surely it must be time for dawn to come. Long night that never ends. Miserable country of holes and dagger-thorns.

At last there is an awareness of change; not so much that the sky lightens, as that darkness has diminished. Then an end to stars, and greyness spreads over the sky to reveal a desolate flat plain, a vast and empty expanse of land, deathly grey and dry after three years of continuous drought. No border fence; no huts, paths, people, nor any sign of life; nothing but straggling dead bushes, their thorns long and bleached; and the cold persistent wind that has blown across thousands of miles of desert to this bleak place.

And we know now that we are hopelessly lost; we have walked through the night and do not know where we are, nor in what direction to reset our course. Somewhere out of sight are men with Alsatians, standing where the land is higher, and scanning the countryside through binoculars. I am not afraid any more, only miserable beyond words at risking so much and coming so far to end up in this wind-scourged, drought-bitter land.

Light, but no sun. We go on walking and after a while find a sandy track, which must lead somewhere; walk along it for a while until Rusty says – look – tyre-marks; this must be a patrol road. In a panic, we quickly walk away from it, look for cover, but find nothing; humps in the ground flatten as we approach, what appear to be bushes dissolve into a thin tracery of twigs. As we search for a place to hide, we see some huts on the horizon. They appear to be part of a farm, which is probably white-owned; the buildings seem more substantial that those of a kraal, so we skirt around them and away. Farther on is an African kraal. No sign of life. We sit down and wait. After some time a man emerges and Rusty approaches him. They walk back towards me. He ways he will show us the way to the border: it is not far, he says, the fence is over there. He is surly, unfriendly. Can we trust him? We walk quickly for about ten minutes, the land dips, and there, clearly visible, almost beyond belief, is the border fence, a double line of barbed wire with a strip of no man's land in between, at the base of two small hills. So we were less than a mile away. We almost run the last few hundred yards; we have thanked our taciturn guide and given him some money. Then we are over the first fence, and over the second and in Bechuanaland.

Helen Suzman

H elen Gavronsky was born on 7 November 1917 in Germiston, near Johannesburg. Of Jewish descent, she is one of South Africa's most famous fighters for human rights. She and her husband, Mosie Suzman, a physician, had three children. Helen entered Parliament in 1953 as the United Party member for the Johannesburg constituency of Houghton, which she represented for the next 36 years. Frustrated at the UP's failure to formulate liberal policies on race, she was one of the MPs who broke away from the party in 1959 to form the Progressive Party. She remained that party's sole (but always feisty) representative in Parliament for 13 years.

Helen Suzman has been internationally acclaimed for her uncompromising stand on human rights, her unremitting campaigns for humane treatment of prisoners, and her sustained and often acerbic opposition to apartheid. As the media and the courts were increasingly reduced to complicit silence by the state, she used Parliament to draw the country's attention to the torture of activists and their disappearance or death in detention. She retired from active politics in 1989. Her portrait (removed soon after the 1994 elections, along with all apartheid-era portraits) was re-hung in Parliament in June 2000. The extent to which she was a thorn in Nationalist government flesh is illustrated by a comment by the former Speaker in the House, Louis le Grange. Ostensibly expressing his regret at being unable to attend the re-unveiling of the Suzman portrait, he reportedly said: 'You can imagine my disappointment that I did not witness your hanging' (*Mail & Guardian*, 23–29 June 2000: 6).

The extract from her autobiography, ***In No Uncertain Terms: Memoirs*** (1993), gives an eyewitness account of the assassination of Prime Minister H.F. Verwoerd in Parliament in 1966.

Confronting Verwoerd, Vorster and Botha

During the years that I was the lone Prog MP, two Prime Ministers held office: Dr Hendrik Verwoerd, who was Minister of Native Affairs and then Prime Minister from 1958 to 1966; and Balthazar John Vorster, Minister of Justice and then Prime Minister from 1966 to 1978. I also had the dubious honour of coping with P.W. Botha, Minister of Coloured Affairs and of Defence before he became Prime Minister from 1978 to 1983 and State President from 1983 until 1989.

Verwoerd, Vorster and Botha were as nasty a trio as you could encounter in your worst nightmares. They were ably assisted by a posse of equally unpleasant Ministers of Bantu Administration and of Police and Justice. Special mention in this regard must go to M.C. Botha and Jimmy Kruger.

Dr Verwoerd was an extraordinary man. He was not South African by birth, but came to the country with his Dutch parents when he was two years old, and lived his life as a devoted Afrikaner. He harboured a deep conviction that he had a divine mission to maintain White civilisation on the southern tip of the Black continent of Africa.

I have to admit Verwoerd was the only man who has ever scared me stiff, and I suspect he had much the same effect on his own caucus and on the United Party, then the official opposition. Here was a man who could stand up in Parliament and talk for more than two hours without a note, building up an argument so convincingly that one sat there nodding one's head like a zombie, until one realised that his entire argument was built on a false premise, for example, that there were no urbanised Blacks, that they all belonged in their ethnic areas and that was where they must exercise their political rights. In practice, the policy aimed at 'freezing' the number of Blacks living in the urban areas, restricting further migration from the rural areas and utilising only migrant Black labour in the urban areas. To this was added Verwoerd's ruthless implementation of forced removals – one of the most appalling aspects of apartheid. It involved the forcible uprooting and 'resettlement' of Black communities into the Native Reserves or Bantustans. The policy aimed *inter alia* at eliminating the so-called 'Black spots'. These were usually rural lands which had been acquired by Black tribes through purchases from White farmers before the Land Act of 1913 (extended in 1936), which severely restricted the right of Blacks to acquire land.

In some cases 'Black spots' consisted of land granted by the government of the day in recognition of services rendered, such as that given by the colonial government of Queen Victoria to the Mfengu people of Tsitsikama in the eastern Cape, for their support of the White settlers during the Sixth Border War (1834) against other Black inhabitants. This gesture of gratitude did not prevent the removal at gunpoint of the Mfengu people some 143 years later, from their fertile lands to an area more than 250 miles away – land which could not provide for them even at subsistence level. (Their own land was sold to White farmers for an average of R229 per hectare. Today the land is valued at R5000 per hectare and the Mfengu are engaged in a determined fight to regain their ancestral home through appeals to the government and by court action. They may well succeed in the 'New South Africa'.)

Verwoerd's Grand Apartheid scheme included the relocation of urban Black townships into other urban areas already so designated, such as the removal of the Sophiatown community to Meadowlands in Soweto. The endorsement out, or expulsion of 'illegal' Black town-dwellers, was yet another part of this heinous scheme.

The Native Reserves into which removals took place were already heavily overpopulated and overstocked with cattle and other livestock. There was scant preparation for the reception of people 'resettled' in those distant areas: often only the erection of row upon row of tin latrines on small demarcated plots. Their former homes, schools and churches were demolished and livestock disposed of with minimal compensation. Entire communities, together with their meagre possessions, were loaded on to trucks under the supervision of armed police and transported many miles into the Reserves.

From the middle of the seventies Dr Verwoerd's Grand Apartheid scheme had been partially accomplished, as four of the ten Bantustans became 'independent': Transkei, Bophuthatswana, Venda and Ciskei (known as the TBVC states). Of course they were independent in name only. They relied on the Republic of South Africa for the major part of their revenue, so-called 'foreign aid', and they were dependent on the earnings of migrant workers in the Republic. Moreover they were recognised as independent states only by each other and by South Africa. Six Bantustans remained as self-governing areas.

I had a number of sharp exchanges with Verwoerd when he was Minister of Native Affairs as well as when he became Prime Minister in September 1958. That year he made his famous prediction about the future of Blacks in so-called White South Africa, saying that from 1978 Black migration to the cities would be reversed and Blacks would be returning to the by then prosperous homelands: 'The rising graph (of migration into the cities) will continue to rise until the year 1978 and then it will fall.' Five years later I challenged Verwoerd with a more realistic assessment of the consequences of his predictions, asking

> If thousands of Blacks went streaming back to the Bantustans, leaving White farmers deprived of their labour force with fields and livestock untended, and mine owners with their empty compounds and stationary shaft wheels; and factory owners with their silent, motionless, machinery, whether all the guns of the Defence Force would not be used to stop these people, and to turn them back into the White Republic of South Africa so that they once again could dig our gold, plough our fields and man our factories, as they have always done, and as they always will do.

To which Cas Greyling (National Party MP for Ventersdorp) replied: 'That is her death knell that has tolled. The speech of the Honourable Member of Houghton is a picture that could only be conjured up by a lunatic.'

Verwoerd also informed Parliament that the Afrikaner would rather be poor and White than rich and mixed. I was sorry he was not alive to witness how wrong he was when the boycotts by Black customers in Boksburg and Carletonville took place in 1980 after the far-right Conservative Party tried to put the clock back and reintroduce apartheid in those small mining towns.

Threatened with bankruptcy, the White shopkeepers soon accepted the repeal of the Separate Amenities Act, Verwoerd's assessment notwithstanding.

When, in 1966, Verwoerd spoke sympathetically about Ian Smith's Unilateral Declaration of Independence in Rhodesia (to which he never gave *de jure* recognition), I said that the less we in South Africa had to do with those rebels, the better. Verwoerd then told me he had written me off. I retorted, 'And the whole world has written *you* off.'

In 1960 there was an attempted assassination of Verwoerd at the Witwatersrand Agricultural Show at Milner Park in Johannesburg. An English-speaking South African named David Pratt shot Verwoerd at point-blank range as he stood on the podium after making a speech. Pratt sent a .22 bullet through Verwoerd's face, but did not succeed in killing him. Verwoerd's burly bodyguard fainted. (Pratt, who was charged with attempted murder, but never stood trial, was sent to a mental institution. The following year he committed suicide.)

Verwoerd was taken to hospital and returned to Parliament less than two months later, when he proceeded to give one of his customary lengthy speeches, minus notes. A friend who was sitting in the Visitors' Gallery during this *tour de force* said to me afterwards, 'Good God – didn't that bullet do anything to Verwoerd?' 'Sure,' I replied. 'It cleared his sinuses.'

Verwoerd made one of his first public appearances after the attempted assassination at the fiftieth anniversary celebrations of Union on 31 May 1960 in Bloemfontein. He was obviously more convinced than ever that divine guidance was with him, a sentiment not shared by the dove which he tossed into the air crying, 'There goes a symbol of South Africa's peace and prosperity.'

The astute bird dropped like a stone.

On 6 September 1966, the House assembled to discuss the Prime Minister's portfolio. We were anticipating a long and busy afternoon as Verwoerd always talked at length on such occasions. In the event, the afternoon session ended abruptly.

The bells were ringing, as they do at a quarter past two every working day in the South African Parliament (except on Fridays when they ring at ten a.m.), when we all trooped in to take our seats. I sat down on my front bench, and a messenger handed me a letter, which I began to read. The Prime Minister came in and took his seat. Suddenly I heard a strangled cry and looked across the aisle of the House, only a few yards from my seat, where a small group had crowded around the Prime Minister's desk.

'Good Lord, what's happened?' I asked my neighbour on the next bench, a member of the National Party, who replied excitedly, 'Didn't you see that man attack the Prime Minister?'

I wondered for a moment whether one of the members of the United Party had gone crazy, leaped across the floor and punched Verwoerd on the nose. I then heard another strangled cry, and as the group opened out I saw somebody being dragged along the aisle of the House by a few Members. It was the man who had attacked the Prime Minister, not an MP but a parliamentary messenger. Before my astonished eyes he was dumped opposite my desk, while Members pulled at his clothes and pummelled him. After another scuffle, he was dragged out and presumably handed over to the police in the Lobby of Parliament.

While I was watching all this with utter amazement, down the aisle of the House from the direction of the Prime Minister's desk dashed the Minister of Defence, P.W. Botha, arms flailing and eyes bulging. He stopped opposite me, shook his finger at me and yelled in Afrikaans, 'It's you who did this. It's all you liberals. You incite people. Now we will get you. We will get the lot of you.' And he blundered out of the House. I was astounded at this attack and said to the Members on either side of me, 'Good God, did you hear that?' Those on the right of me, who were United Party members said, 'Yes, what a thing to say.'

One of the MPs went to the Speaker's dais (the Speaker came in only after the Members were seated and the bells had stopped ringing) and announced, 'The Prime Minister has been seriously injured. Will you all kindly vacate the Chamber?' Soon afterwards the Prime Minister was rushed to hospital by ambulance.

When I went out into the Lobby with everybody else, I was beside myself with rage at Botha's accusation and the threat implicit in what he had said. I decided I could not let it go unchallenged. I went to see R.J. McFarlane, the Secretary of Parliament, who was a sympathetic official, always helpful and responsive. I told him of Botha's attack on me. He took a strong view of the matter and said, 'Well, my goodness me, one can't threaten a Member of Parliament the way he threatened you.' We agreed that he would report it to the Speaker.

By then we knew that Verwoerd was dead. Parliament was adjourned for the day. The following morning, I received a message to go at once to see the Speaker. On my arrival in Speaker Klopper's chambers, I found Botha there as well.

The Speaker turned to Botha, and said very sternly, 'Well, Mr Botha?'

Botha glared at me and growled, 'In terms of the rules of the House, I apologise.'

I lost my temper on hearing what I regarded as the most ungracious apology imaginable. I turned to the Speaker and asked, 'Do you expect me to accept an apology like that?'

The Speaker was distressed and said, 'Oh, please, calm down. We're all in such a nervous state. I do ask you to accept this apology. It would be very bad if we had any more scenes in Parliament.'

I turned to Botha, 'How dare you talk to me the way you did?'

'What did you expect?' he replied. 'There was my leader dying at my feet.'

'I'll tell you what I expect,' I said. 'I expect you to control yourself. You're the man behind the guns in South Africa. You're the Minister of Defence. It would be a sad day for all of us if you can't control yourself.'

He got up in a rage and said to the Speaker, 'Well, I've apologised and she can take it or leave it.' He flounced out of the room.

I turned to the Speaker again, 'Now, do you really expect me to accept that apology?'

'Well,' he said, 'I know he did the wrong thing. And he didn't apologise properly. But I do ask you to accept it in view of the circumstances and particularly as I myself want you to do so.'

Had I taken the matter further, in terms of the rules of the House, I would have had to use the first opportunity to move that a parliamentary select committee be set up to enquire into Botha's accusation and threats. That opportunity would have been immediately after the expressions of condolence by members of the different political parties.

The Speaker had always been more than fair to me, and I therefore felt I had a certain obligation not to put him through this ordeal. I promised to let him know and left his office.

I then consulted my two advisers in Cape Town: Colin Eglin (who had taken over the leadership of the party) and Harry Lawrence. Both advised strongly that I accept Botha's apology, however unsatisfactory. I sent a note to the Speaker: 'In deference to your wishes, and because of the unfortunate circumstances surrounding this whole incident, I have decided to accept Mr Botha's very unsatisfactory apology.' Within about ten minutes, the Chief Whip of the National Party, J.E. Potgieter, appeared in my office and said, 'I want to tell you we are very sorry about Mr Botha's outburst and we wish to thank you for not taking the matter any further.'

Although I felt better after Potgieter's visit, I vowed never again to speak to Botha on any personal basis; only on official business would I have anything to do with him. And from that day I never greeted him, though I had much to say to him across the floor in Parliament, especially after he became Prime Minister in 1978.

Patricia Nxumalo

Like Jane Hoko and Selestina Ngubane, whose stories are to be found in a later section of this book, Patricia Nxumalo was a student in an adult literacy class in the early 1980s. Caroline Kerfoot, the editor of **We Came to Town** (1985), a compilation of literacy students' life-writing, says that many of the stories were first written or taped, then discussed in class and rewritten until the writer felt happy with the result.

Patricia Nxumalo, whose story is reproduced here in full, describes her experience of forced removal and poverty in the late 1960s – experiences that were shared by millions of South Africans.

Moving Homes

We lived in a small place belonging to the Mission. It was nice. We liked it. The land was fertile. You could plant practically anything from a carrot to a head-sized cabbage. We had cattle, goats, hens and some had sheep. We grew up there and loved the place.

Then came 1968. We were moved to a place called Limehill. There were no houses provided. We were dumped into tents – dads, mums, children and furniture, each family into one tent. The place itself was like a desert. People died like flies. The water was horrible.

That is what anyone being moved should expect. No care is taken whether you are old, widowed or blind.

You have to start from scratch.

The People Rise Up

1970 to 1979

By 1972, the South African Institute of Race Relations estimated that at least 1 820 000 Africans had been forced to leave their homes, while a further 600 000 coloured, Indian and Chinese (and 40 000 white) people were moved in terms of the Group Areas Act. The 1970s saw the final phase of the government's policy of outright denial of citizenship to Africans in South Africa by forcing them to become 'citizens' of ethnically exclusive 'independent homelands', run by chiefs and headmen whose appointment had to be approved by the apartheid government. The Transkei led the way, being granted independence in 1976, followed by Bophuthatswana (1977), Venda (1979) and the Ciskei (1981). Others, like KwaZulu (1977) and Lebowa, obtained self-government but refused to consider 'independence'. Significantly, with the exception of QwaQwa, none of these bantustans comprised a single block of land; they consisted of numerous pockets of black states within a largely white South Africa, serving as convenient labour reserves. Well over half their economically active men worked as migrants in South Africa.

None of the bantustans were recognised internationally as sovereign states; indeed, all required substantial hand-outs from Pretoria. These 'independent homelands' enabled the creation of a powerful black élite, whose regimes were notorious for corruption and whose territories were generally overpopulated and unsustainable rural slums.

Despite its apparent successes regarding the creation of an all-white South Africa, in the 1970s the apartheid regime faced mounting adversity. For years it had been protected from hostility from the north by a ring of buffer states controlled by whites, but as independence from Portugal loomed in Angola and Mozambique (obtained in 1975), it became increasingly anxious about military threats from exiles and from its neighbours. The ANC and its Namibian ally, the South West African People's Organisation (SWAPO), had opened military bases in Angola in 1976. The South African government thus ignored the International Court of Justice's 1971 ruling that its occupation of South West

Africa (later Namibia) was illegal and, between 1973 and 1978, it authorised numerous cross-border raids by the Defence Force in Namibia and Angola. In 1977, the UN imposed a compulsory arms embargo against South Africa. Finally accepting the inevitable, in 1978 South Africa acceded to the plan for Namibia's transition to independence – though it continued to attack SWAPO bases in Angola.

However, trouble was brewing within South Africa's borders too. Whereas in the 1960s there had been minimal union activity owing to state repression, 1973 saw the re-emergence of independent trade unions, and between 1972 and 1974 South Africa was rocked by a wave of violent strikes by black workers that hit the economy hard. Moreover, in 1976, MK resumed operations inside South Africa.

Many commentators have identified 1976 as the beginning of the end for the apartheid regime: this was the year in which the Soweto riots erupted. Afrikaners had apparently failed to learn from their own history that attempts to force a language and culture on people would inevitably provoke the opposite effect. Early in the twentieth century, the British High Commissioner had embarked on a policy of 'Anglicisation', compelling schools to use English as the principal medium of instruction. The outrage felt by the Boers helped to fuel developing Afrikaner nationalism. However, disregarding the lessons of history, in 1976 the Afrikaner Nationalist government ruled that Afrikaans should be used on an equal basis with English as the medium of instruction in state schools for Africans. This was the last straw – on top of the inferior system of 'Bantu education' and the injustices and deprivations of apartheid – that sparked the Soweto uprising. On 16 June 1976, police opened fire on marching schoolchildren. Thirteen-year-old Hector Petersen was the first fatality. Rioting, boycotts and school stay-aways rapidly spread to more than 200 townships and cities across the country over the next 15 months. More than 600 protesters and bystanders were killed by police while thousands streamed into exile, seeking military training. In 1977, Steve Biko (who had not been formally charged with any crime) was murdered in detention, and 17 organisations (including the Christian Institute) were banned, along with three newspapers.

The tide of unrest caused a clamour of international calls for economic sanctions and cultural and sports boycotts. Winnie Mandela's much-publicised banishment to Brandfort in 1977 was eclipsed by international condemnation of Steve Biko's death. In addition to attempts to muzzle the media, the government embarked on a propaganda programme. Corruption within the apartheid state's ranks began to emerge when, in 1978, the Information Scandal (a multi-million rands attempt to whitewash South Africa's policies both at home and overseas) broke. B.J. Vorster was forced to resign and P.W. Botha became Prime Minister. By the late 1970s, some Afrikaner leaders had tentatively retracted their commitment to apartheid, largely because the co-optation of some blacks (especially coloureds and Indians) was seen as necessary for the continued maintenance of white supremacy. Moreover, in an attempt to appease black workers, unions for blacks were legalised in 1979. Since gross abuses continued, and since many union organisers, black and white, still suffered detention and banning, from the outset unions were as much concerned with larger political issues as with labour-related matters.

Bessie Head

Bessie Amelia Emery was born on 6 July 1937 in the Pietermaritzburg Mental Hospital. Her white mother had been committed while she was pregnant, apparently because she had demonstrated her 'insanity' by sleeping with a black man. Bessie was raised in Pietermaritzburg by a foster mother, Nellie Heathcote, with whom she lived until the age of 13, after which she was removed and sent to St Monica's Home (an Anglican mission school for coloured girls) in Durban. She taught for four years and then worked briefly in Johannesburg for the *Golden City Post*. In 1962 she married journalist Harold Head, with whom she had a son, but the relationship foundered. Charged with subversive activities for assisting in the publication of a pamphlet that was subsequently banned, Bessie's application for a passport was refused and, in March 1964, she left South Africa for Botswana on a one-way exit permit. She remained there with the status of refugee for 15 years before gaining citizenship in 1979. Her struggles to maintain mental and emotional equilibrium were not always successful. She died in Serowe, Botswana on 17 April 1986, aged 49.

Bessie Head published three novels, *When Rain Clouds Gather* (1969), *Maru* (1971) and the semi-autobiographical account of mental breakdown, *A Question of Power* (1973), as well as a collection of short stories and two volumes of social history. Craig Mac-Kenzie has edited a collection of her autobiographical writings entitled *A Woman Alone* (1990). The letters printed below come from **A Gesture of Belonging: Letters from Bessie Head, 1965–1979**, the posthumous publication of her correspondence to her friend, Randolphe Vigne. In this extract she refers to yet another mental breakdown, which she experienced in 1971.

P. O. Box 15, Serowe
29 June 1971

Dear Randolph,

I've just got home. I was locked up in a loony bin for nearly 3 months. Howard is alright.

The truth is I'd lived in a sort of nightmare here for a long time. By end of 1970 I was so broken I could hardly walk. I broke down and poured out the torture in incoherent fashion. I got locked up. At first I just felt relief to seem to have thrown off the horrors that haunted me. But I broke my life here. I am sorting out what to do as the next best thing. I have a little money to keep me going. Howard is alright. Remember I kept on asking you to take care of him? It was that nightmare life. It went on and on with no end and it stemmed from the soul and others were involved. You said not to come to England. I am not sure what to do.

Bessie

P. O. Box 15, Serowe
15 July 1971

Dear Randolph,

Thank you very much for your short note. Please do not worry about my coming to England. For one thing I am too broken down to make the move. For another I feel I have to get to grips with my situation alone. There was a time I used to write panic-stricken letters but I am well aware of one theme to the breakdown. The underlying part was death. The things I said and did at the time were a kind of final howl. They were so bad that I cannot repeat them.

Events were never normal here and I was entirely unprepared for what opened up inside me over a long period – a depth of evil without a name and a height of goodness without a name. The least you get from those good books is platitudes, without fire. People simply want to believe in an infinite goodness without examining the basic ingredients of the soul. I was unfortunate enough to do so and went insane. It is a horrible world of torture and very dangerous. I can't stand pressure over a long period and now it is hard to turn the accusing finger of destiny towards myself, that I was living hell itself and did not know or perhaps I only wanted to accept heaven, without pain. Haven't people done it for centuries and then slaughtered each other? Don't they say in South Africa that they are Christians?

Randolph, I did have a choice. What would have happened? I was not well. I was tortured beyond endurance. For one brief moment I threw myself on the ground and said: 'God, help me.' Then I made an error. In the same breath I said: 'Which God?' As though, subconsciously I had not come to the end of the road yet. That question, the pause and looking over my shoulder, unhinged my mind which was already over-burdened with suffering. I wanted to throw everything overboard in one violent breath, which I did. No one followed what I was saying. It was all an internal torment belonging to me alone. In the confusion I opened up a wide radius of pain for other people.

The loony bin freed me for a brief while from a deep over-hanging sense of evil, as though I had abruptly shaken off the devil, but I am lost in a sorrow too deep for words. When I look back, as I am free to do now, there was a storm behind that gave me no peace. Why did it happen like that? Did I really have to learn so much? Because I sit with the weight of it – don't grab, don't love, don't hate, don't live, don't, don't, don't. I must have been an unusually stupid person to have so many bombs thrown at me.

A beautiful woman looked after Howard while I was in the loony bin. I was talking to her the other day. She told me that a strain, endured over a long period, blows one's personality to bits. She said she felt like that when she left Rhodesia and came to Botswana. Not so long ago we used to share spices from my garden and cookery recipes. It seemed like it was centuries ago and things I would not have thought over, careless remarks about children seem like mountains of information I know nothing about. That's how bad it is at present Randolph. I could not go to England in a state like this. There is only one human nobility left in me. I am not afraid to die.

As ever,
Bessie

P.O. Box 15, Serowe
13 August 1971

Dear Randolph,

Thanks so much for your letters. I'm not as mad and depressed as the last letter I wrote to you. At least I'm standing up on very shaky legs.

God knows how I wish I could go away somewhere. It's just not that easily done, when you have no travel documents and I have been in touch with United Nations for years, especially while living in Francistown. That song: I have to go away has been going on for years and years because all the wrong things were happening. Half of it was one man, then another man, then another man and weird versions of love in the air, accompanied by abnormal sights. *Maru* gives a good insight into the situation. I keep on looking back along the road I've travelled and seem to see no alternative to the disaster, as though it were something I had to go through with, and end. I am only crying about the people who got hurt because it was not so bad when I kept silent but once I started speaking, I said both vile and violent things because I could not endure any more torture. It is what I said that so sickens me. You know, very few people understand deep horror, fanatical possessiveness, the extremes of emotion, a kind of battle where evil is used to outwit the enemy; or if not outwit – then to sever memories. I eventually found myself pulled right down to that level. The terrible thing is that I did it all by myself when I was ill in health. No standards of nobility remained. You wouldn't understand emotional involvement like that because you refer to your better judgement but now I question love and am deeply afraid of it because its other face is evil.

You can come up against a sort of love so vehement and cruel that it is hardly fit for human society. You can find people glued to you like cement and they won't let go and the links were not made now, but centuries ago. The surprise was to pick up those links in a god-forsaken country like Botswana. Everything was here, the past and the future. I was struggling to destroy the past, knowing that it had no place in the future.

Randolph, I deeply value your care and affection and concern for me. Please don't let go of me. There is one thing I can say for myself. I have survived many impossible situations, maybe this is the worst, but I should see my way out of it too because of Howard, for one thing, and because I have learnt so much. It is like saying that really bad experiences create a new perfection. I wouldn't have known the depths of feeling if I had not been dragged down to them and disliked them. I think there is something wrong with superficial goodness and most people are protected by that. I was not allowed that covering and if in the future I say: I can harm no one, I can do no wrong – it is only because of experience, which was real in its way.

I am writing a little and this letter is very much taken from my present themes of thought – that seeing and feeling evil was of value to me, for the future.

You know, the breakdown so much involved Pat that his wife was very nervous about my staying here. I talked to her and she was afraid I would break down again. I hit one of his teachers. I have a house just outside the school fence and things aren't what they were before the crack up. I had lots of friendly people I knew. It was like approaching them and simply crying for help. 'Please take away the nightmare.' A lunatic does not do it the right way but the nightmare lasted for more than three years.

I wish like you say that I could leave Botswana. I don't have that much money. I also wanted to say that the war that was going on was not over B. Head, the living woman, but over the soul and its past wealth. B. Head, the living woman, had little opportunity or occasion to create any beauty, such as I saw behind me, where love was a big flare that lit up the skies and piled up great wealth (that is if you take it that the soul has a long history behind it). I seemed to do little but be swayed this way and that by internal storms and a fierce pull and tug. There was a terrible and persistent theme of obscenity, I think mainly to break me down. I fought it for a long time and what came out over Christmas was the obscenity. What I said then would have made your hair stand on end. It was thought that I was suffering from a form of insanity not yet known on earth but then people know very little about the soul. I knew nothing until I went right through the mill and now I wonder if some years of suffering pay for centuries of hell and that it was well worth it.

Liz Van Rensburg told me she had written you an angry letter asking you to do something about my situation as they thought nothing could cure me. I think it was unease at having me around here, that caused it. From my side I knew how private was the struggle I was waging and to a certain extent I don't follow the whole process that forced it out into the open. I do nothing drastic unless under pressure that gets too great for me. Years and years of my life went in peaceful solitude, of some kind or the other.

Life is a funny thing. There are no clear warnings along the way, even for the very alert and there is something strange about the soul; it won't get relaxed and free and ungrasping unless suffering is so excruciating as to be a big howl. It is at that point that it widens out and becomes beautiful. I half wish to live a little longer because just now the churning around of thought is much more pleasing to me than it was some time ago.

We were still talking about God and church when I went to the loony bin. You said: 'Be still and know that I am God.' God is such a vague proposition in the heat of living and so often when I look back on what has been said, God seems to me to be the personality of individuals. I was also just taken aback suddenly about your going to church and mentioning it because we never discussed such a thing before. Also, when I say the personality of individuals, I mean what they work out for themselves as standards of goodness and some of these standards became universal. God knows I am wild enough to look for the God of the Anglican church: 'Be Still.' I have a habit of talking to something at night, just to get above myself; but peace of heart, the stirrings of wonder, the things that made the earth and the heavens glow, all came from living people. I wish the unknown God could walk in on me sometime, unexpectedly and say: 'Here I am. Now love me.' It might have happened to me in some other age and time but I am following through something just at a point where I am down on my knees – how much is personality because it gets you through so much and when you are really broken that's when you ought to see how you will survive.

Please Randolph, whatever else happens, keep a hold on me somewhere and please keep writing.

As ever,
Bessie

Linda Fortune

The second-oldest of eight children, classified as a Cape Coloured, Linda Gangat
– extreme right, and referred to as Penny in the text – lived in the largely Afrikaans-
speaking community in District Six, Cape Town until its demolition in the 1960s under
the terms of the notorious Group Areas Act. This involved the displacement of 55 000
residents. Such 'slum clearance' as Linda describes in the extract reproduced here (from
The House in Tyne Street: Childhood Memories of District Six, 1996) typically occurred in
'non-white' areas close to exclusively white-zoned business or residential districts. Overall, the forced removals affected millions of South Africans, most of whom were sent to
sprawling ghettoes of badly built 'matchbox' houses on the outskirts of cities and towns.
It is tragically ironic that the land vacated by the razing of District Six remains, to this day,
largely undeveloped. However, resettlement has begun, with nine new semi-detached
homes having been built in early 2004.

First experience with a bulldozer

There were many people in District Six who did not even know that a word like 'bulldozer' existed. Most of them had never seen such a thing, not even on a picture.

Our first encounter with a bulldozer was terrifying. Suddenly one morning this big monstrosity rumbles and roars down Tyne Street and comes to an abrupt halt in Chapel Street.

Most of the neighbours and their children were running behind it, while other grown-ups had gathered outside their homes to see what the noise was all about. It looked as if a space ship had just landed, as if it had come to invade District Six.

'Can you people now see what's happening here? I told you the world is coming to an end!' one old lady shouted.

'No!' a man shouted back from across the street. 'The world is not coming to an end, we here in District Six are coming to an end!'

The driver of the bulldozer shouted at the people to make way for him as he had a job to do.

'I was sent to demolish the cooldrink factory,' he tried to explain. 'Isn't this it?' he asked, pointing at the old building near the Sidney Street corner. 'Now please, get out of the way! People who get in the way will get hurt!'

Slowly the people moved away.

'Oh,' an old man whom I had often seen shuffling along with his walking stick moaned, 'I'm so glad that my wife didn't live long enough to witness what is happening here today. We lived here for sixty years. Sixty years! All gone.' And slowly he walked away.

As the bulldozer rammed it, the building started falling apart bit by bit. First one wall, then a next. Then part of the roof tumbled in.

The bulldozer just kept going like a huge war tank.

My younger sister Patsy had covered her ears because the noise of bricks and timber and iron being torn apart was unbearable.

'No, go away!' she screamed. 'Stop, stop!'

But her small child's pleas were lost in the sounds of destruction.

Most people stood as if they had just received an electric shock. Speechless they gazed at the destruction in front of them. Daisy clung to Mom, petrified that our house would be next.

'I wish I had a gun like John Wayne so that I could shoot that guy on the bulldozer,' Pete hissed. Mom's reply could not be heard as another wall crashed noisily to the ground.

Boeta Bruima had his arms round Motjie Awa. She was sobbing softly, tears running down her wrinkled brown cheeks. He didn't try to console her, he just shook his head from side to side.

After a while we could hardly see. Clouds of dust rose from the rubble. Faintly one could see waterpipes and electric wires standing out like bloodless veins amongst the debris.

Not long after the bulldozer, a cartage contractor arrived to cart the demolished cooldrink factory away. And as soon as the last broken bricks and chunks of cement were taken away, another contractor arrived with a loader truck and started to dig a huge hole where the factory used to stand.

This puzzled the bystanders, and a little boy asked the driver why he was making such a big hole.

'Can't tell you,' the man answered, 'can just tell you that the next building to go will be the Rose & Crown Bar in Hanover Street.' He laughed.

'Why the Rose & Crown? It's still a smart building and people use it,' one of the regulars of the bar objected.

'Don't know why,' the driver said, 'but can everybody please move away so I can get on with my work!'

Nobody moved. Everybody went on watching. A rumour had started to go round that the Rose & Crown was going to be buried in that hole. It made the people even more upset.

One of the women who lived right next to the cooldrink factory said to the driver that leaving such a big hole open would be dangerous with all the small children around.

'Madam, it won't be long before all you people will be gone too, so don't worry about the empty hole. There won't be any children to play in it,' the driver replied, and he laughed again.

The last few months

Ron and Susan got married in July 1971, in the middle of winter. We were all dressed in thick clothing as we went into St Mary's Cathedral at the bottom end of Roeland Street, just across from the Houses of Parliament. Shirley was bridesmaid and Ron's friend Dave was best man.

After the wedding ceremony, the newly married couple, their train, the families on both sides and some guests went to the old Company Gardens in the centre of town to have the wedding photographs taken. Afterwards there was a reception at a private clubhouse in Woodstock. It was a big wedding, with about 150 guests, and it was as happy an occasion as we could have had so soon after Dad's passing away.

The wedding couple spent their honeymoon in Mossel Bay. When they returned, they moved in with Susan's mother in Kensington, near Maitland.

Within a few months Mom had lost her husband and now her oldest son had moved away. She was left with seven children to take care of in a District that was becoming more and more deserted and unrecognisable. People were leaving every week. More and more buildings were being knocked down or closed up.

We missed a man in the house. Before Dad's death Mom never went out. That had now changed. She was forced to go out. Especially after Ron left the house.

I often thought of what Mr O'Connell said when he paid his last respects to Dad: 'Alex, things are really getting bad here in District Six, lots of houses are already empty. It's a pity that you had to leave your family when they're going to need you most.'

When I came home from work one afternoon in October that year, Mom told me that she had had no option but to fill in some forms.

It reminded me that by mistake I had left my beautiful maroon fountain pen with gold trimmings and my initials engraved on the side at home that morning. I had missed it only when I got to work.

'Mom, have you perhaps seen my pen?' I asked.

She was embarrassed. The white official from the Group Areas who brought the forms to the house, she told me, saw my pen on the table and persuaded her to give it to him. 'Penny, I said I could not as it was my daughter's pen and it was a very special gift. But he said if I give him the pen he'll see to it that we get a nice house.'

'Mom, that man had no right to bribe you. I'm not going to move anywhere, and I'm going to find out who his superiors are and report him. You'll see, in the end that pen will make no difference!'

The man had clearly intimidated my mother, saying that if she did not sign the papers and move out as instructed, then he would have to make the necessary arrangements to forcibly remove us.

He needn't have told her. We knew that. We saw the government trucks every time they roared into what was still left of District Six.

'I want no more trouble, Penny. We have no choice. We don't have money for a deposit to buy a house. We have to move soon, whether we like it or not,' Mom said.

'If Dad was alive he would've put up a fight,' I insisted.

She was quiet for a while. Then she said, 'You know, I think it's perhaps better that your father is no longer with us. You know how outspoken he was and not scared of anybody. We might have had more trouble if they threw him in jail.'

So in her own way Mom did try to resist, but she was forced to accept the house that was allocated to us because of the responsibility she felt towards her children.

That night she called us all together and said that we would be leaving Tyne Street. We were moving to Hanover Park.

Time was drawing close. It had turned November and the official from the Group Areas once again came to ask if they could send a truck to remove us.

'No,' my mother said. 'Under no circumstances will we be seen leaving this place in one of your trucks. We will make our own arrangements when it is time to move.'

'When do you intend moving?' he asked.

'You and your people will have to wait till the school-going children have completed their December exams,' she said. 'What's your rush? This place is going nowhere and the ground in District Six is going to lie empty for many years to come.'

The man looked puzzled.

'Just wait and one day you'll understand what I mean!' she said.

Tension was running high in the house. The other children kept mentioning how they were going to miss their window-shopping trips, the walks on summer nights down Darling and Plein and Adderley Streets and up through the Gardens; the visits to the art gallery, the hothouse and the museum.

'What about our church?' they asked. There was no church in Hanover Park; the nearest Catholic Church was in Lansdowne.

At last the younger children finished their exams and the day arrived that one of Ron's friends came with his lorry. Everybody helped to carry the furniture out. We had to leave behind a solid embuia table because it would not fit into the new house. We also had to leave our big black Dover stove and a hall stand. We phoned Uncle Peter to collect these things.

Finally the lorry was loaded. All Ron's friends were there to go along and help carry the furniture into the house in Hanover Park.

I was the last one to leave the old house in Tyne Street. I lingered and could not get myself to walk out the front door. I went from room to room, feeling quite sick.

'Penny!' someone called.

'I'm looking for the cat,' I replied. Meanwhile I was holding Sweety, the stray cat I found after Blackie died, in my arms.

Eventually I walked down the passage and out the front door.

It was not necessary to lock the front door. The house was going to be demolished and Uncle Peter was already on his way to collect the things that were left inside. I didn't even bother to pull the door closed. Number 14 would exist no more, nor would Aspeling, Godfrey or Parkin Streets.

I started to cry. I sobbed as if someone had just died. I didn't care, I was sentimental about District Six. The place was our home, after all.

Someone, I don't even remember who, came and comforted me. She wanted to know what the matter was.

'The cat scratched me,' I said.

'It's okay, Penny,' Mrs Adams said from across the street. 'We all know how you feel because we all have one pain.'

Then a passer-by observed, 'If you remove a cat from familiar surroundings and you rub a little butter on its paws when it reaches its new destination, it will get accustomed to its new home very quickly.'

Oh, I wish it was so simple, I thought.

End

It wasn't that simple.

After twenty–five years most of the ground in the former District Six still largely lies bare. I have often thought that maybe my mother knew something we didn't know when she spoke to the Group Areas official that day.

She died in Hanover Park in March 1988. Aunty, who moved back in with us after we left District Six, died there more than ten years before her, in August 1975.

The two of them would often sit on the modern couch in the lounge of the Hanover Park house with its matching walls and carpet, so different from the old bed-sitter at number 14 Tyne Street, and wonder what had happened to everybody.

Now that apartheid has been abolished and people are free to live where they choose, we children find ourselves scattered all over the Cape Peninsula: Parow North, Hout Bay, Ottery, Mitchell's Plain, Dieprivier, Mandalay.

I am the only one fortunate enough to work on the outskirts of what used to be District Six, doing what I love best: keeping alive, not just my own but also other people's memories of the place we used to love. For in December 1994 the District Six Museum was opened in the old Central Methodist Church in Buitekant Street, and soon afterwards I was employed as education officer.

MaJele

Izibongo of Zulu girls and women

The *izibongo* of Majele, Mcasule Dube and MaMhlalise Mkhwanazi (or *izihasho*, as some scholars prefer to call the praises of ordinary people) were composed and performed in Zulu. They were recorded by Liz Gunner in a number of districts in Zululand in 1975 and 1976. They are drawn from Liz Gunner's and Mafika Gwala's anthology of Zulu poetry, *Musho: Zulu Popular Praises* (1994).

As part of an oral tradition, women's *izibongo* are communal activities and serve to reinforce a sense of community. Gunner and Gwala point out that they share many of the same features as men's praises, but that instead of the masculine war ethos, they tend to focus on other kinds of courage. The scorn they frequently show for male machismo reveals a subversive edge to the genre that is particularly well illustrated in the poems of MaMhlongo and MaMhlalise, reproduced below. For further explanation of this self-representational practice, see the introductory note to Nontsizi Mgqwetho, pages 64–65.

Gunner and Gwala (1994: 211) point out that MaJele was from Madondo in the Hlabisa district in Zululand (northern KwaZulu-Natal). She was the third wife of a chief. She had only been married a few years when she recited her *izibongo*. The switch from first person to third person (or vice versa) when referring to the same person is not uncommon in praises.

I am she who cuts across the game reserve
That no girl crosses.[1]
I am the boldest of the bold, outfacer of wizards.
Obstinate perseverer.
The nation swore at me and ate their words.
She cold shoulders kings and despises mere commoners.

Note

1. Gunner & Gwala (1994: 210) inform us that this refers to the Hluhluwe Game Reserve, which is dangerous to walk through on foot because of animals such as elephant, hippopotamus and lion.

Mcasule Dube (MaMhlongo)

When Liz Gunner recorded these praises at the Dube homestead, Sihuzu, at Ngoye on 25 March 1976, only Liz, a friend of Mcasule's and her eldest son were present (1994: 207).

I am The Wild Staff-Shaker shaken by women and men.
They say, 'They've given it to her down below they've given it to her up above'.
She passes as they're having sex those lousy privates of their mothers.
Those who remain on the earth will live long and be wealthy.
You go and ask that wretched little private parts of her mother because I myself am afraid of the ill-feeling.

I will never pass in front of your gates.
And as for you, young man
if you're talking to me to make us intimate;
there's nothing you can do to me.
(I'm going to continue)
So say I, the Wild Staff-Shaker
the caller of the shots,
of this little part, right close by.
I don't sleep on the high road, I sleep there on the little path
So say I, I am the Cats that eat the greens
I am The-Chickens flapping their wings (in applause) within the
homestead
where I chose my love.
I knelt, I pleaded,
I said, 'Truly boy, I love you,
May the love between you and me never end'.

MaMhlalise Mkhwanazi

These *izibongo* were recorded during a visit to MaMhlalise at Mtshiva, Ngoye, on 22 January 1976. Liz Gunner and Mafika Gwala (1994: 205) note that she was a widow of the late Chief Nikiza Mkhwanazi and had, after his death, become the wife of one of his brothers, Japhane Mkhwanazi. MaMhlalise lived in the crowded, semi-rural area just north of the township of KwaDlangezwa, overlooking the University of Zululand. She lived in a large homestead with her husband, an elderly co-wife and her three sons and their families. Her *izibongo*, which in her old age she did not perform very often, record her great energy and her capacity for organisation and leadership. Gunner and Gwala observe that the scorn for male machismo evidenced in her praises is a common feature of women's *izibongo*; it is often seen as 'useless promiscuity' (1994: 50).

Two years after her praises were recorded, MaMhlalise experienced great personal tragedy when, after a long dispute over access to land, a neighbouring family was burnt to death and her three sons were jailed for the deed (1994: 51).

The Basking Lizard lying in wayward abandon at her sister's,
Nomchitheka.
I am Ribs-Pressed-Me-In
I would have been a well-built girl.
(I am)-Doves-that-woke-and-pecked at the roof.
The High Greenish Grass tufts
that will one day be jumped by the clever ones.
The Mimosa Bush with thorns for keeping out
those wretched vaginas of their mothers! (a burst of laughter from the women)[1]
I am Squish on something and they say, 'She's crapped!'
But she hasn't crapped, it's her co-wife that's crapped!
The Beater of those who stand, legs apart, lazy and stiff-legged like
cooking pots.

I am The Beater of those who use corrugated iron for doors (she pauses and
    continues)
I am what kind of Bull is it
that mounts outside its own kraal
but is useless at home.[2]
Hah! What do you say to that you old Khandempemvu fellow!'[3]

Notes

1. All notes in parentheses are in the original text.
2. Gunner and Gwala point out that the reference to the 'Bull […] that mounts outside its own kraal' refers not to MaMhlalise herself, but is a criticism of a promiscuous man (1994: 50).
3. *Khandempemvu* means 'the greyheaded one' (Gunner & Gwala 1994: 204).

Maria Tholo

'Maria Tholo' is the pseudonym of a middle-class black woman from Cape Town who confided her experiences of political turmoil to a white woman. Given the unbridled tensions that characterised so many black communities of the time, and the high price paid by those branded as 'sell-outs', such anonymity was necessary. *The Diary of Maria Tholo* (1980) was adapted from tape-recorded interviews by Carol Hermer, a journalist and anthropologist, at the height of the 1976 student uprisings in South Africa. These country-wide demonstrations are generally regarded as heralding the beginning of the end of apartheid.

Maria Tholo's early life was spent in Guguletu. This township, whose name ironically translates as 'Our Pride', is a bleak, densely populated black ghetto on the outskirts of Cape Town. As was the case in all townships for blacks in 'white' South Africa, home ownership was not possible and all houses had to be rented from the relevant local authority.

As a young woman, Maria abandoned her nursing studies to marry Gus Tholo (also a pseudonym). They had two daughters. At the time of the interviews, Maria – now middle-aged – was running a crèche for children of working mothers in the Guguletu area.

Maria's Diary, Monday, December 20

We were all a bit anxious about December 16, supposedly our Black Christmas, but it turned out very quiet. People didn't know what to do, whether to celebrate or not. In this situation you never know whether you are doing the right thing. After all, what special place is one supposed to go to on an ordinary Thursday night? Even if someone tells you it's Christmas, it's not what you're used to and you can't just start celebrating for nothing.

Some youths did go around shouting 'Happy Christmas' and beating empty paraffin tins but it didn't last very long – not even the whole morning. And the students had a braai and a meeting to work out their demands and a programme for the 25th.

They have asked us all to show we're in mourning. We must all wear black. If we don't own a whole outfit, we've still got to wear something black, even a scarf. We must wear this every day until New Year and then bury it in the traditional way, like after someone dies. And we're not allowed to go to church on Christmas Day. We must all be at the graveyard instead.

I don't like this interfering with church. Our youth group left this evening for Swaziland, but up to three hours ago it looked as if they weren't going to be able to go. A group of girl students stormed into our Langa mission and demanded to know how come this group of young people could even think of amusing themselves over Christmas when everyone else was in mourning. We had to explain that the whole thing had been booked with the railways more than six months ago, before the troubles in Soweto had started, let alone in Cape Town. So they let them go but they demanded that they be back by December 26. That's impossible. They were very rude to our church leaders. These girls really have no manners.

Saturday, December 25

Not knowing whether we'd be able to go to church today, I went to last night's service. Gus stayed home. He was too scared to move from his home area. Usually the Friday service is packed but last night there were barely 20 people.

The preacher urged us to defy today's ban on churchgoing because it was anti-Christ and anti-religious and this was an opportunity to prove where one stood. I wasn't convinced. It seemed one of those occasions where one should rather wait and see.

I usually find it very difficult to wake up on Saturday, but this particular one we were all up very early. Gus, of all people, was determined to go to church. Last night when everything was fine he was too scared. Today, he was up and dressed in his suit. I tried to reason with him but he wasn't interested, wouldn't even look at me.

I hadn't heard any church bells ringing so I went outside to check around. I had to jump back into the gate as a small Morris car came tearing up our street. It was 6.30 in the morning but the car was packed with youths and they were all roaring drunk. They didn't look like students and we discovered later that the car had been stolen and they were on the run from the police as they had knocked someone down in Langa. But it gave me quite a fright.

There's a Langa High student who lives across the street and she was also up and about. I called over to her.

'What's happening today?'

'I'm going to the graveyard,' she said. 'Everyone's going to the graveyard.'

'But who are we burying?'

'Auntie, it's best for you to go and find out for yourself. Those who aren't there will be noticed. And let me tell you, I wouldn't go to church because when we come from the graveyard woe unto those we find there.'

It was time to fetch my mother but Gus wouldn't let me go.

'You're going out like that, in a suit? You'll come back with those clothes in tatters.' He went, but dressed just in a shirt and trousers. And I know he didn't go straight to Mother's because I decided to follow – and I got there first.

NY 6 was packed. People, mostly youths, all in black, were milling around. The boys wore black lumber jackets and jeans and the girls had on black skirts and t-shirts or blouses. I overheard someone comment that there were already adults and ministers at the graveyard, so why didn't everyone go. But people had been shot dead at the Soweto graveyard so I wanted to play safe and first see how things developed.

Mother was all ready for church but I managed to persuade her otherwise. I made an excuse that it was because of the weather. Gus arrived, cross with me for having walked so far alone. I could have been equally cross with him for having taken so long. He took Mother home while I popped in to warn Jeff about a rumour I'd heard that the youths were going to commandeer his kombis the next day for a beach trip. People go to the beach every Boxing Day, but this was supposed to be a special protest trip to 'whites only' Muizenberg. But he had already heard the rumour and arranged to get the vans out of Guguletu.

I thumbed a lift back with Mrs. Maphila whom I knew would be going my way. She was actually en route to Section 4 to visit a Mrs. Xubi and very grateful to have company as she didn't like the atmosphere. There was a lot of movement around. As we arrived, two of Mrs. Xubi's kids were just coming back from the graveyard, still wearing their black clothes.

I asked them about going to church. Happily, they said that at the last students' meeting it had been agreed that our church could continue with services because for us it was a normal church day, not just Christmas.

We drove back to Guguletu to give the glad tidings. We had to pass the cemetery. There were a lot of students leaving – and the riot squads just arriving. But they didn't do anything, just stood by and watched.

Some boys coming our way quickened their step as they saw us getting into the kombi.

'Excuse me, Auntie,' one asked, 'but how many people does your kombi hold?'

'Well, about eight, but I've taken the back seat out.'

'Not to worry. We are just small boys. We'd like to go to Mnandi Beach.'

Now that wasn't anywhere near but Pamela just looked at me and said, 'I don't have a choice.' Well, what could I do? I couldn't just abandon her. We were both terrified. They've never done anything when they've asked for a lift but you never know what can happen. She couldn't refuse. That's when she would have felt their fury.

They packed into the kombi and we were on our way. 'Do you want us to wait for you or just leave you there?' Pamela asked.

'No, you can just leave us.'

'You know, you boys aren't fair,' I said. 'You tell us not to celebrate, not to go on picnics and here you are going to the beach.'

'No, auntie, we are not going on a picnic. We want to see who has obeyed us. Some people are stubborn. They have gone camping in spite of the warnings.'

I looked at Pamela in dismay. Here we were bringing trouble.

'Look, we can't go all the way with you then. We can't have people seeing that we brought you.'

'No, that's okay. Play it safe as long as you take us near.'

So we were saved. I used the opportunity to clear the air once again over going to church and also complained about the way those girls had behaved on the 20th when our youth party was leaving. The boys agreed that the girls were the rudest.

I asked them what they were going to do when they got there. 'Oh, you'll hear,' they laughed and they were off.

As we turned we were hailed by two young men from Langa who know Mrs. Maphila. They wanted a lift back to the township. They were camping there and had forgotten something. As they climbed into the kombi we said to them, 'You've had it boys. Those comrades have come for you.'

They started panicking. The one had brought his clothes and his portable hi-fi and left them all in the tent. Well, they should have listened. We couldn't very well take them back to fetch their things because we could have been seen and then we'd have been in trouble for warning people.

Mrs. Maphila dropped me at my corner on her way back to Langa. Gus and Mother were sitting there stiff with worry but somehow I couldn't just come straight out and tell them what had happened. In a few moments I'd forgotten about it and it wasn't until Grace arrived that I started to tell my story. Gus was just about screaming. He couldn't get the words out. 'You know, you can sit here thinking someone is around the corner when they are already dead. But I don't know how you get yourself into these things.' Mother was furious, as if I could have avoided the whole thing.

I thought it was time we went to the graveyard. Gus wouldn't budge. 'I'm not going anywhere. I'm not sticking my neck out another minute.' So we did our own sort of Sabbath service in the house and just lay around. But I was feeling miserable.

Finally, I got up and went around to Angela – only to find that she and Linda had gone off to the graveyard, and without inviting me. One of her neighbours was outside. She had just returned. 'The whole town's there, sis,' she said. 'You'd better go. People are afraid that those who haven't gone are being marked. It's safer to go because there's nothing there, no riot squads, nothing. Nothing but people, but I don't want to tell you the whole thing. Seeing is believing. Go yourself.'

I collected Grace's mother and my own and together we went off, all wearing something black. Gus was still stubborn. We met Linda and Angela on their way back. They had thought I was already there. They'd also been told that it would be hell if they weren't seen. They told us the procedure. First we had to go to the graveyard to tidy up the graves and then to a house in NY 78 which has suffered the most recent bereavement in these troubles.

It was one thing hearing it. Arriving was still a shock. I have never seen so many people. I hadn't understood what they meant about tidying up the graves. I thought perhaps we had to clean the graveyard or something. But what it was was that we had to mould the graves, make the mounds of earth on top, because these graves were flat. They weren't like the usual ones, rounded on top. These graves were separate, in three long rows of about fifty in each line. There were so many I couldn't count any more.

Usually at a new grave there is a cross with the name of the deceased, age and date of birth and death. But the graves in these lines were just marked with a stake and a number. Every gravesite has a stake but it's only when someone gets buried that a metal tag with a number is clipped to it. And these were all numbered graves but with no names on them.

Unknown graves. I was too scared to openly ask questions, but you start feeling your way and people start talking. These graves, we heard, were riot deaths who were buried by the police in the night. Some of the comrades used to come and watch. The people of Section 4 said they used to see the police coming along with big plastic bags, those rubbish bags, and bury them there. Some of the comrades dug them up to find already decomposed bodies, sometimes more than one in a bag. So, it was said these were the graves of the unknown people who were just shot at random during the riots.

Well, you couldn't know whether there were also coloureds buried there, or even convicts. But it was still terrible to think that so many people could be buried like that without the parents or people or relatives or anyone knowing.

At the beginning of each line of graves there was a man with a spade with earth on it. You took a handful and put it onto the grave. Now all day from six o'clock in the morning people had been coming to put a handful on each grave. You could tell how many people must have been there, from all the townships, Nyanga, Langa, Guguletu and all, because these mounds were growing.

I counted two out of all those graves that had a flower on them, a lousy little plastic flower, where the family had been to the police station and discovered the number of the grave. All over people were crying. There were those who had lost their relatives or who still didn't know where their children were. They couldn't help but cry to think that maybe it was their child on whose grave they were throwing earth, but which one, which one? There were so many.

All the time there was this low singing, the sad hum of the freedom songs, and all the time more people, coming, coming. I am used to going to funerals but it had never felt so heavy, people milling around singing, others crying quietly.

Some youths stood, lecturing. 'This is what they do to us. This is what they do to us. This is the treatment we get and still when we say to you people, "Co-operate with us," you don't understand. You won't say "Shoo" when someone stands on your corns. You smile and say, "That's good."'

It was quite an effort, all that bending and throwing. It was too much for Mother. We were getting so tired that we tried to dodge the last row. We went on to the house in NY 78. The owner of the house was filling basins with water with which to wash your hands and everyone who passed put down a few coins.

All the way home there were crowds of people talking in low voices about the scene at the graveyard. In the morning they said there had been ministers present and they had given a service. And after that they had gone to their own churches and some had given a Christmas service. None of the churches were intimidated. Ours would have been left alone anyway but we had been too scared to go.

I just had a couple of salads waiting at home for lunch. I had been too afraid to cook. We were supposed to be eating only sour milk and mphokoqo, but I had made a chicken and hidden it away for the next day. People were coming past the house continuously on their way to the graveyard and it was already late. I wanted Gus to go there quickly. Not him. Once he had made up his mind he wouldn't budge. I was cross with him and rather bored so I slipped out and went across to the Motwelas.

What a surprise. They had quite a Christmas dinner ready. They had invited me but they hadn't said why. Everything must have been prepared very quietly.

We were still eating when Shelley arrived to ask whether I was coming home to make something for supper. The Motwelas sent us back with supper for everyone so the evening ended with some slight celebration. But I pray to God never to have another Christmas like this one. It's difficult to forget the heartbreak of that graveyard. There's a sad and quiet feeling right through the township.

Sunday, December 26

I was looking forward to getting back to normal today. Anything but. There is panic here. We first heard about some action when my aunt arrived, just as I had started cooking for lunch. 'I don't know what is going on,' she said, 'but last night there was trouble.' She had seen a group of youths passing her place – she lives in NY 137 near Nyanga. There were boys, girls, the lot, all singing.

Now the minute people saw those youths in a group they stood around to see what would happen next. As they passed, she said there was a low humming, like waves. It was as if there were waves building up, growing and suddenly bursting.

And then fire. As the group reached the corner of her street it broke into two, one lot going to the corner house and the other to Gqiba's place. In no time there was chaos. The corner house was set on fire. She didn't know whether they burned Gqiba's house but windows were broken and his van burned.

Just as she was telling us about this, we saw people swarming our way, lots of people running, and cars loaded. One car went to our neighbours so I thought I would go and ask what it was all about. They'd come from Nyanga East. They told me that a faction fight was raging between the township and the bachelor quarters. As we spoke, the man of the house came out saying, 'Out. Not in my house. Go away and don't offload in my place. There's no room here. Go back to where you came from.'

I thought that was very unfair – without even giving these people a hearing. As I crossed back home I saw others arriving three houses away and a van coming with more people. I went to talk to the driver. My first thought was for Isaac.

'Don't go near the bachelor quarters,' the man said. 'They are on the rampage. Even women and children have been killed. Everybody is fleeing out of Nyanga. We don't care whether people let us pile our things in the yard and sleep in the bathroom. Just as long as we're out of there.'

As more people flooded in, the cries started for all men to go to the borders. A loudhailer went up and down the streets crying, 'Amadoda, Amadoda emdeni.' We had to be on the alert because the bachelors, having had a field day in Nyanga, were coming our way and were just over the hill – nice and drunk and on the war path. One of our church elders was here visiting Father as the loudhailer passed by. He said that their area had already been on border duty all last night so this was really war.

At first the cry 'Amadoda emdeni' sounded exciting, but that was before we knew that the riot police and teargas were also involved. Gus and Pete ran off to go and patrol but what happened was that they were just in and out of here all day. The main scene of action was along NY 5 but they'd get as far as NY 78 and then be pushed back by the teargas and the shooting.

Some of the men were too cowardly to go to the border. They actually ran out of Guguletu, left their families and ran away. There was one man who was caught today wearing a dress, but he was given away by not having shaved properly.

Around three or four in the afternoon we heard a chanting coming from Section 3. It was a mob of women. They were well armed – each was carrying something, a panga or stick or something – and all were wearing loin cloths tied around the waist, which was supposed to show that they were really going to work hard. Most of them were bare-headed which also meant 'ready for action'.

I don't know how they had heard the news so early because they were really prepared, but there had been a rumour that the bachelors were planning to kill all the children of 'these bitches' (onomokwe) and kill their babies too because they would just grow up like their brothers.

They were chanting, 'Baphela bantwana bethu. Our children are being finished so what do we have to live for,' and 'If the men can't quell this, we will do it ourselves. We are the onomokwe. We will go ourselves.'

The woman leading the group comes from NY 112. She's a very fat woman but she looked very strong. You see these films of Zulu wars and as the men go to fight, you hear the women ululating in the background and it fills the air and makes the warriors surge on. That is what it felt like. Even the cowards felt they had to get out and do something. That kind of thing can be dangerous because you stop thinking and you start feeling, 'I don't care if I die – I will be dying in battle.' That was the spirit behind them.

It was very scary. The children were whimpering. The dogs didn't even want to bark. They just disappeared to the back, like when there are fireworks. Everyone amongst us must have felt, 'This is it.'

I think the riot police must have felt that too, because just then the teargas and shooting intensified. A riot van came past hailing, 'All women and children inside.' It went up and down the streets, up and down. Then another van came past with, 'Everyone indoors. Everyone in your own house,' and within ten minutes there was teargas and they started shooting with those bird pellets.

It was all the way around us. The house on the corner really caught it because it is on the route from NY 5 where the heaviest action was. The wife was away on holiday but the husband was home so the house was open. He said people came charging in to get away from the squads. There are holes in all the windows from the pellets. And when the people ran in, the squads followed. They were not only throwing teargas, they were beating up anybody they could see. It is one thing beating them in the street, but why follow them into the houses. This man is quite desperate. He said people climbed onto his bed and turned it over to try and shield themselves from the beating. Now it's broken. So are his chairs.

After that onslaught things quietened down a bit, so much so that I felt it safe to take Mother to work. And safe enough to venture into Nyanga to search for Isaac. I went to one of his friends who lives in Zwelitsha. All along the way were people carrying luggage. Some had prams filled with suitcases, others were in cars, any mobile thing was carrying people into Guguletu.

And there I was, alone in the car, feeling a bit nervous but wanting to check on Isaac. I cut across to the terminus. I looked first and saw nobody, but as I got there three white-doeked people appeared – bachelors. I'm not good at driving in reverse but I reversed out of there like hell. I think it was for more than a mile, then I turned back straight to Guguletu.

The roads were choked with people streaming away from Nyanga. And all along the way youths were disappearing into the bush that makes up the border. They were carrying cans, plastic cans and other containers. I thought they must be manning themselves with petrol bombs. They were exchanging messages with one another in whistles and animal sounds. It was as if the whole bush was alive. And very frightening to drive past.

The people streaming into Guguletu were full of two warnings. Firstly the Bhacas – we now call them the amasoka or bachelors – were on the warpath. And second, that they were being aided by the police. I asked one man, 'What do you mean? How can you say they are being aided? Are the police actually going with them?'

'No. What happens is that there are two groups – the bachelors and the townspeople. The riot squad have been driving along, shooting out teargas at the townspeople who run back in disarray, and as the teargas disperses them the bachelors fall upon them from behind the police.

'And when the people run to the squads they're told, "These people are going to beat you up. These bachelors are good people. But you people – your children and yourselves – are naughty. You are the ones who provoke them. You don't let them drink their beer and have their parties so they are going to kill you."'

Gus was waiting at home. 'Since when does it take so long to get to Thornton? Are you right in your head, woman? I've been sitting here worrying.' I made some excuse. I wouldn't dare tell him that I'd gone to Nyanga. He and Pete went back to their border duty. Our area is another route from Nyanga East so, though the main fighting was along NY 5, Gus and Pete and the other men of our area had to patrol nearby in case the bachelors came along through the bush to NY 108 and got us that way. We didn't like our men going out at night but at least the homes were safe.

Thank heavens, just as it was getting dark, Isaac came. He was tired, ragged. The whole day they'd been at it, trying to fight off the bachelors. His friend was still there, fighting.

He'd seen one terrible thing happen to a man who works at the dairy near him. He was near the shop when he saw a van patrolling. Now the minute people see a van they run because they know this means teargas. So they started running and as they were cowering away from the teargas, they saw this group of bachelors surging towards them.

Isaac thought that because there was a van between them and the bachelors, the police would also fire towards the bachelors and not let them through. But no, the bachelors charged on. This man, the one from the dairy, wasn't quick to run because he was right near the van and thought that meant protection, but the next minute the bachelors were onto him.

He tried to run towards the Methodist Mission and scale the fence of the school opposite, but they caught him and beat him up. People shouted to the squad to stop it but they just looked on. So what must one think? I mean, if someone who is supposed to come and stop a fight just stands and watches it, it does sound as if they are against us. All they are doing is mopping up the pieces of the dead people.

They must be helping them because if these bachelors had to fight on their own, this fight would once and for all show them their place in Cape Town. They have no right to take the law into their own hands all the time. They are not so numerous that the whole township can be beaten up by them. Even those women knew they could have beaten the bachelors of Nyanga because there weren't that many of them.

There was a Sotho chap here too. He lives near the place where it all started. We were discussing what could have set it off. He thought that yesterday the youth must have gone across to the Newlands area which is for bachelors only. They must have found the amplifiers blaring and everyone drinking and asked them, 'What are you celebrating when other people are mourning our freedom fighters?' Now the bachelors weren't going to have anyone interfere with their enjoyment.

So they chased them out of the Newlands bachelor quarters. But being drunk and angry, they moved over to Zwelitsha and that was where they caught people unexpectedly and went on the rampage. No one knew the bachelors were on the warpath. This man said he didn't know what was happening. He saw fire and heard screaming and as it was too close for comfort, he packed some of his belongings in his van and got right out.

But how it started had become unimportant. All we knew was that the bachelors had got out of hand and were killing women and children. There was just one thought – the safety of our families, and that meant stopping the bachelors.

Mamphela Ramphele

Mamphela was born on 28 December 1947 and grew up in the then Transvaal. Her parents were both primary school teachers. She began her medical training at the University of Natal in 1967. It was here that she met Steve Biko, a leader of the Black Consciousness Movement, and they fell in love. Their daughter, Lerato, was born in 1974, but died of pneumonia at only two and a half months of age. When Mamphela was 16 weeks pregnant with his son, Steve was detained; the brutal interrogation to which he was subjected led to his death on 12 September 1977. Justice Minister Jimmy Kruger told National Party followers that he was indifferent to Biko's death: 'He leaves me cold.' Just prior to Biko's death, Mamphela was served with a banning order and banished from the eastern Cape to the northern Transvaal. In 1983 her exceptional work in initiating and running self-help projects was recognised and she was honoured as *The Star's* 'Woman of the Year'. She became Vice-Chancellor of the University of Cape Town in 1996, the first black South African woman to be so honoured. She resigned from this position after three years to take up a managing director's post at the World Bank.

Her publications reflect her shift of interest from medicine to anthropology. They include *A Bed Called Home: Life in the Migrant Labour Hostels of Cape Town (1993)* and *Bounds of Possibility: The Legacy of Steve Biko* (1991). Her autobiography, **Mamphela Ramphele: A Life** (1995), from which this extract is taken, describes a tempestuous period in her life, the obstacles posed to her love affair with Steve Biko by his prior marriage, and the constant police harassment of them both.

[A few days later] Mr Raymond Tucker, an attorney from Johannesburg, then popular in activist circles, called on me at Steve's request. After carefully reading my banning order, he told me that it was in fact a banishment order, restricting me to a foreign part of the country – a treatment which had up to that point been reserved for troublesome chiefs who refused to co-operate with the white authorities in imposing controls over their people. Banishment in this new sense was a distinction I was to share with Winnie Mandela, who was banished later in 1977 to Brandfort, a small Free State town.

Raymond Tucker became visibly excited when he heard about the way in which Captain Schoeman had handled the errors in my banning order. His conclusion was that I was not banned legally, and could go wherever I chose. He also felt that there was a case to be made for wrongful arrest, and he was accordingly instructed to institute legal proceedings against the Minister of Justice and Police, Mr Jimmy Kruger. I was thrilled. My first thought was naturally to go back to King Williamstown. I decided to make contact with Fr Stubbs at the Community of the Resurrection Priory in Rosettenville, for he was in my view the best person to help me return home. But I first had to get directions from him about how to drive to the Priory, without giving away too much on the telephone, for it was known to be tapped by the police.

When I called Fr Stubbs I pretended to need the directions for Raymond Tucker, who I claimed wanted to visit him that evening to report on his discussions with me. Fr Stubbs was very vague. He could not understand why

Raymond Tucker needed directions to the Priory, where he had been a visitor many times before. In the end I had to make do with what he finally gave me. I confided in Fr Mooney about my intention to leave under cover of darkness that night. He was concerned about my safety, but blessed me and let me go.

When I got back to Tickeyline I fortunately found my younger brother, Thomas, who had been asked by my concerned mother to come and see me. He was then a twenty-year-old student, and was visibly shaken not only by my new place of abode, but more so by my plans to leave that very night for Johannesburg. In fact I told him that he would have to drive me out of Tzaneen: it was unusual then for a black woman to be seen driving a car, and I did not want to arouse suspicions or draw attention to myself. This was a case of naked bullying by an older sister, but it was not the time for gentle negotiations.

We left Tickeyline after dusk. Unfortunately, a typical Lowveld thunderstorm descended on us as we entered Tzaneen. Thomas's considerable driving skills were severely tested on the sharp curves of the Makgoba's Kloof area. As soon as we emerged on the straight towards Pietersburg, he stopped on the side of the road, visibly shaken by the stress of events. We had passed through the danger zone, both physical and political, so I drove for the rest of the way. The trip was uneventful but for our getting lost around Rosettenville and having to be directed by a national serviceman. He was blissfully unaware that I was the embodiment of the very threat to national security which he was supposed to counter.

When we arrived at the Priory, Fr Stubbs was caught completely off guard. He could not believe his keen political antennae had missed the hint I was trying to give him earlier that day. In his typically methodical way he set about making us comfortable for the night, especially my poor brother Thomas, who was still overwhelmed by the day's events. Thomas had not even begun to understand what being banned and banished meant when he was pressed into service to break the orders of those restrictions. For a young man with no political education it was too much, but necessity is the best teacher, and he rose to the occasion. Fr Stubbs arranged with Fr Leo Rakgale, one of his brethren, to drive Thomas to the Johannesburg railway station to catch the train back to Pietersburg the following day. He also arranged for our trip to King, which was to start very early the next morning.

The journey offered us time together. We had a long, frank discussion about our individual backgrounds, our fears and personality traits, which drew us closer together than would have been possible otherwise. Fr Stubbs stopped being just another priest to me; he became a human being, friend and counsellor. When we arrived at Zanempilo, Fr Stubbs called the staff to see who his companion was on this unexpected visit. They could not believe their eyes. There was joy and celebration as people came in to embrace me and welcome me back to the fold. Steve, who was called urgently by phone without much explanation, was absolutely astounded. 'Fr Stubbs, I thought I told you to keep her where she was!' But the joy of reunion was everywhere in evidence. We flew into each other's arms and forgot the nightmare we had lived through over the past few days. The comfort of familiar surroundings and faces had the desired effect and the tension which had settled into my frail body began to ease.

After a discussion on the best way to extract maximum political benefit out of this security police blunder, Steve and I sat back and enjoyed our reunion. Many of our colleagues and friends in the region got to know about my return. Yet the vigilant security police remained blissfully unaware for the entire four days I spent in the King Williamstown area. They were embarrassed to read about my presence for the first time in the Monday morning edition of the *Daily Dispatch*. Donald Woods, the editor, had been one of the first people we alerted. He came to Zanempilo for a breakfast meeting on the Sunday. Thrilled to get the scoop, he announced it with a vengeance. The red-faced security police came to Zanempilo that Monday morning to find me revelling in my new-found freedom and acting in my usual capacity.

It was a short respite, but a crucial one on two counts. Firstly, I settled the score with Captain Schoeman: 6-0, game, set, but not yet match! Secondly, I received a gift I was not to know about until a month later – the conception of my beautiful son, Hlumelo, who became the embodiment of all the happy memories of 'a Love Supreme', the poem Steve had written for me during our student days to capture the essence of our relationship. The rude interruption of our lives had upset our plans not to have another love child until our triangular relationship had been resolved, but my contraceptive pills had been left behind in King together with my other essential items. Abstinence was not a proposition. Passion took its course.

With Captain Schoeman nowhere in sight, the police apologised for the manner in which I had been treated earlier, but made it clear that I was going to have to be taken back to Naphuno in the end. They made elaborate efforts to get everything right the second time: spelling of names; identity number; adequate preparation, by mutual consent, for transporting my personal effects. I was also allowed to wind down my responsibilities in King Williamstown, which included securing my brother Molepo's release from another spell of detention. Captain Schoeman had been trying to put pressure on him to turn state witness in yet another of his crazy cases against Steve and other activists.

I even had time to take proper leave of the people of the village, whom I had got to love so much. The staff organised a party for me, and Mamoswazi led the women in singing and dancing. Lein van den Bergh, an official of the Dutch development agency ICCO, was one of the guests who shared this bitter-sweet farewell with me. He was to become a lifelong friend. There was a sense in which the sadness of my departure was tempered by the hope of my return sooner rather than later. It was farewell, but not goodbye. I was convinced that I would be back in King before the year was ended. At least that was how it looked from Steve's point of view and mine after a discussion of our future plans. However, history had other things in store for us.

I finally drove back to Tzaneen in my own Peugeot sedan with Mziwoxolo at my side to help with the driving. We followed the security police car to Pretoria, where we spent the night sleeping in my car parked in the basement of the Compol Police Station. Here we were given access to staff bathrooms in the morning and prepared ourselves for the remaining drive to Tzaneen.

There was a sad reunion with Fr Mooney and Sisters Mary Theresa and Emily at Ofcolaco. They were happy to have me come and stay in Tickeyline while I sorted myself out, but my return signalled the permanence of my restrictions. The Tzaneen security police were thoroughly ashamed of their ineptitude in not having kept me in check. They had only learnt from their King colleagues on the Monday morning with the publication of the news that I was out of their area of jurisdiction. What a disgrace! But it suited me fine: I was one up on them.

I found setting up house in Lenyenye Township, which I had made an absolute condition of my return to the area, an interesting exercise, for it gave me insights into the people I was to deal with for the next few years of my life. The security policemen, having made such fools of themselves, fell over themselves to keep me under constant surveillance. But they were so inexperienced that I would vanish in front of their eyes, and they would later catch up with me with desperation written on their faces. They were also confused by my friendliness. I treated them with courtesy and made a point of greeting them, even when they did not notice me, at the supermarket or other public places.

Nor did the local Township Superintendent, Mr Letsoalo, know how to deal with me. He had never seen an African medical doctor, let alone one who was said to be a danger to the security of the state. His dealings with me were also bedevilled by the open involvement of the security police in the administration of the township, and he did not know the boundaries of his limited authority. He was as helpful as he could be under the circumstances. I was given a house on the edge of the township, with two bedrooms, a living-room, a kitchen, and inside toilet and shower.

The local magistrate, from whom I had to obtain permission to go outside my area to shop or attend Sunday church, also found it difficult to deal with me. Later he became quite friendly and would share his ambivalences with me. He was very helpful in seeing that my requests were met. He was also instrumental in my move to a better house in a newly developed area, which was to be my home for almost eight years. He had come on an inspection visit to my first house and was visibly shocked at its inadequacy. I was sad when he was transferred out of the area during 1978; perhaps he was seen as too friendly. I shall never know.

The people in the area were amazing. Sister Mary-Theresa in her own way arranged with a local parishioner in Tickeyline, Mrs Mangena, to let me have one of her daughters, Makgatla, then about sixteen years old, come and stay with me in Lenyenye. The trust accorded me as a stranger has never stopped to amaze me. Makgatla Mangena stayed with me and my family until the end of 1994, almost seventeen years after our first contact.

My neighbours in Lenyenye, all policemen in the regular service, were very curious about me. I have no doubt that they had been warned about me, and that some of them informed on me to the security police, whom they saw as their superiors. I nonetheless decided to behave as normally to them as one does to any neighbour, which added to their confusion. Why was I not spitting flames of rage, as they may have been made to expect? I had decided on a deliberate strategy of vigilant self-preservation with the least expense of energy unless matters of principle were at stake. [...]

One of the most important ways of maintaining sanity in life is having some real work to do, as many unemployed people so painfully know. The network of support that developed around me in the first few months could not provide the intellectual stimulation and meaning in my life which were essential to survival. I had spent too many years leading a very full life to tolerate endless days of doing nothing. I could not continue to sit and wait for my return to life with Steve.

I was to have another opportunity of seeing Steve in June 1977, when I gave evidence in his defence in a case brought against him for defeating the ends of justice. Such opportunities for meeting were used to the full by political activists across the country, to the great annoyance of the security police, who were powerless to stop us. After all, one was entitled to a proper defence, even under the draconian legal system of apartheid South Africa. I flew to East London, using a small plane from Tzaneen, and connecting with South African Airways in Johannesburg.

It was good to be back in Mamcete's house. We were soon joined by Thenjiwe, who also arrived ostensibly to give evidence. The expected police swoop came earlier than we had bargained for, but they failed to nail us in one another's company – a trophy they coveted. They nonetheless spoilt our fun. We were temporarily detained and released only on the promise that we would be staying in different places. I was by then expecting Hlumelo, and had the opportunity to share this happy event with Steve without the awful distance between us. We also discussed my intention to start a small local health project to keep myself busy whilst awaiting new developments.

We had a huge party in Ginsberg in a house near Steve's home, in celebration of old times. It was attended by all the old party faithfuls, banned or unbanned, who were within twenty-five kilometres of Ginsberg. It was a nostalgic occasion which invoked a past we could not recreate, but it was an important symbolic statement about the bonds which tied us together in spite of the distances imposed upon us. At the end of the hearing it was sad to have to leave King and all the friends. I had to tear myself from Steve, who was, as usual, quite reassuring and urging patience.

Upon my return to Lenyenye, I decided to occupy my time with something creative. So I started a clinic at the back of the local Roman Catholic church, in one of the general offices, in July 1977. Ironically, Fr Thomas Duane, initially a sceptic, had become most supportive of me and had negotiated with the priest-in-charge of the parish for the space. The Black Community Programme, through its banned Director, Bennie Khoapa, generously made money available to me to purchase modest medical supplies in keeping with the temporary nature of the enterprise. The supportive network of political activists continued to operate against all the odds. I was able to start with the help of a local nurse aid, Morongwa Puka, who had been unemployed for some time.

To remain on the safe side I relied on Morongwa to interpret patients' symptoms. Many people stayed away from the service, in spite of their needs, which became clear later on when I got to know the area better. They could not risk the displeasure of the security police, who were clearly trying to discourage this development. It sounded too familiar, and smelled to them like trouble. They were right. But they need not have worried – not yet, in any case.

It is difficult to explain the series of coincidences which began to happen after my return to Lenyenye, other than in terms of what I believe must be telepathy. I started experiencing discomfort around my lower abdomen towards the end of August. I went to see a Swiss missionary doctor who was the superintendent of Shiluvane Hospital, a local hospital near by. He reassured me about my pregnancy, and advised bed-rest. My attempts to contact Steve over the next week or so drew a blank. I became concerned when he did not return my calls. (I had by then installed a telephone in my house.) A few days later I learned that he had been detained en route to King from Cape Town. I was not overly concerned. He had, after all, survived many brushes with the security police and could take care of himself. It would just be a matter of time before they charged or released him.

My admission to Shiluvane Hospital with a threatened abortion coincided with the beginning of Steve's brutal interrogation, which was to lead to his death on 12 September 1977. I was then sixteen weeks pregnant. His death coincided with the intensification of the threat to the life of my expected baby. With much reluctance, and after threats from me, the security police agreed to my transfer on the same fateful day to Pietersburg Hospital, a relatively better equipped institution with specialist services. I remember weeping on the way to the hospital in the ambulance, which left Shiluvane at 4 a.m. on 12 September 1977. I ascribed my weepiness to anxiety about the safety of my pregnancy.

Dr Van den Ende, the obstetrician, was the doctor assigned to look after me. He was a well-built, kindly man who had soft eyes and spoke with a strong Afrikaans accent. He explained to me after a thorough history and examination that I had an irritable uterus which was reacting to both the growing baby and the multiple fibroids (benign tumours) in its wall. He cautioned me about the chances of success in maintaining the pregnancy to term, but promised to do his best. I was put on treatment to suppress the contractions, and confined to bed. The nurses were wonderful. I relaxed towards the end of the day, permitting myself to regard this as time to be nurtured.

The following morning I was taken aback when the nursing sister in charge of my care insisted that I breach the order of strict bed-rest and go and speak to

265

my sister on the phone. She had a major family problem to share with me. I told the nurse that that was precisely the reason why I should not go to the phone: my family had to learn to solve their problems without me. I had enough of my own, I said. But she persisted.

Eventually I was wheeled to the phone. It was Thenjiwe on the line. I thought that she had succeeded again in fooling 'the system' and settled down for an update on the state of affairs. After impatient niceties, she asked me if I was sitting down, and then she said the impossible: 'Steve is dead.' It was as if someone had put a high voltage current through me. A searing fire burned inside me. 'No, it can't be true' was all I remember saying.

I went into a state of profound emotional shock. 'It can't be true' was my refrain. Dr Van den Ende had to sedate me. I fell in and out of a state of nightmarish sleep and wished that I could die. But death does not come to those who need it most. There was no escape from the reality of loss.

I owe the survival of my son to many people, above all to the undying loyalty and love of Thenjiwe. She had correctly anticipated that I might learn about Steve's death when I opened the newspapers on the morning of the 13th. The paper, with bold headlines, was indeed lying on my bed when I returned from the fateful phone call. Thenjiwe followed up her call with a visit a day or so later, to share the grief with me. The risks she took were enormous, but characteristic of this very fine South African.

I also owe a debt to the skill and patience of Dr Van den Ende. He constantly reminded me over the next few days to pray to God for 'Serenity to accept the things I cannot change, Courage to change those I can, and Wisdom to know the difference'. This prayer remains my constant companion. I owe much as well to the support and good care of the nurses at the hospital, who went beyond the call of duty, and to Fr Duane, who came to sit at my bedside day in and day out for two weeks after this tragedy. He just sat there, ready for a smile or tears on my part. I felt utterly lost. My world had collapsed around me. Gone were the anchor in my life and the security I had become so accustomed to.

The seismic event which shattered me on that fateful morning had many after-shocks. It was not just the end of the vibrant life of a gifted person with a sense of destiny, but it was the death of a dream. The dream which was killed had both personal and national dimensions. But it was the personal anguish which preoccupied me in my lonely hospital bed. I had none of the traditional support which one gets from family and friends. My sister's visit, though brief, helped. But the worst aspect of the loss was not being able to bury Steve. I remember being even more distraught the day after his funeral on seeing newspaper reports and photographs of the ceremony. There was a finality about the pictures of the proceedings. But my exclusion from the rituals made acceptance of this finality difficult. I kept hoping for a miracle to restore him to life.

There were other aspects to the exclusion. Not only was I banned and thus unable to travel to King Williamstown, but I would have been too ill to travel. I had to refrain from burying him in order to protect the life of his unborn son. What is more, I was not his widow. How would I have fitted into the rituals, given this fact? It was a bewildering time for me.

The Biko family were also bewildered, not only by Steve's death but by the fact that he and his wife had already separated as part of the divorce proceedings which Steve had instituted a few weeks earlier. In fact they reversed his own decision to end his marriage, by fetching his wife to come and take part in the mourning ritual as his widow. This reversal of Steve's own wishes has run like a thread through the continuing confusion about his life. His widow was put in the uncomfortable position of mourning as a wife someone who had taken steps to end the marriage in real life. It is not surprising that tensions often surface within the Biko family around the ambiguous position they made her occupy.

The film *Cry Freedom* was in one respect an inaccurate portrayal of Steve's political life, which Donald Woods had not understood in the relatively short time in which he had come to know Steve. It also misrepresented his personal relationships. The peripheral role in which I was cast belied the centrality of my relationship, both personal and political, with Steve. What the film did was to perpetuate the lie of Steve as a Gandhi-type person respectably married to a dedicated wife who shared his life and his political commitment. When I tried to stop the filming of this movie in Zimbabwe, my attempts were sabotaged by the eagerness of a number of people in the liberation movement, including senior ANC leaders, who were only concerned about the anti-apartheid statement it was making. It all added to the pain of loss by inventing memories which were not in concert with the reality of his life.

But life had to go on, and would go on, with or without my co-operation. I had to spend the rest of my pregnancy on strict bed-rest, nursed by my caring family and Makgatla Mangena. My sister Mashadi took leave for the whole of October to come and take care of me in Lenyenye after my discharge from hospital. My mother also came to see me over weekends, when freed from her teaching duties. Brothers came to stay at various points, and Molepo finally came back from King to stay permanently with me in Lenyenye from the end of 1977.

The Nationalist government was not satisfied with having killed Steve; they also sought to kill his ideas. All the Black Consciousness organisations were banned on 19 October 1977, together with many other organs of civil society such as the *World* newspaper. Organisations like the Christian Institute were declared 'affected' and thus could no longer receive foreign funding. Major political actors were detained and banned. The season of repression intensified.

I endured the worst summer of my life in 1977/8. The emotional distress was matched by the harsh physical conditions of my new home. Temperatures hovered around 40°C on most days, relieved only by occasional violent thunderstorms. I had to remain indoors in a house with no ceiling to protect me from the low asbestos roof. I relied on an electric fan, which I kept on for almost twenty-four hours, for some comfort. There was no garden to take refuge in, or trees to shade one from the relentless heat. I also had to contend with the constant screeching of crickets at night. I thought that I would lose my sanity at some point. Captain Schoeman had clearly chosen the worst place for me, as part of his extended torture.

Hlumelo, the shoot that grew from a dead tree trunk, was born on 19 January 1978. It was a long and difficult labour. In the end Dr Van den Ende had to use a pair of forceps to aid the delivery of the head, which was in a posterior position and would not come. I was overjoyed when I saw him – a true shoot from that indomitable tree trunk, an exact physical replica of his father, right down to the fingernails. Malusi prophetically gave Hlumelo his name soon after Steve's death. He said that it was suitable for the baby, be it boy or girl. I forgot the immediate pain of delivery and savoured the bundle of life next to me.

I was fortunate to have my mother with me to help with the care of my son. Hlumelo was a difficult child who cried incessantly. The old women of the village ascribed it to my having cried too much during pregnancy. They were convinced that foetuses pick up the mother's unhappiness and become tense and irritable. It was exhausting coping with my son, but I was so grateful to have him that I could put up with anything. Nobandile Mvovo, who came to see him soon after birth, tried to talk to him: *Xhamela intoni uzo sihlaza kude kangaga? Ba za kuthi singabantu abanjanina xa be kujongile? Ilali yonke imamele*

268

isikhalo sakho. Thula mtana ka Dadebawo. Thula Mgcina. (Xhamela [the Biko clan name], why are you disgracing us so much amongst these strange people? What will they think of us? The whole village is listening to your cry. Please quieten down, my child.) Hlumelo remained unimpressed.

The period of forced inaction gave me the opportunity to mourn and yet see my plight in a broader perspective. Many other people had lost sons, husbands and loved ones to the repressive system. I was at least in a better position to take care of myself than most other victims of this wanton destruction. The poverty of the people around me and their generosity filled me with humility. I had to stop feeling sorry for myself and get up and walk.

Caesarina Kona Makhoere

Caesarina Makhoere was born in a township near Pretoria in 1955. Her father was a policeman and her mother a domestic worker. When she was only a few years old, the family was forcibly removed (under the Group Areas Act) to the township of Mamelodi, far removed from the whites-only central business and residential areas (as was typical of black areas under apartheid). Because of the inhumanly long hours her mother worked, the seven children were largely unsupervised, resulting, Makhoere says, in her pregnancy at the age of 16.

After the birth of her son, Makhoere returned to school to complete her education and it was then that she became active in the students' resistance to Bantu Education. She was arrested in October 1976 under Section 6 of the Security Act of 1967, which allowed the police to keep her in detention for six months (renewable) without being charged. A year later, she was found guilty on the charge of recruiting people for military training and sentenced to five years' imprisonment. Not long after, her father, who she says was 'trapped into pointing out my hideout', died. Her mother, who had taken care of Makhoere's young son while she was in prison, died four months after she was released.

No Child's Play: In Prison Under Apartheid (1988) is an account of Makhoere's time in prison. She recounts the petty cruelties, the racism, the beatings, strip searches and spells in solitary confinement, but also the indomitable resilience that arose from her steadfast political commitment. After her release in 1982, she worked for the Black Sash as an advice worker, counselling those who were the victims of apartheid's discriminatory laws. She has also worked in the cultural department of the ANC.

The farce in the internal courts went on; meanwhile the struggle continued in our daily lives as well.

During this time there was the wardress called Mbomvana. You know, I hated her like hell. I don't even remember her real surname. Because she was so red, we just called her Mbomvana, which means red. She had this attitude, that she would deal with [us] brutally. Here was one thing about us: if a person decided to be difficult, to show an iron hand, we would retaliate the same way. I think she made us more stubborn, and for sure we were already stubborn.

Before the internal trials, on 8 June, in the morning, they brought breakfast. She brought us porridge which was not properly prepared, stiff and raw; I think they cooked it for three minutes and served it up. And they came in a big crowd. We were wondering, uh, what is happening? Because here are so many of these people, men and women, just to bring the porridge. They just stood around in the passage. It was clearly not all right.

We called to them, 'This porridge is not okay.' Mbomvana said she had prepared the porridge that morning and she was satisfied that it was okay. We told her, 'You are talking nonsense, man. How can you say this porridge is okay? Have you eaten it?' She replied that she was not a prisoner, she was not going to eat prisoners' food.

So I spelt it out: 'Then you are cooking shit and coming to tell us it is prisoners' food. You are not a prisoner. So you are doing all this deliberately.'

We picked up the quarrel; everybody was after her. Suddenly they changed their line, 'Thandisa must take her stuff, because she is going.' We demanded, 'Where to?' even before Thandisa could ask 'Where?', because we felt she was just part of us. We asked them, 'Where is she going?'

Her cell was unlocked. They got two men, huge men, tall and healthy, who just grabbed her, beating her on the way. I saw them: ta ta ta! Banging on her throat. They dragged her to the isolation section, and dumped her there.

I was the next victim. I was not expecting this, standing in my cell and cursing them for their treatment of Thandisa. Not knowing that they were coming for me. And they just bundled me, too, took me to the cells. On the way I was telling them a lot of things. That they were afraid of our brothers on the borders, let them go to Angola, SWAPO would shoot them to pieces, the bloody fucking cowards, they were just ill-treating women, knowing that we did not have weapons, anything; I'd just smash them to pieces anyway – after liberation. I would just show them. They started beating me. They were hitting me with a baton, seriously hitting, yo! I was dragged into a cell and dropped.

My old cell was stripped. Most of my things were taken away. They only brought the clothes. That was in the morning. They brought lunch. After lunch they left the cells and went away.

That afternoon this Mbomvana came again, in the company of one we called Yita. I don't remember her surname, either. She unlocked the cell. The men were standing in the courtyard. She said to me I could go and have my bath. She took Thandisa for her exercise and locked her into the small courtyard.

I was hardly three minutes in the bath when she came and told me, 'Come, your time is up.' I objected. '*Au, o a hlanya*; you are insane. How can you say time is up, I have not even washed my face? How long do you provide for bathtime?' And she said 'Fifteen minutes.' Then I asked her, 'Do you know the meaning of 15 minutes? Because I have not even started to wash my face and you are telling me that my time is up.' By that time I was sitting in the bath, naked. She locked the grille, went to call the men. And they came.

You know, Mbomvana, this stupid wardress, had a boyfriend, one of the warders at Kroonstad. And her boyfriend, whose name was Roet, came with another man called Else. They swaggered into the bathroom, lugged me out of the bath, naked, water running off me. And they started smashing into me with batons. All over my body. They pulled me to my cell, one on each side, hammering me with their batons. They dumped me there like a sack of potatoes.

That day I was raving mad. In my anger, I swore that I would never forgive these people. Actually I made it very clear to them that after takeover, if I happen to be alive, they are the people I am going to kill. I am going to hunt for them, to make sure. After liberation, if I happen to see it. No, I won't die before killing you. It cannot be otherwise.

Of course, it was not solely her fault, this Mbomvana; brought up with the idea that you are a superior being, that you have to be on top of the black woman or man's head, that a black woman or man cannot say anything, she or he must take what you give because you are the *baas*. These characters are brought up like that; but still she's one of those I can't forgive.

The following day Brigadier Venter came. In fact, immediately after the beating I rang the bell and said I wanted to see the doctor. Because I must record proof, to lay a charge against them. They told me the doctor was not there. And I reminded them that the doctor himself had said to us that if we wanted him to see us he was willing to come at any time. So I didn't see any reason why they said the doctor was not there.

The next day, before the doctor came, I saw Brigadier Venter and made the complaint about the beating. He defended the assault: according to him, I had refused to go into the cell, and he had given instructions that if anyone refused to go into her cell she had to be taken by force. I said: 'I never refused to go into the cell. This woman has a bad attitude towards us, particularly towards me. She thinks she is in a position to discipline us. I had not been long in the bath and yet she came to say time was up. This was done deliberately. And she decided to call her boyfriend and a friend to beat me up.' And I informed Venter that I wanted to lay a charge against them. Then I saw the doctor, who gave me a thorough examination. He wrote down everything. I was really ill.

I want to make it clear that this Mbomvana was a real sadist. We – Thandisa and I – decided to plot against this Mbomvana. Because, with all our sufferings in prison, this sadist managed to make life even more miserable than it normally was. But also because by now we were despairing of ever getting our situation improved unless we could get into court *outside* the prison. At that time we were in the isolation section, just the two of us. And I said to Thandisa, '*Mchana, wa tseba Mbomvana wa tella* (Comrade, you know Mbomvana is full of nonsense). We must just show her.' I wanted to handle her alone, but Thandisa refused. 'No man, this is not the best way. We must just *donner* her (beat her up) together.'

Before they took all the study materials away, Thandisa had gone into her isolation cell with a box of mathematical instruments. We shared the instruments out between us, those with long, sharp needles. I smuggled one into my cell; Thandisa hid the other.

The following morning (it was on a Sunday) Mbomvana unlocked the two of us; bath time. We decided we would ambush her, take her off her guard. We were going to be so meek. When she unlocked us in the morning we would just smile at her, all sugar. And she would be under the impression that we were now subdued, defeated.

She unlocked me, greeted me. I said, 'How's it?' and she got excited – you know, she actually got excited, she could not believe it. That here was someone greeting her so nicely, this one who was her enemy, perhaps this one was now broken. And she got the same treatment from Thandisa.

And she made the most stupid and dangerous blunder of her career – she unlocked the two of us at the same moment. She was confused; she had expected the usual big problems from us, she thought we were the two most difficult amongst the comrades. When suddenly she found only sweetness and light. And she went blind to reality.

The two of us moved politely to our different bathrooms. We had agreed that when she came to lock us up I would pretend I was still in the bath, né? so that she had to pass my bathroom and go to Thandisa's. And she fell into our trap, blind.

So when she came in, still bemused by her petty victory that we had greeted her properly and a bit smiling that morning, she did just what we planned – went straight to Thandisa to lock her up. And then I jumped out of my bath, immediately, without even drying myself, ducked into the nightdress and ran after her.

And I said, 'Eh, Mbomvana, why are you treating us like this?' She turned, 'Like what?'

I demanded: 'Aren't we supposed to get exercise?' and then, before she could answer, I slapped her. Thandisa went for her. We took the instruments; we started stabbing her.

A wardress, Hekal, was standing there. They had by that time closed the grille, the outside grille to the big yard. We gave Hekal a few claps and she just fled, she was absolutely terrified. Man, she made it clear that she did not want to involve herself in Mbomvana's problem.

And we went for Mbomvana. We stabbed her several times with those mathematical instruments. We had made up our minds that this person was not going to treat us like this; we wanted to kill her, there and then. Let us kill her and they can hang us. Because we have had enough of her. We assaulted her for a long time, stabbing her in the face, on the head, on the body, all over. She was bleeding on to the passage floor. After we had satisfied ourselves we went back to our cells.

There was confusion, a lot of confusion, in the passage. Hekal was whistling frantically. Mbomvana staggered down the passage, bleeding, into the other section. The other comrades were hanging on the windows, staring. We passed all the instruments to a comrade outside of isolation. There were two big drains; that comrade threw the instruments into the drains. We wiped up the blood on the floor, on our hands, removed any potential evidence we could see. Everything had disappeared – except for the blood on Mbomvana's body; she was covered in it.

Don't forget that all this was on a Sunday. As Mbomvana stumbled out, common-law prisoners stood there gaping at her. She used to harass everybody, irrespective of kind. During lunchtime we could hear the common-law prisoners ululating, cheering, singing, praising the beating. The other comrades – Aus Joyce, Mama Dorothy, Mama Mita, Aus Esther – all rejoiced. It was a nice fight, with a person who was giving us all a heavy time. She had got it at last, from those who were not afraid of her. The small kids had decided to solve her.

Some 20 to 25 minutes after her ignominious departure they brought their men to bring us back under control. They were surprised: each was already in her cell, very cool, sleeping in her bed as if untroubled by bad dreams. And they were well and truly frustrated, believe you me; they were looking for an excuse to hurt. They could only lock us up and go away again.

The following day, on the Monday, the staff came in as usual for complaints. We gave them the usual list. But later that week they brought the South African Police into the section. The police announced they wanted to take our statements. We replied, 'Nothing doing. We are not going to make any statements. We will talk to our lawyer.' So they went away.

They removed me from the isolation section to the big section – which was also isolation, as all of us were segregated. The day I was taken there they got a shock. They thought I was going to say no. Instead of sending a wardress to tell me that I was supposed to go to the other section, they brought men to escort me. Hai, this time I was determined to act the lady. To be honest I can be a very decent lady if you are a lady to me; but if you decide to be difficult, I am

also willing to be quite difficult. I refuse to be a lady when other people are not
ladies. It is too expensive.

But I sailed gracefully into that other section. When I reached the cell where
I was supposed to stay, Aus Joyce addressed me, 'You know Kona, I think you
are very intelligent. You know these people. I was listening to them but I didn't
know how to pass on the message to you. Because they were planning how they
were going to beat you up.' It was clear that the boyfriend was really furious
because Mbomvana had been seriously wounded. He wanted to retaliate; but I
did not give him the opportunity.

When the South African Police came some time later I was in the big section,
together with Mama Mita and Aus Joyce. Ausi Esther and Thandisa were in
the other isolation section, serving their sentence, spare diet punishment.

Whenever a case in prison involves blood it is always referred to the South
African Police (SAP). This means the case is no longer in the hands of the
Prisons' Department. When you are found guilty your prison sentence is
increased. Depending on its seriousness, the case is heard at either the Regional
Court, or the Supreme Court if it involves murder. In Mbomvana's case it was
to be the Regional Court, which is why the SAP came to us.

I was in the exercise yard when they came, talking to Thandisa through the
windows of the isolation section. Mbomvana approached:

'These police want to speak to you.'

'What for?' I enquired.

'They want your fingerprints.'

'*Uthini Kona? Uthi bafuna ntoni?* (What is it Kona? What do they want?)'
Thandisa wanted to know.

'*Amafinger prints* (They want fingerprints),' I replied.

'*Umgavumi ga!* (Don't let them do this shit)' she said.

'*Asoze ndi vume* (I won't let them).' Turning to Mbomvana, 'My fingerprints!
What for? I don't want this.'

I had hardly finished talking when they were on top of me. They didn't say
anything but started to beat me. They took the fingerprints by force. At that
time we did not know it was illegal to refuse.

And then those policemen started to beat me up. Eh, they went for me.
Thandisa was telling them nonsense through the window; I was telling them
nonsense, too. I told them they were afraid of our brothers on the borders who
were giving them hell. They should go to Angola where our brothers would blow
them to pieces. And that our brothers would be coming back, and they would

never forget what they saw then. You know, some of those policemen looked really frightened – we were telling them about what was actually happening, not forgetting the fact that many of them had joined the police force because they were afraid of being drafted into the army. Here were people talking about reality: that they were in fact losing in Angola; and here they were beating up women.

That afternoon, after they finished with me, they went to Thandisa and beat her up too, forcing her to give them fingerprints.

We said we wanted to see Captain Callitz. She came. I lodged a complaint that I had been beaten up by the SAP, that I wanted to lay a charge against them. Her only reply was that she was not in a position to say anything, as the SAP were handling that assault case. All she could do was to call the man in charge of the SAP.

So a certain lieutenant came, that very same afternoon. And he informed us that it was illegal for suspects to refuse to give fingerprints. So that if we continued with laying a charge against them, he was going to lay a charge against us likewise. All I said was: 'Listen, I have been beaten up; I have evidence. You can see my body is full of bruises. Whether or not you are going to lay a charge against me for refusing to take fingerprints, I am going to lay a charge of assault.'

He went away.

He came back twice, trying to convince us, trying to threaten us with charges. And I just maintained I would go ahead with it.

One day when we were still in the bigger section, Mbomvana took me out for exercise. She was accompanied by Hekal and one warder we used to call Dikaledi. Outside there was a bench which we used to sit on. I took the bench, put it opposite Aus Joyce's cell and spoke to Aus Joyce through the windows. Thandisa was taking a bath and watching me take exercise; Aus Esther was also in her cell. And while I was sitting there Mbomvana marched over.

'You are not supposed to be sitting there.'

'Is this not a prisoners' bench?'

'But you are supposed to be doing exercise.'

'This is not your bench. If I decide to sit down it has nothing to do with you.'

She repeated, 'No, you must get off this bench.' By that time she was standing next to me. She grabbed the bench and tried to pull it out from under me. I knew I was about to fall; I decided to take her with me. I klapped her. We

277

started fighting. Dikaledi and Hekal were there and began to assist her, hitting me with batons. My comrades could only watch us through the windows. Thandisa began screaming at them, telling them to leave me alone.

So they left me in the yard, shouting, to go to lock Thandisa up again. But when they came to lock her up, she demanded to know why they were fighting with me. They told her it was none of her business. At that point, Thandisa said, she had a wet towel in her hand. She slapped Mbomvana with the towel, spat in her face, and slapped her some more with the towel. So they started fighting with Thandisa, too. It was some time before she was overpowered.

You know, this is a real comrade. A comrade who will defend you at whatever risk to herself.

I was still in the big yard. Aaiiee, I was angry, steaming, hatred flowering. They called some men to take me back to my cell. I was seized by the arms and thrown in the cell.

And then came 31 July. Three of them were bringing us lunch. Because Dikaledi had been involved in beating me up, when I fought Mbomvana over the bench, I was furious with him. I pointed a finger at him: 'Why did you beat me up that day?' He did not answer me, but Mbomvana did. I slapped her and we started fighting. All three were armed with batons.

I had never been beaten up like that before. They laid into me. Honestly, né, they took their time and beat me thoroughly. I was pushed into a corner of the cell. Mbomvana and Else both held my hands so I could not fight back. And all of them hit me wherever he or she could. And they continued hitting me for a long time.

No one could help me. I looked for weapons, there was nothing. But I couldn't stop, you know – I did all I could, using a lot of vulgar words, speaking angry, telling them all sorts of things. After some time they decided to shift, to leave off. They left my hands loose. When they had first come into my cell, they had put my lunch on top of the cupboard. I grabbed the plate full of food and threw it into Mbomvana's face. The fight resumed. Aaiiee, the fight resumed. They came back into my cell and they went to town with me. That time, to be honest, I learned what helplessness meant. I couldn't do anything. I was beaten. Every part of my body was screaming.

When they left, I just dropped on top of my bed and cried. Everything was painful; but what made me cry most of all was that I knew that if I had been able to kill Mbomvana, it would have been better for me. At least I would have known that I had killed this one pig who had made my life so miserable.

278

About 15 or 20 minutes after they had locked my cell, Mama Mita and Aus Joyce began to call to me. They were so worried, asking me how I felt, how it was. Because even the wall tiles were broken, even the toilet basin was cracked, the cell was in chaos. How did I feel? 'Eh eh eh eh, Aus Joyce. Really comrade, *kajeno ba mpetditse ha ke batle go bua maaka* (today I was seriously beaten, I don't want to lie).' My eyes were swollen, my nose was big and I had cuts and bruises everywhere.

That lunchtime, Du Plessis, the stupid brigadier, came. He said that because I was a trouble-maker, they now had to put a chute on the door. The room normally had a grille and a sliding wooden door which the prisoner could open for air or close for privacy. They were proposing to lock the wooden door as well as the grille (which was normally locked) and feed me only through a chute. You can imagine what this man was trying to do. There would be no air; he wanted me to suffocate in that room.

My comrades revolted. Aus Joyce and Mama Mita stated simply, 'Nothing doing. You are not going to do that.'

Immediately after he left they came to put the chute in. Then they locked up that section.

Aus Joyce and Mama Mita insisted on seeing Brigadier Venter. The following day the brigadier came in the morning. When he arrived he announced that he would like to see us all together, not one by one. I think he thought it would teach the others a lesson to see how I looked. Because I was a wreck; swollen eyes, bruises, cuts.

Aus Esther, Aus Joyce, Mama Mita, Thandisa, we were so united. They were clear. 'No, we are not going to permit this. No one is going to lock up our comrade like that. This man is not prepared to see peace here. Eventually this comrade will end up going mad if she is locked up like that.'

Brigadier Venter reversed Du Plessis' decision, on condition that these other comrades talk to me, that I stop fighting. So they did not proceed with the chute. If they had continued with that I do not think I would have lasted for long.

After all this the two of us, Thandisa and I, were called into Captain Callitz's office. There we found the SAP and the magistrate and the prosecutor. They announced that we were charged with assaulting Mbomvana, once for the time we had stabbed her, once for the time she provoked me in the exercise yard.

The case would have to be taken to an outside court.

Now this, as I said, had been one of our main aims. If we could, we wanted to create an opportunity to let the outside world know that we were getting this type of treatment inside, that we were discriminated against, and so on. The outside world seemed completely ignorant of what was going on within South Africa's prisons, particularly with regard to the women political prisoners. People just assumed that we were inside, and that it ended there. We had known that if we injured a wardress seriously enough, enough to add time on to our sentence, their rules and regulations called for a proper trial in a proper outside court. With the attendant publicity.

And we succeeded. The case was taken out.

Turmoil

1980 to 1989

S ince the 1976 uprisings, the ANC had been developing a two-pronged strategy: acts of sabotage, combined with the fomentation of widespread disobedience in order to make the townships ungovernable. School and consumer boycotts, stay-aways and protest marches characterised the 1980s. In 1983, the United Democratic Front (UDF) was launched. By 1984 it had the support of approximately 600 organisations and three million people.

In the 1980s, union membership increased at an unprecedented rate, despite police harassment. In 1981, unregistered unions accepted the state's offer of registration, but on condition that they remain non-racial. Many combined to form large organisations such as the Congress of South African Trade Unions (COSATU, formed in 1985), which soon allied itself with the UDF and the ANC. Trade unions became a powerful tool for resistance: in 1986 there were 793 strikes, more than at any time in the previous ten years, and 2 700 trade unionists were detained.

Sectors of the white population that had previously been silent now began to protest against their coerced participation (through compulsory conscription) on the side of the racist state in what resembled a civil war. The End Conscription Campaign campaigned against compulsory military conscription for young white men (non-compliance meant imprisonment) and the Detainees' Parents Support Committee strove during the late '80s and '90s for the release of children detained without trial. Archbishop Desmond Tutu, leader of the South African Council of Churches, was awarded the Nobel Peace Prize in 1984, and more and more Christians rejected the government's attempts to claim moral legitimacy for its 'separate-but-equal' strategy. In 1985, clerics from 16 church groups called on all Christians to participate in the struggle for liberation.

Support for ANC-aligned resistance movements grew; nevertheless, it seemed to many that no end was in sight. The military might of the state seemed invincible. The 1980s saw intensifying state repression, mass detentions and successive states of emergency (in 1985, '86, '87). And in 1988, 18 organisations, including the UDF and COSATU, were restricted and the End Conscription Campaign was effectively banned.

At the same time, P.W. Botha sought to defuse the hostility by repealing aspects of petty apartheid and laws such as the Pass Laws and those criminalising mixed marriage and inter-racial sex. Although continuing to withhold rights to black South Africans, Botha and other Nationalists had begun to realise that Indians would not all disappear to India, and that some provision had to be made for them and coloureds. They thus engineered a new constitution (adopted in 1984) that widened Botha's powers and allowed for the creation of three racially distinct houses of Parliament (178 seats for whites, 85 seats for coloureds and 45 seats for Asians). Even though many whites and most coloureds and Indians rejected the tri-cameral system (Africans were excluded from participating in the referendum), it nevertheless seemed to some that a new, more enlightened era was dawning. Botha's 'Rubicon' speech in 1985 dashed all such hopes, however. In response, the gold price dropped and the lingering recession erupted into a financial crisis as the rand plunged, foreign banks suspended loans to South Africa, and the disinvestment campaign gathered momentum. Unrest erupted afresh; of the 955 people who died in political violence between September 1984 and January 1986, at least 628 had died at the hands of agents of the state.

Conflict escalated beyond black-white hostilities. The Zulu cultural organisation, Inkatha, which had been established in the early 1920s, was revived in 1975 as the Zulu nationalist Inkatha Freedom Party (IFP) by Chief Mangosuthu Buthelezi. It severed ties with the ANC in 1979 because it refused to accept the authority of the leadership in exile. By the end of the 1980s, Inkatha claimed to have 1,5 million members around the country. Although the organisation publicly denounced apartheid, 200 Inkatha operatives covertly received military training from the National Defence Force in 1986. Enmity flared between UDF/ANC and Inkatha camps, with loss of life on both sides.

Censorship had become a way of life in South Africa. Legislation passed in 1974 added a new category of 'possession prohibited' to earlier bans on distributing material, so that mere possession became a crime, whether or not the publication had been acquired legally and in good faith. By 1981, over 100 laws and regulations restricted press freedom, particularly in the reporting of matters concerning the military, the police, the prisons and black politics. In protest, some publications (until this, too, was forbidden) left blank spaces on the page to indicate the omission of certain items due to censorship. By the late

'80s, well over 30 000 works had been banned. However startling it may be, this figure obscures the more profound and pervasive effects of decades of censorship. State control of television and radio, coupled with self-censorship by the mass media in order to avoid prosecution, meant that many South Africans (especially whites) were largely ignorant of political reality. But some fissures in government control occurred in 1985 with the appearance of the *Weekly Mail*, which provided a highly critical commentary on current affairs.

Because of the role of the police in upholding apartheid laws, South Africa at this time was, in effect, a police state. Nevertheless, heightened militarisation was required to bolster state control, and the newly established State Security Council (not answerable to Parliament) established groups of police and army personnel who specialised in anti-insurgency techniques. Normal legal processes were bypassed as these covert squads resorted to state-sponsored terrorism. In 1986, a bomb planted by police destroyed the Johannesburg headquarters of the South African Council of Churches. Deaths in detention escalated, as did the list of activists who simply disappeared or were murdered.

The end of an era was heralded in January 1989 when P.W. Botha suffered a mild stroke. F.W. de Klerk became State President and immediately began a process of reform, releasing eight prominent political prisoners, including Walter Sisulu.

Mildred Mjekula

The stories of Mildred Mjekula, Maureen Sithole, Ma Dlomo Lugogo and Dolly – all reproduced here in full – were published in a collection of black women workers' stories in a generously illustrated book entitled *Working Women: A Portrait of South Africa's Black Women Workers* (1985). The text belongs to a sub-genre of South African autobiography, the worker testimony. Although seldom overtly political (in order to pass by the censors), these collected testimonies of the uneducated or illiterate, usually published by white researchers, served an important political function: they afforded white academics or literacy workers the opportunity to defy apartheid's insistent denial of the individuality of its victims; in publicising the life stories of apartheid's oppressed, they asserted the importance of their lives and exposed the cost of apartheid in everyday, human terms.

In *Working Women*, the author Lesley Lawson and editor Helene Perold provide statistical and historical contexts for the women's brief accounts of struggles at work and at home. Readers may regret the absence of biographical introductions to each of these women, wishing to know more about them; unfortunately, since they are not prominent figures, our knowledge is restricted to what they themselves have written.

Mildred Mjekula was interviewed in October 1983.

I first came to Johannesburg when I was eighteen years old in 1969. I came from Umtata in the Transkei. I have been working in Jo'burg for fifteen years, all the time without a pass because it was not easy to register.

My first job was with a Mrs Cohen, cooking and cleaning the house, and later looking after the children. Then I worked for another family, doing the same thing.

When I first worked here it was easier to work without a pass stamp. All you needed was your pass from the Transkei. But it was still difficult. My first employer used to tell me not to open the door for anybody while I was working. She tried for a long time to register me but they told her, 'No chance.'

I have not got a job now, and that is why I am struggling to be registered. In fact, I have been trying since 1975 to register my pass. I went to the pass office and explained that I had been working in Jo'burg for many years. But they sent me away, saying that I cannot be registered even if I get a job because

I am from Matanzima[1]. They say if you are from the homelands there is no application possible for you. At the pass office they said I should come to Black Sash – maybe they can help me.

In fact I had a job in Westcliff, but then the inspector came. That madam told me if I get registered I can come back and work for her again, because she likes me.

Since I first came to Johannesburg I have always had to look for work with a room because I have nowhere else to stay. When I look for a job I start off looking for a job in a private house, or a flat – I don't mind as long as there's a room. Usually I look in *The Star* and maybe I'll find a telephone number of people who want a maid. I phone them and then they tell me when to come so that they can see me.

While I had these domestic jobs, I used to get one off-day a week, and one weekend a month. I usually had a small room with space for a bed, a wardrobe and one small table. I started in the kitchen at 7.00 a.m. with one hour off for lunch, and then finished any time between 7.30 p.m. and 8.30 p.m. Not all employers are the same. Some do not mind visitors coming to see you. Others don't like it.

I used to get about R110,00 a month. Every month I sent my mother R60,00, sometimes less. My brother also sends her money, but I am especially strong for my mother, because my baby is there with her, and because my brothers are married already.

Six years ago I had a baby. I have only one and she stays with my mother in the Transkei. I worked while I was pregnant but I went home to give birth. Since then I only see her once a year for two weeks in December, or maybe June. I would like to have more children if I could. After my baby was born I took prevention so that I could see the first one grow. Then I stopped taking prevention but I never fell pregnant again. I went to the doctor and he told me that my tubes were blocked. One child is no good. I'd like two or three.

My child does not remember that I am her mother. She knows me, but now my mother is her mother. She doesn't love me too much and this is difficult for me. When I get a chance, I ask my mother to come to Jo'burg with her, and they stay with me in my room. My madam didn't mind for two or three weeks, but after that she said they must go because of the inspectors.

I have a husband. At least I do not have a marriage certificate but he looks after me, so he is my husband! He is a contract worker and lives in a hostel in the township. He comes to stay with me when I have a room – perhaps for two days or a weekend, and then he goes back to the township. He comes from Tzaneen and works at a steakhouse in Rosebank.

Apart from my husband, and an uncle, it is only my younger brother here in the town. He works at the CNA, and has been in the town for ten years. He stays at Diepkloof hostel, so he can't help me with a place to stay.

My sister works as a contract worker in Cape Town. She wrote to me to tell me there is a chance now to make a contract in Cape Town. She has been working there for ten years now, and like me she has worked all the time without being registered. But I don't want to go to Cape Town.

I have a brother and a sister still living in the Transkei. It is not possible to get work in the Transkei. It is too small and there are too many people. That's why we are all coming to the town. In the Transkei you can look for work for one year and you won't find it – there's no work. People are suffering.

And even here in Johannesburg it is difficult to get work. If you are not registered the whites say they cannot take you because the inspector can come and fine them R500 and arrest you.

I have had trouble with the police before. I have been arrested three times. The first and third times I went to court and the magistrate fined me R5,00. The second time I was discharged – I don't know why.

I am afraid to walk in the streets. When the police come, they ask you for your pass and look for the stamp. Maybe you have a stamp for one year only and it is finished when the police look. They just put you in the van and take you to the police station.

If you are arrested, you can ask the police to make a phone call. You give them 30c, maybe 40c and then you can phone. I can phone my brother at work, or my husband, maybe a friend. Then they know you are in prison and they bring you food, and bail money if there is bail. If there is no bail then you can ask them to come to court with money to pay the fine.

You just sit in prison. Over the weekend – if you are arrested on Friday – it is worse. You must wait until Monday. You must wait in the same clothes, with no soap, no cream, no washing water. You are in prison with all types. Each room has fifteen to twenty people in it. Sometimes it can happen that some try to give you trouble, but if you are lucky maybe you'll find nice people to sit with. Then we look after each other and talk. I was very scared when I first went there. And later. Most of my friends have also been in prison.

Last month, while I was still struggling to be registered, I took a job at a house where the madam did not ask me if I am registered. I felt sick. I had no power and she did not like me to be sick. I said to her: 'I have no power and you still want me in the kitchen. You can't even give me three days off to get a rest?' I worked until I was better, but then I left the job. I was weak and couldn't even pick up a cup, and still she didn't give me time to rest. I could only be sick on my off-day, but I was sick before my off-day! I was cross, so I left.

I do not think it is fair that people must have a pass. They are suffering. There are many people looking for jobs. Not many have a pass and many are arrested. I do remember when women didn't have to have a pass. I remember my mother saying – I think it was 1959 – that she was going to get a pass. After that it was difficult getting jobs.

If I don't get registered I can't go back to Transkei. Maybe I will find someone nice who will take me without a stamp. But they are scared of the fine and the inspectors.

I have no other way of making money, except by working. But from now on I want to learn to do something else – maybe learn to drive or to type so that I can get a job more easily.

I don't want to live my whole life here. I want to work now while I am young but when I'm old I want to go back to Transkei.

Note

1. Mildred is using Matanzima as a synonym for Transkei. Kaiser Matanzima was leader of the 'independent' Transkei.

Maureen Sithole

In 1982 Maureen Sithole was an unregistered nursing assistant working in an old age home in Johannesburg. She left her previous job at a factory because she wanted to learn the skill of caring for people. She was interviewed in April 1982.

I work nights, night shift only. We start at 5.30 p.m. and work until 6.30 in the morning. I leave home at 3.30 p.m. I go by bus. The first thing we do is make sure that the ward is tidy. Then you look at your patients to see how they are. Maybe you find bruises or the patient has changed. Then you make tea, feed them – those who can't feed themselves. After tea you go to the kitchen. We wash up and tidy the place. Then back to the wards.

Now we do two-hourly turning, three times a night. You turn them and you rub that other side. Four o'clock and you wake them up and wash them. Then tidy up the beds. Put on clean linen. That's all for the night.

The work is all right, there is nothing wrong with it. And the old ladies are all right – they give us no trouble. With my job I am satisfied. This is a thing

I want to do. But I am not satisfied with the salary. I earn R100 a month. We even have to buy our own uniforms with that R100.

I have liked nursing from childhood, to be of help to the society. Not for my own benefit, not for gain – I mean to have that knowledge of helping the sick. I used to feel pity for a person who can't do anything for herself.

It takes me a long time to get home from work. I reach home at about 8.30 a.m. or quarter to nine. When I get home, the first thing I do is make myself a cup of tea. Then, if my daughter is not home, I must see about the house, tidy up, make the bed. I must clean. After that make some breakfast.

Then I sleep for a few hours. Two hours or three. Sometimes twelve to two. Sometimes eleven to two. But I don't sleep longer than that – that's for sure. On the weekends it is worse. I don't sleep at all on weekends. We have got neighbours this side and that side and they are drinking. They are so noisy. They open their grams and you can't sleep at all when there is noise.

We work seven days on and three days off – seven days you must work it. I am tired at the end of seven days, but I do manage. Sometimes you feel funny. Sometimes you feel fresh. There are days when you feel sleepy during the night. You must feel drowsy, like it or not.

It does affect me. There are days when I feel very, very tired. As if I am not well. I've got thinner from lack of sleep. At the factory I was size forty. Now I am a size thirty-six.

I used to work in a factory – I was a machinist there. I left that job because I wanted to be a nurse. I saw this advertisement in the newspaper. They said they would train a person to be a nurse aide. Now I am here and I find they don't train us formally. I want a nurse aide certificate, but I can't get it here. Although at this place I do all the work that a nurse aide would do. It's just that this place is not registered, so we can't get our certificates from here.

Now I am doing a separate course to get my nurse aide certificate. I have to go to lectures in the day – twice a week. This means that I pay extra. It also means that there are two days in the week when I don't get any sleep at all.

Ma Dlomo Lugogo

Ma Dlomo Lugogo is a widow living in Mehloloaneng village, Transkei. She was interviewed in August 1984.

I was born in this place, at the mission. That was in 1931.

I only went to school for a little bit. I've got Standard Two. Why? Because in my home there was nobody to look after the cattle, sheep and horses. So I had to go and be a shepherd.

We had a lot of cattle. I can't remember how many but there were a lot – and seven horses. But they are all dead now.

I got married in 1950. My husband's father rented a place near here because there was good grass and water for his cattle. He had a good farm in those days. My husband was working and he used to send me some money. We had four children – two boys and two girls.

Life was better in those days. We were ploughing mealies. We had two places where we could plough, but the government took away one field. Even now we've still got that other field, but because of the drought we get nothing from it.

My husband died in 1960. There was an accident on the road. He was digging and he got killed by the machine that builds the roads. They gave me a very little bit of money. It didn't take a year, and the money was finished. We were paying taxes, but the government didn't help me. The money they gave was too little – and yet he was working for the government.

The load was heavy for me. My husband's brother took away my son to go and stay with him in Mount Fletcher. He saw I was struggling to bring up all these children. And he didn't have any sons – so he took him in.

I went to work on a farm near Harding. My brother was the induna there, and he called me. We were planting trees. I used to get R15 a month. But it was worth a lot more because the prices were not so high. I left that place because it was raining all the time.

Once I went to Johannesburg to work. I was employed in a shop in Kliptown. My job was to take fruit and veggies out into the street and sell them. The money was much better than I got at Harding.

I liked it in town – it was very nice. But I couldn't speak all the languages that other people spoke. I like staying here because we understand each other.

I went back home because my daughter was going to have a baby, and there was nobody to look after the children. That's what keeps me here – my children and my grandchildren. If I didn't have children I would stay in Johannesburg and not come back.

Now I am living here with my son, Sibininiza. I am trying to make a nice vegetable garden, but I haven't got the strength. I used to grow pumpkins and a few things, but now I want to have a proper garden. I am interested because there are people here who explain how to grow spinach and all sorts of other things.

It's difficult but I am trying hard. I haven't got enough in my garden because this year I planted late. And a hailstorm came and destroyed everything. So I can't live off it.

I just live, I don't know how I manage. But I do eat. My one daughter is a domestic worker in Pietermaritzburg and she usually sends me money. But now there is a big delay. She hasn't sent me any money for five months and she's the only person I get money from. It's hard because I have to go to my neighbours and ask them for mealie meal.

My other daughter is married, and she doesn't work, so she can't support me. And my other son is still at school in Mount Fletcher.

I've got no cattle, but I do have about six chickens. They are busy hatching eggs, so I'm not eating eggs. I've got eight goats, and I get milk from them when the grass is green. But now they are starving and I don't get enough milk.

Mostly I eat mealie meal porridge and tea. Sometimes there's imifino, but usually there's nothing else to eat. I'm putting all my hopes in the vegetable garden. I hope I can grow enough to sell.

Life here is hard, but not for everybody. For those who have got food and money, it's not so hard. You need money to live here. I can't garden without money to buy seeds and things for the farm.

It is easier for a woman to survive than a man. There are a lot of little things you can do – you can make beer, or look after your neighbour's children. You can plant turnips, peas, beetroot with your own hands, and sell them.

But if a man can't find work he's finished. Unless he knows about carpentry and someone will pay him to build their house – or somebody will pay him to take out their cattle.

The only work that a man will do around here is to get up and go and take the cattle to the veld. If you ask him to make the fire, he'll say no, he won't do that.

After he's taken the cattle, you see him sitting in the sun with a big dish of food. Besides that, all he knows how to do is to get up and go and look for beer. I don't see a man doing anything at home. No, nothing.

I sometimes cut grass out in the fields and make it into bundles. I sell these bundles of grass for thatch – it's R20 for a hundred bundles. There are many women who do this. I do it because I'm all alone. But women with husbands do it, and the husbands don't help. They just stay at home. If the husband helped his wife they could earn more than that R20. But you'll never see a man there where we cut the grass. It's only women.

I think some men are lazy. When a child grows up and begins to work, the man will come to you and tell you, 'This is my child.' He wants the child to support him. But when you struggled to support that child he was doing nothing.

I used to be a big, healthy woman. But now I am getting sick and thin. I have got no aches or pains, but what worries me is that I have sleepless nights. I don't know why I can't sleep, but sometimes I stay awake the whole night, without even dreaming. If I was somebody that drank beer, I would drink so much that I would sleep straight away. But I don't drink.

Last summer, I was struck by lightning. I didn't see or hear anything. All I remember is that I was watching the rain and hail come down. I was sort of unconscious. People tell me that they found me lying on the floor. The chair I had been sitting on was on top of me. I think that chair did a good job that day, because the centre pole of the house was shattered to pieces. The whole roof would have fallen on me.

I was lucky to be found alive, because after that the lightning struck my neighbour, and she was killed. Their whole house burnt down. I was lucky to survive.

Dolly

When Dolly's husband went into jail in the early 1960s, she was forced to do extra work to support her two children. She chose prostitution. Twenty years later, in September 1984, she describes what this job has done for her.

I started working in a glove factory in 1959. The money was so little, and I just couldn't bring up my children. Between 1961 and 1963 my husband was going in and out of jail, for theft.

I became a prostitute through circumstances. I was struggling. Most of the time I had to borrow money. People in the factory would say, 'Oh, here she comes again …' You have to beg for food. What will the children eat? If there's a way out, make use of it.

One night I said, 'To hell with everything. I'm not going home tonight. I must make some money.' That's when I started. I met a man and he gave me some money. I went home and fed my children, and went back to work again. Then it became a habit.

When my husband came back from jail he said that my second daughter was not his. I said, 'Okay, seeing as the second one is not yours, I'll take them both and bring them up myself.'

In 1964 I went on a whoring spree. I kept on working in the factory for a few years, but this prostitution paid me more than my job. A lot more. You could make R80 to R100 a night. They used to pay a lot of money.

You know, these days things ain't what they used to be. Today there's the cops, today there's the customer who tells you he's only got R2 on him. I mean, what can you do with that? Today a penicillin injection costs R5. I mean you've got to look after your health at the same time.

Since there are these young girls coming up, they don't pay anymore. They rather tell you, 'Get me a young girl.' At times they give you R10, R5, R2. Some of them they just take you and dump you right out in the veld when they've had you. Then you are told, 'F … off, you black bitch.' And you must just go. Who wants to get hurt? But if you get a chance, once he's drunk, you just pick-pocket him.

Before it was easier. We used to queue up in Edith Cavell and Bree. There were about ten of us.

The police were not so inquisitive then. There was a place where we used to go – some offices with toilets and bathrooms. We had some pieces of cardboard. It paid, man. Jesus Christ, you can go twelve times in one night! (*laughs*) Stamina!

The next day you feel nothing. Practically nothing. You must just get your injection.

Once I came across a man who was so drunk. I took him to the building and I asked, 'How much?' And he said, 'No, I'll give you R10 and if it's good I'll give you R15.' And then he took out of a bundle of R10 notes – so thick – and I must get one ten rand out of that! I thought okay, I'll fix him up.

So while he was lying there I just went for those R10 notes in his pocket. I put the money under my armpit, and he didn't see. You know, that day I ran all the way to Commissioner Street without my panties on!

These days I don't go round like I did before. I mean, at forty-two? You know one gets tired of lying on your back every five minutes. Ooh, honestly. Unless I've got an appointment with someone I know. I go to his flat on a Sunday morning, or Saturday afternoon. But not at night because it's risky – the police this side, the muggers that side.

I used to operate in Hillbrow a lot. But nowadays I haven't got a place to go to during the day. You've got to go maybe in a passage. It's risky.

It's very risky. Prostitution is not nice at all. It pays … it does not pay. No.

I've been caught twice before. The second time it was 1979, I think. I was on trial for three weeks and I got nine months for soliciting.

Oh well, once you're used to jail, there's nothing wrong. You just do everything they tell you to do if you don't want to be punished. That's all. I was in the Fort here, and then we went to Boksburg. After a few months they sell you – you can work for some whites.

I went with a gang to Brits. Now those are farms! Phew! From 7 a.m. till 8 p.m. you worked. Oh, it was strenuous. We were sowing, reaping, irrigating, doing a lot of things, man. We were being paid maybe 20c a day.

The conditions were horrible. Jesus Christ. The huts, they were so small – and there were four or five of us in there. No curtains, no windows and muddy. They gave you a blanket and two sacks.

In the morning you ate tea and porridge. Lunchtime – spinach and porridge. Suppertime – tea and porridge. Unless you had money and could buy yourself something else.

I was bitten by a dog and they just used some plaster and grease. And I had to work with that, you know. It was painful. When I came out of jail I went straight to the hospital. It was septic, smelling.

Since then I've been to jail for a reference book, trespassing – but not immorality or soliciting. No, I go carefully with it. I have an appointment, I know where to go and I'm careful.

Now I'm not earning enough. I'm looking for a job actually. Domestic, or floor cleaning – as long as I can work. I'm not choosy you know, as long as I can make ends meet. At forty-two, who wants to go to jail again? I'm too old for whoring. It's not life. Not at all.

This prostitution frightens me nowadays. From 1964 – this is my twentieth year. It's a long time. My children are grown up. I'm a granny now.

My daughters went to Botswana long ago. They've both matriculated. One is an accountant in a bakery, the other works in a bank as a teller. I mean they're twenty-three and twenty-one this year. They don't help me, you know what children are – they just want beautiful things and everything.

I don't like to see their father. He always wants them to come to him, now they are big. I don't mind, no hard feelings – as long as he doesn't bother me. What I don't like is whenever he comes across me he says, 'Do you still sell your body?' I say, 'It brought your children up. Never you mind selling it. Today you are proud of them.' He didn't support them at all. You can just believe me.

Now he's selling drugs. I hope he gets caught, honestly. He's so well-off – he's got a Mercedes, he's bought a big house. But I don't want his wealth. I'll keep my poverty with pride.

Most prostitutes have no choice. Especially if you're the only breadwinner. You've got to pay rent, food and everything. You become a prostitute through circumstance.

Most of the men in Soweto are so useless. I don't know why, they're not prepared to work. They just sit around in the house and do nothing.

It's mostly white men I go with. I don't feel anything for them ... pay me first! But once they are used to you, they take advantage. Acting as if they haven't got money, or just dumping you in the veld. It's heartbreaking. We are not inhuman. We've got feelings too.

Jane Hoko

These short accounts (reproduced here in full) of the experiences of Jane Hoko and Selestina Ngubane were published in *We Came to Town* (1985), a collection of short autobiographical accounts by some of apartheid's oppressed. The narrators, about whom we know only what they themselves wrote, were students in adult literacy classes in the early 1980s. Caroline Kerfoot, the editor, says that the text is intended to serve as material for discussion and comprehension exercises in adult literacy classes.

I am a woman.
I come from the Orange Free State.
I attend the Methodist Church.
I am a member of Manyano.
I am the mother of my daughter.
I am the father of my daughter.
I am the grandmother of my grandchild.
I am the grandfather of my grandchild.
Now I want a house of my own, in the homelands or any other place.

Selestina Ngubane

My Life Story

I was born in Natal. I am a Zulu girl. My father died two years ago.

When I was a young girl, I went to school till I was in Standard Three. I had to leave school, because my other friend who had never been at school used to tell me that she earned lots of money from her employer. So I got jealous. I asked my parents if I could also go to work. They didn't let me but I went crazy about work. I was never happy about school anymore.

Then I started to work and I had trouble with a man and I had a baby boy. His name is Pius Zungu.

My child's father sent somebody to my parents to ask if he could bring lobola, so then we could get married. My mother refused that because she had not liked him from the beginning.

She thought my child's father was a 'skelem' because he used to work in Johannesburg for a long time without being married. So that is why my mother never trusted any man from Johannesburg.

He was 32 years old and I was 18 years old, but today I am tired of work.

I wish we could marry but we are not in love any more.

Emma Mashinini

When Emma Mhlolo Ngwenya was born on 21 August 1929, her parents were living in the backyard of the home of a white family in Rosettenville, Johannesburg. They moved to Prospect Township, which was one of the first areas to be subjected to forced removals in the 1930s (long before the advent of apartheid), and then to Sophiatown. This suburb was unusual in that it was multiracial and most black families owned their own land; it was here that Mashinini went to school, leaving at the end of the tenth grade. Demolition of Sophiatown began in the 1950s and the family was then forced to move to Soweto.

Emma married at the age of 18. She had the first of her six children on her twentieth birthday. Three of her babies died of jaundice; another daughter died in an accident when she was 17 years old. Emma was a full-time mother and homemaker until she was twenty-six, but her marriage was in trouble and her husband used to beat her.

She worked as an unskilled garment worker for a few years before leaving her husband. Her second marriage, to Tom, has been a happy one.

Mashinini was a founder and first general secretary of CCAWUSA, the Commercial, Catering and Allied Workers Union (1975–86), which in turn played a key role in the formation of the Congress of South African Trade Unions (COSATU). Detained for six months in solitary confinement in 1981, she continued her efforts in the cause of workers' rights, gaining numerous foreign honours, among them the declaration of 'Emma Mashinini Day' (8 March 1985) by the governor of Minneapolis. In the early 1990s, she served as president of the Mediation and Conciliation Centre in Johannesburg, and in 1995 was appointed commissioner for the Restitution of Land Rights.

This passage, from *Strikes Have Followed Me All My Life – A South African Autobiography* (1989), concerns her attempts to deal with the traumas of detention and the harrowing nightmares and memory lapses she suffered once she was released.

So now it was time for me to go home. It was so exciting. My child Nomsa was there, and my neighbours. My neighbours came in very great numbers, and there was one visit especially which was very important to me. Morris Kagan, who until that time had never been to Soweto, came to my house. He said – it was before the permits were abolished – 'Permit or no permit, I'm going to Soweto. I'm going to see Emma.' All this was very wonderful, but also too much, because in the evening when I went to bed, I was very exhausted from being alone for so long and then all of a sudden having so many people coming.

At night the cars driving back and forth seemed to me now to be interrogators. Every time there was a car I was terrified, and thought that they were coming back to collect me. These people know what they do when they lock you up. You torture yourself.

So the excitement was short-lived. I now had a period when I was very concerned and worried and wanted to run away from my home. My home was no longer suitable for accommodating me safely, because they knew where it was and I thought they were coming back to get me.

We called the doctor, and he gave me something to put me to rest, to sleep. But still that feeling went on, for days. And all the time people were coming to see me. They were coming in their tens, in their hundreds. We actually had to have arrangements to say which people were going to visit on a certain day. People from trade unions, people from the Church, from prayer meetings. It was just traffic, one after another. And international friends. I was one of those lucky people who had a telephone in the home, and all the time there were telephone calls from all angles.

I'm sure people could tell from my speech that I wasn't normal. And in the end my FIET colleagues in Geneva said, 'We want you to come to Geneva, and we are prepared for you to travel with your husband. We are not going to take the risk of you travelling alone.'

In May I was out of prison, and now in June I was to travel to Geneva. And from Geneva I was whisked away to go to Denmark, to a clinic for detainees and people who had been tortured.

In Denmark I was given the most royal treatment one could expect. I had wonderful doctors who paid the most important attention to me, I had a ward which was like a suite, I had everything I wanted.

But to me it was yet another detention. Tom had to leave me there, and he went to Germany to spend a few days with the children and then went back to South Africa. And mostly I just felt I'd been away from my family for too long, and now again I was away from my family. So in spite of all the good work that was done by this clinic – the good work which I appreciated very much – the fact remains that I wanted to be with my family again. I think this was bad timing, for me to go to that clinic then. I think, for all their good treatment, it was another disorientation.

I was with other people who were torture victims, coming from other countries. We could not speak because we knew different languages. Only the doctors and nurses could come and speak to me. And when you look at these people who are themselves tortured and derailed, it does not give much courage. It just put me off.

There were mostly men, from Chile, South American men. Some of them had brought their families with them. You could see their wives and children, and there was a lot of unpleasantness. These husbands had been away from home in prison, where they were derailed, and they were different people now – they were not who they had been. There must be unpleasantness in such a circumstance. So these families did not come excited. There was misery all around.

The doctors there were very nice. I remember they tried to keep my presence a secret, so that it would not be known in South Africa that I was having this treatment. They didn't want to use my real name. They wanted to give me a name to cover up who I was. This I refused. It was important to me that I had come and that my name was Emma Mashinini. I wanted to go down on record. This was very important. I wasn't going to accept another name.

The doctor who started the clinic was Inge Genefke, a woman about ten or twelve years younger than myself, and a very brave, intelligent person. She said the idea had come to her with the aid and help of another woman, who was in Paris. When I was there the clinic was still in a hospital, in a separate wing. But they were building a separate hospital for torture victims.

Inge Genefke used to want me to speak out, to tell her what happened during the whole time of my imprisonment and what the torture was. I had to dig it out. I forgot some of the things, but she was so patient. She wanted me to dig and dig and speak about everything.

But for me I was speaking to a white doctor, and I had spent so much time with white police, surrounded by white people. It was a white woman who had refused me chewing gum, and a white woman who had put those bracelets on me. And it was hard, very hard, to trust her, this new white woman. As well as that, I had been told when I was released never, *never* to speak about my detention. So whenever I spoke I was leaving something out. I was fearful, terribly fearful, that this would leak out and get to them, and I would be rearrested and charged for having spoken about things.

Then the newspapers found out I was in that hospital, and again I had that fear of being betrayed and that the people who said they were helping me would hand me over and return me to prison. The journalist who most hounded me was black. His name was Z.B. Molefe, and he printed an article on 18 July 1982 in the *Golden City Press* in Johannesburg under the headline: 'MYSTERY OF SICK EMMA'.

> Mystery deepened this week about the whereabouts of prominent trade unionist Mrs Emma Mashinini who is reported to be sick in an overseas hospital.
>
> This was after GCP, assisted by the International Red Cross, contacted more than 30 hospitals in Copenhagen, Denmark – where Mrs Mashinini is reported to be hospitalised – but failed to locate her.
>
> The search for Mrs Mashinini was started after this newspaper published a story on July 4 about her hospitalisation in Copenhagen … suffering from what her doctors described as the 'effects of psychological torture' […]

> Trade union sources revealed to GCP that information about Mrs Mashinini's illness has been shrouded in mystery because 'the family perhaps fears for her life after all she has gone through.' ...

It was as a result of this that I had to assume my code name in the hospital. I became Mrs Akhaya, and special security arrangements were made for me. The nurses were instructed not to allow any strange visitors to my bedside. Back at home Tom protested vehemently with Mr Molefe about this intrusion into my private life and the threat he was causing to my safety.

But despite all this I did manage to speak out. I did manage to trust Inge and tell her about my greatest concern, which was that Alan Fine, who was still in prison, would be charged with some offence and that I would be called as a state witness. This sent me totally berserk, to think of being a state witness. So I told her this, and she asked me, 'Why are you so concerned or afraid of being a state witness?' And I said, 'It's because the community can never accept you having been a state witness.' And she was educating me, saying, 'You know that at times people are made state witnesses very much against their will, and they may have broken down, or there may be other very good reasons why they have eventually gone to become a state witness.' After all the trauma, to go back to the community and be rejected again. It means you are killing this person twice over.

Always she wanted me to dig and speak out, and she seemed to enjoy it when I cried. She even laughed when, after all that time of being unable to cry, I did begin to weep. She would just leave me to cry, and she sat and enjoyed it. I didn't at first understand why this was. I didn't understand why she was enjoying something that made me feel so ashamed. I thought that by crying it showed I was weak, and I was humiliated.

She would say, 'Why are you so apologetic? You live for other people. You don't live for yourself. It is important, you've got to think about yourself before you think about the next person.' She would say, 'You've got to be selfish about yourself.'

I was giving her examples to say that yes, I thought I was a selfish person. I said I was a person who could stand up and speak for herself. She said, 'Give me one good example.' And I gave her an example to say that when I wanted to buy a car I had refused to use my husband's name. According to the rules and regulations in South Africa, if you buy a car under hire purchase you have to use your husband's name. But I refused to use my husband's name and said this was my car and therefore it had to be in my name. And I insisted on this until the car dealer really did give in and said it would be in my name, even though it was not supposed to be so. And my husband gave me his support in that. He said, 'Do what you want to do.'

Well, I told her that example. But she said to me, 'That's not enough. That's not being selfish. That is standing up for your rights.'

I tried everything to prove that I can be selfish, and I did not find one thing. And this was a lecture she gave me time and time again. 'Be selfish about yourself. Be selfish. Live for yourself. Stop thinking about other people.'

I try to, but I have not managed to get to that.

I left Denmark prematurely, I know. Inge felt I should stay longer, but I couldn't. I really was longing to be out of hospital and to go back to my family.

From there I went to join Molly in Germany, and I spent about two weeks with her. This made me feel very good, to be with my daughter, my grandchildren and my son-in-law. Only Dudu I had not seen, although I spoke to her on the phone when I was in Geneva, and the craving to see her was greater than ever.

I remember when I first went from Denmark to Germany to see Molly, when I came out of that hospital, I feared for my life. And when I got to Frankfurt airport to fly home again I looked around and saw two South Africans, Dan Vaughan, the assistant of Desmond Tutu, and Allan Boesak, who is now the Chairman of the World Alliance of Reformed Churches. I don't know where they had come from, but they too were travelling to South Africa and we were going to be on the same plane. This gave me great relief, to know that when I got to the airport there would be someone to say, 'We saw her. We were with her.' So I said to them, 'Thank you. I didn't even need to talk to you. It was just a great relief that I saw you.' And they said, 'This does not happen to you alone. It happens to all of us. After our trips, when we go back home, we wonder what is going to happen to us.'

I am sure people are going to die from heart failure, worrying about getting to that airport at Jan Smuts. There is nothing to hide, nothing, but with the thought that people just disappear between airports the joy of going back to your own country escapes you. Only when you get out of that hole – Jan Smuts airport, Customs – do you feel like saying, 'Free, free, free at last!'

Very many people asked me, when I was in Denmark, why I was going back to South Africa. They said I was in a unique position. My children were out of the country. The only person to come and join me would be my husband. And they would say, 'Don't go back to South Africa.'

But I would say, 'I must go back.' And my children felt, 'If you die, your grave is not going to be in Europe. If you must die, you grave has got to be in Africa. It has to be in South Africa.' Because this is my country. They say, 'We are not here to stay ourselves. We've come to Europe to study, and then we'll go back home. And you must go back home. It's vital. We love you.'

So I had to come back home. [...]

Just a Tiny Giant

The doctors told me I should work half-days, or at the most a four-day week, but it was simply not possible. 1982, of all years, was an important one for CCAWUSA. That was the year we made the retailing employers accept that we were here to stay. It wasn't easy. It took strikes at four of the big employers. They were not all triggered by demands for talks on recognition, but that was always the main issue that would emerge during our talks.

The first big strike was at the Edgars clothing chain group, and it began in May, when I was still in prison. It lasted for about two weeks, and one of the first things I did when I was released was to go to Khotso House to pay my respect to my bosses, the workers, who were very angry when they saw me because I had lost a lot of weight and really I was a different person altogether. It was good to be with them, and I encouraged the Edgars workers to continue with the action they were taking. It was for a good cause, and a very important strike in the sense that the workers were doing things themselves, which must have shown management that I was not the evil-doer they may have thought I was. Here were workers out on strike without anybody necessarily having 'instigated' it. The cause was low wages, but that strike was to lead to an agreement between CCAWUSA and Edgars.

Following that came the Woolworths strike, in August, which began when one of the workers, Albert Rammova, didn't come into work one day and was dismissed. I'd been involved with Woolworths before, but this time I came across several senior persons that I had not met.

The negotiations were held in Cape Town, but before we got there to sit round a table and work things out some of the senior executives, including the Personnel Director, Mr R.W. Stern, came to Khotso House, where the workers were gathered. I had told these executives what the workers had told me: that they would not go back unless Albert was reinstated, and that then it was to be without any strings attached – without loss of pay, without anything. But since these people thought I hadn't done enough, they were prepared to come and address the workers themselves, and so I said, 'Okay, I'll arrange that meeting. You come and speak to them here.'

And they came to Khotso House: tall, huge, bombastic, upright – bosses as they used to be. And we were almost 1,000 workers, packed into the hall. I remember so well the scene when the employers walked in and wanted to address us, and all those workers started singing a song to say, 'Emma, we want to know what they want here,' and 'Emma, did you allow them to come and talk to us?' and so forth.

I said, 'Well, let's give them the opportunity. Let them talk to you.'

Well, the workers made their demands. And the employers said, 'If you don't go back to work you're dismissed.' And, 'You're fired – you're all *fired*,' and so forth. And the workers told them 'We're all fired as it is. You keep your jobs.'

So we had to negotiate further. I had a very active Chairman of the union at that time, Isaac Padi, and he also would come in, and we would sit across the night, bargaining with these employers, until we could go no further, and we had to go to Cape Town.

When we got there I met the Director of Woolworths, Mr Susman, who said to me as I came in the room, 'Oh, my God, this person we fear so much. I thought she was a very big ogre of a person, yet it's just a tiny giant coming in.'

Well, he said he found I was someone he could talk to, and indeed we did have a good meeting, at the end of which the workers were reinstated and were also given the 50 rand increase they wanted.

But there was a lot to do there, at Woolworths. Workers in Woolworths had said they would never join the union because they thought that Woolworths was the best company in South Africa, until our unions went in for this dismissal and we began to look at their conditions. And then, believe me, we found many faults.

There were no promotions for black people in the retail stores. You got the job and you stayed in it. And there were only selective wage increases, just for those the management wanted to reward. The wages were terrible. Very very bad. Women suffered from having to go on confinement leave, because you had to have completed two years with the company and to have a very good record as well, or you would not qualify. You never knew if you had that very good record. You would just hear from them that you did or didn't have it. It was like this with everything, management using its 'discretion' the whole time. So we worked to say there should be a structure based on more than management's prerogative.

Even when the workers went back the employers were not happy. I would receive phone calls from them complaining that when the workers walked in they did not say, 'Good morning, sir, good morning, Mr Joseph', and so forth. So I said, 'What did they say?' They told me the workers were saying, 'Good morning, comrade,' and they did not accept this as a form of address to them.

So now the comrade war started. I said, 'What does "comrade" mean? Is "Good morning, comrade" not the same as saying, "Good morning, colleague"?' Of course it was the Marxist association, and someone was saying only recently that 'comrade' was another word for youth now in South Africa. But to them I said, 'Well, you will just have to live with it or reject it. You either greet back or you don't. But the most important thing here is the workers are not assembled there for greetings. They are assembled for being productive at work. They are either productive or they are not productive. So they either greet and you greet them back, or you don't greet them back because you are offended by "comrade".'

Another thing which offended them was that some of the workers when they walked past, instead of saying 'Good morning' at all, said '*Amandla*', which means power, and which has a reply, 'The power is ours.' This was driving them crazy, because they knew that immediately the workers withdrew their power from work that whole place would again be at a standstill. What with this and the comrade war we had phone calls and phone calls, from the most senior industrial relations personnel in Cape Town. But it died down, and we could go on with our real purpose there, which was to use our recognition and carry on with the improvement of working conditions and wages, and have unfair labour practices done away with.

Also in August was the strike at OK Bazaars. Here the starting point was wages again, and this was another long and arduous strike. The feelings of the workers in this country are so strong. They put up with so much, and when they turn around and say they have had enough, my God, they do mean it. So they have it in their hearts and minds that something must happen, and you are caught up in their determination and their fight, but at the same time you have to direct this anger into a constructive dialogue with another very angry group of people, the employers, and this takes all your strength. Once we even had to step in to protect one of the management, who was found spying in a meeting at Khotso House during the second week of that strike, and was punched and kicked by the workers, and even hit on the head by some women, with their shoes, until one of our officials stepped in and rescued him!

But again we won, and again we managed to sign an agreement with the employers. And in October, with these three battles behind us, we had the last of that year's big strikes, at the Central News Agency (CNA). Here a meeting we had arranged with the management to discuss pay and recognition was cancelled when they turned down our request to have three CNA workers accompany the CCAWUSA officials. The following week about 600 workers went on strike, and they were followed by more. This dispute was resolved in just over a week, a week of hard talking and long meetings with the workers, who never wanted just to sit at home if they were on strike but would come into Khotso House and cram themselves into the hall there, because they wanted to be together, and they knew that their solidarity and togetherness were their most powerful weapon. But that was a very long week for me, with that wonderful but demanding union presence at Khotso House and those long, long meetings with management – the last one, I remember, lasted seven and a half hours.

So by the end of that year we had won these four big battles, and with these recognitions we really had in our hands the power to change things. [...]

Those six months [in prison] brought about a great change in me. I tried to get it all out at the time, all the bad feelings and memories, but I could not, and even now there are things that come up, and I remember. These are long-term effects. I have had long-term physical effects, and long-term mental effects.

The first time I had caught sight of myself in a mirror after all that time I had been shocked. I was a different person altogether. I am a very big person by stature, a fat person, though not tall. But now I was so thin and small, and my complexion had gone so fair from being in this shade for all that time, that I couldn't believe my eyes that this was me. It shook me a lot. I thought it was my sister in that bathroom with me, my sister who is very fair.

After the loss of my teeth, caused by the terrible food I was given in Pretoria, I had to be fitted for dentures when I was in Denmark. And I have to put something on my nails to patch them, because they are always splitting and they hurt. And I have a problem with my bladder, from sitting flat on concrete floors for all that time. I'd never had these problems before, not like most women. I've always been a person who was troubled with tonsils, but never with gyny problems. But now I was advised to have a hysterectomy, much earlier than I should have had it because I was suffering with fibroids.

I was admitted to the Johannesburg General Hospital, which was originally a hospital only for whites. But the white community built a very modern, up-to-date hospital for their community and turned over their rundown hospital to black patients. The whites-only hospital which dominates the horizon of Johannesburg stands as a symbol of the attitude of whites to their own health-care and welfare: for their comparatively small community they have built an enormous hospital; our infinitely larger community has inherited their rejects.

On my day of admission a young male white doctor came to my bedside and a tray with instruments was brought. He was joined by another white doctor, an elderly man. They stood on either side of my bed and the young doctor started examining my vagina and seemed to be demonstrating something to the elderly doctor, who was taking notes. While the young doctor was inserting something into me they were talking. Then the elderly doctor left and the young doctor was joined by another white male doctor. The young doctor was now relating what he had previously done to me in the first examination and I realised that he was being examined by a professor. I was inwardly fuming, and when they had finished and were about to move away, I said to them that I regretted that their bedside manner was so horrible. I asked why they never informed me that I was going to be used as a guinea pig for their exams. I added that I had been humanely examined by a gynaecologist the previous year in Denmark, where I was treated as a human being. I said that they had also failed to prepare me for what they were going to do – that the speculum would feel cold and that it would hurt as they inserted it. They answered defensively, saying they did not know that I could speak English, but neither was at all apologetic. [...]

Two other bad things were the exhaustion and the loss of memory. When I went back to work that first time, in August, I was almost like a cabbage. I, who had always been a very productive person, now had to struggle to keep going. For a long time I felt like this. I felt that although I was free, I was still a condemned person.

It still meant so much to me to see my youngest daughter, Dudu. It meant so much, and then I heard from her that Bishop Tutu had made an arrangement for her to come and see me in January. He didn't tell me he had done this, but when I heard I was so happy. On Christmas Day, I remember, I went to the church where Bishop Tutu was preaching, and I thanked him for what he had done.

Coming back from the church, I felt exhausted, from the heat and everything, and when I got home I went to bed. I spent the whole of Christmas Day sleeping, and then Boxing Day as well. On 27 December my husband said he was driving into town. He said later he wasn't aware that I wasn't myself. He told me I said I was coming to town with him, and he said his car was giving him trouble. I said, 'Well, I can take a taxi or bus to go to hospital.' He said I insisted I wanted to go to hospital.

We drove together, and the car broke down somewhere on the outskirts of the city. He said he left me in the car and that he told me he was coming back. Then he went to get somebody to tow him, and when he came back and didn't find me in the car he thought I'd taken a taxi and proceeded to hospital.

I don't remember anything of what happened. I just remember feeling vaguely that I was walking back to Soweto. I know I went to a service station, and I stopped there and asked, 'How do I walk back to Soweto?' And they gave me the directions. I remember that. 'Walk that way, walk that way.' And I was walking, walking.

I must have got tired along the way, and I sat somewhere on the sidewalk. I was very tired and I didn't know what was going on. It happened that Tom's first cousin was driving into town, and he says he saw a person and noticed it was me. He did a U-turn and found me sitting there, and as he spoke to me he could see I was not right in my mind, and he took me into his car.

He drove me straight back to Soweto. There was no one at home so they took me to my brother's house in Dube. My brother's wife and my brother then packed me into the car and took me to our family doctor, Dr Nathatho [sic] Motlana. I don't remember any of this. It is just what I have been told. Dr Motlana told them I was very unwell, and they took me back to their home and started looking for Tom.

When they found Tom and told him, he was surprised. He reported what had happened to the DPSC, and they said I must be taken to hospital. They recommended me to go to Professor Koornhof, who is the brother of Piet Koornhof, but a very different kind of person.[1] Professor Koornhof wrote a letter to another doctor, who had to examine me, and I was then admitted to Johannesburg Hospital.

I was treated with drugs, and I spent most of the time from after Christmas until somewhere around the middle of January sleeping. But as well as the drugs they gave me a similar treatment to Inge's. They said I had still not spoken out, and I was still very much in need of that kind of therapy.

The trouble was, I knew that Dudu was about to come, and I didn't want her to find me in hospital, so when the doctors insisted that I should remain in hospital I refused. I wanted her to find me at home. It was important to me that Dudu should not know that I had, as it was, lost my senses.

I was very pleased that the day she came home she found me there, and that I was myself, a strong person. I was okay. And the week that she spent with me – it was only for a week, she had to rush to go back – was the best of times I've ever had, and I was so grateful to Desmond Tutu for arranging this for me.

I was to suffer more memory lapses, though. They came at a certain time of year, particularly in December. The first thing that I would experience was a feeling of tiredness, exhaustion, and then I would go into a deep sleep. And thereafter I never knew what happened.

One Sunday in the December of 1983 I went out to Tom, who was in the garden, and said I was going to have a rest. I went to bed. I still don't know what happened next, but when I came round on Monday morning there was blood all over the floor and I found I had lost the nail of my big toe and that I had swellings here and there on my body. Tom says the next thing he saw was me walking out of the house, nearly naked. I don't remember that. We looked around for my toenail, thinking maybe if we found it it would provide a clue as to how I got in that mess, but we couldn't find it anywhere.

I had nightmares, too. When I first came out every car move shattered me. And the thought of going back – well, when they say one gets cold feet I really know what that means. It's not just a saying. Sometimes, even in great heat, when I am perspiring and so forth, my feet are so frozen I have to cover them up.

I did manage to break my memory lapses, at least. In December 1985 my husband and family suggested I leave South Africa to see if I still suffered a lapse. So I went to Dudu, and indeed it never did come. I try always to travel at this time of year now.

For a long time I didn't talk to my family about my prison experiences. Neither Dudu nor Molly knew about many of the things I had been through until they saw me in *Mama, I'm Crying*, telling of the terrible time I could not remember Dudu's name. They kept saying, 'Mom, you never told us about this.' They didn't even know about my forgetting Dudu's name. This book will serve as a living memory of the evil of the apartheid regime. It is an opportunity for me to speak to my children.

Note

1. Piet Koornhof was at that time South Africa's Minister of Co-operation and Development. Professor H.J. Koornhof became involved in the DPSC when his daughter Hannchen was in detention. She was charged, in April–May 1982, under the Internal Security Act with passing on a code which could be used to communicate with ANC members in Botswana. She had already been held for seven months as a Terrorism Act detainee.

Anne Paton

Anne was born on 21 October 1927 in London. In 1951 she married South African Paddy Hopkins and, in 1963, together with their two children, they settled in South Africa. A few years later, when in the throes of a painful divorce, Anne felt that she needed a distraction and thus accepted her ex-neighbour's offer of employment. This 'fierce-looking old gentleman', Alan Paton, was 65 and recently widowed when they met. He was already famous for his writing (most notably, *Cry, the Beloved Country*, 1948) and his extensive anti-apartheid work. They were married in 1969.

In the 1990s Anne was the victim of numerous crimes, including car hijacking, car theft (twice), housebreaking and assault. After another attempted housebreaking (in broad daylight, while she was at home), Anne decided to leave South Africa for England in 1999 – a decision which provoked public dissension amongst Paton family members and aroused some controversy in the South African press.

The passages from ***Some Sort of a Job: My Life with Alan Paton*** (1992) recall the early days of their relationship and her attempts to come to terms with his death in 1988.

The last Sunday in October 1988 dawned dull and overcast, in contrast to some of the golden days earlier in the month. Golden days typical of October in Botha's Hill. It was spring in the garden that Alan had created, and I went to the house for the last time, early in the morning, at the time we would have been in church together. There was one last thing I had to do. I opened the front door and walked through the echoing, empty rooms. This was the house that had known all the seasons of our lives together, the wind and the rain, the mist and the damp, the heat, the floods, the cold winters, and the warmth of the spring. Now it was empty.

I went down the passage to our bedroom and Alan's private veranda and on down into the garden. There I sprinkled his ashes in the places that he had loved best. I wandered down the avenue of plane trees, and lingered by particular plants and shrubs that had meant much to him, some of which we had chosen and planted together – the fever tree from the Kruger Park, and the redwood tree from California. I lingered particularly round the most beautiful tree in the garden, the leopard tree, which had been given to us for a wedding present. Over the years it had grown from a sapling to a glorious spreading tree which sheltered the bird-feeder and bird-bath, attracting the birds that Alan loved to watch.

The birds were not singing that morning, not even the hadeda ibis with their mournful, raucous cry; they were not even sitting on the roof of Alan's study as they so often were. The only sound was that of my feet swishing through the damp grass. It was one of the loneliest moments of my life.

Alan and I had often talked about his death and funeral, usually in a fairly light-hearted way. He said that he would like to be buried on the croquet lawn, which he had turned into an arboretum after he stopped playing croquet. I had been under a certain amount of pressure from the church to place the ashes in a Garden of Remembrance, with a proper service of interment. I could not face yet another church service, and did not like the Garden of Remembrance at either Hillcrest (our current parish) or at Kloof (Alan's old parish). I had thought of putting his ashes with those of his first wife Dorrie, but I found that her ashes had been scattered long ago in the Garden of Remembrance at Stellawood Cemetery. I anguished about it, and then decided to do what I know he would have liked best – scatter them in his beloved garden.

He had created a pathway through the trees, a road, he had called it, and as I walked along it I was suddenly struck by its significance. A road had formed such an important part of Alan's philosophy of life. Did he not write those words – 'There is a lovely road that runs from Ixopo into the hills …' He felt that his whole life was a journey along a road towards that holy Mountain of Isaiah. He called the two volumes of his autobiography *Towards the Mountain* and *Journey Continued*, and he often quoted Christina Rossetti's poem 'Up-Hill': 'Does the road wind up-hill all the way? Yes, to the very end. Will the day's journey take the whole long day? From morn to night my friend'. As I stood there I suddenly realised that this road that he had made was a logical extension of his thinking. When he had started to make it, I had laughed and said, 'What on earth do you want a road there for?' He had laughed too and said he thought it would look nice. He didn't explain; maybe he didn't even realise himself why he had felt the need to make a road in his garden, leading from nowhere to nowhere. I was sorry that I had laughed, that I had not understood. There were so many things I had not understood.

I sprinkled the last of the ashes along this road, took some photographs, locked the house and drove out of the gate, closing it behind me. I have not been back again.

And so I closed a chapter of my life that had begun twenty years earlier. A chapter that had its prologue twenty-five years earlier still when my mother had said to me with uncharacteristic firmness: 'You will do a secretarial course, and then you will always be able to get some sort of a job.' […]

This was not the first time I had met Alan Paton. In 1965 Paddy and I and the children rented a house in Kloof which happened to be adjacent to the house where Alan and Dorrie lived. Our respective servants' quarters were separated by a small fence. At the end of Alan's garden lived his much trusted gardener and general factotum, Sikali. This gentleman could do no wrong in Alan's eyes, but Alan's eyes did not see to Sikali's quarters at the end of the garden. Sikali lived a gay life when off duty and there was an endless stream of visitors to his door. My maid, Beatrice, young and pretty, suffered considerable harassment from these merrymakers, and there was frequent turmoil in the night. I did not enjoy being Alan's neighbour. Was he not an anarchist, set on overthrowing the Government? We wanted nothing to do with him. Paddy and I were not inclined to the Liberal Party and I was (and still am) quite apolitical. Alan Paton meant trouble, and that was obvious from the goings-on at the end of his garden.

One day I happened to be standing deep in thought at my window, and over the hedge from the Paton property flew five little birds who promptly dropped dead in my garden. This was too much. This anarchist was obviously a bird poisoner in addition to his other undesirable activities. I looked up his number in the phone book – Alan was never one of those people who thought he was important enough to keep his name out of the telephone directory, got through to him at once and gave him a piece of my mind. I buried the birds and thought no more about it. Later on in the day I noticed a small shabby figure shuffling up the drive, dressed in a regrettable raincoat and a shapeless hat, and carrying a walking stick. Who on earth could this be? I was not long left in doubt. It was my neighbour, Alan Paton.

'Where are the bodies?' he asked.

'Buried, of course,' I snapped, and went on snapping about his gardener, his behaviour, his poisoning of the birds and his general undesirability.

He stood his ground and came out with some cock-and-bull story of how the birds had obviously flown into the white wall of my house by mistake and dashed out their brains. He said he was a bird lover, and he never used poisons in his garden.

'You may not do so, but I'll bet your gardener does,' I said.

He eventually crept away, thoroughly cowed I hoped. He later told me that he went back and told Dorrie that some frightful harridan lived next door …

That should have been the end of our acquaintance, but we had a mutual friend who was to shape our lives in a way that could never have been imagined on that day. My daughter Athene had a friend called Ann Francis, and as a result I got to know her family, her parents Goondie and Susan, and their three children John, Ann and Vicky. They were to be closely entwined with our lives for many years.

Paddy and I were divorced in 1967 and now that I was on my own, and in need of some distraction to cheer me up, Goondie had an idea. He fancied himself as a matchmaker. He had at least two successes to his credit and, flushed with confidence, he thought he would try again. Dorrie died in October 1967 after a long illness, and Alan was utterly bereft and helpless. He desperately needed a secretary. Dorrie had acted as his secretary all their married life, and while she lay dying she would say to him, 'I will be able to get back to work next week.' The doctors insisted that she should not be told that her illness was terminal, and Alan had to keep up the charade. He could not tell her that she would not be back at work next week, and he could not engage a secretary to help him. He longed to tell Dorrie the truth so that they could share it, but he obeyed the doctors – to his eternal regret.

Thus Goondie had two lonely friends, and the solution was obvious to him at once. I should become Alan's secretary. I told Goondie about the incident of the birds and how I was sure Alan Paton would never want to see me again. Goondie must have convinced him that I was not really so bad, because Alan agreed to meet me. On 21 December 1967 I went round to the Francis household and we were introduced. We made a plan to meet in January to discuss the terms of my employment. I do not recall my feelings after this first meeting, and Alan never remembered the meeting at all.

In January he phoned me to arrange an interview, and on 5 February 1968 I went round to his house. I remember clearly what he was wearing because it was so unsuitable – I thought – for a famous and important person. He wore a cotton shirt, shabby and shapeless shorts, shoes and socks, and a straw hat. He took me to his study, took off his hat, went behind his desk and motioned me to sit opposite him. He glared at me and asked me gruffly if I could type well. I said I could, and told him that I had been brushing up on my shorthand during the last few weeks. He agreed to pay me the princely sum of R1 an hour and we got to work at once. He dictated eleven letters at great speed and I rushed home to type them out while they were fresh in my mind. He also gave me a Foreword to type – 'See how you get on with my writing,' he said. I typed it out most beautifully, and submitted it the next morning, full of the satisfaction of a job well done. He looked at it, he looked at me. 'Mrs Hopkins, how do you spell foreword?' he asked.

'F O R W A R D,' I said smugly.

Alan sighed, and explained, with gestures, the difference between 'forward' and 'foreword'. I was stricken. I had surely lost the job, he wouldn't employ me now. I thought I would try and brighten up the atmosphere. 'I really can spell quite well usually,' I said. 'I can spell exorbitant, E X H O R B I T A N T.' I was triumphant. Alan looked quite stunned, and then suggested that the word really did not have an 'h' in it. I was about to crawl away, humble and defeated, when he suddenly laughed. His laugh completely transformed his face, and I realised that the ferocious glare was really a twinkle. He said he thought that we would manage. And so I became his secretary.

There were many, many letters to begin with, most of them dating months back, and the majority were letters of condolence on Dorrie's death. She had been a greatly beloved lady, and the letters were very moving. Every morning I would go along to the Paton home with my shorthand notebook. Alan would dictate, and I would take the letters home and type them out on my faithful

Imperial Portable Good Companion, a machine that to the typing world was what the Ford Model T was to the motorist. It was the workhorse of all typists, and I had had mine for twenty years. Over the years to follow I acquired better and more elaborate typewriters, but it was Alan's constant complaint that none of these magnificent machines could spell. My spelling was certainly a bit of a stumbling block all our lives together, but he coped manfully. In one letter to a friend in England he described the birds in his garden and referred in particular to the sombre bulbul, which I duly typed as Bull Bull. He wrote a postscript to the letter explaining that his new secretary was English – 'a very nice woman, but she does not know much about South African birds'.

We soon settled into a routine. Every morning at 10.30 the maid would bring in tea and usually some tomato sandwiches. After a few days I took over the teapot. Not being sure how Alan liked his tea, I said, 'Shall I stick some more water in the pot?'

'Certainly, Mrs Hopkins. I presume you brought the glue?' was his response, chuckling to himself at his own joke.

And so started what I like to call my tertiary education in English. At his hands my vocabulary doubled and my English improved enormously.

Alan was very difficult to work for because he was so disorganised. He had a little paper diary, the kind that is handed out free by the chemist, and he kept it in his shirt pocket. It was a miracle that it never went into the wash, but he frequently did not have it handy when he answered the phone, and as a result he would sometimes double-date, even triple-date. Many times I would come along in the morning to be greeted with surprise. 'Oh, didn't I tell you I was going to the doctor, lawyer, dentist etc?' No, indeed he hadn't. He would cast around vaguely for some work for me to do. 'Just occupy yourself for a bit, I will be back soon,' he would say. And occupy myself I did. I tackled his study which was a complete shambles of unanswered letters from months back, unfiled documents lying in heaps, unreconciled bank statements, unread proofs, and unrelated papers, crowding every available space.

One morning I tentatively asked him if he knew that he was R5 000 overdrawn at the bank. He was astonished. 'My goodness,' he said. 'I wonder why?' I eventually located the problem, brought order out of chaos, and generally set the pattern for the years ahead. I made myself indispensable, but there was one fly in the ointment. He had to pay me. This was a concept quite foreign to him. Dorrie had been his secretary, and other odd jobs that had been done for him had been done by adoring fans for love. Not me, I wanted payment, and he very grudgingly paid me at the end of every month, R1 an hour – I kept meticulous records.

Work was not all letters, however. At this time he was writing *Kontakion For You Departed* which was about his life with Dorrie. I was the first person to see the manuscript, and I appear in the book on page 77. I took it home and typed it for him, and was fascinated by the change that came over him as the book progressed. Doing it was for him a catharsis. He wrote out his grief and sadness, and when the book was finished he was ready to take the next step forward.

During this time our relationship was slowly changing. During our morning working sessions the time for work grew shorter and the time for talking grew longer. To the day he died Alan hated writing letters, and would use any excuse to get out of doing them. By March he was calling me Anne, but it was some time before I was sufficiently at ease with him to call him by his first name. We met frequently as guests at the Francis home – all part of Goondie's plan, of course, and our association was ripening into friendship. In May Alan went to Mariannhill Hospital to have his varicose veins attended to. I visited him from time to time, joining him for his evening whisky which we drank out of toothmugs, much to his amusement. He was very proud of the great number of stitches they took out of his legs, and he kept them in a jar by his bed for his visitors to admire. I remember remarking that one could admire gallstones, or something concrete, but not stitches. He was a bit crestfallen! All this time my divorce was being finalised and I visited Alan in hospital on the evening after the case had been heard. He was very kind and concerned. When he was well enough to go home it was I who collected him from hospital. Where were all his other friends at this time, I wondered? When we drove home he said he was reminded of how he had felt after being in hospital for 77 days with typhoid in 1934. The world looked new and fresh and wonderful to him.

A few days after his return home Alan gave me a note which I was not to read until I got home. I was in a panic; what had I done? But the note was to say that he was in trouble; his reputation was likely to be damaged, and I might not want to work for him any more. (In my diary I wrote 'Idiot!' How could I not want to work for him any more?) The background to the story was that a few months earlier he had given a lift to an African man and had taken him to [Clermont], a nearby township. The man had grabbed him round the throat and demanded money. Fortunately a Mr Khumalo had come to Alan's rescue, and he escaped with nothing more than a very sore throat. Now the case had come to court and the defence was claiming that Alan had gone to [Clermont] to 'pick up' an African woman. Although this accusation was rejected as absurd, it was very unpleasant and hateful for Alan. He behaved with great dignity throughout it all, and was very grateful to me for standing by him.

And so the days and weeks flew past, and Goondie decided the time had come to make his next move. He and Susan organised that the four of us should go to the cinema together, and at the last minute they cancelled on some flimsy excuse. Alan and I would have to go alone. I was appalled. Who was I to go out with the great Alan Paton? But Alan insisted. I rummaged in my wardrobe for something to wear, and came up with an old velvet maternity dress which had been converted to a different shape. Maternity dresses never convert successfully, but I had tried with this one because I liked the colour. I thought I looked quite elegant. All that Alan noticed (so he told me later) was that the dress got very creased ... We went to see *Whispers* with Dame Edith Evans, and afterwards he took me out to dinner at Saltori's Restaurant, which was a great favourite of his.

He drove me home, and I felt I should invite him in for coffee. It was August, and very cold. I was far too mean to light the fire at 11 o'clock at night however, and he sat and shivered on one side of the room, and I sat on the other. We chatted idly and somehow got onto the subject of his future. I said that I had noticed the interest shown by some of his female correspondents and expected that he would marry again. He gave me what I can only describe as a coy look and said, 'If I marry anyone I should like it to be someone like you.' I was overcome with confusion and took this as a proposal. To the end of his life he would maintain that it had certainly not been intended as a proposal, he was merely making an observation! I was astounded. By now I had fallen under his spell, and was devoted to him, but the thought of marriage could not have been further from my mind. I was in a turmoil: he was too old (25 years older than I), we were unsuited, our backgrounds were very different, and I knew nothing of politics or of intellectuals.

However, Goondie now started to apply pressure. He invited Alan and me together to dinner and lunch on every possible occasion, and there was a great deal of teasing and fun and laughter. Susan didn't think Goondie's plan was such a good idea; she thought we were unsuited. Goondie was undaunted. I did put up a token resistance because I felt it was too soon after my divorce to be thinking of marriage again. I was not sure of my feelings, and was full of doubts. Alan had no doubts, however, and eventually he convinced me that mine were unfounded.

And so I said yes. But it was not all plain sailing after that. We spent a great deal of time together, going for long drives round the countryside, and talking endlessly, getting to know one another, and making plans. There were many problems. First of all, where were we going to live? Alan had expected that I would move into his house in Kloof, and was upset when I refused. But I could not live in Dorrie's house: I wanted us to start afresh. We spent many fruitless days house-hunting. Alan had to have a house with space for a croquet lawn; I wanted to be near Hillcrest so that my daughter Athene could keep her horse. I wanted a reasonably modern house; Alan didn't care. The house at Kloof was rather inconvenient and difficult to run, but he had got used to it. Later in life he was to appreciate the comforts of home, but at that time they were unimportant to him. Eventually, in November we happened to drive past a house in Botha's Hill with a 'For Sale' notice outside. We went in on impulse and within half an hour had agreed to buy it. We were to live in this house for the whole period of our married life.

During this time I was being introduced to Alan's friends. We were not officially engaged, but certain select friends were let in on the secret. There was no doubt about their reaction. They were appalled. What was Alan thinking of, marrying this totally unsuitable person, too young, too flippant, apolitical, light minded, ill educated. I was altogether wrong. I have since talked to some of these friends, who have admitted that anyone would have been wrong for Alan, as far as they were concerned. They were possessive of him, and I was an interloper. They also felt pushed aside in some way, rather like children having to welcome a new stepmother. To put it bluntly, they were jealous!

I was taken to meet Alan's closest friend, and he didn't approve at all. I really would not do, he told Alan. So much did Alan value the opinion of this friend that he was cast into gloom from which he took days to recover. It was at this time that he made the remark that being engaged to me was like setting out on a beautiful sunny morning to walk over a wonderful landscape – and promptly falling into a bog. I am afraid that I did not forgive this particular person for his destructive criticism, and always treated him warily and with reserve. Yet, since Alan died, he has shown more concern for me than almost any of his other friends. I have forgiven him now.

In addition to all our other difficulties there was a problem with the Church. Alan was a staunch Anglican, and attending Communion on Sunday morning was an essential part of the routine of his life. Now he was to be barred from this. Because he was to marry a divorced woman, the disapproval of the Church descended on his head. The Archbishop of Cape Town at the time, the Most Reverend Selby Taylor, appeared to me to be a hard and unforgiving man.

Aware of the Church's disapproval, Alan wrote to him offering to resign from the Order of Simon of Cyrene. This is a most distinguished body limited to fifty Anglican laymen and women who are judged to have rendered outstanding service to the Church. The Archbishop accepted his resignation, and withdrew his plans to invite Alan to sit on the liturgical committee to discuss the new Prayer Book. Alan also felt obliged to resign from the council of St Peter's College at Fort Hare. Alan was not entirely cast out, however: the Archbishop graciously agreed that there was no reason why Alan should not continue with his plans to write the life of Archbishop Clayton.

Once the news of our impending wedding appeared in the press, it revealed the fact that Paddy had been married before. The Bishop of Natal, the late Vernon Inman, telephoned Alan and said that all was well. As I had married a divorced man, I was not married in the eyes of the Church, and Alan was in the clear. To his eternal credit Alan said drily, 'I suppose you would consider that her children are illegitimate?' The Bishop said no more. After a suitable period of penance Alan was restored to the Church, and to the Order of Simon of Cyrene, but it was too late for him to go back on the liturgical committee. Alan was a very forgiving man, and bore all this with fortitude, but it was a most distressing time for him. [...]

In October we went away for a week to Peter and Phoebe Brown's cottage at Giant's Castle in the Drakensberg mountains. Quite what my neighbours thought I don't know – they saw me driving off in the car with a strange man and a mountain of luggage. This was an idyllic holiday. The cottage is remote and private with a wonderful view. It is also very primitive, the Bushman's River being the only source of water, and the lavatory a 'long drop' in the garden. We bathed in the river, walked and read, and Alan did some writing. We had come away to see if a week entirely on our own was supportable. We were going through the usual doubts that beset engaged couples, and in our case there were many difficulties and hazards. We found, however, that we were entirely happy in one another's company, and returned home refreshed and reassured.

I also had to meet Alan's family, his two sons David and Jonathan, and their wives, and their five children. When I was introduced to David's wife Nancy, she said, 'You must be mad or very brave to consider marrying a Paton.' I didn't find this very encouraging.

On 24 November the news broke in the papers. Someone had leaked it to them, and Alan was convinced it was the Security Police. His phone was tapped and his mail investigated in those days, and nothing was hidden from the authorities. Frankly I think Alan leaked it himself. He loved talking to the newspapers, and could not keep a secret. Once the news was out we were hounded unmercifully. This was my first introduction to the ruthless behaviour of the press. I arrived for work one morning and Alan said, 'I am afraid the newspapers are here.' They had cameras of course, and I was horrified. I was not properly dressed for a photograph and my hair was a mess. Indeed the resulting photograph, published all over the country, shows a smugly smiling Alan sitting beside a frumpish female who looks as if she has a hot potato in her mouth. There was one gentleman of the press who was very persistent and kept phoning me up at all hours. Eventually I gave him a vague (and false) date – 'probably the last day in January'. By arranging to get married a day earlier, on 30 January, we thought we were being very clever, but the press found out, as they always do. This particular newshound, who worked for an international syndicate, was only doing his job, but I got very irritated with him. I didn't hear from him again until nineteen years and more had passed, and Alan lay dying. Then he pestered me again. It was he whom I phoned first with the news of Alan's death.

Alan wanted to be married in Church. The Anglican Church would not marry us, but the Methodist Church was much more accommodating, and so we were married on 30 January 1969 in the old Methodist Church in Durban by the Reverend Robert Irvine. Alan decided he would start off the day by cutting the poinsettias in his garden. He got his hands covered in latex, and was in a great state because he could not get it off! It was an extremely hot day, and during the ceremony a bead of perspiration rolled down to the end of my nose. Alan watched this with interest and often joked about it in after years. He could not get the ring on my podgy, sweaty finger and I had to push it on myself. It was a trifle tight, but – being hopelessly superstitious – I never took it off my hand until after Alan died.

Our wedding was attended only by David and Nancy and Jonathan and his wife Margaret and a few close friends, including, of course, Goondie and Susan Francis. We had a celebratory lunch at Saltori's Restaurant, during which Goondie went out into the street and came back waving a news placard: 'Alan Paton Married'. We drove off to Peter Brown's cottage at Giant's Castle for our honeymoon, spending a night at the Imperial Hotel in Pietermaritzburg on the way.

This is the place where one writes that we lived happily ever after, but it was not quite as simple as that.

The New
South Africa

1990 to 2000

In his opening speech to Parliament on 2 February 1990, F. W. de Klerk legalised the ANC, SACP and other opposition parties, and lifted restrictions on listed people. Nelson Mandela walked out of prison in Cape Town a free man on 11 February 1990. In 1991, the De Klerk government repealed a host of apartheid laws, including the Group Areas Act and the Population Registration Act. By this time, at least 3,5 million people had been the victims of forced removal. The about-turn was supported by the majority of whites: in March 1992, 68,6 per cent of those whites who participated in a referendum mandated De Klerk to continue the reform process.

Soon after De Klerk had assumed control, 'talks about talks' began between the ANC and the government to resolve issues such as the release of political prisoners, indemnity for exiles, the re-incorporation of the bantustans into South Africa, and the composition of a government of national unity. Also at stake was the mutual commitment to end violence.

During the transition period (1990–1994) violence escalated: in the first eight months of 1990, more than 700 people died in unrest. As negotiations progressed, right-wing militancy resurfaced and protests, mass action and violence, in particular between ANC and IFP supporters, continued to erupt, leading to massive loss of life. There were also the apparently random massacres of innocent people by what the ANC termed a 'third force': from mid-1990 to March 1994, apparently motiveless train attacks had left more than 600 people dead and 1 400 injured. There were also farm murders and the ringing cries of PAC supporters, 'One settler, one bullet'. It is estimated that between 1991 and 1993 approximately 10 000 people died in politically motivated violence. Although there was much good news, such as in October 1993 when Mandela and De Klerk were jointly awarded the Nobel Peace Prize and when the United

Nations lifted sanctions against South Africa, the years before the first democratic elections were extremely tense: the outcome of the negotiations was never certain, and the economy took a hammering.

Negotiations culminated in a draft constitution for a new South Africa and the re-acceptance of South Africa by the international community. Still, it was not all smooth sailing to the first democratic elections: Chief Mangosuthu Buthelezi of the IFP rejected the arrangement because it seemed prejudicial to his supporters. (Buthelezi's credibility was at an all-time low, however, for in 1991 it was discovered that the apartheid government had been providing funding and military training for the IFP.) The month before the election, IFP marchers attacked the ANC headquarters in Johannesburg and over 50 people were killed. Literally days before the election (set for 27 April 1994), Buthelezi yielded and joined the election battle. (Special stickers had to be hastily printed and stuck onto ballot papers.)

Those who had been 'citizens' of the 'independent homelands' regained South African citizenship in January 1994 so that they could vote and, after the election, these areas were reincorporated into South Africa. The ANC won an overwhelming majority and, on 10 May 1994, Nelson Mandela was inaugurated as President. That year, South Africa rejoined the Commonwealth and the UN General Assembly. It had been a decade stained with the blood of more than 20 000 South Africans.

The idea for the Truth and Reconciliation Commission (TRC) was proposed by the new Minister of Justice, Dullah Omar, in July 1994. The aim was to discover what had led to gross violations of human rights, and to deal with that past by granting amnesty to those who made full disclosure of their deeds. The TRC was set up in 1995 with 17 members, headed by Archbishop Desmond Tutu. One committee investigated gross violations of human rights between 1960 and 1994. Public hearings were held around the country in 1996 and 1997, and over 20 000 statements by victims and survivors were recorded. Another committee heard applications for amnesty by over 7 000 men (no women applied for amnesty). The testimony of victims and perpetrators shocked South Africa: not only were the apartheid regime's secret death squads uncovered, but also torture in ANC camps and the much publicised activities of Winnie Mandela and her personal guard, the Mandela United Football Club. A third committee advised the government on reparations and rehabilitation for victims of gross abuses of human rights. In 2003, the ANC government announced a blanket reparation payout of R30 000 for each successful applicant.

For most South Africans, 1994 marked the birth of a new – and wonderful – South Africa. Integration at schools, in hospitals and elsewhere happened remarkably smoothly and affirmative action employment policies resulted in the increasing Africanisation of all institutions and in an expanding black middle class. With the collapse of apartheid, indigenous languages (for the first time) acquired official status. South Africa now has eleven official languages. Democratic South Africa has been heralded with a new brightly coloured flag and an Africanised coat of arms, and a revised multilingual national anthem. On 10 December 1996, the democratic constitution was adopted. The constitution, hailed as one of the most liberal in the world, abolished the death penalty. In 1999, Nelson Mandela's term ended and Thabo Mbeki became President.

Profound reconstruction notwithstanding, the budding democracy has not, in nine years, transformed all lives: the poorest people are still mostly black and unemployment is high. By 1990, there were an estimated 5–7 million squatters living in shacks. The numbers have since grown. South Africa is reputed to have the third highest murder rate in the world and the second highest rate of serial homicides. In one twelve-month period, between July 1999 and July 2000, police reported 23 832 murders and 51 249 rapes. (Terrifyingly, rape reportage is believed by commentators to be as low as 20 per cent – and, of those reported, conviction rates are similarly poor.) All of this, along with the devastating AIDS pandemic (an estimated 30 per cent of the population is HIV-positive) has seriously tainted, but not destroyed, South Africans' celebration of the 'miracle' of the new South Africa.

AnnMarie Wolpe

AnnMarie Kantor married Harold Wolpe in 1955. They had three children. Harold was a member of the banned ANC and acted as lawyer to Nelson Mandela, Walter Sisulu and other key ANC figures in numerous cases. When he was imprisoned under the Ninety-Day Detention law in 1963, AnnMarie smuggled a saw and files into the prison, thus helping him and three others to escape. AnnMarie and the children fled South Africa in 1963. They lived in exile in Britain until 1991, when the prospect of political resolution led AnnMarie and Harold to apply for indemnity from the apartheid government.

AnnMarie is a leading feminist academic who developed the Women's Studies programme at Middlesex University in the 1980s, wrote *Feminism and Materialism*, and was a founder member of the leading feminist journal, *Feminist Review*. The passages below are taken from **The Long Way Home** (1994). She recounts the difficulties of returning to South Africa after decades of life in exile. She and Harold lived in Cape Town until his death in 1996.

We are caught up in an euphoria about what is happening in South Africa. First Walter Sisulu and Ahmed Kathrada and other Rivonia trialists freed. And now Nelson Mandela, who retained the Presidency of the ANC even though he was serving such an inhuman sentence. Mandela handles the international press as though he has always been in the spotlight. It is awe-inspiring to watch and listen to this regal man, particularly recalling how he spent more than twenty years on Robben Island, for fifteen of which he was forced to break stones at the quarry. I recall seeing Robben Island, a little blob in the distance off the coast of Cape Town – a place that was a refuge, a source of food for passing seamen, and finally a prison for the insane, the criminals, and now political prisoners. […]

March 1990

Harold is getting decidedly excited about the thought of returning to South Africa. He is not one to be overtly enthusiastic: his hallmark is restraint and level-headedness. There are not many things that get him really worked up. One is bad driving in London; another is a really good intellectual argument. He is like a terrier, worrying at the problem and never giving up. The cross-examination skills he acquired as a barrister stand him in good stead. The children get furious with him if they have an argument. 'We can't win. He's impossible,' Nicholas complains, and I tend to agree. Sometimes I have to pacify wounded feelings when people take his arguments as personal attacks. They never are; Harold just loves a good discussion. We are so very different. I get excited; he remains composed. Unlike me, he seldom gets worked up over situations or events or people, and is irritated by what he calls my extreme responses. Just as well. It would be impossible if we were similar.

'I'm bored at Essex,' he says. This is only part of the story. He is disenchanted with the department, which fails to give him any tangible recognition for things he has written which have had a major impact in South Africa and among Africanists in general. 'Essex Sociology Department appears singularly unimpressed. The trouble is that what I write is not regarded as sociology,' he adds, somewhat wistfully. This was evident in his belated promotion to Senior Lecturer and then never getting a chair. 'And I have to retire in a few years' time, in any event. I might as well go to South Africa, where it seems I can go on and on working.' Of course there are other, even stronger reasons pulling him back, chiefly a sense of obligation. 'They're going to need people like us, with our expertise. There's so much work to be done when the apartheid system goes. While the problems are going to be enormous, it will be tremendously exciting helping to build a new South Africa. It isn't going to be easy,' he adds, anticipating my doubts about people in our age group having enough stamina to cope with the difficulties, even assuming that the political harassment by the state ceases. 'I have been free all these years. I owe it to the others. I can't say now: Tough shit, you get on with the work while I enjoy life in London and Europe. I can't do it. It would deny all that I believe in. It would make a mockery of my political beliefs, and everything I have stood for and done in the past.'

I understand that and believe, as our children do, that his politics have always been his driving force. The children are proud of Harold, and respect him. I, even more than them, am aware of the extraordinary integrity, selflessness and honesty by which he has lived his life. Acknowledging that does not make it easier for me. The payoff is zero financially. It certainly doesn't help with the bank balance. Worse than that, the struggle against apartheid had been a particularly bloody one and left a trail of broken lives, and the impact on us has not been inconsiderable.

It is quite simple: I don't want to go back. 'I wouldn't mind seeing the place, but live there – never. Anyway, it won't be safe. There's bound to be someone who wants to get you.' I say all this unconvincingly, because I know now without any doubt that he wants to return. Any move by us will have massive repercussions for Peta, Jonny, Tessa and Nicholas, and I am torn by misgivings.

April 1990

In March I thought spring was here, but the weather is always deceptive. A blossom comes out, the sun shines falteringly for a day, and the birds cavort around. Then we're plunged cruelly back into cold, dreary, gloomy days. 'It's at times like this,' my eccentric neighbour Phoebe once said, 'that people commit suicide. They think everything is getting better. They are fooled – it doesn't.' Now it really is spring, and I understand well the old saying I used to hear as a child, and which never made sense: 'Ne'er cast a clout till May is out', because the temperature doesn't equal the burgeoning new growth. The darkness has lifted, the days are getting longer, blossom is everywhere, although the horse chestnuts are late this year. I always feel better when summer is round the corner.

There is little doubt now that sooner or later Harold will go to South Africa although, of course, the question of his indemnity has yet to be resolved. 'It's impossible to get any clarity,' he complains. 'No one knows whether the co-conspirator charge had been proscribed. Even if it has, there's always the possibility that they will find some other reason to detain me.' I worry less about formal imprisonment than about his being on a hit list. I have yet to be convinced that the change of heart extends to those people who have been responsible for the murders of so many apartheid opponents in the past.

After more than thirty-five years of marriage, being with someone becomes something of a habit. That isn't what our relationship is all about. I can't say simply: I love him, and will follow him to the ends of the earth. It isn't like that after all these years. Our lives are inextricably tied up with our children, although Nicholas and Tessa in particular complain that Harold's involvement in politics takes precedence over everything else. And there are times when I have felt the same. From time to time I have craved his undivided attention, but have had to share it with all his other responsibilities, including his political ones. I would down everything for him in a crisis. I had never been absolutely sure that he would do the same for me, until I had the hip operations. He was incredibly supportive over the long recovery period. It must have come as a huge shock to see me so vulnerable and dependent. Normally I have been strong and able to bear all sorts of adversities. He is not demonstrative, yet I know that he depends on me every bit as much as I depend on him, although for very different reasons. We share many interests, and are excellent companions. He has been my mentor, and now he is my sharpest and most reliable critic, even if I always throw my hands up in horror and threaten to give up academic life after he has dissected what I have written. He is used to my histrionics, and I am used to his low-key responses.

Could I possibly allow him to go to South Africa without me? Could I really not go with him? Every now and again I entertain the idea. Contrary to my expectations, I unexpectedly loved living on my own in Berkeley when I taught at University of California, Davis in 1985. I wallowed in the freedom of being answerable to no one, coming and going when I liked, buying my own car, having my own bank account, eating when I felt like it – although it was a bit lonely, and I would set out my tray in front of the TV. I did not have to think about anyone except myself. That was for a limited period. Could I do it now, calculatingly, going on sixty? Somebody I know separated from her husband recently, and she says she is deliriously happy doing her own thing. Harold and I enjoy being with each other, we have fun, and we have our serious moments. Being with Harold is a consolidation of years of trials, tribulations and love. I can't leave him.

The trouble is that I do not feel duty bound to return to South Africa. I have always had doubts about the role of white people, particularly in my age group. I doubt whether black people would welcome the likes of me back. If I was black, I think I would feel hostility towards all white people.

Then, of course there are Peta and Jonathan, Tessa, and Nicholas. Our departure would disrupt their lives as much as it would mine and Harold's. Tessa is the most blunt: 'I hate South Africa for what it has done to our family and to all our friends. And I am angry with you for being involved.' She directs her remarks to Harold. Her unhappiness is transparent. Late at night Harold and I talk about this and wonder whether it wouldn't be a good thing for her to be separated from us. She seems to have been the one most affected by our exile. Perhaps she would finally come to terms with it and live her own life. [...]

May 1990

[...] The phone calls between Harold and South Africa don't abate. Harold is now being coerced to agree to take up a post either as Professor of Sociology or as a director of a research unit at UWC. It seems a *fait accompli* that he is returning to South Africa. Somehow we don't sit down and talk about my desires or hopes or wishes. It seems to be taken for granted that I too will return. Harold is vague, but says there should be no problem in my getting a job as well. I certainly won't entertain the idea of going out to South Africa if I don't have a job waiting for me. [...]

South Africa will be a foreign country. I will be a stranger in my home country. I find myself trying to catalogue in concrete terms what I will actively miss, and I have games with myself as I drive along the streets of London trying to work out exactly what it will be. It is difficult, because there is so much one takes for granted, like the specialist shops. I know where to buy the best Turkish sweetmeats, I know who the best fishmonger is. It is having oysters for starters and goose for Christmas. It is knowing which bargains to go for at the

January sales. It is walking in the back streets of Mayfair and marvelling at a gem of a house that you suddenly come upon. It is the annual summer Channel crossing and drive through sleepy French villages, remembering the siestas that go on from midday through to 2.30. It is our friends and the interesting and stimulating intellectuals; exotic meals cooked by Sami, one of my closest friends; browsing in Camden Lock, and always returning to my favourite stalls, where I know I will find the right present for someone; instant access to books hot off the press; my teaching and my students. It is the delight of the flower market in the East End on Sunday mornings; the best TV in the world; our best friend Roy, who visits us regularly when he has a gig on in or near London.

Perhaps most importantly, it is far from the violence and the red dust and the heat and the noise and the children who run barefoot though the veld.

Going home. Those words, once spoken spontaneously, are no longer in the same league as 'I want to visit the Far East', 'I want to go to Mexico', 'I would love to see what Johannesburg looks like now', or 'Wouldn't it be lovely to go and stay with my sister, Betty, and walk on the squeaky white sands of Clifton Beach'. Going home is no longer fantasy.

Nicky Arden

Nicolette Schey was born in the 1940s in Durban. In 1966 she and her husband emigrated to the USA owing to their disillusionment with apartheid. After suffering chronic and severe depression for a period of two years, she returned to South Africa. On a visit to a game reserve, a chance encounter with a *sangoma* led to her undertaking a two-year training course in traditional African medicine.

The passage from ***The Spirits Speak: One Woman's Mystical Journey into the African Spirit World*** (1996) begins when she is still in training. Her mentor, Joyce, is a full-time domestic worker for a white family in Johannesburg, seeing her clients in her *khaya*, the tiny servant's room still found in the backyard of whites' homes all over South Africa. When they first meet, Joyce is wearing characteristic maid's garb; at the next meeting, she is transformed, wearing a red skirt fringed with beads, and beads across her chest, around her neck and head; she watches as another *sangoma* ascertains from the ancestors that Arden 'has the spirit' and may thus embark on training. But Arden must learn not only how to allow the spirits to work through her; she must also grapple with her Western value system.

A month of nights with Joyce goes by quickly.

'You must try and *phalaza* again,' Joyce said a couple of times, and I begin a modified version, working with small amounts of the pink liquid. I also continue to inhale the deadly snuff, though my nose is still constantly blocked or running, and every now and then it suddenly bleeds, no matter how small a pinch I take. Often now the region of my third eye feels aroused, drawn forward, in a sensation that is almost painful, and occasionally the east calls and I face the morning sun and meditate on light, on enlightenment.

And one morning while I meditate, eyes closed over the wisping smoke curls of the *imphepho*, my shoulders curve into a different shape, my nose lifts differently to the air. A rolling motion begins, starting with my shoulders; it is strange, yet familiar. And I am gone.

My front legs tread in sure footfalls, shoulders rolling. I walk on substance, yet in space; untethered, unleashed from belonging. All is consumed in the motion, in the liquidly repetitive padding, in the smooth sweep of the shoulders.

As with the snake, this creature has become me, my body – her host. We travel through an insubstantial surround where no sound penetrates, where there is no sense of time.

The return is slow, reluctant. Sound returns first, then sensation. When I open my eyes, the contours of the furniture seem hard and square.

Joyce looks at me long and hard when I tell her. 'What kind of animal?' she asks.

'I'm not sure,' I answer, 'not a lion, more like a leopard.' She nods but doesn't answer.

Ron is due to arrive shortly, and for these last few days alone I'd been worried. All my concentration had been going into working with Joyce; there was no one else to tug at me.

And indeed, once he is here I seem to feel immobilized. During the day I don't eat the foam regularly or inhale the *imphepho*; my attention is split between the *sangoma* work and him. Not that he does anything to distract me, it is just the fact of his being here. From the beginning Joyce had been clear that we were not to have sex while I was in training, and aside from the occasional nudges, he holds to the agreement.

I soon feel mired. The thought of driving to Bordeaux becomes galling and I stall and arrive late. When I dance I am slow to see.

'Your spirits are not coming up today,' Sylvia says one night after a laborious session of dancing and divining.

'No, they're not.'

'Don't worry, we all go through times like this while we are training. Sometimes it feels like we just want to say, forget this, but you must fight this feeling, just fight it and keep going, and the spirits will come back up.' And I feel relieved that it's not just me.

One evening after I have been particularly slow and sit in embarrassed silence, a woman comes to visit Joyce. Her name is Emily. She is plump, dark-skinned and pink-cheeked.

As she and Joyce speak in Zulu, I become increasingly aware that my hands feel hot and prickly, my face sweaty, my mouth dry, and somewhere in my legs an ache begins. After a while I interrupt. 'Emily, do your hands sometimes feel hot and prickly?' I ask.

'Yes,' the woman answers.

'And your face,' I ask, 'does your face also sometimes feel hot and your mouth dry?'

'Yes,' she says again, and she says something to Joyce in Zulu. Now they are both looking at me.

'And your body also,' I say, as the heat moves from my face down my chest.

'Yes,' she answers.

'Your legs, they also hurt you?'

Her eyes are wide.

Something clicks in my head. 'Do you drink a lot of water?' I ask.

'Yes,' she says, 'even at night.'

I am suddenly sure that she is diabetic. But how to say it? How to leap across the cultures? Also, I cannot undermine Joyce, and I feel that by saying something I would be doing just that.

Later, when she is gone, I ask Joyce if she has been prescribing anything for her. Yes, she says, she is giving her herbs to *phalaza* and steam herself, but, she adds, the sickness is because she must take the spirit and become a *sangoma*. Her spirits are calling her.

That night I wrestle with the conundrum of my western worries and traditional practices. What if this woman is diabetic? What if she goes on believing it's the spirits calling her? The next morning when, back at the flat, I see Jean out watering her little garden below, I go down and talk to her about it.

'This is why doctors can't stand *sangomas*,' she explodes. 'Here this poor woman could well lose her sight or her legs. You've got to say something to Joyce.'

For a few days I mull this over, unsure of how to raise the issue. Finally, one night I tell Joyce of someone I knew who had similar symptoms and was diagnosed as diabetic. 'Perhaps Emily should go and have a blood test,' I suggest, 'because it's something that could become dangerous.'

But Joyce's eyes close down and I know this will go no further.

My dreams lately have been filled with images of men with no legs or with only stumps for legs. When I tell Joyce about them she says that it is my spirits. 'Your spirits want to be picked up again, because when Ron came they went down, down, down.'

'What must I do?'

'No, you just keep eating your foam and doing your herbs and you will be all right.'

Later on we talk some more about dreams.

'If somebody keeps dreaming she's having a baby or she's sleeping with a man, or a man with a wife, that's not good.'

'Why?' I ask.

'That means,' Joyce answers, 'that there is somebody sending you horrible things. It's when you dream that same thing again and again.'

'How,' I ask, 'do people send these bad things?'

'I don't know,' she answers, 'because I don't know how to do it.'

'Why do people do these things?'

'Because they're jealous,' she responds. 'Like I'm working, and maybe they think I'm getting lots of money and they want the job. Or they want my house or the things inside. It's only the jealous ones who do those things. They go to people who are willing to do bad things, and they pay the money and they take *muti* and come to your house and put it around there. And that's why I give someone *muti* to spray outside their house; it's to kill those bad things.'

'When you spray, will it take care of it forever?' I ask.

'No,' Joyce answers, 'you see, when you spray, then the bad things will go back to the one who sent it. They'll see those things coming back in a dream, or they will start itching, and they will say, "Oh, I see these things are coming back to worry me," and they will try again.'

'So it's a case of who can last the longest,' I say.

'Yes, who can last the longest. You see, instead of taking the money and buying something nice, like a dress or something for the house, they buy the *muti* to do the bad things.'

Later, when I'm lying on the foam mattress, I think about the conversation I had with Pip Erasmus six or seven months ago about *sangomas*. He had said then that so much of their belief is based on superstition. That, for example, if your car drives over a nail and your tyre is punctured, it is not a random act of chance, rather it is that the nail was 'put' there by somebody because they were jealous of you or had a grudge against you.

And I remember his almost cavalier attitude toward *sangomas*, and then the story he told about being awakened one night with his bed shaking and continuing to shake until he commanded the spirits to leave. And here I am now, wedged between my western being and experiences for which there are no explanations.

The amount of time we spend on the herbs is less now; most of the time is given over to dancing and divining. One night while divining, as soon as I drop onto my knees to say '*shaya ngikutshele*', a picture of the pug dog that lives across the road pops fully formed into my head. And when I say it, Sylvia throws up her arms and shouts, 'Oh, my God', and breaks into a high, loud ululatation, and she and Joyce throw themselves into each other's arms, then into my arms. This is the first time that an image has revealed itself so quickly.

Eventually Joyce regains control and starts to sing again as I reach for the imaginary dog and place it on the floor in front of me. I then take a pinch of ash and sprinkle it on the spot where I put the dog, place each foot on the ash, and begin dancing. And there are other times now when the picture of what Joyce is thinking appears almost immediately, like a photograph, in my mind.

Oh strange, strange process, strange only to me though, swaying in some never-never land, neither an unquestioning African disciple nor Eurognostic.

One evening, while we cook, we talk about customs. Sylvia tells how, in her culture, a girl passes from childhood into womanhood. When a girl has her first period, she is kept at home for ten days, after which she is led to the river where she washes herself and puts on new clothes that are special for the occasion. Young men, from the ages of seventeen to twenty, are taken up to the hilltop where they are circumcised by the medicine man. They stay there, usually in a group of eight to ten, for about three months, until they are healed.

Sylvia says that her son is now nineteen and will soon have to be circumcised. She will probably take him to a hospital to have it done, she says, rather than back in the village.

And I am just amazed at the transition Sylvia represents, that so many of these women represent, one foot planted in the world of old tradition and the other in the white, western ways of being.

And I wonder whether they have given up more than they have gained. [...]

Meanwhile, my other, daytime life continues. Ron and I spend days looking at furniture or pictures for the flat. He has a hard time walking around with me in my *thwasa* wrappings, but he enjoys the attention. 'That skirt makes you look like a sack of potatoes,' he says. But he is good-humored about it.

Often we drive to Hillbrow, that Haight-Ashbury of Johannesburg, where we have delicately flavored Greek lunches, or toasted cheese sandwiches at sidewalk cafés and watch a world sometimes as strange as *Star Trek* revolve by. Burly Greek men with their shirt sleeves rolled high and their biceps bulging; slim young men of indeterminate color in skintight pants sway by sensuously.

A young man dressed in leather with studs and with bleached hair carries a monkey on his shoulder; two brown prostitutes come to blows over a pale German tourist; every now and then an armoured car with men in green carrying rifles. Black men, some boys, some old, hustle to direct cars into parking spaces for small change, and two-storied buses cloud the narrow street with fumes.

While the country gentles into fall, the days have been sunny and warm. Everywhere there is a mix of hope and despair. The radio is filled with optimistic talk of the new South Africa. Cars sprout bumper stickers calling for peace. Meanwhile, in the townships, on the trains, the blacks kill each other.

Among our friends, it is the white men who seem to be having the hardest time with the upcoming transition, moving farther and farther to the right, their speech peppered with epithets such as 'kaffir,' their jokes diseased with racism.

But not all of them. Dennis, Ron's brother, says, 'We are witnessing a most remarkable period in history. Do you know this is the first time a government will be voting itself out of power?'

When I go for my twice-weekly Zulu lessons I watch Mehlo's mouth making sounds that I know mine will never wrap around.

'*Chk*,' she says, '*chk*, like you're calling a horse.'

'*Chk*,' I repeat, perfectly able to make the sound unattached to the rest of the word, but once attached, my tongue and lips fail.

And the rules! 'If the left-most of any vowel juxtaposed is either *i* or *u* or *ou*, it changes into a semivowel; or, if the left-most of two vowels is *a*, *e*, *o*, and the right-most is *i*, *u*, then *i* becomes *e* and *u* becomes *o*.' And I had been told that Zulu was the simplest of the African languages!

One night when I come into Joyce's little kitchen, there are two men waiting to be 'fortuned.' This evening Joyce tells me that I will start, and I am immediately panic-stricken.

We go into the little bedroom while Sylvia, who is also at Joyce's, waits outside. Joyce wraps the *ibayi*, the traditional white shawl with the red sun in its centre, around my shoulders.

The men sit on the floor on the reed mat in front of the pink-bedspreaded bed, their legs stretched out in front of them. Their socks have holes in them. The lighter-skinned one moves with a nervous quickness; he holds a match between his teeth that he rolls with his fingers every now and then.

Joyce lights the *imphepho* and I breathe deeply, hoping that its sweet smoke will bring some illumination into my mind, which at this stage is frighteningly empty. Nothing comes. Dear spirits, I beg, a little illumination, please. Joyce gestures to the candle and I push it into the centre of the room.

The one with the lighter skin places a ten-rand note on the floor between us and I tell him to light the candle. I sit looking first at its flame, and then long into his eyes. He looks directly back at me, mockingly. I wait. He rolls the matchstick between his lips. Then I start, and I talk without thinking, allowing the words to come out of my mouth.

'You have a tightness around your head.' He shrugs slightly. 'You get headaches here,' and I gesture to over my eyes. He shrugs again, and I don't know whether he is saying yes or no. 'Your neck often feels tight, and your shoulders.' Again he shrugs. Joyce says something to him in Zulu, and he responds by answering, 'Sometimes.'

I feel him thinking, *No white bitch is going to tell me what's going on – least of all a white trainee.* But I continue. 'There is a sadness deep in your belly,' I say. He takes a while to answer, rolling the matchstick between his teeth, then nods and says, 'Yes,' almost mockingly.

'This sadness has to do with someone else in your life, someone close to you.'

Again he rolls the matchstick around in his mouth. Then, 'My life partner,' he says.

Joyce tells me that is enough now, and she calls in Sylvia. I move to the stool.

Sylvia comes in and goes to the sacred corner where she takes down the whisk, and two sets of beads that she pulls over her head so that they cross her chest. She wraps an *ibayi* around her chest, and faces the corner where the *imphepho* smokes.

Deep growls rise up, like smoke, from her belly, move cavernously through her chest and out, filling the small room, warm and musky now with its five bodies, with its labouring animal sound. Her eyes are closed, she is on her knees, the candle is before her.

She begins to flail at herself with the switch, hitting from shoulder to shoulder. Then she starts: '*Shaya ngikutshele, shaya ngikutshele.*' The words erupt as deeply cavernous as the growls; she crawls this way and that on her knees, hitting her shoulders with the whisk, eyes closed, head moving from side to side like an animal sniffing the air.

The sound crowds out all thought; we are riveted to her, melted down by the depth, the primitive essence. She begins to speak, first to the light-skinned one who has quickly taken the matchstick out of his mouth. She speaks rapidly, in Zulu; he answers, she talks. While she talks to him her voice is normal, then '*Aiyeh, aiyeh,*' she wails, pushing the air out of her body, panting, as though in the throes of labour. Again her eyes close, she moves from knee to knee, sweat pours from her face. She whips the switch. And again she talks.

I am awed by it all, wavering in and out of thoughts of theatre. How lame I must have seemed. This is worth something. For half an hour she continues, then she is done and she sits panting, wiping her face with her fingers. The men put on their shoes and leave.

When they've gone I say to Sylvia, 'Wow, that was incredible. What did you see?'

'That man has got a lot of problems. His head here,' she motions to her forehead, 'is very tight, and down his neck and across his shoulders is very tight.'

'You did see this also,' Joyce says to me.

'Yes, but he was having no white dame tell him what was wrong with him.'

They laugh. 'You're right,' Joyce says, 'and some people don't want to have someone who is in training working with them.'

Sylvia continues, 'He wants his wife to leave the house they are in, but if he forces her out, the comrades will come after him and kill him. She is a schoolteacher and she can get the comrades to do this.'

'Why doesn't he just go see a lawyer and take care of it legally?' I ask.

'Because he is afraid that then the comrades will get him,' Sylvia answers. Those 'comrades', the ones who would kill for a song, are often no more than children. They are the ones who have seen too much: too much violence, too much hatred. They are easily manipulated towards whatever cause, political or personal.

'What did you tell him?' I ask.

'No, it's very difficult,' she says, 'he should be putting *muti* down around the house, but if he does, she will find it, so he can't do anything at home.'

After we eat and watch television for a while, Joyce helps Sylvia prepare to make a home safe. Sylvia has a client in Bloemfontein who has been experiencing strange things around her house: footsteps on the roof, fleeting figures that she sees out of the corner of her eye, strange sounds and strange illnesses.

Joyce has gathered about sixteen five-inch sticks made from small branches that she has sharpened at one end, and six smooth river stones. Joyce takes a beaded horn out from among her *muti* bottles, and with her finger reaches in and hooks out lumps of a black, tarry-looking substance. I ask what it is. 'It is herbs,' she says.

She puts the horn aside and opens a small jar and hands it to me. 'This is lion's fat,' she says. I smell it. It smells musty. She adds half a teaspoon. Then she opens a second small jar. 'This is horse's fat.' I smell it also. It smells rancid. She adds a small amount of that as well. Then from a small, slim bottle she pours a half teaspoon of a dark liquid. 'It looks like old car oil,' I say.

'Yes.' She mixes the ingredients and then takes each sharpened stick and smears the mixture around them, leaving the sharpened ends free. Then she takes the river stones and spreads the mix on them.

While she is preparing the sticks and stones, she explains that Sylvia will dig holes around the house and bury them, creating a barrier against anything bad that someone might be sending.

Once those are done and packed away in a plastic bag, she rummages in her *muti* cabinet and pulls out a handful of aloe leaves and snake-lily root. Sylvia begins pounding the leaves on a large flat stone with a smaller round one until what she has is a mushy mess. The bulbous roots are roughly grated. Joyce gives it a final looking over, then scoops it into a plastic bag and ties the ends together tightly.

Now Sylvia needs to be made safe so that she will not absorb any of the bad things, so she will be immune. She takes off her top and her skirt and tucks her petticoat into her panties. Joyce looks among her bottles and pulls out a small packet from which she takes a razor blade. I note that it is not a new one. Joyce stretches out the blade towards me. 'Do you want to cut her?' she asks.

'Oh, God,' I say, 'I shake too much, she'd have zigzags.'

Sylvia kneels, and Joyce parts the hair on the top of her head, then quickly makes a tiny cut with the razor. Then at the wrist, elbow, shoulder, throat, between her breasts, on the hips, knees, and instep. She waits a minute to make sure drops of blood have formed. Then she takes a black creamy substance from a small bottle and rubs it into each cut, starting with the head. When she is done Sylvia stands still with her arms out from her sides.

'Does it hurt?' I ask.

'It stings,' she says. She stands until the *muti* has dried and then dresses again. She will leave the next morning for Bloemfontein.

The man who has been complaining of the sensation of spiders' webs around his face and a pain around the side of his abdomen has been coming every second day for his regimen of steamings. He strips down to his underpants and sits over the simmering herbs for fifteen minutes.

'*Hai, uh uh,*' he answers, shaking his head, when I ask *Unjani,* 'How are you?' 'The pains are getting worse,' he says. Again I'm wracked by my western worries that something is clinically wrong, and also by guilt, that I'm not doing anything to help him get to qualified help. Then I shake my head. As far as he is concerned he is getting qualified help. *Oh God*, I pray, *let his belief be sufficient.*

While he is steaming, Joyce says that he is very worried because his peepee won't stand up. 'Well,' I say, 'if he is very worried, then it won't stand up for sure.'

She laughs and slaps my hand. 'No,' she says, 'I must make him some *muti* to drink to help his peepee, and tomorrow he must *spuyt*.' She scrunches her lips and points to her butt. As hard a time as I have with *phalaza*, Joyce has with enemas.

In the little shower area I'd seen the white metal jug with the pipe coming from it, ending in a small spoon-shaped lip. I wonder whether she uses the same insertion tip for everyone. I'm sure she does, but better not to ask.

When he leaves we both sit scratching at our faces, at the sensations of spiders' webs he has left behind.

Marike de Klerk

Marike Willemse was a honeymoon baby. When she and her brother were still little, her father, a university lecturer, fell in love with one of his students, and when she was five years old, her parents were divorced. Both parents remarried; however, the children felt unwanted in both homes. When Marike was at Potchefstroom University she met a young law student, F.W. de Klerk. They were married on 11 April 1959. They had two sons and adopted a daughter. After a long career in the Afrikaner Nationalist government, in 1989 F.W. was inaugurated as State President. Within months he announced the unbanning of the liberation movements and the unconditional release of Nelson Mandela.

The autobiographical text from which these passages are taken – *Marike: A Journey Through Summer and Winter* (by Maretha Maartens, 1997) – was originally published in Afrikaans. Much of the narrative is addressed to her grandchildren, and explains why they should not judge their grandfather harshly for his role in apartheid. The narrative ends in 1998 with her attempts to come to terms with her husband's decision to divorce her after 38 years of marriage.

Marike was murdered – and probably raped – in December 2001. A young security guard at the housing complex in which she lived was convicted of her murder and sentenced to two terms of life imprisonment.

Like most of my school friends, I simply accepted that black girls went barefoot, wore worn-out clothes and later on worked as servants in white homes.

Like all educated and Christian Afrikaans children, I never swore at any black person, maltreated them, refused them a meal or deliberately behaved badly towards them.

I calmly accepted that black women sat on the floor instead of on chairs or benches in whites homes; that black people died illiterate; that coloured people differed from me.

I in my environment and they in theirs, I thought as did most of the children in my class. Of course there was a deeper reason underlying this. We knew how few of us there were. We were scared of the sheer overwhelming number of black South Africans. Perhaps the fear of domination and loss of identity affected the collective conscience of the Afrikaner and finally, their ability to discriminate. For this sin your grandfather, also publicly, asked forgiveness before God.

Your grandfather was a thinker. How he experienced the apartheid ideology as a child and a young man and the ensuing mental growth in his life, he told you long ago in his own way. All that remains to be said is that this grandmother of yours had no *road to Damascus* experience. Life with your grandfather, years of reading and study (what a blessing that I am an eternal student!), your grandfather's sense of justice, seeing his struggle with the truth, our endless conversations about the will of God for the Afrikaner but also the will of God for all the people of this country, converted me.

You know what follows on conversion: expiation, new responsibility, involvement. You also know that true conversion is lifelong, that you can never go back to the way of life that you regarded as right and normal. You know about the vituperation which follows on conversion. Not everyone applauds you. There are people who tell you that you should have your head read. Not to mention the cats that have been let loose in the quiet dovecote of our existence. There will always be people who tell you that it would have been better if you had not been converted.

Because your grandfather saw analogies, struggled with God and had the courage of his convictions to unlock the concentration camp gates of our traditions and open our own Brandenburg gate, because he destroyed our own Berlin Wall, because he sent out bulldozers to remove the great atrocities as well as the smaller, more subtle injustices against the creations of God, our compatriots, he, with Nelson Mandela, received the Nobel Prize in 1995. […]

The evening before the Nobel Prize for Peace would be awarded, the recipients, their partners, office-bearers, interested parties and the press were received by the adjudicators for an official motivation of their decision regarding the joint award. One by one the committee members took the floor. I was impressed by the profound insight shown by the committee member responsible for the historical research.

What I expected? Can anyone, who lives in the sun as we do, have any idea of what a function of this kind encompasses?

There was a repetition at ten o'clock in the morning. At two in the afternoon we sat in the kind of hall which you could easily picture within the European-Scandinavian context: somewhat sombre, the kind of friezes and wall paintings one could find in the older parts of Prague, Budapest, Madrid and Berlin. I looked up at wall paintings with sombre scenes from the Second World War, at the square, sad figure of some or other Norwegian king. Was this hall with its gloomy depictions of human suffering and soldiers marching, the most suitable place for awarding the Peace Prize?

The South African ambassador flew in a ton of proteas. We looked straight at them and smelt the veld at Betty's Bay, Cape Point and Hermanus. Outside on the square, the thermometer measured minus 10 °C.

'Look at the beautiful flowers!' I had cried ecstatically that morning to Princess Zinani, Nelson Mandela's daughter. 'Do you know these flowers grow in the veld where we have a home!'

'Is it?' she had said.

The King of Norway, I noticed during the ceremony, had had a bad night. He and the Queen sat right in front of me. I saw his head nodding, saw him fall asleep.

Nelson Mandela was the first to receive his award, make his speech.

Then it was my husband's turn. He walked forward, suddenly stood so endlessly alone before the audience. *Look at the proteas, FW*, I wanted to say to him. *Smell the smell of our veld Afrikaner*, I wanted to cry out. And again:

Afrikaner, believer. You are the difference FW; do you believe it now? It was all worthwhile: every sacrifice, every return when Codesa was on the edge of collapse, all the sleepless nights, all the lonely struggles at your desk.

Then he quoted the poet, NP van Wyk Louw and all the sadness, the greatness, the language and the soul of my country washed over me. He read it in Afrikaans and then the English version:

O wide and woeful land
beneath the great South stars
will soaring joy ne'r rise above
your silent grief?

Will ne'r a mighty beauty rise
above you, like the hail-white summer clouds
that billow o'er your brooding peaks
and in you ne'r deed be wrought
that over the earth resounds
and mocks the ages in their impotence?

In what he then said, I recognized the speech he had written at the dining-room table as the new leader of the NP: 'Our goal is a new South Africa: a totally changed South Africa; a South Africa that has rid itself of the antagonisms of the past; a South Africa free of domination or oppression in whatever form; a South Africa within which the democratic forces – all reasonable people – align themselves behind mutually acceptable goals and against radicalism, irrespective of where it comes from.'

I heard the applause which followed his speech and my heart wanted to break with pride and gratitude.

And suddenly we were outside in the dark Norwegian winter. As always we were surrounded by security forces. We drove back to the hotel and heard that a candlelight ceremony would be held on the square in front of the hotel before dinner.

When we heard the sound of many voices, we went out onto the balcony.

Thousands of candles were lit in the cold; we looked down on something like the reflection of a starry sky in a bottomless pool.

The crowd started chanting: 'Mandela ... Mandela ...'

Someone began to sing *Nkosi sikilel' iAfrika.*

Nelson Mandela gave the raised fist salute to the crowd. Later FW and I went back into the room.

In the room FW took off his coat and said thoughtfully: 'Do we still belong here?'

MaGumede

Izibongo/izihasho

Predictably, facets of the indigenous tradition of praising have adapted to radical social change in South Africa. Some contemporary praises have adopted the westernised notions of author and authority (and ownership), and have recorded texts in print or on record/disk. Some, such as those reproduced below, have largely removed the sacred aspects of the genre. They deal with contemporary issues, social problems that have emerged from the massive destruction of traditional societies arising out of colonialism, apartheid and mass urbanisation.

The *izihasho* (a sub-category of *izibongo*) of MaGumede, MaSitHole and Bella Mshibe were recorded by the students of Noleen Turner, an academic in isiZulu Studies. Turner says that while the *izibongo* of Zulu women often contain satirical references, the *izihasho* reproduced here – though particularly extreme – seldom cause more than mild embarrassment to the subject because the criticisms (usually not self-composed) are couched in poetic forms that are perceived to obviate any malicious intent. Also, when they are recited, the performer usually emphasises the humorousness of the images. The subject of the poem thus derives a sense of pride from being the focus of attention. 'Being known by her "praises" provides [a woman] with a distinct identity, a sort of recognition and support which is important to her ego and psyche' (Turner, 1995: 73).

Turner (1995: 70) notes that MaGumede's iron will made her the object of ridicule for, in a patriarchal society such as is found amongst the Zulu, it is extremely rare (and abhorrent) to find a woman who dominates the household or her husband. The praises would also be recited in order to rebuke the husband who had allowed such a thing to happen in his household, and would be a spur to him to address the situation. The criticisms notwithstanding, MaGumede herself recited her praises with glee.

MaGumede, woman that hits men!
Railway bus of the Whites
Dominator in the household.

MaSithole

Turner (1995: 61) remarks that the most commonly censured practices in urban areas are promiscuity (as in MaSithole's poem), laziness, gossiping and drinking. She comments further that MaSithole's poem is of particular interest because its structure closely resembles that of traditional *izibongo samakhosi* (the praises of warriors) – but instead of conquests in battle, the poem alludes to MaSithole's love conquests, the men who are discarded, in much the same way that heroes of old dealt with adversaries in battle (1995: 63).

You who have no fixed place to live
Because of your promiscuity.
Prostitute you upset me,
You do not sleep at home because of men
The lover of men,
The changer of different men,

Who rejected Sipho
By accepting S'fiso
When she had already admitted John.
Who rejected John
By replacing him with Sabelo.
Sabelo ran away
And was followed by Vezi.

The changer of different men
Who rejected Mdu
And changed him for Zakhele.
All men belong to me!
The lover of men,

You have men in Durban
You have men in Johannesburg
You have men in Olundi,
You have men in Port Shepstone,
You have men in all spheres of the world.

Bella Mshibe

Bella Mshibe was living in Umlazi, a sprawling matchbox-house 'location' for blacks working in the Durban area. She had come from a rural environment to town to join her husband. Because of her traditional Zulu attire, she was taunted by the township women. In these praises, which were, Turner explains (1995:71), self-composed, it is the township women whom she derides for their whiteman's clothing and loss of their own culture.

You low-classed women of D-Section, what are they doing?
They wear rags
When did you last see a Whiteman wearing a headring?
Hololo! Hololo! No leave me alone!

Antjie Krog

A ntjie Krog was born on 23 October 1952 in the *verkrampte* (conservative Afrikaner) town of Kroonstad, Orange Free State. She and her husband, John Samuel, have four children. Antjie is an Afrikaans poet, writer and journalist. Several of her works have been translated into other languages and have won both local and foreign prizes. She made her debut with *Dogter van Jefta* in 1970. Her first prose work, *Relaas van 'n Moord* (1995), was published in English as *Account of a Murder. Down to my Last Skin: Poems* (2000) is the first collection of her poems to appear in English. Her most recent work of prose is *A Change of Tongue* (2003).

In her capacity as a radio reporter for the South African Broadcasting Corporation (SABC), Antjie covered the Truth and Reconciliation hearings around the country for more than two years, from the legislative genesis of the Commission, through to the testimonies of victims and of victimisers. She recounts her experiences in the multiple prize-winning **Country of My Skull** (1998). In the passage reproduced here she describes the early days of reporting on the TRC in the mid-1990s, and then her absorption of the narratives of trauma that surrounded her at the hearings.

Instinctively, one knew that some people would deliberately cut themselves off from the Truth Commission process. And it would be quite possible to do so, by reading nothing about it. But very few people escape news bulletins – even the music stations have a lunchtime news report. So it is crucial to us that the Commission and its narratives be captured as fully as possible on ordinary news bulletins. Even people who do no more than listen to the news should be given a full understanding of the essence of the Commission, and hear quite a few of its stories. This means that the past has to be put into hard news gripping enough to make bulletin headlines, into reports that the bulletin-writers in Johannesburg cannot ignore. To do this we will have to use the full spectrum of hard news techniques and where necessary develop and reform them according to our needs.

A bulletin generally consists of three audio elements: ordinary reporting read out by a newsreader, 20-second sound bites of other people's voices, and 40-second voice reports sent through by a journalist. How can these elements be moulded to our aims? An expert needs to come help me, I plead. And they send Angie.

I sit next to her in the media room at the city hall in East London. It is the first day of the hearings. Angie types codes and passwords into her laptop computer to log on to the network. We wait: little lights flash and scratchy shrieks issue from the modem – sounds of broken glass. 'We're on – we're logged on!' For the rest of my life I will remember this scene: the members of the radio team, each wearing earphones, recording the translation of their assigned language, and Angie on a cushion, so that she can reach the unusually high table, making a furious assault on the day's first news story – furious, because Angie is someone who types with all ten of her fingers. And as those pinkies squirrel away on the keys, the testimony of the first victim of the first day, Nohle Mohape, goes through to Johannesburg – in time for the eleven o'clock bulletin.

Thus our labours over the next two years will be structured. The first actuality programmes are around one o'clock. We do short packages, text with sound bites or live interviews for the afternoon programmes, and in the evenings we work on longer pieces for the following morning. Meanwhile the news bulletins keep flowing through. Stories, complete stories with beginnings, middles and ends, are told for the first time over the news; in a 40-second voice report, we relate how Phindile Mfeti told his wife that he was going off to have his jeans shortened, and then disappeared without a trace. How she later found on his desk the glasses and pipe that he always took with him. How she asked the

Commission for something to bury – even if it was just a piece of bone or a handful of ash.

We also learn quickly. Bulletin-writers and newsreaders squirm away from whatever is not fashionable or harmlessly clinical. For words like 'menstruation' or 'penis' there is no place on the news; a phrase such as 'they braaied my child on a fire' is out of the question. We are told that the writer Rian Malan has complained that he doesn't want to mix 'breakfast and blood' in the mornings. This is just the encouragement we need. We write the first lines of the hard copy: 'The missing hand of ANC activist Sicelo Mhlawuli dominated the testimonies before the Truth Commission hearings in East London today. Mhlawuli's hand was last seen by a fellow detainee.' Then the recorded comment: 'I saw the severed hand of a black activist in a bottle at a Port Elizabeth police station. The police told me it was a baboon's hand. They said to me: "Look here, this is the bottled hand of a Communist." But I know that Sicelo Mhlawuli, one of the Cradock Four, was buried with his hand missing.' This is a perfect sound bite. (How quickly our own language changes – fantastic testimony, sexy subject, nice audible crying …) then the newsreader concludes the story: 'The daughter of Sicelo Mhlawuli, Babalwa, has told the Truth Commission how a certain policeman, Cloete, came to her mother's house every day and stood next to her mother howling like a dog – all the time waving his hand loosely in the air while all of them laughed.'

We also insist on the use of 'Truth Commission' rather than 'TRC', which would conceal the essence of the Commission behind a meaningless abbreviation.

We pick out a sequence. We remove some pauses and edit it into a 20-second sound bite. We feed it to Johannesburg. We switch on a small transistor. The news comes through: 'I was making tea in the police station. I heard a noise, I looked up … There he fell … Someone fell from the upper floor past the window … I ran down … It was my child … my grandchild, but I raised him.'

We lift our fists triumphantly. We've done it!

The voice of an ordinary cleaning woman is the headline on the one o'clock news.

Week after week; voice after voice; account after account. It is like travelling on a rainy night behind a huge truck – images of devastation breaking in sheets on the windscreen. You can't overtake, because you can't see; and you can't slow down or stop because then you will never get anywhere.

It is not so much the deaths, and the names of the dead, but the web of infinite sorrow woven around them. It keeps on coming and coming. A wide, barren, disconsolate landscape where the horizon keeps on dropping away.

And this is how we often end up at the daily press conferences – bewildered and close to tears at the feet of Archbishop Tutu. By the end of four weeks they are no longer press conferences. He caresses us with pieces of hope and humanity. We ask fewer and fewer critical questions. Perplexed, we listen to the sharp, haughty questions posed by foreign journalists – those who jet into the country, attend one day's hearings, and then confront the Commission about its lack of judicial procedures and objectivity.

The first sign of the International Journalist in your midst is the subtle fragrance. Male or female, overseas journalists can obviously afford a perfumery that you won't find on the shelves at Pick 'n Pay. The second sign is the equipment. Microphones like cruise missiles on launching pads appear in front of interviewees, and you have to find space next to them for your humble little SABC mike. They are equipped with recorders that produce fully edited sound bites and reports at the push of a button, computers they can carry in their inside pockets and cellphones no bigger than lipsticks. And they know something really big is happening in East London, they pick up the vibes – but nothing fits into their operating frameworks. 'How can you report *anything*?' a Belgian journalist struggles to keep the scepticism out of his voice. 'South African journalists keep on bursting into tears all around me in the hall.'

The Story of the Century, they tell us. With heroes and villains; well-known and unknown characters; the powerful and the powerless, the literate and the illiterate. Hung with laptops, tape recorders, bags, notebooks and reels of cable and tape, we limp into hotel foyers long after midnight.

[…]
dare I sit in this grape dark
during this return journey where my body is overcome
by grief my heart coagulate resigned
write I – a blue slit against this all …

The word 'Truth' makes me uncomfortable.
The word 'truth' still trips the tongue.

'Your voice tightens up when you approach the word "truth",' the technical assistant says, irritated. 'Repeat it twenty times so that you become familiar with it. *Truth is mos jou job!*' ('Truth is your job, after all!')

I hesitate at the word, I am not used to using it. Even when I type it, it ends up as either *turth* or *trth*. I have never bedded that word in a poem. I prefer the word 'lie'. The moment the lie raises its head, I smell blood. Because it is there … where the truth is closest.

The word 'reconciliation', on the other hand, is my daily bread.

Compromise, accommodate, provide, make space for. Understand. Tolerate. Empathize. Endure … without it, no relationship, no work, no progress is possible. Yes. Piece by piece we die into reconciliation.

However – neither truth nor reconciliation is part of my graphite when sitting in front of a blank page, rubber close at hand. Everything else fades away. It becomes so quiet. Something opens and something falls into this quiet space. A tone, an image, a line mobilizes completely. I become myself. Truth and reconciliation do not enter my anarchy. They choke on betrayal and rage, they fall off my refusal to be moral. I write the broken line. For some brief moments of loose-limbed happiness everything I am, every shivering, otherwise useless, vulnerable fibre and hypersensitive sense come together. A heightened phase of clarity and the glue stays … and somewhat breathless, I know: for this I am made.

I am not made to report on the Truth and Reconciliation Commission. When I was first told to head the five-person radio team covering the Truth Commission, I began to cry, inexplicably, on the plane back from Johannesburg. Someone tripped over my bag in the aisle. Mumbling excuses, fumbling with tissues, I looked up into the face of Dirk Coetzee. There was no escape.

After three days a nervous breakdown was diagnosed. Two weeks later, the first hearings on human rights violations began in East London.

The months that have passed have proved my premonition right – reporting on the Truth Commission indeed leaves most of us physically exhausted and mentally frayed.

Because of language.

Week after week, from one faceless building to another, from one dusty, godforsaken town to another, the arteries of our past bleed their own peculiar rhythm, tone and image. One cannot get rid of it. Ever.

To have the voices of ordinary people dominate the news. To have no one escape the process.

We sleep between one and two hours a night. We live on chocolate and potato chips. After five years without cigarettes, I start smoking again.

In the second week of hearings, I do a Question and Answer with an actuality programme. I stammer. I freeze. I am without language. I put the receiver down, and think: resign. Now. You are clearly incompetent. The next morning the Truth Commission sends one of its own counsellors to address the journalists. 'You will experience the same symptoms as the victims. You will find yourself powerless – without help, without words.'

I am shocked to be a textbook case within a mere ten days.

'Exercise regularly. Take photographs of loved ones with you to come home to in the hotels. Take your favourite music with you. And talk to one another ... be one another's therapists.'

We develop techniques to lessen the impact. We no longer go into the halls where the hearings take place, because of the accumulated grief. We watch on the monitors provided. The moment someone starts crying, we start writing/ scribbling/doodling.

One hotel room drifts into another. One breakfast buffet provides the same sad fruit as another. One sorrow-filled room flows into another. One rental car smells like another ... but the language, the detail, the individual tone ... it stays.

[...]

Wordless, lost. While Afrikaner surnames like Barnard, Nieuwoudt, Van Zyl, Van Wyk peel off victims' lips. The question they keep asking: What kind of person, what kind of human being, keeps another's hand in a fruit-jar on his desk? What kind of hatred makes animals of people?

It is ordinary people who appear before the Truth Commission. People you meet daily in the street, on the bus and train – people with the signs of poverty and hard work on their bodies and their clothes. In their faces you can read astonishment, bewilderment, sown by the callousness of the security police and the unfairness of the justice system. 'We were treated like garbage: worse even than dogs. Even ants were treated better than us.'

And everyone wants to know: Who? Why? Out of the sighing arises more than the need for facts or the longing to get closure on someone's life. The victims ask the hardest of all the questions: How is it possible that the person I loved so much lit no spark of humanity in you?

A mother stumbles on to the fact that her child is dead. She sends one child to go and buy fish. He hears on the street: 'They shot your little brother just now.'

The abnormality of South African society strikes Commissioner Mary Burton. 'In a normal society if your child is not at home in time, you think he might still be at his friends. But under Apartheid you go and look at the police station, then at the jails, then at the hospital and eventually at the morgue.'

What gradually becomes clear is that the Apartheid system worked like a finely woven net – starting with the Broederbond who appointed leaders. In turn these leaders appointed ministers, judges, generals. Security forces, courts, administrations were tangled in. Through Parliament legislation was launched that would keep the brutal enforcement of Apartheid out of sight.

It is striking that no politicians attend the hearings. Is it because they respect the independence of the Commission, or do they simply not want to know what price ordinary people paid for the end of Apartheid and the new dispensation? Many of those testifying are unemployed and live in squatter camps.

Now that people are able to tell their stories, the lid of the Pandora's box is lifted; for the first time these individual truths sound unhindered in the ears of all South Africans. The black people in the audience are seldom upset. They have known the truth for years. The whites are often disconcerted: they didn't realize the magnitude of the outrage, the 'depth of depravity' as Tutu calls it.

Where does the truth lie? What does it have to do with reconciliation and justice?

'For me, justice lies in the fact that everything is being laid out on the same table,' says my colleague Mondli. 'The truth that rules our fears, our deeds and our dreams is coming to light. From now on you don't only see a smiling black man in front of you, but you also know what I carry inside of me. I've always known it – now you also know.'

'And reconciliation?'

'Reconciliation will only be possible when the dignity of black people has been restored and when whites become compassionate. Reconciliation and amnesty I don't find important. That people are able to tell their stories – that's the important thing.'

'For me, it's a new beginning,' I say. 'It is not about skin colour, culture, language, but about people. The personal pain puts an end to all stereotypes. Where we connect now has nothing to do with group or colour, we connect with our humanity ...' I keep quiet. Drunk or embarrassed.

'Let us drink to the end of three centuries of fractured morality,' says Mondli and lifts his glass. 'Here people are finally breaking through to one another and you and I are experiencing it.'

'And maybe this is how we should measure our success – if we manage to formulate a morality based on our common humanity.'

Mondli laughs and says: 'We're all starting to talk like Tutu.'

Time and time again the name crops up: the A-Team of Tumahole, the township at Parys on the banks of the Vaal River. 'I only heard there was this thing called the A-Team. They were people against the UDF. They used to drive through the township in their cars – they started this A-Team to work with the police. At night we saw police vans delivering booze to their houses. The A-Team wore their names on their chests, they carried hammers, pangas and guns to bring death to their own community.'

According to witnesses, the activities usually started on a Saturday afternoon. After drinking and taking some drugs they would target their prey. Torture and killing were never part of their vocabulary; instead they took their victims to what they called 'The Open Field' – all in the name of discipline.

David Nhlapo, an ordinary resident of Tumahole, says the A-Team picked him up one evening. They took him from Parys to Sasolburg. 'That's where they put a tyre on me, poured me with petrol and they said I should be naked. I undressed myself and they said, "You are now going to feel the pain the other policemen felt." They sliced my friend's neck with a spade.'

In stories about KwaZulu-Natal, the name of another gang often comes up – the Amabutho. They also had special attire that singled them out – balaclavas and colourful overalls. Their weapons were knobkerries, spears and axes, and they worked with Inkatha and the SADF. Their rituals were steeped in tradition. Before going after their victims, they drank and splashed on war potions to make themselves invincible. They also didn't speak of 'killing', but used euphemistic phrases like 'to remove obstacles' and 'to purify the fields'.

A survivor of one of their attacks remembers: 'And one of the Amabuthos said: "Let me see who has an axe ..." and I heard they were chopping down our door and they were coming inside ... I don't know when Kumbolani died because at that stage I was hiding. I wasn't hiding under the bed, because I realized if they find me under the bed, they will kill me more cruelly, they must kill me standing. So I stood behind the door and I was hiding, and they got inside, they chopped him ... they chopped him in his face with an axe and on his chest ... they opened up his chest with an axe.'

The Amabutho often removed body parts to brew a concoction with which to cleanse themselves of the murder. The operational tactics of both the

A-Team and the Amabutho echo some of the Vlakplaas rituals described by Dirk Coetzee. Men bonding in groups. Drinking, choosing a victim, arming themselves and then getting together to make the Big Kill.

Tutu reads an anonymous letter in Afrikaans sent to the Commission during the second week of hearings. '*Dan huil ek vir dit wat gebeur het, al kan ek niks daaraan verander nie. Dan soek ek in my binneste om to verstaan hoe is dit moontlik dat niemand eenvoudig geweet het nie, hoe is dit moontlik dat so min iets daaraan gedoen het, hoe is dit moontlik dat ek ook maar baie keer net toegekyk het. Dan wonder ek hoe is dit moontlik om met daardie skuld en skande van die binnekant te lewe ... ek weet nie wat om te sê nie, ek weet nie wat om te doen nie, ek vra u hieroor om verskoning – ek is jammer vir al die pyn en die hartseer. Ek sê dit nie maklik nie. Ek sê dit met 'n hart wat stukkend is en met trane in my oe ...*'

('Then I cry over what has happened, even though I cannot change anything. Then I look inside myself to understand how it is possible that no one knew, how it is possible that so few did something about it, how it is possible that often I also just looked on. Then I wonder how it is possible to live with this inner guilt and shame ... I don't know what to say, I don't know what to do, I ask you to forgive me for this – I am sorry about all the pain and the heartache. It isn't easy to say this. I say it with a heart that is broken and with tears in my eyes ...')

The texts grow next to one another in the vapour of freshly mown language. Nomonde Calata, Priscilla Zantsi, Isabel Hofmeyr, Nontuthuzelo Mpehlo, Nqabakazi Godolozi, Elaine Scarry, Feziwe Mfeti, Nohle Mohape, Art Spiegelman, Govan Mbeki, Phyllis Maseko, Ariel Dorfman, Lucas Sikwepere, Abdulhay Jassat, Johan Smit, Ms Mkhize and Ms Khuzwayo, Marta Cullberg Weston, Cyril Mhlongo, Bheki Mlangeni's mother, Colette Franz, Yehuda Amichai.

Some journalists ask to be deployed elsewhere. Others start to focus on the perpetrators. Some storm out enraged at parties, or see friends fleeing from them. Some drink deep gulps of neat brandy, others calm themselves with neatly rolled *daggazolletjies*. After four months most of us who travel frequently become ill – lungs and airways. The Chairperson has bronchitis, the Deputy Chairperson pneumonia. It's the planes, someone says, they are germ incubators. No, it's the constant adapting to different climates and altitudes. We are becoming a family. I board a tiny propellered plane and sit next to one of the interpreters. In the back sits the Arch with his Anglican bodyguard. While we ascend shakily, I see how Tutu bows his head and prays and I just know, somehow, we're going to be fine.

I walk into my home one evening. My family are excitedly watching cricket on television. They seem like a happy, close-knit group. I stand in the dark kitchen for a long time. Everything has become unconnected and unfamiliar. I realize that I don't know where the light switch is.

I can talk about nothing but the Truth Commission. Yet I don't talk about it at all.

Until the day in Queenstown. It is bitterly cold. Coated, scarved, duveted, we listen to one necklacing experience after another – grim stories, a relentless procession of faces in a monotonous rhythm.

A man testifies about a bomb explosion in his restaurant. He says, 'The reason why only one person died that day is because of the top-quality tables that we have at the Spur.'

And I start to laugh.

'My friend came to me and said: Lucas, I wanted to come to you …'

'… but I couldn't find my legs,' I say to myself and collapse with laughter.

A local journalist puts some tea in front of me and asks tentatively: 'Have you been covering the Commission for long?'

I take two weeks leave.

We tell stories not to die of life

The man sits alone. He is wearing a cheap jacket. In a formal, old-fashioned Afrikaans he says he cannot tell the story of how an ANC bomb wiped out his family and friends.

'I can deal with it only in the form of questions. Do you know, you the Truth Commissioners, how a temperature feels of between six and eight thousand degrees? Do you know how it feels to experience a blow so intense that it forces the fillings from your teeth? Do you know how it feels to look for survivors and only find the dead and maimed … Do you know how it feels to look for your three-year-old child and never, Mr Chairman, never to find him again and to keep wondering for the rest of your life where he is?'

Towards the end of the eighties, the Van Eck and De Neyschen families went on holiday on a game farm near Messina on the northern border of South

Africa. One afternoon the two families went out in the bakkie to look for game. The back wheel on the right – the exact spot where the three-year-old Van Eck boy was sitting – struck a landmine.

'We were immediately in flames. When I came to myself I saw my baby boy of eighteen months was still alive … he was lying quite still, but looking at me. Mr De Neyschen was lying on his steering wheel … his hair burning, blood spouting from his forehead.'

Van Eck pulled them all through the window, and then he went to look for survivors.

'Right behind the vehicle I found my wife and Martie de Neyschen. Both severely maimed and killed outright. I searched further. I came upon little Kobus de Neyschen who had some life in him. I went back to his father and said: 'The child is still alive, but severely maimed and burnt.' His father asked there on the scene to let his child go … which is what happened. Then I noticed Mr De Neyschen's daughter Lizelda walking towards us out of the veld … She had a cut across her face and she limped. Then I searched further for my son of three years, but could not find him … until today I could not find him … I and my son buried our two family members and the next day our two friends. Since then it has been down the hill for me all the way. I sit for days … I simply sit … I lost my business. I am reduced to a poor white.'

The small side hall accommodates the electronic media. The translation is channelled to our tape recorders. We see Van Eck on the monitor. I write the news copy. I decide on a sound bite. I dictate the hard copy over the phone. I read: ' … and never comma Minister Chairman comma never to find …' A catch in my voice … My throat throbs heavily. My breast silts up, speechless.

I give the phone to a colleague and flee blindly among the cables and electronic equipment … out on to the stoep overlooking Nelspruit. I gasp for breath. Like two underwater swimmers, my eyes burst out to the horizons … the mountains lit in a blushing light-blue hedge of peace. I am drowning. My eyes claw at the trees, the kloofs … see, smell … the landscape of paradise and a language from paradise: *mispel, maroela, tarentaal,* I whisper. The air is drowsy with jasmine and *kanferfoelie.* I sit down on the steps and everything tears out of me. Flesh and blood can in the end only endure so much … Every week we are stretched thinner and thinner over different pitches of grief … how many people can one see crying, how much sorrow wrenched loose can one accommodate … and how does one get rid of the specific intonation of the words? It stays and stays.

360

I wake up in unfamiliar beds with blood on my flayed lips ... and sound bites screaming in my ears.

I receive a call. 'They say the story is really powerful ... can we possibly send another sound bite? Shall we send the one about the fillings or the one about the daughter coming towards them?'

I wipe my face. 'Send the one about how he just sits – and remember to add that the newspapers of the day said pieces of his son's hair and eyes were found in a tree near the bakkie.'

My hair is falling out. My teeth falling out. I have rashes. After the amnesty deadline I enter my house like a stranger. And barren. I sit around for days. Staring. My youngest walks into a room and starts. 'Sorry, I'm not used to you being home.'

No poetry should come forth from this. May my hand fall off if I write this.

So I sit around. Naturally and unnaturally without words. Stunned by the knowledge of the price people have paid for their words. If I write this, I exploit and betray. If I don't, I die. Suddenly my grandmother's motto comes to mind: when in despair, bake a cake. To bake a cake is a restorative process.

I snip into a bowl glacé pineapple, watermelon, ginger, green figs, dates and walnuts. Big red and green cherries, currants, sultanas. I let it stand in a cool dark cupboard – a bowl full of glistening jewels soaking in brandy. I relish the velvet of twelve eggs, butter and sugar. I bake a fruit cake and eat small fragrant slices in the blinding blue Cape summer heat.

And I think up delicious lines of lies and revenge.

Charlene Smith

On 1 April 1999, multi-award winning journalist Charlene Smith was raped at knife-point in her Johannesburg home. In spite of strenuous attempts to silence her (some by high-ranking members of the ANC government, amongst others), Smith (the mother of two young-adult children) embarked on a brave campaign to speak out about South Africa's horrific rape statistics, and about HIV/AIDS. Her book, *Proud of Me: Speaking Out Against Sexual Violence and HIV* (2001), is not 'about me because my experience was not mine alone' (xi). She uses her experiences 'as a link … to tell the story of the people of my country and of my continent' (ix). She urges her readers: 'help us stop the worst holocaust the world has ever faced – AIDS'. This pandemic is, she reminds us, 'fuelled in Africa, and in a good deal of Asia, by sexual violence' (x).

The Endless Night

The day I was raped was a special day.

It began before dawn with my son and me warbling 'Happy Birthday' down the phone to my daughter who was celebrating her twenty-first birthday one thousand kilometres away.

It ended with me – naked but for a thin gown, blood congealed on one hand, torn masking tape around my pulse points – arguing with a doctor in a crowded emergency room.

In some ways there had been portents. An astrologer who told me a 'lover' would arrive unexpectedly on my doorstep. An AIDS fieldworker who suggested I write an article about the fact that antiretroviral drugs should be given to rape survivors. Trying, but not succeeding, to get a rape survivor to talk to a television film crew about her experience. I became annoyed because I was certain that the rape organisations I phoned had never asked any woman for her views because they believed raped women would be ashamed. And so they entrenched and, in a sense, contributed to that view.

And there were the phone calls.

Ten days before I was raped, as my son and I were preparing to go out for lunch, the phone rang. I answered and a man asked, 'How are you?'

I asked who was speaking.

He said, 'Aaron.'

I did not recognise the name, so I asked, 'Can I help you?'

He said, 'I love you.'

I put the phone down.

After our return from lunch the same deep voice spoke from the answering machine: 'If you won't speak to me, I will fuck you.'

I phoned the police. They said there was nothing they could do. I thought I was probably over-reacting, but there was something about that voice that unsettled me.

I did what everyone should when their instinct speaks to them – I listened to it. I noted in my diary the details of the first call and the time, the names of the police officers and police station. I removed the tape from the answering machine and said to my son: 'If anything happens to me, you must remember where the diary and tape are.'

In two decades of covering violence in townships, of being shot at, teargassed, arrested countless times, threatened with death and assault, little unsettled me – but those calls did. I phoned a security consultant that week and explained that I was uneasy about the calls. I asked him to check the security at my house when he had time. He promised he would, but in the busy world that Johannesburg is, he never got a chance.

The day before I was raped, a Wednesday, I had a dinner party and mentioned the calls and my unease to friends. We laughed it off. I was just being silly.

On the afternoon of the following day, Thursday 1 April 1999 – the eve of the Easter weekend – a French television crew I had assisted phoned and asked me to join them for a farewell drink that evening. I agreed. My son was going to dinner and the cinema with friends. He would be back at 11 pm. He left at 6 pm, I left at 6.30 pm.

I am sure the rapist was already watching the house and that he entered a short while after I left through bars that he had probably already filed off the back door; then through a double-locked outer door, and then through a locked interior door – with no signs of forced entry.

The French TV crew parked their car directly opposite the pavement cafe where we met. 'We 'ave 'eard crime is very bad in Johannesburg and we don't want to lose our equipment,' they explained. It was a beautiful autumn evening but I felt inexplicably melancholy. At 8.15 pm I made my excuses and left.

By the following day, Good Friday, I had begun a four-day process of writing the following article. It was the first time I had written about myself. I never want to write a similar article again.

Every 26 seconds in South Africa a woman gets raped. It was my turn last Thursday night.

Before I began writing I took Retrovir (AZT), 3TC and Crixivan – the triple therapy recommended by the Centers for Disease Control (CDC) in Atlanta, Georgia in the USA. According to the CDC, based on studies of needlestick injuries, the use of triple therapy will reduce the possibility of HIV infection in those who complete the 28-day course by 81 per cent – significant odds.

AZT, 3TC and Crixivan will hopefully lessen the potential of me getting AIDS from the rapist, assuming of course, that he is HIV-positive. In a country where 1 800 people contract HIV every day, it's a gamble I refuse to take. But the difficulties I encountered in getting the drug and the treatment I received from medical staff at private hospitals and the district surgeon's office are an indictment against health care policies and the medical profession. I need to take these drugs for a month, within two weeks they will be making me feel very ill and depressed. The therapy will cost me around R4 000. I am a freelance journalist with medical aid for hospitalisation only, not this.

With the three antiretroviral drugs I am also on antibiotics in case the rapist had a sexually transmittable disease aside from HIV/AIDS. The district surgeon, a quiet Congolese who admitted she has to go for therapy because she cannot cope with what she sees, also gave me 'morning after' tablets because I was raped while I was ovulating. She gave me yet another 12 drugs I had to take simultaneously, I don't know what they were for. I need drugs to sleep and tranquillisers for when I become very fearful or tearful.

A general practitioner gave me Valoid to stop nausea and vomiting. Since the rape I frequently feel nauseous, my stomach aches from where he pushed me. But also I feel as though I have something terrible in my stomach that I have to get rid of, I wish someone could scrape out my insides.

This is about the rape:

I come home at 8.30 pm after meeting with a French television crew I had given some assistance to. I am tired. My three dogs act as normal. I open the door, walk in and lock it again. I notice there are more lights on than I had left on, an expensive mustard-coloured leather jacket with sheepskin lining that I had bought in Argentina is in the middle of the lounge floor. I thought my son had come home needing a warm jacket and had, for inexplicable reasons, left the jacket on the lounge floor. I go to his room and note the lights are on instead of just his lamp. I leave them.

I go into my room, put my bag, car keys and cellphone on a chair next to the telephone and go to the toilet kicking off my shoes as I go. As I stand next to the toilet to flush he is there. He stands briefly in the doorway as if wanting me to admire him in the jacket. I begin screaming. He walks towards me holding an elaborate silver Argentine gaucho's knife that is usually in a display among paintings in the lounge, and says, 'Keep quiet. I have a knife.' No ordinary kitchen knife for him.

I obey. He pushes me out of the bathroom holding the knife close to me. 'Where is the money?'

'I don't have any,' I say. 'I am poor.'

He looks in my bag, I have R10. He is furious and throws it on the floor. 'Is this all?'

'Yes,' I say.

Where is my ATM card? I give it to him.

'Give me the number, and don't lie.' I do as he says.

'I can take you there in the car,' I say. (I just want to get out of the house.)

'No,' he says. He grabs me by my arms which, days later, still ache. 'Is anyone coming here?'

'Yes,' I say.

'When?'

I think, if I tell him it is soon he might panic. 'In an hour or two.'

'Is it your husband?'

'Yes.'

He asks, 'Where is your son?'

'He is sleeping at friends tonight.'

'Don't move, I'm going to tie you up.'

He opens my cupboard. He's going to bind me with scarves or stockings, I think. But this is a man who has prepared while waiting for my return; thick masking tape normally kept in a kitchen cupboard is waiting in my bedroom cupboard. He ties my hands behind my back, making the tape go round and round my wrists and hands.

'First', he says, 'we are going to have sex.'

He is a tall man, about two metres, good looking, not very dark skin, the pale tones of a Xhosa or Tswana, with a thin moustache. His eyes have a slightly almond shape. He has a thin gold sleeper earring in his left ear, he wears a good quality long-sleeved green polo neck type shirt, he wears an expensive pair of brown corduroys.

He takes off my slacks and underwear, and undoes his pants.

He pushes me on to the bed. I remember reading of a woman who told a would-be rapist she had AIDS and he left her alone. I try the same thing. He says, 'I'll wear a condom.' He does not. He cannot get a full erection. I am very dry, making full penetration difficult. He begins swearing. He has to stay in control, I think.

I soothe: 'It's not your fault, it's the AIDS, it does this.'

'How old are you?' he asks. I lie and say I am considerably older; it occurs to me that he knows menopausal women could be dry. (A friend disagrees. She believes he thought older white women are less likely to be HIV-positive.)

I lie there thinking, be calm, be calm. He finishes and does up his pants.

'Now I'm going to get the money, but I will only be 15 minutes. Don't do anything stupid because I will kill you.' He winds tape across my eyes and around my head.

'Don't put the tape over my nose,' I say. He winds it over my mouth and around my head, binds my ankles and my knees. Throughout, I speak in a calm, level voice.

(*At this stage in writing my heart begins pounding and I begin vomiting. My son finds me crouching next to the toilet, crying; it is now night and the bathroom looks the same as when the rapist entered. I continue writing the next morning after a sleep aided by a tranquilliser and sleeping pill and the twenty-four-hour security guard and new alarm system a friend has installed. A kind neighbour has changed the locks on the doors.*)

I can hear him go to my bag and rifle through it. 'Don't you have any credit cards or other bank cards?'

'No, I told you I am poor.'

I hear him pocket my cellphone. He picks me up as if I weigh nothing (I'm 1,62 metres and weigh 57 kilograms). 'I'm going to lock you into the toilet so you don't try anything.' The silver fingerprint powder on the door later shows that he had big hands. He puts me on the ground. I realise I must look like a victim. I am crouching [forward], knees bent, head down. In fact my pose is not of submission but of intense concentration, listening to and analysing every sound.

'I'm going. I will be only 15 minutes.' He closes the door, but does not lock it, this tells me he will not leave the house immediately. I hear him lifting the lids of Chinese urns in the lounge. He is still looking for money – but he has left my laptop on the bed where he raped me, a radio on a living room couch, a brand new mountain bike, antique earrings in my ears. He took off my watch but dropped it on the floor. His real motive is not robbery. He speaks well, he is clean. He has planned this all so carefully.

He comes back into the bathroom. 'Where are the front door keys?' I can't speak so I indicate with my bound hands. 'You're not tied up well enough.' He comes back and applies more layers of masking tape to my hands and wrists.

He slides a latch across the bathroom door. I hear him quietly leave, and lock the front door. He leaves through the front door, on to a patio blazing with light in full view of the street.

I wait a while in case he returns to check on me, and then I struggle to free myself. I am not a person of much physical strength, I get men to open the lids on jars, or even tins. The first victory is when the ties around my ankles break free, and then my knees. I can't see which of our two bathrooms I am in, but I guess. I flounder around with my eyes bound, I have to get my hands free, it is unbelievably hard, at one point I stop, I'm exhausted, I'm terrified, I feel like giving up. But I think, if you give up, he will come back and kill you. I continue, finally I get one hand free, I push the tape over my eyes up, and that over my mouth down, I can't get my other hand free, it is bound not only to my back, but in some strange way to my jacket, he's done something so that it continues to restrict me. I ignore it and begin kicking the door. I realise I don't have the strength to smash it. I open the window and begin tugging at the burglar bars, I'll never pull them out.

I begin screaming. 'Help me, please somebody help me!' I have a quiet voice and even when I raise it, it is not very loud. He has put me in the middle bathroom furthest from neighbours, it is also the beginning of a long weekend, my neighbours may have gone away. Not even dogs bark when I shout. No one seems to hear.

I kick the door some more. 'Please God, let me live,' I pray under my breath. The lights are off but I feel for something in the bathroom cupboard to break the window, perhaps that sound will carry further than my voice. The first few containers I use have no impact, and then I take one that makes the glass break, I keep smashing the glass out of the frame. 'Help me, someone please help me!' I think of murder victims, they must feel like this before they die. There is a glow from my neighbours' outdoor lights but I know those are electronically controlled, the night is soundless and dark.

I can't smash out the top window frame, my strength seems to be failing. At one stage my mouth goes absolutely dry and no sound leaves my lips. I drink water from the tap and carry on shouting. Suddenly I see a torch glow and hear the voices of men at my back gate. At first I'm terrified, is that him back with more? And then I recognise the voice of a neighbour.

He says, 'What is wrong?'

'Call the police!' I shout. 'I've been raped, he has a knife, please get me out of here, he is coming back. Be careful, he has a knife ...'

They manage to get to the window. 'Help me, please. Get me out of here. I'm locked in the bathroom and I'm terrified.'

'We've called the police. How do we get into the house?' they ask.

'I don't know, break the doors or the windows but please get me out.'

Seconds later I hear voices in the passage. I'm frightened again, it must be him in the house. But it's them. The back door was wide open.

They unlock the bathroom door and stand looking at me in horror. I'm wearing only a longish top, the lower part of my body is naked, I have masking tape all over my head and my body, my left hand is bleeding where the knife slashed me but is still attached to masking tape and my jacket, hampering my movements.

I cry, 'I'm terribly sorry, but he raped me. I don't have my clothes with me.'

My white neighbour goes to fetch his wife. My black neighbour leads me gently away.

'Please cut off this masking tape. I can't move properly.' I try to move my bloodied hand. My black neighbour gets something and with the greatest gentleness cuts off the masking tape and frees my hand.

I tell you the race of my neighbours because I want you to know that rape is not about race, as some South Africans think. It is not about what men do. It is about what a few sick individuals do, it has nothing to do with race or malehood. Indeed, for the most part men treated me better than women that night.

The police arrive, I can see shock on their faces. They ask for details. I am still astonishingly calm, I know it's important that I should be. They immediately begin broadcasting details on their hand radios; one dashes out. My neighbour's wife arrives and holds me. I want to put on my clothes, at least underwear, but she cautions me not to, she helps me find a gown.

I keep saying to them and the police, 'I've got to get AZT fast so that I don't get HIV.'

I find my doctor's phone number, I call him, he's away for the weekend. I phone a close friend, her answering machine is on. I phone another, I tell her what happened, and ask her to try and find my doctor. She is concerned and confused. I tell her I am fine. I just need AZT.

The police ask me not to remove the remaining masking tape because they want to fingerprint it.

A young police reservist takes me outside. A neighbour and his wife drive by. They stop and ask one of my rescuers what is going on; he speaks quietly to them. Another comes and also speaks to him. The streets are dark and I don't know if he is somewhere watching me. I am uncharacteristically terrified. I don't mind the neighbours knowing what happened; they and their families must be warned of the danger in this otherwise quiet neighbourhood. But I don't want anyone looking at me.

I have all my medical aid details, the police have radioed ahead to Milpark Hospital telling them I'm a rape victim (how I hate the word victim) and that I want AZT. I hate getting out of the car and walking past the people in casualty, who stare at me. My left hand is caked in blood, I am wearing a gown and have masking tape in my hair, around my wrists, neck, ankles and knees. A young nurse guides me into a private cubicle and leaves me. I don't want to lie on a bed, I don't want anything to do with beds. I don't want to sit down because I feel moisture between my legs, even though I do not believe he achieved orgasm. I realise I'm standing with my arms at my sides facing the wall saying quietly over and over, 'I'm alive, I'm alive.' The young nurse comes in and gently pulls me away from the wall and puts her arms around me.

Maria Ndlovu

We know little of Maria Ndlovu, whose testimony is reproduced here in full, beyond the fact that she is HIV-positive and brave enough to make her status public. The book in which it appears, entitled *Living Openly: HIV Positive South Africans Tell Their Stories* (2000), seeks to rip away the shroud of secrecy that prevents those who are HIV-positive from speaking out. Such disclosure is uncommon: at funerals around the country, the cause of death is unspoken or misrepresented. The tragic death of Gugu Dlamini serves to illustrate the taboo: in 1998, she was killed by a mob near her home after she publicly declared her HIV status. Charlene Smith, whose account of her own rape appears earlier, points out:

It's not good to be a woman in Africa. Most people infected with Aids on the continent are women. Six times more girls are HIV-positive than boys. And in South Africa, 30% to 36% of pregnant women are infected. [...]

Around the continent the rape of virgins (children) is soaring based on a myth that a man who rapes a virgin will be cleansed of HIV. [...] In South Africa we stopped publishing the statistics, but the Medical Research Council says the incidence of child rape has doubled in the past year and with it infection rates.[...]

Because a third of all pregnant women are infected, the incidence of HIV in babies is very high.[...] The SA Paediatric Association says 200 babies are born each day infected with HIV. (*Mail & Guardian*, World Aids Day Supplement, 1–7 December 2000: 5)

As if to bring home with particular force the fact that AIDS reduces life expectancy, the same publication in which Smith's article appears announces the death, just a few days earlier, of Queenie Qiza, whose testimony appears in the same book as Maria Ndlovu's.

Maria Ndlovu
Diagnosed 1996. Disclosed 1998.
The first time I disclosed was to a group of students. There was this film by UNAIDS, 'I Can Hardly Wait', and it showed things that the youth do. So we'd watch the movie and then discuss in groups and find out what issues affect them, including AIDS. I came in as the reality and told them my story as somebody living with HIV.

I had made the decision to disclose some time before, but I just had not had the chance to do it. My decision came quickly ... two weeks after my diagnosis. My original thought was that I won't talk about it. I'll wait until I get sick and then tell people.

It was when I went to an HIV clinic and it was so silent and quiet. It was like we were sitting in an electric chair waiting to die and we would not talk or greet as we would in other queues, like in the casualty for example, where you would see somebody and you would ask what is happening. It was then that I made up my mind that this needs to be talked about because it is not right to feel as if you are dying when you are not. I wanted to normalise the situation.

For me it's a calling to do this. I feel an urge in me to help other people or to at least help them get through acceptance. I especially feel for the youth that they try to be as preventative as possible.

I am fortunate. My experiences were not negative in the sense that people were harsh on me, but they were negative in the sense that I did not attain what I thought I would attain. Like when you speak to a group there will be people that say, 'I don't believe you, you look so fit, it can't be true. They must have given you money to say this.' Then there are some men that say, 'I would like to taste it on you,' like there is any flavour. At least when I was infected I didn't notice any certain flavour.

At the workplace the negative was not directly towards me but a reaction of a people in denial. That's how I see us in South Africa, I see a people in denial. Each time we have something going on around HIV, the response is better than the last one. So I think we are making an impact.

It is important to joke about HIV because it's a positive outlook. It's not like one feels like one is going to die tomorrow. It puts a bit of life into it. You see it is normal, and it is normal because not everyone who is HIV positive dies of AIDS. Some die of something else, and those that are negative also die of something else. Eventually we all die … it is more about how responsible we are about how we die.

One of the reasons why I wanted to talk about my HIV is because of how I got my virus. Everyone knows that people are being raped in South Africa every day and so they know that is the reality.

When I was raped, I kept quiet for some time. I spoke more of my HIV status than I did of my rape, and then I thought, 'Why am I keeping quiet? Am I protecting the rapist, and why should I?' So I started talking about it the way it really is. It's not like I'm blaming because it doesn't help anybody to blame, but it's more accepting the situation and doing something about it.

There are lots of women who keep quiet about rape. It was really a trauma when I was raped and I didn't get counselled as early as I should have. It is when I talked about it that I got help. If you are silent, people don't know and can't help. For me it was difficult to talk about HIV because I was still dealing with my rape when I knew about my status.

I actually saw the rapist twice after my rape. I think I wasn't the only person this guy raped, I think he raped a few others. He wanted to die with others.

For me, rape and HIV go hand in hand because if you are raped, you are already at risk because a rapist doesn't come to you with a condom. In fact, you are not in a situation where you can negotiate using a condom because you are not in a relationship.

Even in a relationship sometimes it's difficult to negotiate. That is one of the reasons I felt I needed to talk about it, not to talk and say it's a bit better that I didn't get infected any other way because I feel that whatever way one is infected, the fact still stands that one is infected. It is how one deals with it, how one accepts it and lives positively after going through whatever they have gone through.

Glossary

ag nee wat (Afrikaans): oh no, but that doesn't matter …
aikona (pidgin Zulu): oh no; no way
amabele (Xhosa): sorghum beer
amadoda emdeni (Xhosa): men to the border
aus, ausi (from Afrikaans *ousie*): sister

baas (Afrikaans): master
bachelor: migrant worker living in single-sex hostel
baphela bantwana bethu (from Xhosa *baphel' abantwana bethu*): they are finishing our children
bhuti, boeta (from Afrikaans *boet*): brother
braai (Afrikaans): barbecue
burgher (Afrikaans): citizen; Boer soldier in the Anglo-Boer War

CNA: Central News Agency, a nation-wide chain of booksellers and stationers
COD: Congress of Democrats, allied to the African National Congress
comrade: township activist, usually young, with ties to ANC or UDF

daggazolletjies (Afrikaans): marijuana cigarettes
dhobi (Hindi): washerman
doek (Afrikaans): headscarf
donner (Afrikaans): thrash
DPSC: Detainees' Parents Support Committee

FIET: International Federation of Commercial, Clerical, Professional and Technical Employees

harmel (Afrikaans *hamel*): a wether (a castrated ram)

imifino (Xhosa): wild 'spinach'
imphepho (Zulu): incense
induna (Xhosa): foreman
inspan (Afrikaans): harness a team of oxen

kak (Afrikaans): shit

kanferfoelie (Afrikaans): honeysuckle

kaross (from Afrikaans *karos*): cloak or rug of animal hide

Khaki-Boer (Afrikaans): Boer/Afrikaner who sided with the English in the Anglo-Boer War

Khakis (Afrikaans): British soldiers in the Anglo-Boer War

klapped (Afrikaans): slapped

kneidlach (Yiddish): matzah balls

knobkerrie (from Afrikaans *knopkierie*): club

kombi: mini bus

konfyt (Afrikaans): jam, preserve

koppie/kopje (Afrikaans/Dutch): a small rocky hill

kraal (Afrikaans): cattle enclosure

lobola (from Zulu *ilobolo*): bride price

lucky-bean: the scarlet and black seed of the Coast Coral Tree

marhewu (Xhosa): sour milk

maroela (Afrikaans): fruit of the marula tree

mealies (from Afrikaans *mielies*): maize; crushed and dried in 'stamped mealies'

mispel (Afrikaans): medlar

MK: Umkhonto weSizwe; 'Sword of the Nation', the military wing of the African National Congress

monotocca: a genus of Australian trees and shrubs

morena (Sotho): chief; a greeting

môtjie (Malay): Indian lady shopkeeper

mphokoqo (from Xhosa *umphokoqo*): dry, crumbly porridge

M-Plan: an ANC strategic document prepared by Nelson Mandela

muti (*umuthi*) (Zulu): medical preparation or 'charm' made by a sangoma

natuurlik (Afrikaans): naturally

necklace: tyre doused with petrol, placed around the neck and lit

nkosazana (from Xhosa *inkosazana*): princess; first-born girl

Nkosi Sikelel' iAfrika: God Save Africa (title of South Africa's national anthem)

ntate (Sotho): father

ntombi (from Xhosa *intombi*): girl

outspan (Afrikaans): unharness and make camp

pad kos (Afrikaans): food for the road; provisions
panga: a long flat blade
papa (from Afrikaans *pap*): maize porridge
phalaza (from Zulu *ukuphalaza*): drink medicine to induce vomiting
platteland (Afrikaans): 'flat land'; the interior
poffertjies (Afrikaans): fritters

SADF: South African Defence Force
sangoma (from Zulu *isangoma*): a traditional diviner
SB: Special Branch, the police department set up to spy on activists
shaya (amathambo) ngikutshele (Zulu): beat (the bones), so that I'll tell you –
    ... said when throwing bones/divining
skelem (from Afrikaans *skelm*): crook
slim (Afrikaans): clever, cunning
spuyt (Afrikaans *spuit*): squirt
stoep (Afrikaans): front verandah

tarentaal (Afrikaans): guineafowl
thwasa (from Zulu *ithwasa*): a student diviner
tsotsi (from Zulu *utsotsi*): township hoodlum

umsebenzi (Zulu): the worker; work

VAD: Voluntary Aid Detachment
veld (Afrikaans): field, countryside
verneukery (Afrikaans): fraud, trickery

wilde (Afrikaans): wild, savage, fierce

Sources

Primary sources

Arden, Nicky

From *The Spirits Speak: One Woman's Mystical Journey into the African Spirit World*. New York: Henry Holt, 1996: 100–13. Copyright © 1996 Nicky Arden.

Baard, Frances

From *My Spirit Is Not Banned*. Harare, Zimbabwe: Zimbabwe Publishing House, 1986: 71–79. Copyright © 1986, reprinted by permission of Zimbabwe Publishing House.

Bernstein, Hilda

From *The World that was Ours: The Story of the Rivonia Trial*. London: SA Writers, 1989: 263–73. Copyright © 1989, reprinted by permission of Hilda Bernstein.

Dhlamini, Ntombi

In, *Words that Circle Words: A Choice of South African Oral Poetry*, ed. Jeff Opland. Johannesburg: Ad Donker, 1992: 65. Copyright © 1992, reprinted by permission of Jonathan Ball Publishers.

De Klerk, Marike

From *A Journey through Summer and Winter*. by Maretha Maartens, trans. Maretha Maartens and Madelein van Biljon. (Originally published in Afrikaans.) Vanderbijlpark: Carpe Diem Books, 1997: 167–68; 192–94. Copyright © 1997, reprinted by permission of Carpe Diem Books.

Dolly

In, *Working Women: A Portrait of South Africa's Black Women Workers*, eds. Lesley Lawson and Helene Perold. Johannesburg: Sached Trust / Ravan Press, 1985: 90–92. Copyright © 1985, reprinted by permission of MacMillan South Africa.

Dube, Mcasule

In, *Musho: Zulu Popular Praises*, ed. and trans. Liz Gunner and Mafika Gwala. Johannesburg: Witwatersrand University Press, 1994: 207. Copyright © 1994, reprinted by permission of Witwatersrand University Press.

First, Ruth

From *117 Days: An Account of Confinement and Interrogation under the South African Ninety-Day Detention Law.* London: Bloomsbury, 1988 (1965): 50–57. Copyright © 1988, reprinted by permission of Bloomsbury.

Fortune, Linda

From *The House in Tyne Street: Childhood Memories of District Six.* Cape Town: Kwela, 1996: 122–30. Copyright © 1996, reprinted by permission of NB Publishers Limited.

Dr Goonam

From *Coolie Doctor: An Autobiography by Dr. Goonam* (and Fatima Meer). Durban: Madiba Publishers, 1991: 60–66. Copyright © 1991, reprinted by permission of Fatima Meer.

Gordon, Lyndall

From *Shared Lives.* Cape Town: David Philip, 1992: 122–29; 132-35. Copyright © 1992, reprinted by permission of New Africa Books.

Head, Bessie

From *A Gesture of Belonging: Letters from Bessie Head, 1965–1979,* ed. Randolph Vigne. London: S.A. Writers and Portsmouth, N.H.: Heinemann, 1991: 142–48. Copyright © 1991, reprinted by permission of Randolph Vigne.

Hobhouse, Emily

From *Boer War Letters,* ed. Rykie van Reenen. Cape Town: Human and Rousseau, 1999 (1984): 196–201. Copyright © 1999, reprinted by permission of NB Publishers Limited.

Hoko, Jane

In, *We Came to Town,* ed. Caroline Kerfoot. Johannesburg: Ravan Press, 1985: 2. Copyright © 1985, reprinted by permission of MacMillan South Africa.

Joseph, Helen

From *Side by Side: The Autobiography of Helen Joseph.* London: Zed Books, 1986: 133–41. Copyright © 1986, reprinted by permission of Zed Books.

Kitson, Norma

From *Where Sixpence Lives.* London: The Hogarth Press, 1987: 8–15. Copyright © 1985, 1986 Norma Kitson.

Krog, Antjie

From *Country of My Skull.* Johannesburg: Random House, 1998: 31–33;
36–37; 44–49. Copyright © 1998, reprinted by permission of Random
House.

Lugogo, Ma Dlomo

In, *Working Women: A Portrait of South Africa's Black Women Workers,* eds.
Lesley Lawson and Helene Perold. Johannesburg: Sached Trust / Ravan Press,
1985: 101–3. Copyright © 1985, reprinted by permission of Macmillan
South Africa.

Magona, Sindiwe

From *To My Children's Children.* Cape Town: David Philip, 1990: 65–72.
Copyright © 1990, reprinted by permission of New Africa Books.

MaGumede

In, 'Censure and Social Comment in the *Izihasho* of Urban Zulu Women,'
by Noleen Turner. *AlterNation* 2 (2) 1995: 70. Copyright © 1995, reprinted
by permission of Noleen Turner.

MaJele

In, *Musho: Zulu Popular Praises,* ed. and trans. Liz Gunner and Mafika
Gwala. Johannesburg: Witwatersrand University Press, 1994: 211.
Copyright © 1994, reprinted by permission of Witwatersrand University
Press.

Madikizela-Mandela, Winnie

From *Part of My Soul,* ed. Anne Benjamin, adapted by Mary Benson. First
published in Germany as *Ein Stück meiner Seele ging mit ihm* by Rowohlt
Taschenbuch Verlag, 1984, Penguin Books 1985: 57–61. Copyright © 1985,
reprinted by permission of Penguin Books Limited.

Makhoere, Caesarina Kona

From *No Child's Play: In Prison Under Apartheid.* London: The Women's Press,
1988: 60–69. Copyright © 1988 Caesarina Kona Makhoere.

Mashinini, Emma

From *Strikes Have Followed Me All My Life: A South African Autobiography.*
London: Women's Press, 1989: 90–96; 100–3; 105–10. Copyright © 1989,
reprinted by permission of Emma Mashinini.

MaSithole

In, 'Censure and Social Comment in the *Izihasho* of Urban Zulu Women,'
by Noleen Turner. *AlterNation* 2 (2) 1995: 62. Copyright © 1995, reprinted
by permission of Noleen Turner.

Makanya, Katie

From *The Calling of Katie Makanya* by Margaret McCord. Cape Town and Johannesburg: David Philip, 1995: 238–42. Copyright © 1995, reprinted by permission of New Africa Books.

McMagh, Kathleen

From *A Dinner of Herbs, Being the Memoirs of Kathleen McMagh*. Cape Town: Purnell, 1968: 14–19. Copyright © 1968 Kathleen McMagh.

Mgqwethu, Nontsizi

In, *Xhosa Poets and Poetry*, ed. and trans. Jeff Opland. Cape Town: David Philip, 1998: 201–2. Copyright © 1998, reprinted by permission of New Africa Books.

Michael, Marjorie

From *I Married a Hunter*. London: Odhams Press, 1956: 54–59.

Mjekula, Mildred

In, *Working Women: A Portrait of South Africa's Black Women Workers*, eds. Lesley Lawson and Helene Perold. Johannesburg: Sached Trust / Ravan Press, 1985: 77; 79; 81. Copyright © 1985, reprinted by permission of Macmillan South Africa.

Mkhwanazi, MaMhlalise

In, *Musho: Zulu Popular Praises*, ed. and trans. Liz Gunner and Mafika Gwala. Johannesburg: Witwatersrand University Press, 1994: 205. Copyright © 1994, reprinted by permission of Witwatersrand University Press.

Mshibe, Bella

In, 'Censure and Social Comment in the *Izihasho* of Urban Zulu Women,' by Noleen Turner. *AlterNation* 2(2), 1995: 70. Copyright © 1995, reprinted by permission of Noleen Turner.

Ndlovu, Maria

In, *Living Openly: HIV Positive South Africans Tell Their Stories*, by Susan Fox (interviews) and Gisèle Wulfson (photographs). Pretoria: Beyond Awareness Campaign, HIV/AIDS and STD Directorate, Department of Health, 2000: 4–5. Copyright © 2000 Department of Health .

Ngubane, Selestina

In, *We Came to Town*, ed. Caroline Kerfoot. Johannesburg: Ravan Press, 1985: 8. Copyright © 1985, reprinted by permission of Macmillan South Africa.

Ntantala, Phyllis.

From *A Life's Mosaic: The Autobiography of Phyllis Ntantala*. Berkeley, Los Angeles: University of California Press, 1992: 17–25. Copyright © 1992, reprinted by permission of Phyllis Jordan (née Ntantala).

Nthunya, Mpho 'M'atshepo

From *Singing Away the Hunger: Stories of a Life in Lesotho*, ed. K. Limakatso Kendall. Pietermaritzburg: University of Natal Press, 1996: 1–3; 28–34. Copyright © 1996, reprinted by permission of University of Natal Press.

Nxumalo, Patricia

In, *We Came to Town,* ed. Caroline Kerfoot. Johannesburg: Ravan Press, 1985: 11. Copyright © 1985, reprinted by permission of Macmillan South Africa.

Paton, Anne

From *Some Sort of a Job: My Life with Alan Paton*. London: Viking Penguin, 1992: 1–2; 7–16. Copyright © 1992, reprinted by permission of Penguin Books South Africa.

Podbrey, Pauline.

From *White Girl in Search of the Party*. Pietermaritzburg: University of Natal Press/ Hadeda Books, 1993: 83–96. Copyright © 1993, reprinted by permission of University of Natal Press

Raal, Sarah

From *The Lady who Fought: A Young Woman's Account of the Anglo-Boer War*, trans. Karen Smalberger. (Originally published in Afrikaans as *Met Die Boere in Die Veld*, Nasionale Pers, 1936.) Cape Town: Stormberg, 2000: 43–49. Copyright © 2000 Stormberg Publishers.

Ramphele, Mamphela

From *Mamphela Ramphele: A Life*. Cape Town: David Philip, 1995: 126–38. Copyright © 1995, reprinted by permission of New Africa Books.

Resha, Maggie

From *'Mangoana Tsoara Thipa Ka Bohaleng: My Life in the Struggle*. Johannesburg: Congress of South African Writers, 1991: 112–18. Copyright © 1991 Maggie Resha.

Sagan, Leontine

From *Lights and Shadows: The Autobiography of Leontine Sagan*. ed. Loren Kruger. Johannesburg: Witwatersrand University Press, 1996: 27–34. Copyright © 1996, reprinted by permission of Witwatersrand University Press.

Sithole, Maureen

In, *Working Women: A Portrait of South Africa's Black Women Workers*, eds.
Lesley Lawson and Helene Perold. Johannesburg: Sached Trust / Ravan Press,
1985: 50–52. Copyright © 1985, reprinted by permission of Macmillan
South Africa.

Slovo, Gillian

From *Every Secret Thing: My Family, My Country*. Great Britain: Little,
Brown and Company, 1997: 62–68; 75–80. Copyright © 1997, reprinted by
permission of Time Warner Books UK.

Smith, Charlene

From *Proud of Me: Speaking Out Against Sexual Violence and HIV.* Sandton:
Penguin, 2001: 1–9. Copyright © 2001, reprinted by permission of Penguin
Books South Africa.

Smith, Pauline

From *Secret Fire: The 1913-14 South African Journal of Pauline Smith*, ed.
Harold Scheub. Pietermaritzburg: University of Natal Press, 1997: 11–18.
Copyright © 1997, reprinted by permission of University of Natal Press.

Smith, Prue.

From *The Morning Light: A South African Childhood Revalued*. Cape Town:
David Philip, 2000: 74–78; 114–15; 117–18; 130–32; 135–38. Copyright
© 2000, reprinted by permission of New Africa Books.

Solomon, Bertha

From *Time Remembered: The Story of a Fight*. Cape Town: Howard
Timmins, 1968: 223–26. Copyright © 1968 Bertha Solomon.

Suzman, Helen

From *In No Uncertain Terms: Memoirs.* Johannesburg: Jonathan Ball, 1993:
65–71. Copyright © 1993, reprinted by permission of Helen Suzman.

Tholo, Maria

From *The Diary of Maria Tholo*, by Carol Hermer, Johannesburg: Ravan Press,
1980: 164–75. Copyright © 1980, reprinted by permission of Carol Hermer.

Wolpe, AnnMarie

From *The Long Way Home*. Cape Town: David Philip, 1994: 7; 9–13; 15; 17–18.
Copyright © 1994, reprinted by permission of New Africa Books.

Sources of historical and literary information

Barker, Brian Johnson, Paul Bell, Bruce Cameron, Chiara Carter, Allan
  Duggan, Vivien Horler, Vincent Leroux, Portia Maurice, Cecile Reynierse,
  Hugh Roberton, Peter Schafer and Lee-Ann Smith. *Illustrated History of
  South Africa – The Real Story*. Third edition, second printing. Cape Town:
  Reader's Digest, 1995.

Canonici, Noverino. *Zulu Oral Traditions*. Durban: University of Natal, 1996.

Chapman, Michael. *Southern African Literatures*. London and New York:
  Longman, 1996.

Gunner, Elizabeth. *Ukubonga Nezibongo: Zulu Praising and Praises*.
  Unpublished PhD thesis. University of London, 1984.

Opland, Jeff. *Xhosa Oral Poetry: Aspects of a Black South African Tradition*.
  Johannesburg, Ravan Press, 1983.

Saunders, Christopher and Nicholas Southey. *A Dictionary of South African
  History*. Cape Town: David Philip, 1998.

Turner, Noleen. *Oral Strategies for Conflict Expression and Articulation of
  Criticism in Zulu Discourse*. Unpublished doctoral thesis. University of
  KwaZulu-Natal, 2004.

van Wyk Smith, M. *Grounds of Contest: A Survey of South African English
  Literature*. Kenwyn, South Africa: Juta, 1990.

Walker, Cherryl (ed.). *Women and Gender in Southern Africa to 1945*. Cape
  Town: David Philip and London: James Currey, 1990.

Index